GW00322883

BUSINESS Superbrands

AN INSIGHT INTO BRITAIN'S STRONGEST B2B BRANDS

VOLUME I

Australia • Holland • Ireland • Japan • Philippines • United Kingdom • USA

Editor-in-Chief
Marcel Knobil

Managing Editor
Blair Hamilford

Author
James Curtis

Art Director
Adam Selwyn – Creative & Commercial Communications

Published by Superbrands Ltd
64 West Yard
Camden Lock Place
London
NW1 8AF

Printed in Italy

ISBN 0-9528153-4-6

Contents

Marcel Knobil

Chairperson, Business Superbrands Council
Chairperson, Superbrands
Chairperson, Creative & Commercial Communications

The Business Superbrands book is published by the Superbrands organisation, the independent arbiter and authority on branding. It promotes the discipline of branding and pays tribute to exceptional brands.

The Superbrands organisation has published three books addressing consumer Superbrands. In recognition that branding has at last become highly respected amongst many companies targeting businesses and organisations, Superbrands has identified those who have best capitalised upon this crucial discipline.

There are many companies which have still not recognised the importance of branding in the b2b world. Of those who have, many have yet to apply the discipline. And of those who have attempted to do so, few have done so with a combination of strategic and creative flair.

Through the following pages of this book you will gain an insight into many of the most admired business brands.

The brands have been awarded Business Superbrand status by the Business Superbrands Council. The Council is made up of eminent figures from the world of branding with a particular emphasis on business. Each member has a deep appreciation of what makes a great brand and keeps the following definition top-of-mind:

'A Business Superbrand has established the finest reputation in its field. It offers customers significant emotional and/or tangible advantages over its competitors which (consciously or sub-consciously) customers want, recognise, and are confident about investing in. Business Superbrands are targeted at businesses and organisations (although not necessarily exclusively so).'

Superbrands explores the history of these brands, observing how they have developed over the years and highlights their marketing, advertising and design achievements.

The Superbrands organisation is present in territories throughout the world (including Australia, Holland, Ireland, Japan, Philippines, United Kingdom and USA) and has featured analysis of over 350 brands in its publications. It is no accident that by far the majority of these brands have been built upon a high quality product or service, lived up to their promises, stood for something distinctive, generated considerable awareness, defined a clear personality, and consistently remained faithful to their brand principles.

There is, however, no simple formula for becoming and remaining a Business Superbrand. But, through evaluating many of the greatest Business Superbrands in Britain, numerous lessons can be learned.

B2B Branding

Why strong branding is crucial in the business-to-business market according to members of the Business Superbrands Council

Claire Allen

Marketing Director
Andersen Consulting

"2b, or not 2b?" At least Hamlet had time to ask the question. These days, if you are in the business-to-business market, you have no time for deliberation. Competition in this sector has exploded, and one way to gain market dominance is through paying much more attention to branding. Why? Nay-sayers argue that branding belongs to the experiential purchase of the consumer. Not so. This leaves the business purchaser in a communications void, needing to make an often very expensive, highly customised, and therefore fairly risky buying decision. Without giving him or her clear messages and points of differentiation businesses make their customers rely too much on emotive - and sometimes political - purchasing instincts: effectively, the purchasing choice is being held to ransom.
So; there's the rub. Add a much stronger branding component to your marketing activities, and help your business buyers put your business as their first preferences.

Anthony Carlisle

Executive Director
Incepta Group & Citigate Dewe Rogerson

The arguments for brand in business-to-business are no different to those for business-to-consumer. It is the nature and scale of audiences that differ. And since businesses' corporate and commercial audiences frequently tend to be more concentrated and influential, than the customer audiences, individually if not collectively, the power of brand matters is a strategic imperative. Essentially, brand is the summation and expression of corporate personality, purpose, values and qualities. You can enter a room unknown and unannounced. Or you can enter a room with your position, reputation, qualities and significance preceding you. It is the same for companies presenting themselves and their products, services and investor delivery. The cumulative impact and halo effect of brand are indeed influential. As we harness the information age to business of all kinds, the strategic imperative of brand only grows that much stronger.

Stephen Carter

Chief Executive Officer
J Walter Thompson

If there is one phrase from the dictionary of the New Economy I would underscore for the leaders of the business world, it is the phrase 'Open Access.' It has suggestions of vulnerability, lack of mystique, price transparency and customer control. These are all things that are historically felt acutely in the classic consumer markets. However, more recently the business-to-business world is seeing and feeling the impact. Suddenly Professional Service Firms, Consultants, Investment Bankers and Asset Managers are living in a world where there is progressive Open Access. This environment demands differentiation, a tangible customer proposition, and a clear set of values and principles; in short it calls for business-to-business Brand Management. As the capital markets continue to demand real growth, innovation and increasing returns the need to move from category to category and country to country will increase. The powerful and meaningful brands will find these conditions easier to manage.

John Mathers

Executive Vice-President Branding & Corporate Identity, Fitch

Great companies understand that their reputation and their brand are synonymous and that the way they behave, as an organisation must reflect what they stand for.
This simple truism exists for business-to-business brands as much as it does for consumer brands. Everything they do has to deliver against that promise, the products and services they develop, the way they communicate to their external audiences as well as their own people, to the way they organise and run the company.
They also understand that building a great brand is not just about the short term. It becomes a way of doing things that delivered over time sets them apart from their competition.
The Superbrands on the following pages not only understand this, they embrace it wholeheartedly.

Rufus Olins

Editor
Management Today

We are a long way from the days when a brand was burned into the hide of a steer to mark ownership. Back then the value was in the beef; today the brand itself is often the meat. Spot a Gucci watch, a pair of Camel boots or Calvin Klein sunglasses and one quickly appreciates the power of a name in the consumer market. The same applies in the business-to-business market.
In today's digital age, when one is groping for a word for a search engine, what comes to mind more easily than a recognised brand? And when one has to make decisions in the ether, when many of us are moving into uncharted territory, is there anything more comforting than a name that is tried, tested and trusted?

Andrew Robertson

Chief Executive
Abbot Mead Vickers BBDO

Brands have value because they enable human beings to make choices. Business people, despite their best attempts to appear otherwise, are human beings.
They are faced with a choice of many more options in any category than most consumers are – think about how many law firms there are, for example, and compare that with instant coffee brands.
And the decisions they make are usually big ones – with far-reaching consequences.
Is strong branding crucial in b2b? Hello.

Conor Dignam

Editor
Marketing

If you want to be a Superbrand and you're not, then ask yourself this: what promise does your brand make to your customers, and how well does it keep it? The strongest of brands enters into a pact with its customers and says 'trust me, choose me and I will reward your decision by meeting your needs'. Superbrands have a very clear sense of their own identity, values, and personality.
They are ferocious when it comes to protecting and preserving these core values against imposters and rivals. Superbands are consistent and communicative. A Superbrand, like any brand, will make mistakes. But the measure of a Superbrand is to recognise the error, recover lost ground, and regain customer trust. So they listen to their customers and hear what they say, because to stop listening is to stop learning. Superbrands have a relationship which make them the preferred choice in their market because the customer trusts them to deliver on their brand promise.

Royston Hogarth

Group Marketing Director
Logica plc

To date, business-to-business brand development has largely been based on rational benefits such as price, quality and value; whilst consumer brands have focussed on building a 'personality' around emotional factors. But 'people are people' - everyone is ultimately a consumer and customers in the b2b market act just as emotionally. They demand the same things from a brand - trust, understanding, a feeling that they are dealing with 'people like them'.
To date, few b2b companies have applied the emotional as well as the rational factors to building their brand. I believe there is opportunity for real differentiation for those that redress this balance now. A more emotional brand will not only inspire potential clients, but also staff.
Once the brand has been built, reliably delivering on the brand promise is essential - just as in the consumer arena.

Deborah Kiely

Global Head of Advertising
UBS Warburg

Truism # 897: We live in the age of branding. At home, labels jostle for room on our bodies, in our kitchens, in the garage. At work, not only our hardware, but even the information we receive on it has its own brand values. Quickly, make your mind up. Do you get your news from Bloomberg, or CNBC? Do you get your market alerts from WSJ.com or FT.com? Are you a Nokia person or an Orange person? What does your on-line trading service really say about you? When you float your dot.com, which investment bank is the right name to drop in the gym? Who will build your fabulous new headquarters in Frankfurt? No, Germany's so 20th century: make that Dublin. Which of the big accountancy firms will handle your liquidation? Take a deep breath. Relax. Surrender to the brand.

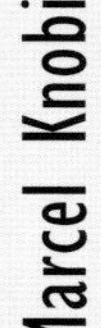

Marcel Knobil

Chairperson
Business Superbrands Council

Whether sitting at home playing with my children, or sitting at work playing on my computer, I am still the same person.
Whether walking down the aisles of the Supermarket, or flicking through the various proposals for a new office computer network, I still have to make a choice.
Whether I am buying something for my home or business I need to be confident that I am making the right decision. A strong brand will reassure me – I can trust it to deliver.
As more and more brands manage to achieve a similar standard of product and service they must battle to get noticed by me and earn my confidence. Whether it be a consumer or business brand is irrelevant. Those that win the battle will invariably be the ones that have capitalised upon prudent branding.

Stuart Smith

Editor
Marketing Week

B2b. It's becoming the increasingly eligible sister of b2c, once the cynosure of lascivious venture capitalists, eager to get into bed with the latest hot Net property. But, if not exactly on the shelf, spendthrift b2c has cash-burnt out the ardour of the capital markets, which are now thirsting for a fresh conquest. B2b had better watch out, because the same golden rules, so woefully neglected during the b2c affair, will apply in its own case. Successful branding is paramount to the success of any business-to-business enterprise, new economy or not. That doesn't mean profligate expenditure on an ill-thought out high profile advertising campaign; it means rigorous application of all the classic rules of brand marketing. A brand is only as valuable as its weakest link to the customer, whether that customer is a businessman or member of the general public.

Dr Hamish Stevenson

Compiler of Fast Track 100, and Virgin Atlantic Research Fellow, Templeton, Oxford

My experience of identifying and analysing the fastest-growing unquoted companies in the UK for the Virgin Atlantic Fast Track 100 league table published annually in The Sunday Times suggests that the strength of their brand is as important for these emerging companies as for the largest corporations. Most of their customers are large blue chip corporations, which demand particularly high levels of service and credibility. Whilst most companies on the league table may not yet be recognisable brands, it is based on the American Inc 500 league table, which first identified rising stars like Microsoft 18 years ago. Emerging brands on our league tables include the microchip company, ARM, which recently shot into the FTSE 100, bagless vacuum cleaner company Dyson and niche retailer Carphone Warehouse. In the interests of competition it is encouraging to see these and other private companies such as Virgin and easyJet gazumping the brand dinosaurs....

Helena Sturridge

Publisher
Computer Weekly

Are business brands treated as the poor relations? Probably, in the past the level of attention lavished upon them has not matched that of consumer brands. But not any more. Attitudes have had to change very sharply. And the web is the driver. Those with strong brands have every reason to be thankful. As the extremely unforgiving spotlight is pointed at every business model, and every product and service has to go back and the central question: what is the value the customer is getting, is shown into stark relief. Knowing and understanding your brand, knowing its strength and building on it will be the only way to retain your surefootedness as e-business reshapes the economic landscape.

Lord Watson CBE

Chairman/Europe
Burson-Marsteller

The arrival of digital communications has had a revolutionary impact.
The way we do business with customers and suppliers, run our homes, bank accounts and leisure time has been changed irrevocably and it has happened incredibly fast. Michael Dell talks about his company in terms of 'Dellocity' and it's velocity that characterises this market.
Speed is the issue that makes brand building so vital in the business-to-business marketplace. Products and services can be introduced and replicated by competitors in a matter of months. No matter how unique the technology, it is the brand that gives the buyer the guarantee of quality, longevity and more importantly reliability.
Ask the b2b dot coms.

Market

The travel market has never been healthier, with more UK people taking holidays abroad and becoming increasingly adventurous in their choice of destinations. More countries around the world have opened themselves up to tourism, air fares are cheaper and people have a higher disposable income to spend on travel.

All this has contributed to steady growth in the number of UK residents booking package holidays. Back in 1980, just 6.2 million people took package breaks, but, in 1999, this figure had reached 17.6 million. Holiday bookings act as a rough barometer of economic health, with a sharp dip seen during the recession of the early 1990s before continuous annual increases since 1997.

The package holiday explosion has been one of the most remarkable social phenomena of the post-war years. International tourism, based to a large extent on the package tour, has become what is probably the greatest single growth industry.

As the travel industry grows, there are more and more ways for consumers to book holidays and, correspondingly, a greater need for security and confidence in the companies they use. This is why the Association of British Travel Agents has such an important role to play in building consumer trust in the travel industry. According to research by MORI, 72% of package holidays are booked via travel agents and tour operators, and four out of five holiday makers say that when they do book via an agent, it is important that they are a member of ABTA.

An increasing number of people are booking holidays over the internet, or at least using it to search for good deals. Many travel companies, have invested heavily in their internet operations to take advantage of this and to compete against web-only operators. People are also booking later, hoping to take advantage of last minute deals. These are just some of the factors that make the travel industry more competitive than ever.

Achievements

ABTA is the second largest travel trade association in the world. Together, ABTA members are responsible for the sale of more than 90% of UK-sold overseas package holidays.

With over 7,500 travel agent branches in the UK, ABTA has become one of the most trusted brands in the travel business, with unrivalled credibility among trade partners and consumers. Also, according to MORI, it enjoys extremely high awareness levels, with 88% of package holiday makers saying that they have heard of the organisation. This ranks ABTA's awareness level above that of the TUC (77%) and NATO (76%). Three-quarters of holiday makers agree that 'my money is safe when booking a holiday through an ABTA tour operator' and three in five believe that there are distinct advantages in booking a holiday through an ABTA agent. Indeed, if a travel agent was to withdraw from ABTA, two-thirds of holiday makers say they would not deal with them again.

The association has become a model of industry self-regulation, and is frequently held up as an example for other self-regulated sectors to follow. It has helped raise standards among UK travel agents and tour operators, which, in turn has inspired consumer trust in the industry and boosted overall spend on tourism.

Key factors that have helped ABTA achieve its pre-eminent position and high consumer profile include the provision of financial protection for the holiday maker. This was a crucial move, made in response to the growing need to protect consumers against the financial instability of some travel companies during the 1980s and early 1990s. Not only has this raised the profile of ABTA, but also helped avert damage to the reputation of the UK travel industry as a whole.

This is not the only work ABTA does to improve the industry's standing - it also battles against legislation which may be damaging to the trade and promotes the image of members through external public relations. The scope and effectiveness of its work has made ABTA the envy of travel associations around the world.

History

ABTA was founded in 1950. The body was formed during the post-war boom which, together with the dawn of the jet age, fuelled demand for international travel.

In 1965, ABTA introduced a rule guaranteeing financial protection for consumers. Known as the Stabiliser, the rule stated that if ABTA member tour operators wished to sell their foreign inclusive holidays or other travel arrangements through third parties, they could only do so through ABTA Member travel agents. It also stated that ABTA travel agents could only sell the arrangements of ABTA tour operators. Naturally, this led to most tour operators and travel agents seeking to join ABTA, which, in turn, led to the association's safeguard for the travelling public being spread as widely as possible. In 1976, the Office of Fair Trading referred Stabiliser to the Restrictive Practices Court, but, in 1982, it was ruled that the policy was in the public interest.

With this in place, ABTA was able to build up its strength and continue to protect the interests of its members' customers and of the UK travel industry as a whole. In 1992, with the introduction of the Package Travel Regulations which provided similar levels of protection, the Stabiliser rule was removed. This was a European Community initiative which sought to harmonise consumer protection schemes for package travel across the EC.

Another important development in ABTA's history was the introduction of an industry Code of Conduct in 1960. The codes have been progressively strengthened over the years as the travel industry has grown in size and complexity.

In 1975, ABTA introduced an arbitration scheme for the travel industry. The purpose of the scheme is to provide a simple and inexpensive way of resolving disputes without having to take the matter to court.

The current ABTA logo, designed by Landor, was launched in November 1987 and was soon to be widely recognised by the UK travelling public. In 2000, ABTA celebrated its 50th anniversary.

Product

Membership of ABTA is open to UK travel agents and tour operators which can meet its criteria. Currently, the association has 7,575 Travel Agent Office branches and 796 Tour Operator members, which have a combined turnover of £32 billion.

A cornerstone of ABTA's product is financial protection. It takes great care in checking tour operator's finances to reduce the risk of things going wrong. If anything does, ABTA's scheme of financial protection allows holiday makers' trips to continue as originally planned. ABTA will make sure travellers are never stranded abroad. People who have not yet started their holiday will get their money back or, where possible, ABTA will make arrangements for them to continue with the planned holiday.

Another core feature of ABTA's service is its Code of Conduct. This ensures that members work to the highest standards of service and

quality. All members must ensure that their products meet comprehensive guidelines to ensure clarity and accuracy. Also, ABTA members are required to provide advice on insurance, visas, passports, health requirements, and alterations to travel arrangements.

Measures such as this are key to confidence in the ABTA brand. Training is another important element of this, and members are required to employ properly qualified staff. ABTA's Travel Training Company provides courses for staff at all levels.

Dealing with complaints is another plank of ABTA's service. ABTA provides a low cost independent arbitration service to its members' clients. Administered by the Chartered Institute of Arbitrators, this is a simple, inexpensive way to reach a legally binding solution, and does not require complainants to attend court. However, the service does not affect people's rights to resolve a dispute through the courts if they wish, it is simply a further choice available.

ABTA members have access to a wide range of support services and products. These include the British Travel Agents' Accommodation Register, covering over 2000 hotels throughout the UK and free access to ABTA's mailing list of members. It also provides special phone services for members, with competitive rates and flexible tariffs. Other services include business finance for purchases, off-site document storage and reduced prices for office supplies.

HOLIDAY PROTECTION ABTA

All ABTA travel agents are members of our financial protection scheme. So you can go ahead and book your holiday knowing that, should they fail financially, you will still get the product you booked. Or your money back. For a leaflet containing the full story on what ABTA offers you, call **020 7307 1991.**

LOOK BEFORE YOU BOOK ABTA

LOOK BEFORE YOU BOOK ABTA

When you see the ABTA symbol, you know your holiday is protected. Every travel agent and tour operator in our membership operates under our strict codes of conduct and has passed our rigorous checks on their financial security. So in the unlikely event that they should fail financially, we'll ensure that it is not your holiday that suffers. For a leaflet containing the full story on what ABTA offers you, call **020 7307 1991.**

Recent Developments

ABTA recently teamed up with the English Tourism Council and the Scottish and Wales Tourist Boards to launch a new training manual. The programme, called 'Britain - We Have The Knowledge', was sent free of charge to ABTA Members.

The package was developed by ABTA's Travel Training Company, together with UK travel agents, tour operators, hotels, transport companies and other suppliers to build up the industry's knowledge of what Britain has to offer and how to sell it successfully.

ABTA also entered an agreement with the British Hospitality Association to publish a suggested code for travel agents and hoteliers. The code sets out suggested practices to assist members of both associations in their dealings with each other. Currently, ABTA Members have only an estimated 8% of domestic hotel bookings. Achieving a higher share of the market, and boosting domestic sales of UK holidays, depends on improving links between travel agents and hoteliers.

1999 saw a big increase in the number of applications for membership. A total of 118 applications for membership were received during the year - a 13.5% rise on 1998.

ABTA recently worked with The Reward Group to produce their first annual survey of pay and benefits for the travel sector. This enables the travel industry to compare itself to other industry groups, helping to ensure that it offers competitive rewards to people working in the business.

With more and more business taking place over the internet, ABTA is working with Trust UK to 'kitemark' all ABTA Member sites in order to inspire trust in their customers. ABTA has already updated its Code of Conduct to include specific provisions relevant to internet trading so that customers can be confident in dealing with ABTA companies online.

Promotion

ABTA promotes itself principally via a mix of public relations and advertising. It has a heritage of brand-building advertising work, having run high-profile campaigns in the 1970s and 1980s.

In 1974, it invested £100,000 on a TV advertising campaign which combined images of the drab realities of everyday life with the slogan 'See your travel agent'. In 1985, when package holiday sales were enjoying a boom period, ABTA enlisted the services of top model Sam Fox for another campaign.

With ABTA celebrating its 50th anniversary, there have been plenty of PR opportunities. ABTA's senior personnel regularly provide input into media interviews and documentaries about the travel industry, providing valuable platforms for ABTA's voice to be heard. Other PR tactics include product placement, including a deal which saw ABTA's logo displayed in a travel agent's set in Coronation Street.

ABTA's most recent advertising uses the slogan 'Look Before You Book', urging travellers to only use ABTA-registered agents and operators.

ABTA also works with other businesses on cross-promotional opportunies. For example, for its recent report on travel industry remuneration, it sought sponsorship from companies like Avis Rent A Car, Best Western Hotels, Blakes Holidays and the Forte Hotel Group.

The association's members also receive the monthly 'ABTA Magazine', which features news and developments and features about the travel industry.

Brand Values

'Building Confidence in Travel' underlines everything that the association does. With its guarantees of protection for the traveller, 'Peace of Mind' is another important element of the ABTA brand. It is also closely linked to self-regulation and acting in the consumer's interest.

Things you didn't know about ABTA

ABTA's Information Bureau receives 70,000 calls per year.

In 1998, ABTA dealt with 18,400 complaints. Of these, 1600 went to ABTA's independent arbitration scheme.

In 1998, ABTA paid out £1 million in respect of travel agency failures and £200,000 in respect of tour operators' failures.

As a measure of its financial protection for consumers, ABTA currently has bonds valued at £184 million for travel agents and £113 million for tour operators.

ABTA member companies employ approximately 45,000 staff.

Cruising is the fastest growing sector of the travel market. The only country which cruises more than the UK is the US.

47% of package holidays booked by UK travellers are to Spain.

The most common question ABTA's Information Department is asked is "Is this company a member of ABTA?".

Market

If you asked a group of people to say what the word 'ACAS' made them think of, they would most probably say 'strike' or 'conflict'. This response is easy to understand, as the Advisory, Conciliation and Arbitration Service is frequently in the news as it seeks to resolve national disputes. Some of the most protracted and bitter disputes in memory have all seen ACAS take centre stage – the miners' strike, the national dock strike and the steel industry dispute are just three examples. These disputes were well publicised because of their potentially damaging effects on industry and the economy, and, inevitably, ACAS made the headlines at the same time. More recent disputes experienced by London Underground and British Airways have again highlighted ACAS's continuing role on the national stage.

The days of flying pickets, closed shops and frequent large-scale industrial disputes are gone, but the demand for ACAS conciliation has remained fairly constant. In the last few years, a climate of increased competitiveness has developed in the business world, with the emphasis on cost-efficiency and employee performance. There is also the impact of new legislation from Westminster and the European Union – not least a greater emphasis on employee rights. These factors create different types of problems between employers and employees, requiring ACAS to change with the times too.

This more complex legislative environment is reflected in the fact that individual employment rights disputes are now the busiest source of work for ACAS, dealing with well over 100,000 cases per year. Every year, the service handles thousands of new cases involving complaints of unfair dismissal, race and sex discrimination and wage deductions.

ACAS is now as involved in working to prevent disputes as it is in resolving them. It is shifting its focus from cure to prevention, making the most of the 'Advisory' role that is the first letter in its name. However, industrial disputes do still take place. ACAS is involved in resolving over a 1000 per year.

Although sponsored by the Department of Trade and Industry, ACAS is a non-departmental body and is fully independent and impartial. It employs around 760 staff, based at fourteen offices throughout the UK. ACAS is directed by a council made up of twelve members from industry and trade unions as well as from a variety of independent sources. These eminent members help ensure that ACAS remains impartial.

Achievements

Over the last 26 years, ACAS has led the way in understanding and helping to improve employment relations. It has been involved in some of the highest profile disputes in UK history and helped to resolve them. Hundreds more never made the headlines, thanks to ACAS's behind-the-scenes work. In its history, ACAS has resolved around 50,000 industrial disputes. In 1998, in 95% of collective disputes in which ACAS conciliated, industrial action was avoided altogether.

The number of cases dealt with in the area of individual employment rights has risen sharply in the last twenty years. Cases dealt with in the 1980s were on average 42,000 per year – now it is over 100,000 per year. Employment disputes are very costly to both employers and employees. Subsequently, ACAS's role in preventing and resolving around 75% of such actions has helped save considerable public expense.

History

A voluntary conciliation and arbitration service was launched by the government in 1896 and augmented during the Second World War by the provision of free advice to employers and unions on industrial relations and personnel problems. From 1960, this was known as the Industrial Relations Service.

Having been renamed the Conciliation and Advisory Service in 1972, Secretary of State for Employment, Michael Foot transferred the service out of government and placed it under the control of an independent council in 1974. It had become difficult for ACAS to be part of a government department that was responsible for Income Policy and Public Sector Pay when a large part of its workload was dedicated to resolving pay issues. Its new independent status marked a watershed in British industrial relations.

In 1976, it was put on a statutory footing, giving it a duty to promote the improvement of industrial relations and assist with the avoidance and resolution of collective and individual employment disputes. To reflect its new statutory role and wider range of functions, the word 'advisory' was added and the now well-known acronym ACAS was born.

Soon, in the turbulent industrial days of the 1970s and early 1980s, ACAS became a household name, even making its debut in the Oxford English Dictionary. The miners' strike of the mid-1980s saw ACAS mediating between the National Coal Board and the National Union of Mine Workers for over a year. In the same year, 1984, ACAS was involved in two protracted disputes over teachers' pay. The following year, ACAS was involved in the 'Battle of Wapping', when Rupert Murdoch broke the print unions' control of Fleet Street.

During the 1990s, as trade union membership declined, and the old adversarial style of industrial relations gave way to a more modern style of workplace co-operation, the focus of ACAS's work shifted away from resolving collective disputes to preventative work, training, and, with the arrival of more complex employment laws, settling individual disputes. However there is still plenty of demand for ACAS's skills in mediating on large-scale industrial problems as illustrated in ACAS's 'Towards better employment relations' publication.

Product

ACAS's work falls into four main areas. Firstly, it provides information and advice to employers, employees and their representatives, with the aim of promoting a better understanding of workplace issues and thereby preventing confrontation and disputes. This advice is largely dispensed via ACAS's national network of Public Enquiry Points (PEPs).

These eleven centres in Scotland, England and Wales handle telephone enquiries on subjects as varied as maternity leave, redundancy, discrimination and pay. PEPs handle around 750,000 calls per year. For more detailed enquiries, PEPs refer callers to a variety of ACAS Handbooks and Advisory Booklets. This ongoing series of Advisory publications reflect current developments in the workplace and cover topics such as teamwork, discipline, absenteeism and appraisal.

The second area of ACAS's service is preventing and resolving industrial disputes. The service has developed ways of helping employers and employees foster constructive relationships, holding workshops where both parties can discuss their feelings and agree on potential barriers to long-term goals. Where this preventative action fails, ACAS will conciliate in disputes. Where conciliation does not work, ACAS can arrange for a disagreement to be settled through arbitration. This process involves both sides setting out their case in writing followed by a hearing. Each side has to agree to accept the arbitrator's decision as binding.

The third and largest area of ACAS's work is in the area of individual employment rights. It handles around 100,000 new cases per year, mainly involving allegations of unfair dismissal, discrimination and wage deductions. When someone makes a complaint to an Employment Tribunal, an ACAS conciliation officer is sent a copy of the complaint and then offers to help the parties settle without the need for a tribunal hearing.

ACAS also offers workshops and seminars for small firms, running special events for small businesses all over the UK. They are designed for those without expertise in personnel issues and they tend to focus on topics such as employment contracts and discipline. They are non-profit making, so the costs of the seminars are kept low and typically run for half a day.

On top of all this, ACAS's web site (www.acas.org.uk) is a central resource of help, advice and information.

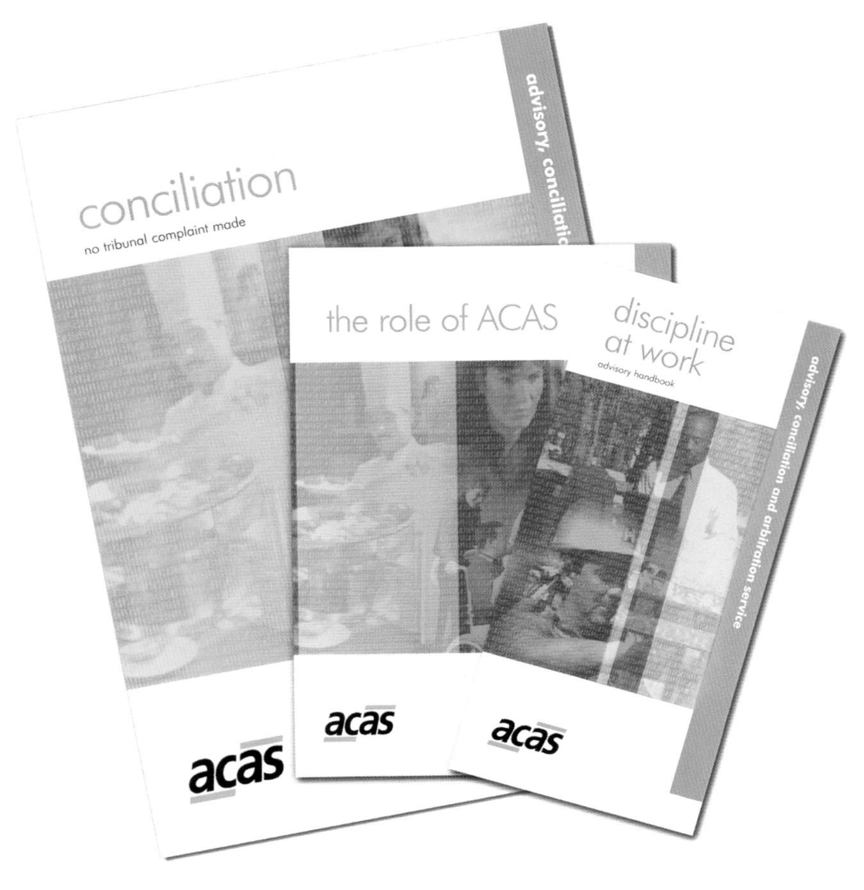

Recent Developments

In November 1999, ACAS celebrated its 25th anniversary. To mark the occasion, the service held an anniversary conference, attracting speakers including Cherie Booth and Secretary of State for Trade and Industry, Stephen Byers. Mr Byers launched a new ACAS product, a publication entitled 'Towards better employment relations – using the ACAS advisory service'. The publication gives clear examples of how prevention has worked and describes some of the techniques used. Cherie Booth also used the occasion as a platform to call for employers to take a more consultative approach to workplace relations.

In summer 1998, ACAS's work was affected greatly by the introduction of the government's 'Fairness at work' White Paper. This had significant implications for ACAS as it contained a raft of proposals aimed at increasing the rights of individuals in the workplace.

In 2000 ACAS introduced a new service for unfair dismissal claims called the Arbitration Alternative. Where conciliation has not succeeded, parties have the option of having their case heard in private by an ACAS-appointed arbitrator instead of at a tribunal hearing. In comparison to tribunal hearings, arbitration is confidential, informal, non-legalistic, and speedier to arrange and conduct.

Promotion

In 2000 ACAS implemented a new corporate visual identity that reflects and projects the modern ACAS personality. The style has been incorporated throughout all new publications and has strengthened the ACAS brand making it instantly recognisable. ACAS plans to promote its services more pro-actively in the future. In 2000 ACAS employed a leading communications consultant to create a PR campaign. The initiative aims to give ACAS a greater voice in a wide variety of employment issues and ensure that the ACAS viewpoint and name is never far from an employment story in the media.

As its history of involvement in well-known disputes has shown, the ACAS name has become synonymous with conflict resolution and conciliation, generating a great deal of goodwill and awareness for the brand. The challenge ACAS now faces is to develop its corporate identity to reflect the growing awareness of its advisory role in preventing disputes.

Brand Values

The ACAS mission is 'to improve the performance and effectiveness of organisations by providing an independent and impartial service to prevent and resolve disputes and to build harmonious relationships at work'.

ACAS is a modern service that stands for conciliation over confrontation and, very importantly, impartiality and confidentiality. With 25 years of promoting the improvement of industrial relations ACAS has become known as knowledgeable, understanding and trustworthy.

Things you didn't know about ACAS

ACAS's longest conciliation in one sitting was 27 hours.

Pay issues are the most common cause of workplace disputes.

Categories in complaints to Employment Tribunals which grew the most in 1999, were Protection of Wages and Unfair Dismissal.

A woman talking to ACAS about accusations that she was rude to customers said: "I've never been rude to anyone. It's not in my bloody nature."

Market

Market research is a $13 billion industry worldwide. ACNielsen is the largest firm in the industry, with an 11% share. Several large firms offer syndicated research services, tracking product movement, purchasing behaviour and media audiences on a continuous basis. A wide range of smaller firms provide customised research, assessing consumer attitudes, usually through unique, one-off studies.

The industry continues to grow rapidly, fuelled by strong global demand for marketplace information and consumer insights. Within the consumer products industry, a number of trends are driving this demand, including globalisation of client businesses; retailer and manufacturer consolidation; growth in the number of distribution channels, including the internet and its availability to consumers; greater reliance on micro and one-to-one marketing in highly competitive mature markets; and continued expansion in emerging markets.

Achievements

As the company that introduced new concepts in market research in the 1930s, ACNielsen's achievements are manifold. The company invented the concept of tracking retail sales as a measure of competitive performance in the consumer products industry, an innovation that transformed the concept of market share into a practical and important measure of business success. It also created the first ever broadcast audience ratings system and placed the first commercial order for a mainframe computer in 1947.

ACNielsen has built an unrivalled reputation in the market research industry and is often cited as the benchmark of measurement and the industry standard in many sectors.

In the UK, ACNielsen was the first market research organisation to incorporate retail scanning information into its services. ACNielsen is at the forefront of the retailer-supplier partnership. Information is critical to this process, and ACNielsen plays a key role in providing retailers and suppliers with a common language through provision of data, services and tools.

ACNielsen is unique in its combination of global reach, the breadth of its services covering traditional and new media, and the depth of knowledge in local markets.

History

Arthur Charles Nielsen, Sr, founding father of modern market research, established the company that bears his name in Chicago in 1923. From provision of efficiency and performance surveys for industrial clients, Nielsen adapted his research techniques for the retail sector, convinced that consumer goods companies spent considerable sums on advertising without knowing if it worked. They needed market research to guide them.

In 1933 Nielsen introduced his revolutionary Retail Drug Index, whereby auditors visiting a set sample of stores counted the merchandise and audited the purchase invoices, enabling accurate tracking of sales of all the brands in specific product categories. In 1934, he added a Food Index and a Department Store Index, which, with the addition of other sector measurements, eventually became the Nielsen Retail Index. Eventually, Nielsen extended the service to assessing the effects of displays, promotions and advertising on the sales of products. The crucial element of this research was to inform a brand owner of sales performance relative to the competition over time – in other words, market share analysis.

Although retail marketing research has always been the company's largest business, Nielsen is best known for creating the 'Nielsen Ratings' system of measuring TV and radio audiences in the United States. Radio audience measurement developed in the late 1930s as radio advertising began to take off - a device called an Audimeter recorded, minute by minute, where the dial on a radio was set. Despite industry doubts, Nielsen argued and proved that measuring the listening of a representative sample of households – say 1,500 – could accurately reflect the behaviour of millions. By 1950, ACNielsen expanded its US audience measurement services to television.

Even as his business was growing in the United States, Nielsen set his sights on international expansion, opening the first international office in the UK in 1939. ACNielsen's global growth continues to this day: the company currently offers market research services in more than 100 countries.

After the war, ACNielsen was instrumental in the commercialisation of mainframe computers. In the US Army, Nielsen's son, Arthur Jr, had seen a machine used to perform complex ballistic calculations. He persuaded his father that the company could use such a machine to make the generation of its statistical reports more efficient. A contract to build it was signed in 1947, but the machine was not ready until 1951. By this time its cost – $1 million – had

greatly exceeded the company's original budget and the computer ended up being used by the US Census office. It is now in the Smithsonian Institute.

Nielsen, Jr, became president of the A C Nielsen Company in 1957. In 1977, the company introduced the first retail measurement service using information collected from checkout scanners, which automatically read universal product codes printed on packaging. This allowed ACNielsen to electronically collect retail information at the point of sale.

In 1984, another giant in the information industry, The Dun & Bradstreet Corporation, acquired ACNielsen. By this time, ACNielsen had a presence in 24 countries and its international sales were bigger than its US activities.

In 1988, ACNielsen introduced the first household panel service using hand-held scanning technology. Participants in the company's Homescan panels record all bar-coded purchases from every store they visit.

The company's international expansion received another boost in 1994, when ACNielsen acquired Survey Research Group, the leading customised researcher in Asia Pacific.

In 1996, Dun & Bradstreet split into three separate public companies. Since then, ACNielsen's successful turnaround in the United States, substantial quality and service improvements in Europe, and streamlined, more efficient operations in Asia Pacific have transformed it from a turnaround company to one with sustainable long-term growth prospects.

ACNielsen more than doubled its operating income, net income and earnings per share in 1997, and increased those measures of profitability by more than 50% in 1998 and by more than 30% in 1999.

Today, ACNielsen is the world's leading market research firm, offering measurement and analysis of marketplace dynamics, consumer attitudes and behaviour, and new and traditional media in more than 100 countries. Clients include leading consumer product manufacturers, retailers and service firms, media and entertainment companies and the internet community.

More than 9,000 clients worldwide rely on ACNielsen's information and insights, proprietary research methodologies and professional services to make better business decisions, manage marketing and sales activities and improve performance. During 1999 the company generated revenues of $1.5 billion, with 43% coming from the Americas, 39% from Europe, Middle East and Africa and 18% from Asia Pacific. ACNielsen is the largest player in the $13 billion market research industry, with more than 21,000 employees worldwide.

Product

ACNielsen markets its products and services through four business segments. The cornerstone of the business is retail measurement service, providing continuous tracking of consumer purchases from food, drug, mass merchandise and other retail outlets in more than 80 countries. Clients rely on both ACNielsen's Scantrack service, which uses data from checkout scanners, and the company's in-store audits, to provide detailed information on actual purchases, market shares, distribution, pricing and merchandising and promotional activities.

Related services include key account reports; decision support services, including the Inf*Act Workstation; Spaceman merchandising services, and marketing and sales applications. Multicountry reporting is also available.

ACNielsen also offers consumer panel research, which tracks the buying behaviour and demographics of more than 135,000 households in twenty countries, primarily through the use of in-home scanners. Panel information reveals who is buying, what they are buying and where they shop, and includes details such as method of payment, use of coupons, and participation in frequent shopper programmes.

Customised research delivers information and insights about consumer attitudes and purchasing behaviour in more than 60 countries. Quantitative and qualitative studies are conducted through surveys, focus groups and other methods to explore a broad range of marketing issues, including customer satisfaction, brand awareness and advertising effectiveness. ACNielsen BASES and ACNielsen Market Decisions, acquired in 1998 and 1999, respectively, offer test-marketing services to launch new products or reposition existing brands.

ACNielsen's media measurement services, offered through ACNielsen Media International, deliver detailed audience and advertising information that serves as the currency for negotiating advertising placements and rates in more than 40 countries. Services include television audience measurement in eighteen countries, radio audience measurement in eleven markets, and advertising expenditure measurement in 30 countries.

In 1997, ACNielsen acquired Entertainment Data Inc, the pre-eminent source of box office information for the worldwide motion picture industry. ACNielsen EDI tracks receipts from more than 45,000 movie screens in twelve countries, covering Europe, Latin America and Australia.

In 1999, ACNielsen formed ACNielsen eRatings.com, a venture with NetRatings, Inc, to measure internet audiences, advertising and user activity. Through the Nielsen//NetRatings service, the venture aims to become the global industry standard for internet measurement, providing information about who's online, which sites they're visiting, which ads they're viewing and clicking on, and how much time they spend surfing per site.

In addition, ACNielsen markets a broad range of advanced decision-support software and modeling & analytical services, helping clients integrate and evaluate large volumes of information, make judgements about their growth opportunities and plan future marketing and sales campaigns.

Recent Developments

In 1999, ACNielsen expanded its scanning-based retail coverage in Latin America, Eastern Europe and Asia Pacific, and launched Retail Warehouse Solutions for US retailers and FreshTrack for measuring fresh-food sales in Canada. The UK continued to augment its portfolio of expertise with the introduction of ACNielsen's Catering Wholesale Service in 2000, an innovative tracking service which measures the wholesale sector within the foodservice market.

1999 was also a busy year for ACNielsen's media and entertainment services, with consolidation of global media operations under the new name of ACNielsen Media International. As well as acquiring Media Monitoring Services, the UK's leading provider of advertising expenditure measurement, the company completed a ten-city expansion of television audience measurement services in China and acquired full ownership of Media Services Korea. It also won television audience measurement contracts in New Zealand, Hong Kong and Finland.

ACNielsen EDI launched ReelResearch.com, a new service that uses the internet to test movie trailers and advertising.

Moving at internet speed, ACNielsen eRatings.com will launch the Nielsen//NetRatings internet measurement service in more than 30 countries, covering about 90% of the world's internet audience, by the end of 2001.

On the customised research side, 1999 saw ACNielsen acquire full ownership of Market Decisions, the US leader in controlled market and in-store product testing. The organisation also expanded ACNielsen BASES' E-Panel online research capabilities.

As part of its commitment to develop people, the UK company recently reinstated its Graduate Trainee Programme, through which graduates have reached senior level and board positions in the UK and Europe. In July 1999 the UK business achieved the government's recognised status as an 'Investor in People'.

Promotion

ACNielsen derives most of its promotion from the use of its information and its people in the public domain. As the industry standard in many countries, ACNielsen, and indeed its clients, frequently provide selected data and insight to the media for publication. ACNielsen people are regularly quoted in the press commenting on issues of the day as well as appearing on numerous conference platforms throughout the world as industry and issue experts.

The company also co-operates with respected trade magazines to publish influential surveys, which are widely reported in the media and used for reference by the trade and brand owners. The annual Biggest Brands Survey, published in the UK's Marketing magazine for the past decade, ranks consumer goods brands by sector. A similarly well respected editorial endorsement for ACNielsen's information over the past decade is the annual Top 100 UK Grocery Brands survey in Checkout magazine.

Brand Values

ACNielsen aims to help its customers turn information into insights, insights into knowledge and knowledge into actions that drive profitable growth. Its vision is to be recognised wordwide as the premier professional services firm in market research, supported by the core values of integrity and honesty, respect and development of people, and excellence and innovation.

Things you didn't know about ACNielsen

In 1918, Arthur C Nielsen Sr graduated from the University of Wisconsin with a degree in engineering. His grades were so high that, to date, no one at the university has ever equalled his grade point average.

Antarctica is the only continent in which ACNielsen does not operate.

ACNielsen was the first company to use electronic scanners – in 1967, to input type-written information into a computer.

In 1954, ACNielsen became the first company to use a computer – an IBM 650 - for commercial business.

In 1964, ACNielsen was the first market research company to equip home workers with computers.

The UK was the first market ACNielsen entered outside the US, in 1939.

ACNielsen invented the broadcast audience 'ratings' system and was instrumental in the commercialisation of mainframe computers.

ACNielsen is the largest operator of consumer panels worldwide, covering more than 135,000 households in twenty countries.

Corporate Services

Market

American Express is one of the world's most famous brands. Best known by consumers for its charge and credit cards, 'Amex' is also a formidable brand in the business to business sector. Its Corporate Services division provides global expense management programmes and Consulting Services to 83 of The Times Top 100 companies and two thirds of the Fortune Top 500. It provides a raft of services to companies to help them manage their purchasing, employee expenses and travel budgets. As well as these services, American Express provides consultancy for its corporate clients and payment solutions for retailers and merchants.

European businesses spend about £20 billion every year on travel and related expenses, accounting for nearly a third of all their indirect operating expenses. With these costs in mind, companies are understandably keen to implement careful management of their travel and expense budgets. Companies spend millions on corporate travel – air fares account for nearly half of a typical corporation's travel expenditure – and, in the UK, where corporate travel costs are the highest in Europe, companies need all the help they can get to keep expenditure down. Corporate travel policies – whereby a company centralises its travel booking and works with designated partners to benefit from special discounts – are used by 83% of global corporations. Corporate cards – allowing employees to charge business expenses to a company account – are used by 79% of all corporations. Corporate purchasing cards – allowing companies to simplify the process of purchasing goods and services – is another important area, allowing companies to cut purchase-processing costs by up to 80%.

The internet is expanding American Express' market in important ways, with heavy investments in web-based ventures, and providing online services to corporate clients and merchants to help them manage and reduce costs.

Achievements

Having begun as a rough and tumble freight forwarding company in 1850, American Express has grown into a leading global financial and travel services company and one of the most recognisable and widely used international business brands. It is ranked as one of the top twenty world brands.

It has developed a worldwide financial services network and built the most widely recognised charge card in the world, with over 47 million cards in use and over £254 billion spent on them every year. Having launched its corporate card in 1971, it is ten times as big as its closest corporate card competitor and the American Express Corporate Card continues to be the recognised leader for managing business travel and entertainment expenses the world over.

During its 150 years in business, American Express has also built itself into the world's largest travel company, with over 3,200 Travel Service Offices. It has made it easier for businesses to manage their increasingly global activities, through providing cost-efficient, easy to manage travel solutions.

History

American Express was founded by Henry Wells in 1850. Originally established as an express freight company, American Express has links to such famous names as Wells Fargo and The Pony Express. In those days of the Wild West, companies such as these were needed for the safe and speedy transport of goods, valuables, and money.

Operating under the slogan 'Safety and Dispatch', and with a bulldog logo, American Express quickly became a trusted and recognisable brand. During the American Civil War in the 1860s, it undertook the dangerous business of delivering election papers to the troops in the field, and, in 1892, developed a system of underwriting money orders as a safer alternative to shipping cash.

Towards the end of the century, American Express helped US immigrants by opening banks around Europe, making it easier for them to send money back to relatives at home. This started the bank's international expansion rolling, and, in 1891, it launched the now world-famous American Express Traveller's Cheque – the first of its kind. This was a true innovation, allowing US dollar cheques to be converted into a variety of currencies and offering the ability to get a refund or replacement if the cheque was lost or stolen. Around this time, American Express freight offices in England, France and Germany started selling tickets for trains and transatlantic ships.

Before long, the company had a network of European agents making it easier for customers to send and receive money and goods around the world. After the First World War, the company expanded its travel organisation and extended its financial operations into Latin America, the Far East and further into Europe.

The famous green American Express charge card was launched in 1958 and immediately became a coveted status symbol. The company introduced its Corporate Charge card in 1971 and its success quickly mirrored that of the consumer products.

Product

American Express Corporate Services focuses on helping companies to manage their expenses via a variety of tools. The three principal areas are Corporate Card, Corporate Purchasing Card and Corporate Travel.

The American Express Corporate Card is an expense management tool which saves companies time and money by streamlining the way expenses are reported and processed. Using the card, employees can charge expenses to a central account which the company then settles with American Express. This is far simpler than having to check and process receipts and, thanks to value-added tools that come as part of the service, allows companies to keep a close eye on their expenses. It eliminates the need for cash advances and requires fewer administrative personnel. One client, Seagram, cut $15 million from its corporate travel bill when it started using the Corporate Card.

In the corporate travel area, American Express offers a Travel Management portfolio of services to help companies control their travel expenses. The American Express Interactive Travel service (AXI) offers corporate clients an online travel planning, booking and approval tool. Highlighting preferred partners and suppliers – such as airlines and hotels with which the company has agreed special rates – AXI Travel makes it easier for clients to manage their travel requirements in real time and wherever they are in the world.

In April 2000 American Express was awarded "Best Use of

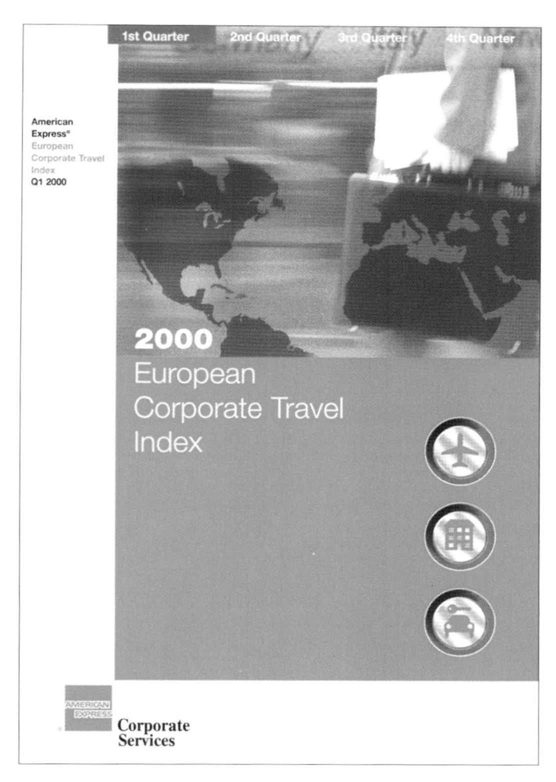

Technology" for this product, during the travel industry's Year 2000 Agent Achievement Awards. AXI Travel won in recognition of its best use of technology based on sales performance and customer care.

Another travel tool is Jaguar – a point of sale system that automatically pulls up a profile of a corporate customer and makes sure that their travel bookings adhere to the company's travel policy. There are also pre-trip and post-trip analysis and reporting tools which allow travel managers to monitor travel costs, keep track of trends, generate reports and pay attention to details such as ensuring not too many senior executives are on the same flight. Travel Services also offers specialist consultancy to help companies drive down their travel costs and database services which can simulate spend patterns, collate historical information and cross-match competing deals.

The Corporate Purchasing Card simplifies the way in which companies buy goods and services. Employees authorised to buy using the purchasing card can quickly buy direct instead of requesting supplies from a purchasing department which takes time and costs more. According to a study by American Express and Ernst & Young, companies can reduce administrative costs by 80% by using a purchasing card and up to 95% if they combine this with online purchasing.

American Express' Consultancy Services study a company's expense management processes from beginning to end, identifying areas of potential saving, helping to implement new processes and assessing results. It is a combination of their ability to capture global spend data with the ability to turn it into actionable strategies that can cut indirect operating costs by 40%. With one client, their consultants implemented a hotel programme that drove compliance rates up to 89% and saved £2.7 million pounds on total annual hotel costs.

Another important area of American Express is its Merchant Services. Millions of merchants around the world welcome American Express cards and receive a package of services in return. These include internet-based programmes, such as the E-Commerce Resource Centre, providing merchants with tips on how to develop and implement online business strategies.

Recent Developments

In 1999, the company launched American Express @ Work, a corporate desktop portal that helps business customers manage their Corporate Card and Corporate Purchasing Card programmes online. For purchasing, this acts as a business-to-business e-commerce tool, allowing companies to buy goods and services online.

In April 2000, American Express launched its Partner Corporate Loyalty Programme for small and medium-sized businesses. This is the UK's first expense management travel programme specifically for SMEs, and promises to save them up to 21% on air travel, 7% on hotel accommodation and 10% on car hire costs. Because SMEs are too small to negotiate special deals from large travel suppliers, this programme allows them to benefit from the type of savings enjoyed by larger companies. American Express has calculated that European SMEs spend around $30 billion a year on travel and related expenses.

Promotion

With one of the most famous corporate identities in the world, the American Express 'blue box' is a powerful icon. The company has always been a high-profile advertiser, with one of the most famous lines in advertising history – 'American Express? That'll do nicely.'
More recently, this has been replaced by the Blue Card TV campaign. Although these campaigns are clearly targeting consumers, they also serve to raise American Express' profile among corporate customers, especially merchants who are considering accepting the card.

The company's website is another strong promotional tool for corporate services, outlining all of the company's offerings to large and small companies and to merchants.

An effective way for American Express to promote itself is via PR, commissioning reports to highlight issues which underpin its position as the industry thought leader. For example, last year it teamed up with Ernst & Young to produce the American Express Purchasing Process and Automation Study to illustrate how much companies can save on administrative costs by using corporate purchasing cards. It also publishes an annual Global Travel and Expense Management Survey, highlighting the importance of managing travel and expenses in the corporate sector. Other regular reports cover business travel, such as the American Express Year 2000 Travel Trends Survey. All of these raise interesting points and reveal trends which are picked up in the wider media.

Brand Values

The hallmarks of the American Express brand are trust, integrity, security, quality and customer service. The company takes the maintenance and consistent implementation of its brand values extremely seriously and conducts annual brand audits to track the health of the brand, and also recently unveiled an employee training programme focusing on brand management.

Service is at the core of the brand and the promise that the training programme hopes to instil in American Express staff is 'making customers feel respected and special through unsurpassed service, expertise, and integrity'.

The corporate vision is to be the world's most respected service brand. Built on this foundation are five core principles: customer commitment, quality, success, trust and integrity and security. All of these factors work towards the ultimate goal, which is to facilitate customers' success.

American Express has a Brand Management Team and Brand Facilitators to ensure that these values are expressed and implemented throughout the company's 88,378 employees in 120 countries.

Things you didn't know about American Express

Annual spending on American Express cards is nearly four times higher than on Visa and Mastercard products.

Globally, American Express is ten times the size of its nearest corporate card competitor.

$254 billion was spent on American Express cards in 1999.

In Paris, the American Express office helped 150,000 Americans get home safely when they found themselves trapped at the outbreak of the First World War. When the war got worse, American Express cheques were often seen as a safer alternative to cash.

American Express is the world's largest travel management company with over 3,200 Travel Service offices, Corporate Travel Centres and representative offices worldwide.

It won 'Large Travel Agent of the Year' award in April 2000 at the industry's Year 2000 Agent Achievement Awards.

Andersen Consulting

Market

Management and technology consulting is a $300 billion plus industry (Source: Dataquest), in which Andersen Consulting is one of the biggest players. With revenues of $9 billion and 65,000 personnel working in 48 countries. Andersen Consulting is a global powerhouse.

It is a true giant in the increasingly high profile and valuable management and technology consultancy sector, working with some of the biggest names in business across a dozen industries, offering services in strategy, process, technology, change management, and e-commerce consulting, as well as in business process management.

In today's networked economy, businesses need more help than ever to develop their strategies, technological infrastructure and people to compete on the global stage. Andersen Consulting is the undisputed leader in providing this expertise.

The firm works with more than 4,500 organisations around the world, including 91 of Fortune's 1999 Global 100 companies. It works with 95% of Fortune's top telecommunications organisations and 85% of its top utilities companies and 78% of banking firms. Clients also include more than half of the Industry Standard 100 most important companies of the internet economy. In the UK clients include The London Stock Exchange and Prudential.

Achievements

In 1998, Andersen Consulting celebrated its first ten years as an independent brand. In its first five years of independence it reported revenues of $3.4 billion and 32,000 personnel. After ten years, these figures had more than doubled.

At the end of 1999, when revenues reached $8.9 billion, the firm's success in the new e-commerce sector became evident. It reported e-commerce related revenues of $1.5 billion – a massive increase on the $500 million it had earned from this sector in 1998.

As shown by its success in e-commerce, Andersen Consulting has the muscle, expertise and global presence to apply itself to almost anything that a company wishes to improve upon. It has built a particularly strong reputation in the technological consultancy sector, working very closely with major computer and software manufacturers, including Microsoft.

External indicators reflect the firm's achievements. In 1998, it was ranked the world's leading consulting firm by three newsletters covering this sector: Consultants News, Global IT Consulting Report, and Management Consultant International. In addition it came out on top in a Landor/Harris ImagePower study in the US.

History

Andersen Consulting originated as the consulting arm of the accountancy firm, Arthur Andersen, in 1942. In its earliest years, it did not operate under a separate name or brand, and, in 1951, was simply called Administrative Services. However, even at this point, the growing need to advise companies on the development of systems, methods, and new management theories quickly grew the unit's business.

In the 1950s, Administrative Services was influential in helping companies use technology to improve their operations. In 1953, it installed

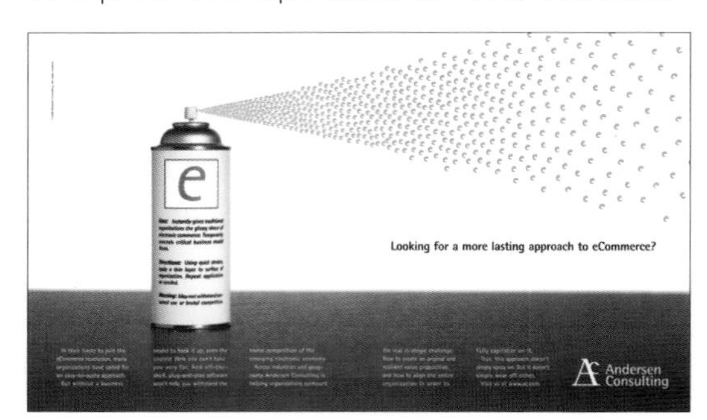

the first ever computer for business applications at General Electric. The system, called General Run, is regarded as one of the earliest forerunners to modern computer operating platforms. In 1957, Administrative Services installed the Bank of America's first computer system. At the same time, it recommended the creation of a new type of credit card, called the BankAmericard, which later became known as Visa. Also, during the 1950s, the division expanded overseas, opening offices in Europe and Australia.

In the 1960s, the firm started to formalise its consulting operations, with the creation of a consultancy training school in Chicago. At this time, the division was also influential in helping major US companies expand abroad, such as Ford, for which it helped develop its European manufacturing and parts distribution network.

In the 1970s, international expansion continued apace, especially in Asia Pacific, where it opened offices in Hong Kong and Singapore. (Today, Andersen Consulting is the largest consulting firm in Asia Pacific.) In the 1970s, Administrative Services also became an authority in 'Just In Time' manufacturing, passing

on techniques it used with Yamaha of Japan to the US motorbike company, Harley Davidson. During the 1970s, the company also helped manage the integration of British European Airways and British Overseas Airways Corporation to form British Airways in 1975.

In 1980, with Administrative Services now a thriving business, the company renamed it the Management Information Consulting Division. At this stage, the division had revenues of $192 million and 3,600 personnel. As a result of this growth, in 1989, the partners created Andersen Consulting as a legally separate commercial enterprise devoted to management and technology consulting. By 1994, Andersen Consulting was reporting revenues of $3.4 billion and employing 32,000 personnel.

In 1998, following an eighteen month comprehensive brand exploration, a new corporate identity was launched, supported by a global brand building campaign. This involved the design of the firm's first logo, positioning statement and personality traits. At the end of 1998, the company reported its most successful ever year, with revenues of $8.3 billion.

Product

Andersen Consulting's services are divided into five business units: Financial Services, Products, Resources, Communications and High Tech, and Government. The biggest market is Financial Services, generating $2.5 billion (28%) of total revenue. Products, which includes automotive and industrial, food and consumer goods, retail and pharmaceutical categories account for 18% of revenue, while Resources (including chemicals, energy, utilities and natural resources) generated 18%. Communications and Hi-tech is a 28% sector, while Government work accounts for 8%. Government and communications are the fastest growing areas, increasing by 35% and 29% respectively in 1999.

Examples of Andersen Consulting's work in the financial services sector include a major project for Germany's fourth largest bank, Commerzbank AG. Andersen Consulting helped the bank transform its retail banking business, installing a 24-hour call centre and introducing internet-based services. In Communications and High Tech, it worked with Hong Kong Telecom to create and dominate a new sector in interactive TV services. Other prominent clients include Prudential, Fiat and DuPont.

Andersen Consulting also offers clients unique capabilities to help with specific needs. For example, its Retail Ideas Exchange is a centre in

Chicago where clients can explore innovative solutions – including new technology – for the food and packaged goods industries. Its Knowledge Xchange is a tool which allows employees to share information from a central computerised resource. Today, it features 1.5 million pages in fourteen global libraries.

Recent Developments

In December 1999, Andersen Consulting formed AC Ventures to invest in new electronic businesses. This entity gives new media start-ups and spin-offs access to $1 billion in capital and know-how. To further invest in the new media age, the firm also launched over twenty Dot-com Launch Centres in February 2000. These are production studios that help new start-ups mature into successful operations. Additional launch centres will be opened in the near future.

In March 2000, Andersen Consulting announced a $1 billion global alliance with Microsoft designed to stimulate enterprise in the electronic economy. The new joint venture company, called Avanade, is dedicated to designing and building business solutions based on the Microsoft enterprise platform, which includes Microsoft Windows 2000.

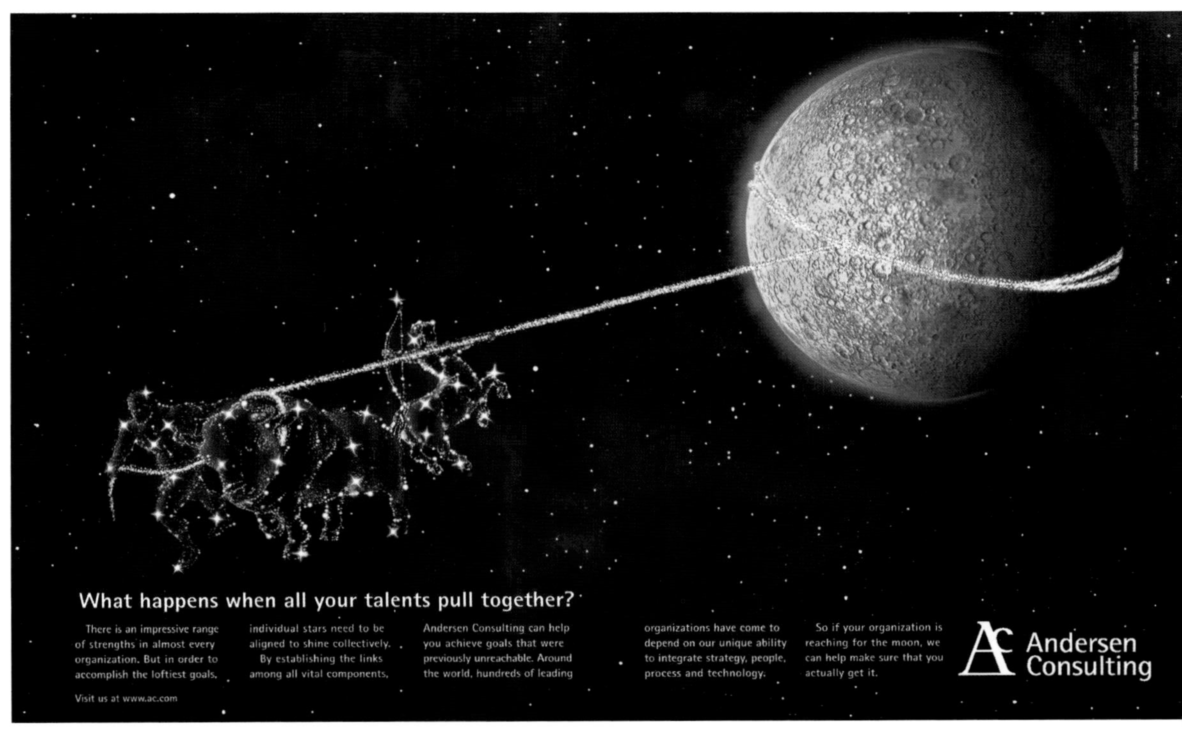

Promotion

Andersen Consulting's high profile marketing and global brand building makes it an innovator in its sector. Professional services companies have not been particularly active in business-to-business marketing over the years, but Andersen Consulting broke the mould by advertising heavily in above-the-line media commencing in 1988.

Over a period of ten years, Andersen Consulting's marketing and communications efforts have positioned Andersen Consulting as the leader in the management and technology consulting arena. In 1998, with an aspiration of becoming one of the world's leading business-to-business brands, the firm launched a new brand identity supported by a $100 million marketing effort. This major marketing initiative helped reinforce Andersen Consulting as the leading management consultant in the world and became a springboard to its more recent efforts which are aimed at positioning Andersen Consulting as the leader in the e-commerce marketplace.

Andersen Consulting has also invested in event sponsorships, focusing on world-class events such as Formula One Grand Prix, in which it became a lead sponsor of the Williams team. In 1998, it was the sole corporate sponsor of the three-month Van Gogh exhibition at the National Gallery of Art in Washington DC. The firm became a global sponsor of the Andersen Consulting World Golf Championships in 1999. In the UK, the firm also sponsored the Snowdon Exhibition at the National Gallery.

As part of its new brand identity launch, Andersen Consulting redesigned its corporate website (www.ac.com) and introduced an internal communications programme designed to embed the values of the firm's new identity into the culture of the company and its employees.

The firm also invests in 'thought leadership' as part of its promotional activities. This involves promoting the quality of its thinking through packaged research reports, conferences and high-profile partnerships with organisations like The World Economic Forum at Davos and the Smithsonian Institution.

Brand Values

Andersen Consulting aspires to be the world's most admired business-to-business brand. Its brand is based around the excellence of its thinking, the quality of its people and its place at the centre of a new business age.

It goes to great lengths to ensure its values are applied consistently throughout the company. It has over 1,200 'brand champions' – marketing people and key influencers – who focus on consistency of brand communication inside and outside the company. It has a 72-page document describing the firm's positioning, called Building Our Brand, and keeps image and documentation libraries stocked with resources to provide material which can be used in branded communications. There is also a Global Brand Database – a resource which houses all brand information – which is supported by the firm's Global Brand Hotline. This resource answers all internal questions relating to the brand. Externally, the strength of the brand is measured by an annual survey among Fortune 500 executives in 24 countries.

NB 2001 sees a change of name and identity for Andersen Consulting.

Things you didn't know about Andersen Consulting

In 1994, a team from the firm's London office helped the Moscow Bread Company's bakers, drivers and factory managers resolve the city's bread shortages. This work established the firms' reputation in Moscow and it opened an office there shortly afterwards.

In 1957 it helped the Bank of America create the worlds' first credit card.

Between 1982 and 1995, Andersen Consulting helped Harley Davidson increase its share of the US motorcycle market from 30 to 60%.

An astonishing 90% of blue jeans produced in the world move through production processes benefiting from Andersen Consulting supply chain work.

Half of the world's mail is processed with the help of Andersen Consulting.

One third of the world's passenger airline tickets are processed by Andersen Consulting through PRA Solutions, a wholly owned Andersen Consulting enterprise that provides technology and services to the airline industry.

AVIS

Market

Avis is synonymous with vehicle rental. Alongside Hertz, Budget, Europcar and Sixt, it dominates the sector, especially when it comes to renting to business customers.

Corporate clients account for around half of the total vehicle rental market, with rental firms usually providing cars on a contracted basis. Today's global corporations need support from suppliers with similarly international reach, a wide product portfolio and high service levels. As the top rental company in Europe, with 2,700 locations, Avis is the only one of the majors to rent cars in every European country. Overall, the European car rental market is worth nearly £3.3 billion annually.

Worldwide, Avis has 4,200 rental locations and a fleet of 370,000 vehicles in over 160 countries. Annually, it completes around sixteen million rental transactions, generating an annual gross revenue of approximately £1.7 billion. In Europe, 84% of revenues comes from corporate clients in the UK, France, Germany, Spain and Italy.

This network helped to make Avis a brand that 75% of Europe's top 500 companies do business with. The company is constantly expanding its network to further improve service, mostly by granting licences to local franchises. This is a flexible and safe route for it to expand into more diverse territories, like Africa, Asia and the Middle East.

Achievements

From humble beginnings at Detroit Airport, Avis has built itself into a world-leading brand. It is not only an instantly recognisable name to consumers and business users all over the world, but also market leader in Europe, Africa and The Middle East, with the largest fleet and widest choice.

The company has successfully pioneered car rental in several international markets, including Central and Eastern Europe, where it subsequently expanded its operations. It was the first car rental company to open an office in East Germany after the fall of the Berlin Wall – a move that helped it springboard into neighbouring former eastern bloc territories, like the Czech Republic and Romania. It has achieved a similar goal in the former Soviet Union and, when it opened an office in the Ukraine in 1997, it became the first and only car rental company to have an office in every European country. This gives it an unrivalled European network - including presence at all 75 major European airports.

The company has been similarly pioneering in Africa, where it now has representation in over 85% of the region. Again, this has given it greater coverage than any of its competitors. In the Middle East, it is represented in 90% of the region, and in Asia, is licensed to operate in 27 territories.

Avis has been similarly pioneering in its commitment to high customer service levels since the mid-1960s, and the introduction of the first computerised reservation system Wizard, in 1972. It has also built one of the best partnership structures in the business, with over 50 airline partners.

History

Warren Avis opened the first Avis office at Willow Run airport, Detroit, in 1946. At that time, he had a grand total of three cars, but it was the world's first ever car rental operation at an airport.

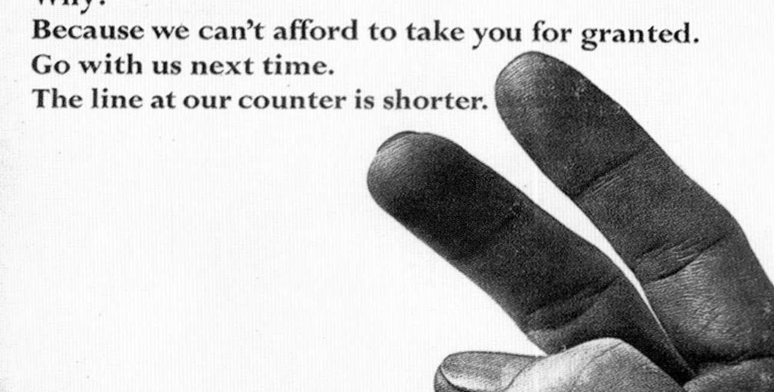

By 1953, Avis was the second largest car rental company in the US and already expanding overseas - opening franchised operations in Mexico, Canada and Europe. By 1963 it was struggling with a 10% US market share, compared to 75% for Hertz. It launched an advertising campaign that proved crucial in turning its fortunes around. The slogan, 'We're only No.2. We try harder' emphasised its commitment to customer service and remains at the core of its brand today. The slogan has subsequently been recognised as one of the ten best of all time.

In 1965, Avis officially launched Avis Europe to look after its growing operations in Europe, Africa and the Middle East. By 1973, it was market leader in these areas – a position it still holds today.

In 1979, Avis entered a worldwide advertising and marketing agreement with General Motors, and began featuring GM cars in its fleet worldwide. In 1986, Avis Europe legally separated from its owner, Avis Inc, and became the first ever car company to float in the London Stock Exchange. In three years, it tripled its market value, before reverting to private ownership again in 1989.

In 1987, Avis Inc became employee-owned, with a £1.2 billion Employee Stock Ownership Plan – this made it the largest employee owned company in the US and a role model for other companies to follow.

In 1996, the company's impressive technological track record continued, when it became the first car rental company to launch a website – www.avis.com. The following year, Avis Europe re-floated on the London Stock Exchange to fund expansion of the business. In the same year, Avis Europe licensed its name for use in 27 new Asian markets and signed a partnership deal in the Ukraine.

Product

Avis was an early leader in technical support systems, with the introduction of its Wizard computerised reservation system in 1972. This is still in operation today and is the most extensive online, real-time reservation, rental and management information system in the industry. Wizard controls the fleet, knowing where every car can be found, who they are rented to and when they will be returned. Wizard is also invaluable when it comes to managing company fleet costs and travel policy. Reports can be customised for corporate customers so they can optimise the management of their rental costs.

Avis has special arrangements for corporate clients, packed into its Corporate Contract service. Corporate accounts are given priority and each client assigned a Corporate Account Manager to tailor services to a company's needs. This service also includes monthly reports which help clients manage their account more efficiently.

Thanks to partnerships with major airlines, Avis offers streamlined services at airports. For instance, with British Airways at Heathrow, customers can return their car and check-in for an onward BA flight all at the same desk. With services like Avis Preferred, customers can enjoy some of the quickest service in the industry. Having completed a personal profile just once, customers can call ahead and then arrive at a Preferred desk to find a car pre-assigned with all the paperwork completed. Returning a car is just as quick – the Rapid Return Service allows the vehicle details to be entered into a hand held terminal, which automatically calculates the bill and issues a receipt before the customer even reaches the desk.

Avis also offers services tailored for smaller businesses, like Avis Advance, and Maxi-Rent – a flexible programme for long term rentals designed to facilitate fleet management.

Recent Developments

Avis has recently launched its on-line rental booking service - www.avis.co.uk allowing customers to make or modify a booking wherever they are in the world. Frequent travellers will be able to enter their itineraries into the site so that a car is always ready for them when they need it.

Avis will soon make further use of the internet in a joint venture with US-based Navidec to sell ex-rental cars on-line. Avis will have up to 40,000 cars each year for sale over the site.

In March 2000, an all-new central reservations centre, based at Salford Quays in Manchester, went live. Staffed by 300 agents, the centre is designed to take over two million calls and make over 400,000 outbound calls in its first year. Agents can speak English, French, German, and also handle fax, post and email reservations.

Avis is also working to safeguard the environment, promoting responsible car usage through a variety of schemes. A major market intelligence report, called Traffic Ahead, is designed to help companies adopt an environmentally responsible transport policy and examine the role car rental can play in achieving this. It also examines how government transport policy affects individual companies and the impact of the Budget on the fleet industry. Avis has also introduced a car-sharing club, called CARvenience. This allows club members - who pay an annual membership fee – to pick up cars from specially allocated points as and when they need them. It is designed to be a cost-effective alternative to car ownership or long term rental.

Promotion

Avis is one of the most promotionally active of the major car rental brands, making extensive use of media including press, outdoor, and sponsorship.

A major recent initiative was a joint promotion with British Airways, offering BA customers money off and prizes every time they rent an Avis car. This was particularly attractive to business users as it offered members of BA Executive Club the chance to drive classic cars, including Porsches, Ferraris and Lamborghinis. The promotion was advertised in the press and by direct mail, using the slogan 'The Road to Riches'.

The company has also entered into joint promotions with Kodak, and made use of product placement in films, including James Bond's 'Tomorrow Never Dies'.

Brand Values

The company is driven by a singular vision – established in 1965 - 'to be the best and fastest growing company with the highest profit margins in the car rental business'. These values are enshrined in the 'We Try Harder' slogan.

From the 1960s, when Avis made a virtue of being second biggest but the best in terms of service, it has put the customer at the centre of the business. Empathy (understanding customer needs), Honesty (value for money and integrity) and Humanity (putting the customer first) underpin the 'We Try Harder' philosophy. These values have contributed to Avis having one of the strongest and most consistent corporate cultures in the world.

Things you didn't know about Avis

Over 40% of Avis's licensee partners have been associated with the group for twenty years or more.

Warren Avis got the idea for airport-based car rental during World War II when he was a bomber pilot. He used to carry his motorbike in the bomber so that he could always have transport wherever he landed.

Avis is planting up to 26,000 trees in the UK to offset carbon dioxide emissions made by cars. Last year it planted one tree in the UK for every car in the fleet.

Avis Europe offers 60 models from twenty manufacturers.

Avis has 57 travel partners worldwide and more airline partners than any other car rental company.

Avis was the first car rental company to operate a 100% lead-free fleet.

Bartle Bogle Hegarty

Market

The UK market for advertising has grown by nearly 10% since 1999 to reach a value of almost £11.6 billion. Advertising expenditure is strongly influenced by economic conditions and periods of high consumer spending create conditions for higher corporate profitability. This in turn increases the resources available to advertisers for the promotion of their brands. As the UK's economy improved following the recession of the early 1990s, the advertising market saw ever-increasing growth rates.

The market is dominated by collections of advertising agencies who are members of groups, such as WPP Group, Interpublic Ltd and Omnicom UK Ltd. However the agencies within these groups operate as separate entities battling for market share. The lead agencies include Abbott Mead Vickers, BMP DDB, J Walter Thompson and TBWA GGT Simons Palmer.

Founded as an advertising agency in London in 1982, Bartle Bogle Hegarty has grown into a major international communications group.

BBH Communications is now the master brand for a group with offices in London, Singapore, Tokyo and New York, and subsidiaries specialising in media, design, brand consultancy and, of course, advertising.

In total, BBH employs 452 people, recorded global billings of $505 million in 1999 and is 51% privately owned by its employees. The remaining 49% was acquired by the US-based advertising agency network, Leo Burnett, in 1997.

The flagship of the group remains the London agency, based in Kingly Street, Soho. In terms of UK billings it amounts to £165.5 million in 1999 (Source: MMS). The important metric for BBH is its reputation for creativity. In this respect, it leads its field, coming top of Marketing Week's Clients Top Agency for Creativity for the past eleven years.

Achievements

BBH has created some of the most iconic advertising of the last two decades. Few people can forget its work for Levi Strauss, a campaign that began in 1985 when Nick Kamen walked into a launderette, kicked off his jeans, put them in the washer and sat back to the sounds of Marvin Gaye's 'I heard it through the Grapevine'.

This campaign not only revived the fortunes of Levi's – boosting sales of 501s by 800% – but also changed the face of British advertising. That ad symbolised a new place for advertising at the heart of pop culture. The campaign is widely regarded as one of the best bodies of work for any advertiser. BBH's awards for Levi's include eight Golds at Cannes International and a Gold and Commendation in the highly regarded IPA Advertising Effectiveness Awards.

Thanks to work like this, it is not surprising that Levi's has been with BBH since its foundation in 1982. But the agency has two other clients that have also been with it since the beginning – Audi and Whitbread (which has since been bought by Interbrew UK). Thanks to the unforgettable line, 'Vorsprung durch Technik', Audi's ads also go down in the advertising hall of fame and have won numerous awards. Over the years, BBH has helped to change Audi from a bland 'Euro-car' into a highly desirable brand with a reputation for technical innovation and daring design.

For Interbrew UK, BBH's work for Boddingtons, using the line 'The Cream of Manchester', has helped the brand break out of its home North West market to become a national favourite. Within eighteen months of national rollout, Boddingtons was the number one take-home bitter. TV, press and poster work has been honoured at Cannes International and won the IPA Gold in 1994.

The agency's work for other clients, such as Elida Faberge deodorant, Lynx, reflects a similar mix of creative excellence and business effectiveness. The highly amusing 'Lynx Effect' campaign, running since 1995, has consistently boosted sales.

In a recent survey by Campaign Magazine, BBH's ads for Levi's, Audi, Boddingtons and One 2 One were voted among the Top 100 British ads of the century. BBH was also one of only two agencies to achieve two entries (Levi's and Boddingtons) in the 'Top 10 Ads Ever' poll carried out by Channel 4 and The Sunday Times in May 2000.

As well as countless industry awards, BBH's work has helped it become the only advertising agency ever to win the Queen's Award for Export Achievement, in 1996 and 1997. In April 1997 the agency was named International Agency of the Year by Advertising Age.

History

BBH was founded in 1982 by John Bartle, Nigel Bogle and John Hegarty.

The agency's 'rock-and-romance' ads for Levi's soon put the agency's name on the map and sent jeans sales through the roof. In 1987, it was voted Campaign magazine's Agency of the Year and Hegarty – the creative force behind the campaign – began to become something of a celebrity. During the 1980s, when advertising was regarded as the sexiest of all businesses and leading agencies were growing phenomenally fast, Hegarty joined Maurice and Charles Saatchi as one of the key faces of British advertising.

During the early 1990s, the agency continued to win important new business despite its belief in no creative pitches, like Boddingtons in 1991, Electrolux in 1993, Coca-Cola in 1994 and Lynx and One 2 One in 1995. Its work put it at the top of the industry magazines' creativity leagues and advertising effectiveness leagues, winning IPA Golds in 1994 for Cadbury's Roses and Boddingtons. BBH was named 'Agency of the Year' at the Cannes International Advertising Festival for two years in succession (1993/1994).

SUPPLEMENT TO ADVERTISING AGE APRIL 1997

Advertising Age International

http://adage.com

Bartle Bogle Hegarty

International Agency of the Year *Page i-3*

Dial 011-800-GO-GLOBAL: Multinational marketers to get standard numbers in 20 countries i-8

Middle East Special Report: Israel embraces Americana; pan-Arab TV war erupts; high-tech booms i-11

Focus on Airline Marketing: Reborn Pan Am rises from bankruptcy to win back international travelers i-23

In 1995, BBH hived off its media department into a new stand-alone subsidiary, Motive Communications. In 1996, the agency began its international expansion, becoming the first independent agency to set up a regional office in Asia Pacific, based in Singapore. The aim was to serve international brand names, as opposed to local business. At this stage, half of the agency's income was generated from international clients – a factor that helped it win the Queen's Award for Export Achievement in that year.

In 1997, as BBH's scope of international assignments increased, the agency actively sought a partner to provide global media delivery for its clients. That agency was Leo Burnett, which, with offices in 83 offices in 72 countries, gave BBH access to the global media market. Retaining the majority stake, the deal allowed BBH to continue to operate independently and continue its expansion abroad. In 1998, it opened an office in New York, serving clients including Reebok, Johnnie Walker and Unilever.

In January 2000 Motive (BBH Group) and Starcom (Leo Burnett Group) merged to become Starcom Motive Partnership offering an independent objective media service for clients in a vastly changing media landscape.

Product

Bartle Bogle Hegarty believes in the power of 'Creativity' to create big advertising-led ideas that change consumer perceptions and alter their behaviour. Big ideas are rarely constrained by medium or by geography: they are, by their very nature, holistic, embracing above and below-the-line applications equally and crossing borders with ease.

Big ideas are famous ideas and BBH believes that brands need fame – common understanding and emotional involvement that everyone can relate to. Fame is what makes people talk about soap operas – it also guarantees we all know what driving an Audi 'means'.

Recent Developments

The agency's work for Levi's continues to win praise and awards. The 1999 'Flat Eric' campaign, for Levi's Sta-Prest, made Levi's cool again and grew Sta-Prest sales across Europe. Flat Eric, a fluffy yellow puppet (which became a cult figure on the net and a best selling toy in the shops) helped Levi's win Campaign magazine's Campaign of the Year, in 1999. Indeed the song 'Flat Beat', which accompanied the commercial, rose to the top of the charts in April 1999.

One of the network's recent success stories is BBH US which opened its doors in New York in September 1998 and has grown rapidly in under two years. The agency employs 57 people, has twelve clients and bills $180 million. It boasts clients such as Reebok Classic (on a global basis), Lipton Foods, Johnnie Walker and the successful teen portal, Bolt.com.

Promotion

BBH's own marketing is focused on a Business Development Unit, which looks after internal and external communications. It is in charge of fostering new client contacts, using a mixture of direct mail and face to face meetings. It is also in charge of the agency's PR, building BBH's profile in the media.

It produces a range of material to keep existing and prospective clients informed about the agency's work. These include the BBH website, a regularly updated creative booklet, showreels, case histories on key accounts and PR cutting books.

Furthermore, the Elixir Programme is BBH's investment in development of innovative thinking on brands and communication. The programme aims to develop forward-thinking intelligence that will attract the attention of the wider marketing community, the media and, of course potential clients. The programme consists of three types of activity: internally generated thought pieces on key issues; ad-hoc BBH funded research projects on key areas of interest; and a BBH funded service which uses a network of contacts around the world to monitor cultural trends and how they reflect and impact on brands.

Brand Values

All along, the BBH brand has been founded on a firm belief in its creative principles and the importance of effectiveness. It has a reputation for successfully working with clients that share in its belief and way of doing things.

BBH's beliefs are as follows: the power of creativity and the primacy of the idea; encouraging ideas from any source; the right of everyone to be listened to; the fundamental importance of effectiveness and accountability; processes that liberate creativity; client relationships that encourage equal status, allowing best advice; an organisation without politics; providing opportunity, stimulation and consideration to all who work with them; the need for honesty, decency and integrity in all that they do; and the obligations these beliefs place upon them.

Things you didn't know about **Bartle Bogle Hegarty**

John Hegarty became so well known in the 1980s that he appeared as a guest on the chat show, Wogan, in 1987 and on Radio 4's Desert Island Discs.

The agency was responsible for projecting a nude image of Gail Porter onto the Houses of Parliament. This appeared on the front cover of every tabloid newspaper across the UK.

Between 1985 and 1995, BBH produced 22 ads for Levi's that spawned eleven top ten single releases, including six number one hits. Hits created or revived by Levi's ads include Mr Boombastic by Shaggy, Wonderful World by Sam Cooke, and I Heard it through the Grapevine, by Marvin Gaye.

Pop star Robbie Williams was persuaded to don a pair of false breasts by BBH in TV and press ads for the Institute of Cancer Research. The ads raised awareness for testicular cancer.

BBH was attacked in early 2000 when a press ad for Barnardos depicted a baby preparing to inject himself with heroin. The campaign was designed to encourage early intervention into childhood problems.

In 1999 a giant pair of knickers was erected in Oxford Street for FHM. This ended up as an entry into Guinness Book of Records for the largest pair of knickers.

Market

The telecommunications industry is probably the fastest growing and the most competitive in the world. In the UK, BT leads a sector estimated by Keynote Research to be worth £23.5 billion in 1999, which is 58% more than in 1994.

This rate of growth can be attributed to telecoms moving beyond the realms of providing traditional voice telephony and into the rapidly expanding worlds of mobile communications and the internet. The world of communications is moving from narrowband to broadband, from fixed to mobile and from voice dominated communication to a data and internet dominated environment.

These factors are illustrated by looking at where the major telecoms companies derive their revenues. According to Keynote, 49% of telecom incomes were from fixed lines in 1994 – a figure which shrank to 36% in 1999. Conversely, the cellular sector has seen dramatic growth, with its share of revenue increasing from 16% to over 28% in the same time period.

This is radically changing the nature and structure of the industry. For one thing, previously separate technologies are converging – broadband and mobile, internet and mobile, broadband and internet. Also, the industry is consolidating, and merger and acquisition activity is rife, as players join forces to compete on an ever-larger stage. As markets are liberalised and technology makes boundaries and time zones increasingly irrelevant, the communications industry is a truly international business.

E-business has the potential to change everything about the way companies work: how they communicate with their customers and suppliers, how they buy materials and turn them into products, how they market and how they sell, and how they communicate with their employees and their shareholders. BT's product offering ensures it is keeping pace with the demands of this exciting new business culture.

Achievements

BT is one of the best known, most powerful brands in Britain. Its ambition is to be the most successful communications group in the world.

In research, its brand scores highly in terms of awareness. In Marketing magazine's long-running Adwatch survey (which ranks advertising on levels of unprompted consumer awareness) BT has been one of the most consistently strong performers, especially with its long-running 'It's good to talk' campaign starring Bob Hoskins. This campaign won the top prize in the highly prestigious Advertising Effectiveness Awards, held by the Institute of Practitioners in Advertising.

Operationally, BT has made important strides as it tries to transform itself into a new-wave communications company. This requires it to have global strength and a focus on the high growth areas of the internet, mobility, multimedia, data and solutions. To achieve this, it has been investing heavily in building new, high bandwidth networks as well as expanding its activities outside of the UK.

As a result, BT now boasts a worldwide operation which includes some 30 equity-based ventures and nearly 50 distributors, as well as having its own operations in key markets. Directly or indirectly, BT has gained access to 85% of the European and 100% of the Asia-Pacific region's addressable markets.

It has also created backbone networks which are capable of carrying massive volumes of internet traffic as well as voice calls. In the UK, it has spearheaded the move towards the provision of broadband services, with major investments in creating a broadband internet protocol (IP) network, and in mainland Europe it has created a major pan-European high-speed network. Concert - it's new global joint venture with AT&T - is rolling out one of the most advanced high-capacity IP networks in the world.

History

For many years the UK's telephone service was provided by the General Post Office. In 1969, the Post Office became a state public corporation and was split into two separate entities. The corporation responsible for telecommunications took on the trading name British Telecommunications and in 1984, British Telecom, as it was then known, was privatised.

At the time, it was the first state-owned telecommunications company to be privatised in Europe. In 1991, British Telecom was restructured and relaunched as BT with new branding and a new logo.

In April 2000, BT announced a radical restructuring to create a number of new international businesses, each with its own character and priorities, but working together to meet customers needs.

The new organisation is structured as follows. Ignite is an international broadband network business, focused primarily on corporate and wholesale customers. BTopenworld, is an international mass-market broadband internet business, operating with Asymmetric Digital Subscriber Line (ADSL) technology. BT Wireless is an international mobile business, with a particular emphasis on mobile data. Yell.com, is BT's international directories and associated e-commerce business.

Concert, BT's global joint venture with AT&T, started operations at the beginning of 2000. It meets the global communications needs of multinational companies, carriers and internet service providers.

Product

BT is one of the world's leading providers of telecommunications services to residential and business customers. Voice calls still form an important part of its business, but an increasingly large proportion of revenue now comes from new-wave areas such as the internet.

BT's products and services are suitable for a wide range of business applications, including one-person home-based companies, small and medium sized enterprises, and the largest multinationals.

Developing the products and services that its business customers need to compete in the world of e-business is a central plank of BT's offering. Business-to-business activity is by far the biggest area of e-commerce and BT is well positioned to serve demand. Knowing that different customers will have different experiences and different needs, BT has been careful to have something in its portfolio for all kinds of business wanting to compete in this sphere.

For example, smaller businesses can use the 'btclick for business' portfolio to find new suppliers, research markets, discover local business resources and set up a website. Products such as BT Business Manager and BT People Manager enable companies to access the very best software for functions such as stock management or payroll processes. Such application service provision products are predicted to form an increasingly significant part of the communications market.

Larger businesses can use BTnet services – powerful, large-scale services which can keep thousands of people online from a variety of locations.

BT's solutions businesses, Syntegra and Syncordia, help large businesses get the best from their communications and information systems. For example, Syntegra developed the first seamless worldwide automatic referral service for Visa and has launched a new e-business air logistics information technology system. Syncordia won a £250 million contract to provide and manage Barclays Bank's internet protocol network and has worked with the frozen-food retailer Iceland on their internet home shopping service.

Mobile services are becoming an increasingly important part of BT's offer and the BT internet phone was the first commercially available wireless access protocol (WAP) service in the UK. A wide range of services are available, including BT's own Genie Internet – already a leading mobile information service which sends information, such as sports scores, share prices, travel news and e-mails, to users' phones.

The BT Cellnet Business First calling plan is aimed at businesses of all sizes. Instead of having to manage a variety of mobile phones and pricing packages, business customers can opt for a single plan that offers the best savings for that company.

Recent Developments

BT has recently made major acquisitions in Japan, Canada, the Republic of Ireland and the Netherlands, largely in the new wave areas of mobility and the internet. It has also invested significant amounts in new high-bandwidth networks, primarily in the UK and continental Europe.

BT also recently acquired a licence from the UK Government to operate so-called third generation mobile data services. These allow BT to offer broadband data transmission to mobile users, enabling users to access the internet, and enjoy the download speeds and data capacities previously only available on powerful personal computers.

BT has recently introduced new products designed to reduce prices and to simplify its price structure, and also introduced new options to give customers greater choice and control over how they are charged. For example, the BT Together range of pricing plans provides residential and smaller business customers with competitive prices, inclusive call allowances and other value features for a single monthly fee. BT has also introduced a commitment to deliver competitive prices to the corporate business customer.

Building on the momentum created by BT Together, it has introduced BT SurfTime. This offers unlimited internet calls for a fixed fee and means that accessing the internet in the UK is cheaper.

Promotion

For some time, BT's overall marketing strategy has been to stimulate overall communication, be it by the phone or the internet. As its market share is ultimately limited by government regulation, it does this in order to grow the size of the total market.

The long-running 'It's good to talk' TV advertising campaign was a classic example of this approach, as is the more recent 'Stay in Touch' campaign, featuring ET. Aimed at increasing call usage and the penetration of the internet, the campaign has addressed many communications issues, including the launch of a special website designed for people who work from home.

BT's website www.bt.com is increasingly used for marketing and promotion and as a channel that customers can use to contact the company. It has been the destination for customers to register interest in forthcoming launches, resulting in a steady increase in orders, particularly for additional exchange lines.

For businesses the 'You Can' campaign has highlighted the improved efficiency and effectiveness that telecommunications makes possible and the role that BT can play in helping customers find solutions to their communications needs.

The brand was also supported by being the lead sponsor of the BT Global Challenge, the 30,000 mile yacht race which started in September 2000.

Brand Values

The essence of the BT brand is rooted in the basic human need to connect. That means connecting with people, places and things that matter at home and at work. Connected to information, experiences, ideas and feelings, to the familiar and to the new and to the world in general. The brand encapsulates connection in every sense of the word, helping people to live their lives to the full.

BT aims to be the guide to the potential of communications, today and for the future, wherever people are, and whatever their need. BT has always been actively involved in all kinds of communications across all walks of life. Its heritage, knowledge and breadth of experience means that it is uniquely placed to guide people – to show them all kinds of ways to stay in touch so they can get much more out of life.

This is how BT fits into the basic human need to feel connected and why its brand proposition is all about being a guide. The BT brand consists of three key attributes, which are inherent in the notion of guide: Trust, Potential and Freedom.

The guide proposition is also reflected in nine brand values – Expert, Progressive, and Trustworthy (the way BT does things). Empathetic, Imaginative and Proactive (the way BT works with customers). Friendly, Helpful and Enthusiastic (BT's personality and the way it behaves from day to day).

Things you didn't know about BT

www.bt.com receives over one million hits per day.

BT's famous 'piper' corporate identity makeover was the biggest and most expensive of its kind when it was undertaken in the early 1990s.

BT's growing international activity is reflected in the fact that its non-UK income in 1999 was 18% of turnover, compared to 10% the year before.

In the UK, BT has 28.5 million customer lines. Of these, twenty million are residential and 8.5 million are business lines.

In March 2000, the Organisation for Economic Co-operation and Development (OECD) researched the best internet access prices offered by the largest national operator in each member country. It reported that the BT Internet package provided the cheapest off-peak internet access amongst all 29 countries.

Car and Van Rental

Market

Founded in 1958 to cater for the cost-conscious customer, Budget has grown to become the third largest car and truck rental company in the world. In the UK, Budget is also one of the biggest players in its sector, with an airport market share of 18%.

In Europe, according to Datamonitor, the car rental market is worth around £5 billion per year. This is a growth market, and strong demand is expected to push its value to nearly £7 billion by 2004.

Business to business custom is a massive revenue stream in the car rental sector. Business rentals – combining airport and non-airport revenue – account for around 50% of the European market.

One of the fastest growth areas for car rental firms is in the business fleet market. As corporations seek a more flexible approach to fleet management, they are increasingly turning to leasing and car rental companies. This business is worth nearly £5 million per year in Europe alone and is growing fast. In fact, it is one of the most important factors driving growth of the rental sector overall.

Airport rental business is also growing in line with international air travel. As deregulation in the airline sector causes fares to tumble and a host of new operators to burst onto the scene, the airport car rental sector prospers. Regional and international airports are seeing strong passenger growth and show no sign of slowing.

Furthermore, in markets where there is still low rental penetration – like Spain, Italy and Greece – there are strong opportunities for growth.

Achievements

From humble beginnings, with a fleet of just ten cars, Budget has grown into an international giant, employing 24,500 people and operating a fleet of over 268,000 cars and trucks. It operates a network of 3,200 rental locations, including 825 airport sites, in over 120 countries and territories. World-wide, Budget's revenues are around £2.9 billion.

The company has successfully managed a process of expansion and change, developing from a primarily franchised structure to an operating company, embarking on a large-scale franchise acquisition programme, helping to increase the consistency and quality of its international product offering. Now it is truly global in terms of its strategic approach, product and service.

These factors have helped Budget win a number of industry awards. For example, it has been voted 'Best Business Car Rental Company' and 'Best European Car Rental Company' by Business Travel World and the Institute of Travel Management, and 'World's Best Car Rental' by Condé Nast Traveller.

Budget's success has helped it claim leadership in several international markets. It is market leader in Canada and Holland, as well as many other countries in Europe, Latin America and Asia Pacific.

Budget has led the field with its commitment to protecting the environment. It was one of the first international rental companies to make substitute energy vehicles available for rental, introducing electric cars in France in 1996 and LPG (Liquified Petroleum Gas) vehicles in the UK in 1998. It introduced the first ever fleet of electric cars for rental to the US market in 1998.

Budget has also led the way in introducing 'driveshare' solutions, designed to encourage commuters to share vehicles and so reduce air pollution. The company has won several awards for its pioneering environmental initiatives, including the Fleet News 2000 Awards 'Environmental Initiative of the Year' for a car sharing initiative launched in Edinburgh in 1999.

History

Budget was founded in 1958 in Los Angeles by Morris Mirkin, as a rental car company for the 'budget minded' customer.

It broke into an already crowded market, where three established airport-based competitors charged $10 a day and ten cents a mile. Morris and his wife – running a fleet of just ten cars – priced their off-airport service at $4 a day and four cents a mile. From the start, the Budget brand lived up to its name.

By 1960, with an expanded fleet, the Budget Rent a Car Corporation was formally established. The business model was based on a mixture of wholly owned and franchisee-owned rental locations.

Budget first arrived in the UK in 1966, opening offices in Croydon and Ilford. At this stage, Budget was still basing its rental offices in town centres as opposed to airports. It changed this in 1968, when it opened its first airport site in Minneapolis, US, followed in 1969 by the first European airport location in Zurich. By this stage, the company had 636 locations in twelve countries, making it the world's fourth largest rental company. It had also changed ownership, being acquired by the US transport company, Transamerica.

From very early on, Budget made truck rentals an important aspect of its service, introducing 55 into the system in 1968 and establishing truck rental at 120 UK locations in 1973.

By 1979, with 62,000 vehicles and 1,200 locations, Budget had become the third largest car rental company in the world and the biggest in Canada. At this time the company introduced its famous 'You're #1 at Budget' slogan.

In the mid-1980s, Budget underwent several changes in ownership, including a leveraged buy-out in 1986 and an

Initial Public Offering of its stock in 1987. By 1989, the size of Budget – with 225,000 vehicles and a 19.5% market share – had attracted the attention of the motor giant Ford, which bought a stake in the company. This interest remained until 1997, when Ford sold its interest to Budget's largest franchisee, Team Rental Group.

Product

For business customers, Budget offers a range of tailored packages. One of its longest established is CorpRate, which was first developed in 1968. This is designed for businesses of all sizes, from small start-ups to multi-national corporations. The programme offers companies guaranteed fixed rates all over the world. It includes unlimited mileage, a dedicated freephone reservation number plus a delivery and collection service. Silver and Gold CorpRate membership offers additional benefits for high-volume users.

Budget's Driveshare and City Car Club services are other important business services. These are designed to help companies make efficient use of cars for their employees without damaging the environment.

In March 1999, Budget and the City of Edinburgh Council teamed up to launch City Car Club, the first ever commercial car club in the UK. This 'pay as you drive' scheme is designed to be an attractive alternative to owning a car or, for companies, to providing company cars for employees. For an annual membership fee of £99, members can call up a reservation line and request a car whenever they need it, with as little as fifteen minutes notice. They pay an hourly rate and can pick the car up and return it to convenient city centre locations. The aim of the scheme is to reduce the number of cars on the road.

Budget's Driveshare is a commuter transportation scheme that is also an attractive, environmentally friendly, option for corporate customers. Rather than every employee travelling to work in their own car, the scheme is offering the opportunity to travel in shared minibuses which have privileged access to bus lanes to escape traffic congestion. Driveshare also reduces the number of parking spaces required at a company's location and enhances its green credentials. Figures show that participation in the scheme also helps reduce absenteeism and lateness.

Budget's online service (www.budget.com) is another attractive option for business users. This acts as a centralised booking resource for business and leisure customers around the world, including up to date information on airline and hotel partnership deals.

Budget's WorldClass fleet – comprising luxury and speciality vehicles – is another attractive business option, including models from Jaguar, Mercedes, BMW and Lotus.

On a purely business to business level, the Team Budget programme is designed to help travel agents develop their car rental business. Providing training, communication and business-building tools, Team Budget provides agents with guidance and support in all aspects of car rental business.

Recent Developments

Budget recently launched an important new service for corporate customers, Budget Business Club. Targeted particularly at small and medium size enterprises (SMEs) the programme offers better rates, service and rewards.

It grants members automatic enrolment in Budget's global reward programme, Perfect Drive. This is a unique benefit, as no other car rental company offers a global reward programme on top of a value for money rates structure and service levels expected by frequent business renters.

Business Club offers discounts of up to 45% and access to Budget's 'Fastbreak' service, a paperless express service for frequent renters. Fastbreak has been a great success in the US and was rolled out in Europe in summer 2000.

With the Perfect Drive reward programme, points collected every time customers rent, can be redeemed against rewards including golf equipment or free car rental.

Operationally, an important recent development is the termination of Budget's partnership with Sixt Car Rental in Germany. This means Budget is building up a new network of rental locations across Germany, with around 150 opened at the end of 2000.

Promotion

To target business travellers, Budget's advertising in and around airports is a valuable tool. This is mainly poster work, although the brand has done some TV work in the past, mainly in the US market.

Frequent flyer programmes are another important promotional tool and Budget is a partner in over 20 of them, including British Midland Diamond Club, Lufthansa Miles and More, United Airlines Mileage Plus and Virgin Atlantic Flying Club. Budget also has a preferred partnership with the low-cost airline Go, which is proving increasingly popular with business travellers. As part of these partnership arrangements, Budget is able to link up on regular direct mail campaigns and special promotions targeting business travellers.

The company also derives promotional mileage from its partnerships with the loyalty schemes of international hotel groups, including Best Western, Choice Hotels Europe and the Starwood Sheraton Group.

Budget's Perfect Drive global reward programme – the first of its kind in the car rental business – is another valuable promotional tool, offering attractive benefits for business users and co-marketing opportunities with other brands.

Brand Values

Budget's core brand value has always been enshrined in its name. Providing value for money vehicle rental without compromising on product quality and service is the company's mission. The company's famous slogan 'You're #1 at Budget' reinforced the company's focus on individual customer needs. That has been replaced by the 'Get out of the ordinary' slogan, introduced in 1997. This reflects the company's aggressive worldwide approach to customer satisfaction and its extraordinary product and service levels. This change was accompanied by a new corporate identity, replacing the old familiar black and orange stripes with a more dynamic orange and blue triangle logo.

Things you didn't know about Budget

Budget is the first car rental company to commit to promoting alternative fuels and transport methods. It was the first major rental company to introduce LPG vehicles into its UK and French fleets in 1998.

The first ever Fly/Drive programme developed by Budget International was in the UK.

Budget is the largest global renter of Jaguar cars. It began renting them in 1993.

Electric cars can travel 100 miles before they need to be recharged.

An LPG car will travel 423 miles on £25 of fuel, compared to 262 miles on petrol.

Each car used in Budget's City Car Club scheme in Edinburgh has the potential to replace up to six other vehicles.

PerfectDrive is the first truly global car rental reward programme.

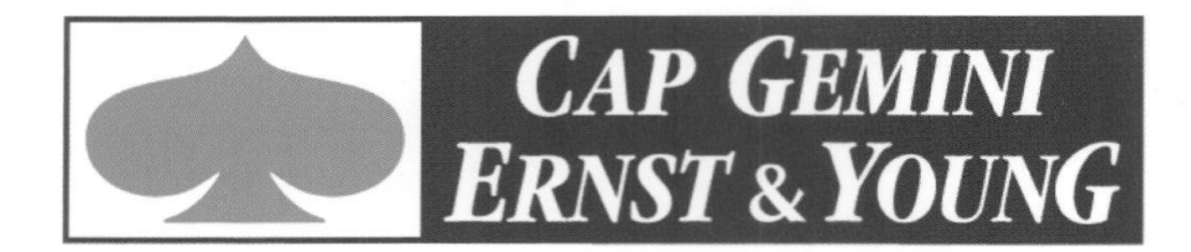

Market

Sometimes said to be the company that makes Europe compute, Cap Gemini Ernst & Young is the largest European IT services and management consultancy company.

As a consultancy which ultimately aims to help its clients' businesses run better, Cap Gemini Ernst & Young works in a wide variety of markets. The main areas of its operations are in telecommunications and media, utilities, financial services, manufacturing and life sciences (such as pharmaceuticals). Deregulation and technological progress have profoundly affected each of these markets, boosting demand for management and IT consultancy.

In today's 'network economy' businesses rely on technology to give them a competitive edge. Consulting on business strategy and then mixing this with its IT expertise to help clients execute their plans is Cap Gemini Ernst & Young's key strength.

Internet and e-commerce related consultancy is growing fast as more and more companies seek to cash in on the dotcom boom. In Europe, the internet and e-commerce services market is exploding, growing from $2.5 billion in 1999 to a predicted $22 billion in 2002. In terms of overall IT services, the UK is the fastest growing and second largest market in Europe, worth an estimated $18.6 billion (Source: IDC).

Cap Gemini Ernst & Young itself is the only European player to be ranked in the global ten biggest IT services companies.

Achievements

The personal achievement of the group's founder and president, Serge Kampf, in turning the company he founded in 1967 into a £2.83 billion company (1999) with 40,000 employees is impressive to say the least. Kampf has taken it from a tiny company operating from two rooms in Grenoble to one of the largest IT services companies in the world. Cap Gemini

has also proved to be one of France's biggest business success stories on the world stage.

IT services is one of the most crowded and competitive sectors in business and any company that can carve out a leading position for itself, as has Cap Gemini Ernst & Young, is worthy of acclaim. Critics point to Kampf's early appreciation of the importance of globalisation as a key to its success. The acquisition spree

of the 1980s gave the group crucial leadership in local markets.

The group has also been praised for sticking to its expertise – IT services and consultancy – and not losing focus during its rapid period of expansion. This has allowed it to gain an enviable reputation in two key areas of business that have never been in more demand than they are in today's networked economy.

History

In May 2000, Cap Gemini acquired Ernst & Young's consulting business. The newly formed organisation – Cap Gemini Ernst & Young – employs more than 57,000 people worldwide and reports global revenues of €7.7 billion (1999). The acquisition also provides the new group with a strong presence in the US.

Cap Gemini's roots trace back to 1967 when Serge Kampf founded Sogeti in Grenoble, France. Sogeti was to specialise in services related to the development and implementation of computer applications. Even in its earliest days, Sogeti offered more than just technical assistance, expanding into facilities management and consulting.

In 1976, after a decade of rapid growth for Sogeti, Serge Kampf gained control of CAP, his biggest competitor in France in the IT services market and already a powerful European player. Shortly afterwards, Gemini Computer Systems joined the group, leading to the creation of the pan-European business, Cap Gemini Sogeti, in 1975.

Following the merger, the new group grew rapidly, opening an office in the US in 1978. During the 1980s, the group developed skills in systems integration and acquired a major French competitor specialising in this area – Sesa – to give it market share. Sesa was one of the earliest companies to specialise in data transmission, and at one point in the 1980s – controlled half of the world's data transmission market.

By this stage, Serge Kampf – still in charge – had gained a reputation as one of France's most dynamic businessmen. He had turned the company into a multinational with subsidiaries in eight European countries and the US and had accumulated a $100 million 'war chest' for expansion, leading him to buy a string of IT companies around Europe.

In the 1990s, rapid change in the global IT industry – such as the explosion of microprocessing and intensified competition – prompted the group to implement a top to bottom overhaul of its operations. Globalisation of the IT sector meant that the group's markets were shrinking, demanding a more efficient structure. For the first time, the group posted losses, making it vulnerable to predators. In 1991, Daimler-Benz acquired a share in the group and it soon became clear the German giant wanted to become a majority shareholder. In 1997, this threat disappeared as Daimler Benz sold its share and the group headed back towards independence. A crisis had been averted.

Around this time, the company launched its 'convergence' strategy, building strong links between its consultancy and IT services arms to offer clients a seamless approach to business transformation. This remains the strategy driving growth for Cap Gemini Ernst & Young today.

Product

The Cap Gemini Ernst & Young Group defines its businesses as: management consulting, IT consulting, systems integration, software development, outsourcing and training otherwise expressed as 'Advise, Design, Build and Run'.

These products fall into two principal business units: management consulting and IT services. On the management consultancy side, the company helps its corporate clients through periods of change through a variety of methods.

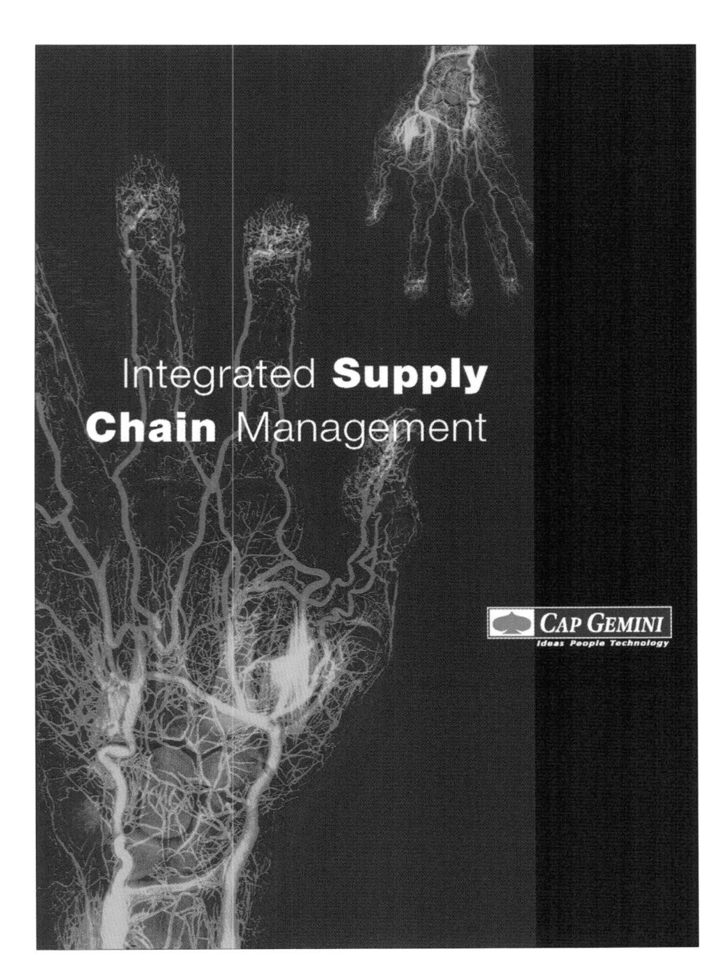

These can be in the areas of: strategy formulation and implementation, process improvement and redesign, re-organisation of human resources, implementation of automated systems and overall information management.

The key function performed by IT services is in advising companies what IT they need to perform better, implementing and integrating the systems into their business and, if necessary, managing it on their behalf. Applications Management, the outsourcing of IT-heavy functions like running applications, is a growing area in many business sectors and is one of the group's most successful activities.

The principle business units – namely management consultancy and IT services – do not act in isolation. With so much of the latest business thinking closely linked to the use of technology, there is inevitably a high amount of crossover between advising on business strategy and IT services. Some of the biggest issues facing business, such as customer relationship management and e-commerce, are heavily reliant on IT to succeed, creating excellent opportunities for Cap Gemini Ernst & Young to offer clients a two-pronged service.

As such, the group offers clients what it calls 'Concurrent Transformation' – merging business and system transformation into a single service. Concurrent Transformation enables a company to run a change management and systems management project simultaneously (as opposed to sequentially) in a seamless process.

Recent Developments

In February 2000, Cap Gemini teamed up with Microsoft in a new strategic global alliance focusing on opportunities in e-business. The alliance combines Cap Gemini Ernst & Young's consulting expertise and e-business knowledge with Microsoft's newest generation of technologies. Initially, the alliance is focusing on solutions in the retail market and e-commerce.

Furthermore, Cap Gemini Ernst & Young has recently been involved in some major deals. In March 2000, it signed an agreement with Cisco, the worldwide leader in networking for the internet, to form a new company dedicated to driving the internet economy. The deal means that Cisco is investing $835 million in the Cap Gemini Ernst & Young Group. Together, Cap Gemini Ernst & Young and Cisco is lending their IT expertise to companies wishing to capitalise on the growth of the internet.

Promotion

Cap Gemini Ernst & Young's promotion takes a variety of forms, using a mixture of media and events to raise its profile among key decision-makers in its target businesses.

Examples of recent work include 'A Blueprint for Financial Services'. This was a comprehensive report into the future of banking and insurance including comment and opinion from industry leaders and some of the solutions offered by Cap Gemini Ernst & Young. The idea was to establish Cap Gemini Ernst & Young as an authority in all aspects of banking applications.

When positioning itself as an expert in the media sector, it sponsored a supplement in Broadcast magazine about new opportunities in digital TV. Called the 'Digital Nation', the supplement brought together views from industry experts and contained news of initiatives by Cap Gemini Ernst & Young. The supplement was also direct mailed to enhance its effect.

The group also uses live events to promote itself across sectors. The most notable example is the Director's Forum – a closed door meeting between directors from the public and private sectors. The Forum aims to explore new approaches, share best practice, and allow directors to talk openly about the future.

The company also uses direct mail and the internet to conduct regular communications with clients and prospects in the cluttered telecoms sector. The newsletter, called Broadsheet, demonstrates the use of cutting edge technology and business solutions that can help telecoms compete in the new media marketplace.

Brand Values

Cap Gemini Ernst & Young has a core brand proposition – 'Ideas, People, Technology' – which, it hopes, has resonance throughout the organisation. More broadly it sets out its values as: honesty, boldness, trust, freedom, team spirit, modesty and fun.

The company encourages its staff to be innovative and creative through strategy and technology. It wants its brand to communicate that enterprising people with intelligent solutions are its key resource. It is very careful with its choice of visual imagery, always keen to convey these core values and the importance of people. Its brand guidelines stipulate that no piece of communication should be produced which does not have people as its focus. Images should be bold, brave and challenging and never obvious or mainstream.

Cap Gemini Ernst & Young wants its brand to challenge preconceptions of management and IT consultancy, never portraying its employees as 'suits' or using management jargon in its communications.

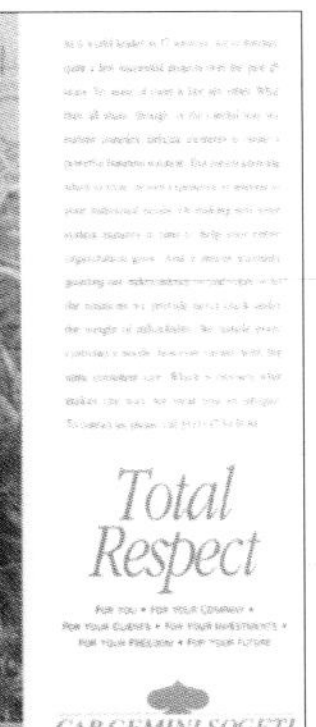

The company has a special unit devoted to maintenance of the brand. Cap Gemini Ernst & Young University plays an important role in ensuring these values are consistently applied throughout the group. It aims to harmonise methods and practices to ensure they all reflect brand values, as well as giving newcomers a grounding in them when they arrive.

Things you didn't know about Cap Gemini Ernst & Young

The company's clients include some of the biggest names in business, including Corus, Virgin, BT, McDonald's, General Motors Europe, Saab and Open TV.

Cap Gemini was awarded European Company of the Year in 1999 by the European Press Federation.

The children of employees are always thrilled to learn that Geoff Unwin, the CEO's first job was as a chocolate taster.

Geoff Unwin is also unique in the business world as being one of the few Englishmen to run a French owned company.

Cap Gemini Ernst & Young invented the concept of applications management which is still a major product stream and revenue earner.

When Cap Gemini Ernst & Young's marketing department wanted to test how famous their brand was, they decided to test it out on London taxi drivers. Because the group's London head office is included on famous black taxi 'Knowledge' test, all drivers should know where the office is. Suffice to say, London staff only have to say "Cap Gemini" to a cab driver and they will be taken straight there.

The company runs a comprehensive community programme. Over 2,000 UK staff or 25% gave time in 1999 to this programme.

Market

Castrol is something of an anomaly amongst oil companies, as it has been purely focused on formulating and supplying industrial, automotive, aeronautical and marine lubricants. Whether it's in the engine of your car or the manufacturing tools of the factory that made it, Castrol's lubricants are keeping machines and vehicles running smoothly all over the world.

The company is part of Burmah Castrol Plc, which has sales of £3 billion and employs 19,000 people in 55 countries. Around 55% of the company's profit is accounted for by Castrol Consumer, which supplies the car and motorcycle oils the brand is perhaps best known for. This market alone consumes eleven billion litres of lubricants, oils, transmission and brake fluids every year and, with an 11% market share, Castrol is number one in the sector.

However, industrial, commercial and marine are also important areas of the business, and the Castrol brand enjoys a strong position in many segments within these markets also.

Industrial, where Castrol supplies specialist lubricants for industrial equipment, is a twelve billion litre market and Castrol's share is around 8%. The brand also has a 12% share of the marine sector, supplying lubricants, greases and cleaners for all types of vessels, from a port tug to the QE2. As well as these areas, Castrol also supplies its products to the commercial vehicle markets.

Geographically, nearly 40% of its profit comes from Europe, with 28% generated in North America and 29% in Asia Pacific. Its main international competitors include Mobil, Shell, Texaco, BP and Chevron.

Achievements

In over 100 years, Castrol has built one of the world's best known brands and leadership of the specialist lubricants sector. Its distinctive brand identity is recognised around the globe. In India, for example, it has 85% unprompted brand awareness. Castrol GTX, launched in1968, is the most famous motor oil brand in the world.

This fame has been achieved thanks to the consistency and power of its marketing, but is also down to the excellence of its product. Testament to this are Castrol's close links to some of greatest feats achieved by man and machine through its long-term support of sporting and record-breaking initiatives.

In this respect, it is fair to say that Castrol has played a key role in the development of the transport industry.

Castrol has a long tradition of supporting speed record attempts, on land, sea and air, and the technological advances made in these endeavours have often led to engineering improvements that we all benefit from.

Just some of the record-breakers who have relied on Castrol lubricants include Sir Malcolm Campbell and the current land speed record holder, Andy Green, who, in the Castrol-lubricated Thrust SSC, was the first man to go supersonic on land. It has also partnered sporting winners like the Williams Formula One racing team, Castrol Honda in the World Superbike Championship and the Toyota Castrol World rally team. High performance applications like this have always acted as a test-bed for Castrol, helping it refine its product for commercial and consumer markets.

Castrol has also helped other historic events such as partnering the Anglo-French consortium that built the world's first supersonic airliner, Concorde, and providing specialist lubricants to the Hoverspeed Great Britain 'Seacat' catamaran, which won the Hales and Blue Riband Trophies for the fastest-ever Atlantic crossing in 1990. The SeaCat is now operating regular services to France and Ireland.

History

Charles Cheers Wakefield founded Castrol in 1899. He resigned from the Vacuum Oil Co (which later became Mobil) to set up his own business. He set up CC Wakefield & Co in London, where he had been an agent for Vacuum.

The business got off to a good start, selling oils and blended lubricants, mainly, at first, to the railway industry. However, in the early 1900s, the developing motor industry caught Wakefield's eye. He could see that the motor car and cycle were set to revolutionise society, and so, in 1909, he launched a motor oil specially designed to lubricate the engines of these 'new fangled' machines. It was called Castrol. The new range of Wakefield Motor Oil (Castrol Brand) used the distinctive red, white and green colours from the very start. It was available in three grades, Castrol CW for cars, Castrol C for motorbikes and Castrol R for aero and racing engines.

It was this latter group that took to using Castrol first. In 1909 Louis Bleriot had become the first man to fly across the English channel, putting aviation on the map. In October 1909, Leon Delagrange, won the first aviation prize to be awarded in Britain, for speed and distance, using Castrol oil. From that point on, the history of Castrol and the history of advances in transport were firmly linked. Over the years, Castrol has helped set speed records on land, sea and air.

By 1960, the name Castrol had become so famous that CC Wakefield & Co changed its name to that of its major brand. In 1966, after years of international expansion and buying up smaller companies, Castrol was itself taken over, by the giant Burmah Oil Company. But it didn't

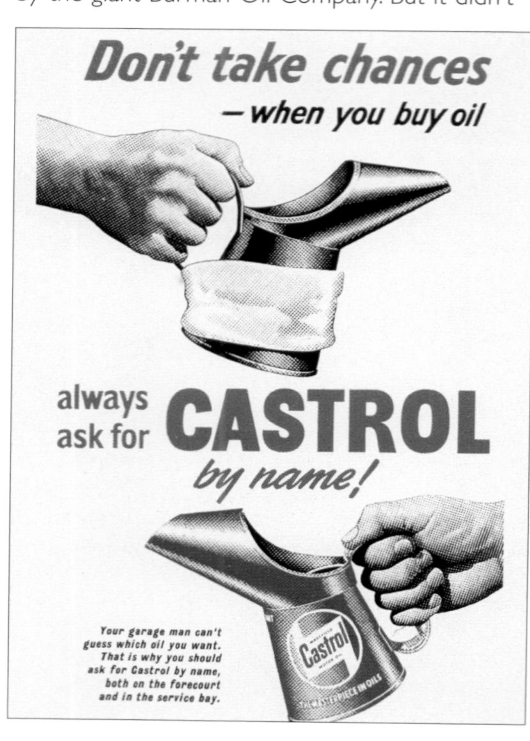

affect the power of the Castrol brand and, in 1968, the name that still resonates today was born – Castrol GTX. The genius of this oil was to be suitable for every car, under every condition of operation.

During the 1980s, Castrol focused its broad lubricants business onto five core sectors: consumer, commercial, metal-working, industrial and marine. It was at this time that Castrol started to make massive in-roads into the industrial sector, providing specialist lubricants for factory machinery, such as Castrol Syntillo R – a soluble lubricant for metal cutting.

By 1990 Castrol was the biggest and most successful part of Burmah Oil, prompting the parent group to rename itself Burmah Castrol Plc. Now, the giant that took over Castrol has been eaten up itself, by BP.

Product

There are over 5000 Castrol formulations – engine oils, gear oils, coolants and greases, to name a few – which the company blends to suit the requirements of whatever sector it is supplying to.

Castrol Consumer is the world leader in the supply of motorcar and motorcycle lubricants and services, marketing to workshops and retail chains, auto accessory stores and petrol stations. Its principal products are engine oils, including Castrol GTX, as well as tranmission and brake fluids.

Castrol Marine supplies specialist lubricants and fluids to the international marine market. Customers include some of the world's largest ship owners and cruise operators. Products include the Castrol TLX range of engine lubricants and Castrol Spherol.

Castrol Industrial is a world leader in the supply of specialised products and services to metalworking industries such as transport and metal component manufacturers. Cutting fluids, release agents and cleaners are essential to the smooth running of any manufacturing plant and Castrol's range meets all possible needs. It also supplies the food, mining, power generation and offshore gas and oil production industries. Castrol Chemical Management Services is a leading player in the growing market for outsourced chemical fluid management for production plants.

Castrol Commercial supplies products to commercial on and off-road vehicles, such as trucks and buses, earth-moving equipment, agricultural, quarrying and forestry equipment. Brands include Castrol Agri for tractors and Castrol Turbomax for heavy trucks.

Recent Developments

The biggest news to affect Castrol is its acquisition by BP in July 2000. BP agreed to purchase the company for £3 billion, in a move designed to strengthen its global lubricants business. Castrol has become BP's leading lubricant brand, distributed through the group's 28,000 retail sites and to the group's industrial and marine customers around the world. In the meantime, to prepare itself for stiffer competition in all of its sectors, Castrol is transforming its organisation. This sees a tighter focus on the four core business units (Consumer, Commercial, Industrial and Marine), making each more accountable and directly-led.

Promotion

From the start, Castrol's promotional strategy has been to associate its brand with the motoring, aviation and marine successes to which it has contributed. From record-breaking speed attempts to motorsport, Castrol has been a committed partner, providing commercial and technical support to some of the fastest people on the planet.

The Castrol Achievements annual booklet, published since 1912, summarises the sporting or record-breaking endeavours with which Castrol has been associated. The result is that Castrol's brand has become synonymous with boundary-pushing performance and technical innovation.

As such, its involvement in motorsport is one of its most powerful promotional tools. Castrol's heritage in world rallying has seen it sponsor a host of teams, making its brand synonymous with high-performance and endurance. Most recently, it signed a deal with Hyundai to partner the car manufacturer in the Hyundai Castrol Rally Team.

Castrol's promotional links with motorsport are firmly focused on strong business-to-business relationships. The best example of this strategy is Castrol's worldwide partnership with BMW. This partnership involves Castrol as Technical Sponsor of the BMW Williams F1 and BMW V12 American Le Mans racing teams. In order to provide the highest quality lubricants for these cars, BMW and Castrol work together on developing and testing new lubricants for BMW engines, as well as products for other components, like steering and brake fluids. The partnership invests in the joint development of new industrial products and production methods.

But this is a relationship which goes beyond racing alone. Castrol is the official strategic partner for lubricants with BMW and its products and research are also used in BMW's production cars and after sales service. The depth of the relationship is demonstrated by the fact that Castrol even supplies industrial fluid management solutions for BMW's manufacturing plants. The link with BMW, bringing two of the world's most important automotive brands together, is an important promotional and business platform for Castrol.

Castrol's extensive advertising has given it a reputation for excellence in brand management and marketing and its founder, Charles Wakefield, is credited with being one of the world's first great marketers.

Nowadays, each of the product lines does its own advertising, such as Castrol Industrial, whose print campaign is for AquaSafe corrosion protection. They also make use of promotions, such as an initiative for buyers of agricultural machinery lubricants from Castrol Commercial to collect and redeem vouchers.

This, combined with its famous advertising campaigns – like the 1980s 'Liquid Engineering' campaign for Castrol GTX – help drive awareness of the brand for business as well as private consumers.

Brand Values

Castrol's core brand values are High Performance, Premium Quality and Technology-led. Given the fact that Castrol has been the chosen oil for breaking world speed and endurance records, the value of High Performance needs no more explanation.

Premium Quality refers not only to its product range, but also its high standards of customer service and advice.

Technology-led has always been a by-word for Castrol, which has extensive research and development facilities around the world. As well as its R&D headquarters in Pangbourne, Berkshire, it also works with leading universities and technical centres. It lays great emphasis on research and development and producing environmentally-friendly products. It has a strong record of developing products that protect the environment, like nitrite-free soluble cutting fluids and engine oils that prevent damage to catalytic converters.

Things you didn't know about Castrol

Sir Malcolm Campbell's 245mph land speed record, set in 1931 in his 'Bluebird', was achieved using Castrol oil. In 1935, the nine-time land speed record holder declared, "If there were a better oil than Wakefield Castrol, I should use it."

In 1932, Castrol's founder, Charles Wakefield, paid for Amy Johnson's record-breaking flight from Australia to England in a plane lubricated by Castrol R.

In 1967, the QE2 was launched. It was the world's largest liner at the time, and its engines were lubricated by Castrol.

In 1950 Castrol provided the motor oil for the winner of the world's first Formula One race – an Alfa Romeo.

Castrol has a track record of developing products designed for motor racing for the mass market. An example is its SRF Brake Fluid, which was initially developed for Formula One.

CLIFFORD CHANCE

Market

Clifford Chance is a giant among law firms. In fact, after its merger in 2000 with Rogers & Wells in the US and Pünder Volhard Weber & Axster of Germany, it is now the world's largest integrated law firm.

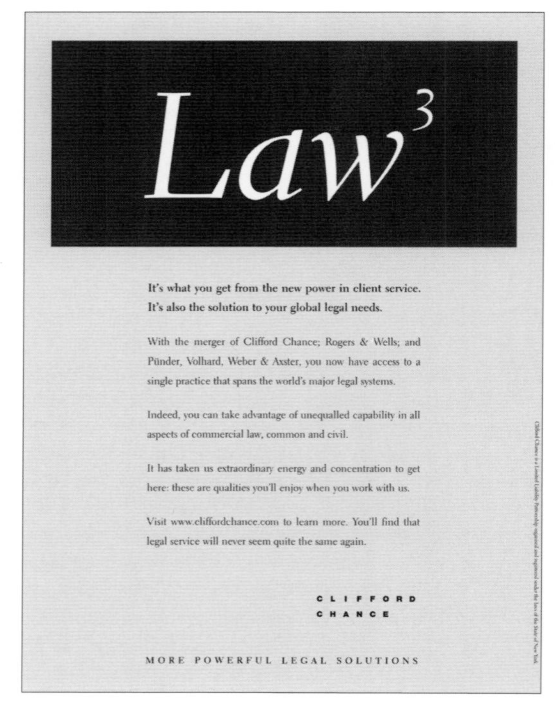

Expanding (in terms of global capability) has never been more important in the legal industry, with the emergence of international law firms following the trend towards globalisation in business itself. Factors like deregulation and technology have reduced barriers to entry, making companies increasingly see the world as a single market, and not surprisingly, look for professional service suppliers to have an equally global mindset and reach.

Following the merger, Clifford Chance has become the first integrated law firm to cover all the world's major financial centres. Its traditional speciality is banking law, but it has established expertise across all aspects of law which affect every company in business today, such as finance, capital markets, litigation, employment and real estate.

As more companies seek to expand on the international stage, mergers and acquisitions activity is driving the international market for legal services. Clifford Chance works with many of the world's largest corporations to help them successfully achieve their expansion goals.

Achievements

Clifford Chance has built one of the strongest global brands in the legal profession. In the UK, where competition among law firms is particularly intense, it has emerged as the biggest international player, well ahead of its closest rivals, Linklaters, Freshfields, Allen & Overy, and Slaughter and May.

The firm's reputation is not only built on the basis of its geographical reach and size. It also has an unsurpassed reputation across multiple industry sectors. According to the 'Chambers Guide to the Legal Profession', 114 of Clifford Chance's lawyers are recognised leaders in their fields, and the firm is ranked first in sixteen specialist areas. The areas in which it is particularly well regarded include banking, litigation and property.

The firm's tenacity in expanding the reach of its brand beyond the UK market has been particularly impressive, especially in 2000, when it announced not just one, but two massive mergers. These deals propelled it into the international super-league and stunned the industry. The merger made Clifford Chance the world's largest integrated law firm, and, in the process, showed how UK law firms have become world leaders, thriving in the face of worldwide competition.

Its foresight in reacting to the trend towards globalisation has put it ahead of its closest UK competitors which are now looking to follow its example. For example, Freshfields' merger with the German firm Bruckhaus Westrick Heller Loeber to create a pan-European entity.

Clifford Chance has been ahead of the game for some time. The 1987 merger between Clifford Turner and Coward Chance sparked the trend towards law firm mergers which continue to this day. It also set the trend for international activity, stating its intention to create the first genuine pan-European law firm as long ago as the late 1980s, then to create the world's premier law firm in the 1990s.

History

Clifford Chance's history begins with two London firms – Coward Chance and Clifford Turner. Coward Chance dates back as far as 1802, while Clifford Turner was formed in 1900.

The two firms grew rapidly, both at home and overseas. Coward Chance built an extensive banking practice, which was a major factor in its success. Clifford Turner, on the other hand, had a strong and expanding corporate practice.

Both firms were aware of the need for better balanced practices and that changes in the financial world frequently required corporate and banking lawyers to work together. A merged firm could also offer competitive advantages in other areas of work where large teams of lawyers were required, including those in specialised areas.

The merger between Clifford Turner and Coward Chance was announced in February 1987 and took the City and the legal profession by surprise. In 1986, rumours were rife about several firms merging but the Clifford Chance merger was successfully kept secret.

In 1992 Clifford Chance moved into purpose-built new offices at 200 Aldersgate Street, London.

Between 1988 and 1990 Clifford Chance developed a strategy for its development in Europe and internationally which provided the broad framework for the firm's next phase of expansion. It envisaged an integrated network of local offices in the principal European countries, each office containing a mix of UK and leading local lawyers.

As far back as 1987 Clifford Chance had offices in Brussels, Paris, Amsterdam, Madrid, Hong Kong, Tokyo, Singapore and Dubai. Since then it has expanded rapidly, opening offices in Frankfurt, Moscow, Warsaw, Barcelona, Budapest, Shanghai, Milan, Rome, Prague, Bangkok, São Paulo and Washington.

Clifford Chance's post-merger aim, set out in a ten year plan published in 1987, was 'to be the leading European-based international law firm'. Having achieved that, Clifford Chance then rolled out its new ten year vision: to become 'The World's Premier Law Firm'.

Recognising that clients want to be able to use one law firm worldwide for major transactions and projects, Clifford Chance merged with Rogers & Wells and Pünder Volhard Weber & Axster.

Product

Although Clifford Chance is a global giant, it balances international strengths with the capability to serve local markets through its network of 29 offices in 21 countries around the world.

The firm's main international areas of practice are: finance, capital markets, corporate, litigation and dispute resolution, real estate, taxation, pensions and employment.

The finance practice is the largest in the world, with partners and solicitors located in every major commercial and financial centre. As global business deals become ever more complex, it is the first fully integrated firm to be able to assemble teams of lawyers from Europe, the US and Asia to advise on national and

international regulatory issues. As such, it acts for all the world's leading investment and commercial banks.

The corporate practice handles some of the world's largest and most complex mergers and acquisitions transactions, as well as advising business on private equity, insurance, real estate, media and telecommunications.

The firm's international team of 500 litigators is the largest and most comprehensive of its kind, with experience in virtually all segments of the business and financial markets. As well as working with clients to resolve existing disputes, they also advise on developing programmes to minimise future litigation risks. Some of the world's largest actions in areas including anti-trust, competition and intellectual property, are frequently handled by Clifford Chance.

In the fast-changing real estate market – Clifford Chance acts for banks, property companies, hoteliers, as well as local and public authorities.

The firm's tax practice is also the largest of any international law firm, providing advice on international and domestic taxation, covering a wide range of financing, investment, corporate and commercial issues, together with advice on tax litigation, disputes and transfer pricing.

As well as these areas, the firm advises providers and fund managers on pensions. The employment practice also assists clients on all major employment issues, ranging from appointments and severance of senior executives to immigration, discrimination and employee benefits.

Recent Developments

The biggest recent change to affect the firm was undoubtedly its merger with Rogers & Wells and Pünder, Volhard, Weber & Axster. The new firm came into being on January 1st 2000. The three-way merger, created the world's largest integrated law firm, with over 3000 lawyers worldwide, commanding fees of over $1 billion.

The new firm is called Clifford Chance in the UK, Asia and parts of Europe, Clifford Chance Rogers & Wells in the US and Clifford Chance Pünder elsewhere in Europe.

However, this is not the only big deal which Clifford Chance has completed recently. In December 1999, it also merged with a leading Luxembourg firm Faltz & Kremer. This firm has a pre-eminent international finance and corporate practice, and particular expertise in local litigation and private banking.

Promotion

Historically, professional services companies have not been major users of mainstream promotional tools to convey their brands to business clients. However, that has changed in recent times as more of the big players in the fields of management consultancy, accountancy and law have invested in the benefits of marketing and brand-building.

Clifford Chance is an example of this trend. With such an important development as its recent merger to communicate, the firm has rolled out a global communications programme, with a new brand identity.

A multi-media campaign targeting the legal and business communities, as well as its own staff was launched worldwide. It included road-shows, allowing senior management to present the new firm's capability to clients around the world. In addition a new firm brochure, new signage and stationary for all offices around the world was developed, as well as a new corporate website and intranet. An internal 'launch pack' was sent to all 7000 of the new firm's employees.

As well as these initiatives, the firm has taken advertising in international business press titles such as the Financial Times, the Wall Street Journal, The Economist, Handelsblatt and Frankfurter Allgemeine.

The advertisements communicate how the combination of the three firms provides more powerful legal solutions. Simple, clean messages like 'Concentration³', 'Energy³' and 'Law³' formed the theme of the ads referring to the strength of the firm post-merger, underlined by the stapline 'Simply more powerful solutions'.

Complementing this diverse suite of communication tools, the firm hosts seminars on key legal issues and releases a wide range of publications and newsletters on recent legal developments.

All of this carries the firm's new corporate identity, incorporating the names of the three firms and a new global symbol illustrating the unity of the new firm.

Brand Values

The new brand of Clifford Chance is designed to reflect the best of the three firms involved in the merger, whilst at the same time creating something powerful and new. The core values of Clifford Chance are defined as excellence, integrity, focus, commitment, support, loyalty, multi-cultural and entrepreneurial.

These are combined with values which the firm believes differentiate its services in the legal sector, namely: open-mindedness, enthusiasm, determination, innovation, positivity and courage.

These values were used to launch the newly merged firm, which aimed to communicate three key messages. Firstly, that the firm is a single organisation offering a seamless, global and local, service. Secondly, that it is breaking new ground in the scale and scope of services it can offer to multinational clients. And, thirdly, that it can make the most complex matters more simple for its clients.

Things you didn't know about Clifford Chance

Clifford Chance was the first British law firm to establish a pan-European practice, develop a regional presence in Asia, open offices in Frankfurt and Moscow and establish a US securities practice.

Clifford Chance advised Merrill Lynch in its groundbreaking 50:50 partnership with HSBC Holdings to create the first global online banking and investment service.

Clifford Chance advised on the development of Canary Wharf at London's Docklands.

Clifford Chance acted for fourteen years for the liquidators of BAH, the principal foreign subsidiary of the collapsed Banco Ambrosiano. The outstanding outcome represented an 86% recovery for 109 creditor banks, with approximately $537 million recovered.

Clifford Chance advised in connection with the privatisations of British Coal and British Rail.

Clifford Chance advised on the mergers between Glaxo and Wellcome, and UBS and SBC.

Clifford Chance was the first law firm to pull off a three way transatlantic and pan-European merger and thereby change the face of the legal profession.

Clifford Chance in London has outgrown its City premises and is planning to move to Canary Wharf in 2003.

COMPAQ

Market

Compaq is one of the best-known brands in the world and a true giant in the IT sector. It is the world's number one PC manufacturer and the second largest computing and services company overall, behind IBM. Compaq is a $40 billion company, employing 85,000 people around the world. Having shipped 15.7 million computer systems in 1999, Compaq has a 14% share of the total world computer market.

Compaq supplies software and hardware, including high-end corporate servers, storage solutions, commercial desktop computers, as well as portable products and consumer PCs. With such a wide range of products and services, it is a major player in the consumer and business-to-business markets.

As the network economy takes off, and businesses around the world look to take full advantage of e-business opportunities, Compaq aims to be the brand building the infrastructure. To be the company laying the tracks of the information superhighway requires size and muscle. As a result, today's IT sector is all about global strength and Compaq has aggressively pursued this strategy.

The prizes for being strong in this sector are high. Thanks to surging demand for networked computing solutions, servers are now the fastest growing sector of the computer industry. Overall, global purchases of IT services are expected to grow from $301 billion to $622 billion by 2002 (Source: Gartner Group/Dataquest).

In today's market, Compaq and its competitors have to be much more than just computer manufacturers. They have to deliver e-business solutions for the enterprise market, providing much more than hardware alone. Companies need computing partners for the internet age, helping them deliver the non-stop operations and capability on which today's e-business solutions are built.

Achievements

Compaq set the business world alight following its 1982 launch. After just one year, it had sales of $11 million, making it America's fastest growing start-up company ever. In 1998, it set another record, becoming the first company to post annual sales of $1 billion after just five years trading. In just over ten years in business, it became the world's biggest PC manufacturer, in 1995.

The key to Compaq's success was that it was among the first to identify that the IBM-compatible PC would set an unstoppable standard for the whole industry. It knew that this standard would be too big for IBM to dominate alone, and saw the gap for making perfectly compatible products. It did so with panache, launching the first ever computer to combine true portability with professional-level power and the world's first desktop PC to be built around the next generation 32-bit Intel 8386 processor. This ground-breaking product DeskPro 386, with three times faster processing speeds, saw Compaq storm ahead of the competition and set new standards in the industry.

In 1998, it greatly strengthened its claim to be the leader in business computing solutions when it acquired Digital Equipment Corporation for $9.6 billion. This was the biggest take-over in the history of the computer business and the move gave Compaq Digital's expertise in high-end business servers and networks.

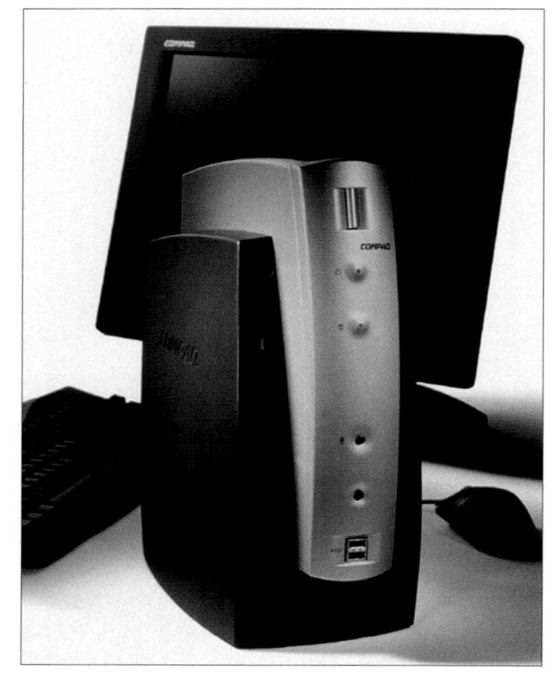

The deal stunned the industry and instantly catapulted Compaq into a position to challenge IBM and Hewlett-Packard for dominance of the entire computer market. It was also a very wise move, as it showed Compaq recognised that the higher margins and room for future growth was in the business server and enterprise computing sector.

In the UK, Compaq's achievements are closely linked to the guidance of Joe McNally, Chairman of UK and Ireland. He is credited with turning Compaq from a $1 company in 1986 to £1 billion in 1997. In just six years, he pulled Compaq alongside IBM as a leading supplier of business PCs.

But Compaq has combined this breakneck pace of growth with industry-leading environmental practices. In 1993, it became one of the first computer manufacturers to eliminate CFCs from worldwide manufacturing operations, and in 1997, it was awarded a Gold Medal for International Corporate Environment Achievement.

More recently, Compaq's ethical record was further strengthened when President Bill Clinton recognised it as a leader in bridging society's 'digital divide'. This was thanks to work Compaq has done with Tech Corps – a non-profit organisation that aims to bring the internet into more schools.

History

Compaq Computer Corporation was founded by Rod Canion, Jim Harris and Bill Murto in Houston, Texas, in 1982. At the time, Canion said, "We view ourselves as a large company in its formative years, not a small company with the potential to grow." Consequently, Compaq became one of the fastest growing companies in business history.

The founding aim of Compaq was to make an affordable computer that could do everything that IBM's PC could and in 1983, it introduced the first-ever portable computer.

From the very early days, Compaq broke new ground not only in its product but in its marketing, setting out to de-mystify the business of buying computers. The ads, supported by end lines like 'Simply Works better' and 'We'll never cease to amaze you', quickly established Compaq's credentials as an innovative barn-stormer in the computer business.

In its first year, the computer manufacturer broke US business records by recording £111 million in revenue, and in its second year, it set a computer industry record with sales of $329 million.

By 1987, it had manufactured its millionth computer, established a European headquarters in Germany and announced plans to build its first manufacturing plant outside of the US, in Scotland. In 1988, with sales topping $1 billion, Compaq had grown faster than any other company in the world, and, by 1991, it had become the UK's biggest PC vendor. Its brands, such as the 286, DeskPro 386, SystemPro and LTE 286 were by now making big inroads into the business market.

In 1993, it entered the consumer PC market with its world-famous Presario range. This was one of the first home computers to come with CD-Rom as standard, introducing the concept of the multimedia computer. The following year, announced a $10.5 million expansion of its Scottish manufacturing facility.

By this stage, Compaq was making $1 billion in the UK alone, and it was the world's biggest PC manufacturer.

In 1995, it sought to strengthen its position in the high-end business computing sector by acquiring Tandem Computers for $4 billion. Tandem extended Compaq's reach into mission-critical solutions and doubled its sales and service resources. The deal spurred Compaq's growth further, reporting sales of $24.6 billion in 1997 and a market of 85 countries and 15,000 sales outlets. The following year, it launched its Workstation Division and Professional Workstation 5000. These forays into the high-end business market prepared the ground for Compaq's massive acquisition of Digital in 1998.

Product

For the business customer, Compaq's product range is about much more than hardware such as notebooks, desktops, workstations, servers, monitors and storage solutions.

Compaq's Enterprise Solutions and Services Group provides the infrastructure, applications and know-how to enable businesses to implement non-stop e-business. The group combines Compaq's strength in servers, storage, networked products and professional support services to deliver high-performance, tightly integrated solutions.

In the enterprise server sector, Compaq has one of the broadest product lines on the market, ranging from entry-level, single processor servers for small businesses, like the NeoServer, to multi-processor, high availability enterprise-class servers like the Himalaya. It is servers such as these that many ISPs, websites, search engines and ATM cash networks rely on for 24-hour reliable performance. The Himalaya has a number one market share among fault tolerant systems and is used by 24 of the top 25 banks in the US.

In the storage market, in which Compaq is an undisputed leader, Compaq's products include the StorageWorks RAID line and the StorageWorks Enterprise Backup solution.

Computers for businesses range from the Prosignia to the more powerful DeskPro desktop range. Armada notebooks are also powerful enough for business applications. Higher level machines include the DeskPro, Alpha and Professional workstations. There is also the recently launched iPAQ desktop, which is primarily aimed at corporate network environments that use PCs for mainstream office productivity applications and corporate internet/intranet access.

As well as these core product lines, Compaq has a powerful Services Division, integrating the combined skills of the group to deliver total services including systems integration and operations management. Compaq's 27,000 service employees provide support to customers from 550 locations in 114 countries.

Recent Developments

As part of its strategy to target more small and medium sized businesses (SMEs), Compaq launched its new Prosignia range of PCs, servers and notebooks in 1999. It also launched a new simplified business PC, called iPaq, a revolutionary new, legacy-free PC, designed specifically to meet the needs of the internet user.

Promotion

Compaq set new standards in computer advertising, with John Cleese starring in a long series of highly amusing TV ads in the 1980s. At that time, the language of the industry – bits, bytes and chips – was meaningless to all but tech-heads. The John Cleese ads tackled this head on, satirising the jargon and focusing on a simple message – Compaq computers perform better.

In 1996, Compaq ran another ground-breaking campaign, running with the line 'Compaq costs you less than cheaper computers'. While the rest of the industry had traditionally focused on messages of raw price and performance, Compaq introduced the idea that reliability and quality would save customers more money through reducing down time and maintenance costs. The campaign was targeted at IT managers

and was backed up by a detailed booklet about the cost of business PC ownership.

The brand's recent campaigns, using press, TV and radio, present Compaq as a one-stop shop for business solutions and the company that makes modern e-business 'tick'. Focusing on the non-stop, 24-hour nature of the internet economy, Compaq uses the ads to show how it provides the computing backbone for the world's busiest websites, search engines and cashpoint networks. They use the end-lines 'Compaq, better answers' and 'Compaq. NonStop™'.

This 'NonStop' message has also been supported by sponsorship, including a deal backing a yacht in the round the world race, BT Global Challenge. The 30,000 mile race, which began in late 2000, is one of the most gruelling in sport, and ideally suits Compaq's NonStop brand values. Compaq is also principal sponsor of the BMW Williams Formula One racing team. The deal is intended to reflect how Compaq helps companies always be 'up and running' and make real-time, mission-critical decisions.

Brand Values

Compaq's founding mission was to make personal computing affordable and available to everyone, providing solutions that took the complexity out of computer systems but at the same time pushing the boundaries of performance. Nowadays, in the age of the internet, one of Compaq's most important values is to be seen as 'The NonStop Internet Company' which provides its customers with 'Better Answers'. Its mission is 'To ensure our customers' success in the 24x7 internet world by delivering, with our partners, the best infrastructure, access and solutions'.

As well as this internet-specific message, Compaq's brand is based on the core values of being: smart, gutsy, human and a pacesetter.

Things you didn't know about Compaq

Compaq's computing is behind four out of five of the world's most popular websites and four out of the five busiest search engines.

75% of the world's cash machine transactions are underpinned by Compaq's computing.

Fifteen million people interact with Compaq-powered web sites every day.

Compaq invented the PC server.

Compaq is the largest single provider to Internet Service Providers. Six of the eight largest ISPs have standardised on Compaq.

66 of the 68 largest stock exchanges are run on Compaq computers, with $3 trillion passing through them every day.

Over 60% of the world's currency trading takes place over Compaq systems.

Compaq is the UK's sixth biggest exporter.

Dun & Bradstreet

Market

Dun & Bradstreet is the largest business information company in the world. Companies all over the world use D&B's data to manage customer and supplier relationships. It boasts a global database covering more than 59 million businesses worldwide, underpinning a wide range of services that provide insight and intelligence for D&B's customers.

Information is a key competitive asset in today's market. Businesses need to know what their competitors are doing and gauge their financial strength. They also need to evaluate new business opportunities, identify prospects, assess credit and risk and, when necessary, chase bad debt.

As a $2 billion company providing information to over two million customers in 230 countries, D&B is able to meet all these needs. Until the 1980s, D&B was the undisputed leader in its field and there was little competition. However, as company data became more easily available, the business information sector has become much more competitive and D&B continues to lead the field.

With the internet making information a global currency instantaneously available at the touch of a button, D&B's market is being transformed by new technology and new competitors. Other established brands in the market, coming from different specialist backgrounds – such as Equifax or Reuters – are jostling for position in the business information sector. In this battle, the power of brands will count for a great deal.

Achievements

Dun & Bradstreet has an unsurpassed record for anticipating and preparing for technological change long before it transforms the wider market and this foresight continues to keep ahead of the competition today.

D&B is continually innovating and embracing change. In many ways, it prepared itself for the internet age long before anyone knew it was coming. It was the first information company to make data available to customers over the internet and the first in Europe to deliver data over an extranet. Efficient delivery of information to customers in whatever format they desire has always been a key D&B strength and it still leads the way in harnessing new technology to continually improve its service.

It was also one of the first companies to make truly sophisticated use of the database technology that has become so central to business today. Likewise, it was a pioneer in call centre technology, anticipating the explosion in telebusiness that occurred during the 1990s.

One of D&B's most important achievements is building its unparalleled database of 59 million businesses worldwide. Doing this requires it to constantly update and refine the information, which it does through a variety of channels, all dedicated to maintaining the quality of the database.

A key element of the database is also one of D&B's most important achievements. The company's unique way of identifying companies, the Data Universal Numbering System (D-U-N-S), has become a world standard for identifying and keeping track of different businesses and one of the most important contributions to database technology. The D-U-N-S® Number, which is accepted as standard by the International Standards Organisation, the European Commission and the United Nations, is much more than an identification number. It allows you to trace the linkage of a company and plot its structure. It is also invaluable in preventing duplication of records in giant databases and for cleaning records. The D-U-N-S® Number is increasingly being used to help companies make significant savings in the management of their most valuable asset – their data.

History

Dun & Bradstreet started life as The Mercantile Agency, founded in New York in 1841. The company was the world's first credit agency, founded on the belief that credit should be sought and granted based on sound information gathered professionally and methodically. The Mercantile's founder, Lewis Tappan, was a religious man who wanted to introduce probity to the credit business, which, at that time, was a haphazard and unprincipled affair.

By 1857, the business was going so well that further offices were opened in London and Montreal. The company was now run by Benjamin Douglass, who, in 1859, sold his interest to his brother in law, Robert Dun. He changed the company's name to R G Dun & Co. In 1933, a British competitor, The Bradstreet Company, merged with Dun & Co, eventually giving birth to the company's current name.

During the 1960s, Dun & Bradstreet entered a period of rapid expansion in the US. It acquired the Reuben H Donnelley Corporation – the company that revolutionised the use of telephone directories as sources of business information – in 1961. This merger also gave D&B access to Donnelley's direct mail division. In 1962, D&B acquired Moody's Investors Service – another revolutionary business, which introduced the idea of providing investors with sound information on companies in order to guide their decisions.

In the 1970s, D&B expanded dramatically in the UK, with turnover trebling between 1973 and 1977. New technology was the stimulus for growth, allowing the company to increase the capacity and collection capability of its business information services. In 1983, D&B UK produced the first computerised Business Information Reports, and, in the late 1980s began to build the centralised business database that now forms the core of the company's operations.

In 1990, D&B opened its European headquarters in High Wycombe, and in 1995, opened its hi-tech call centre in Newport, Gwent.

Product

Dun & Bradstreet's core asset is its database of 59 million businesses in 230 countries. This is updated nearly one million times per day. In the UK, the database covers over 2.1 million businesses.

The database helps D&B provide UK and international business information reports and provide The D&B Rating, coupling scoring technology with research to give a shorthand guide to a company's future performance. D&B also provides a monitoring service to alert customers to changes in a trading partner's performance which might affect their own.

As well as using D&B's data for credit and risk management, customers can use it for marketing and sales purposes. The information can be sliced and diced using 48 different selection criteria, and used to support direct mail or telemarketing campaigns. It is available on CD Rom, over the Internet or by using D&B's directories. It is also published in directories like Key British Enterprises, and Who Owns Whom and 30 different Regional Business Registers. D&B's data can also be used by purchasing professionals to source, evaluate and manage supplier relationships.

D&B's access to information about companies in 230 countries, updated by 40 centres, allows customers to compete in international markets. This includes D&B Country Reports, which evaluate the characteristics and risks of potential export markets and provide in-depth analysis to help customers plan business activity.

As well as these services, D&B has a Commercial Debt Collection business. This is the largest in the world, incorporating a range of services designed to help businesses recover money owed to them.

Recent Developments

D&B is developing more and more internet-based services. For example, D&B recently developed an internet-based credit information service called ComputaNet for the computer sector. It combines up to date payment information, industry specific company and market information with an online reference facility.

Likewise, D&B's CommsNet is the only credit information service specifically designed for the communications industry. It is a 'shared information network' available via the internet, providing 24-hour access to specialist credit and industry data on manufacturers, operators, distributors and resellers within the communications industry.

D&B is also forming alliances with an increasing number of 'e-partners'. It is teaming up with software vendors, such as Oracle, SAP, Siebel and the SAS Institute, on projects which see D&B data embedded into a range of applications. These deals mean that end users can access D&B's data seamlessly via their own systems.

Further associations with Onesource, Ask Alex and Mondus see D&B forming the information backbone for exciting new internet-based business-to-business services.

Promotion

As the business information market has become more competitive, D&B's investment in promoting its brand has increased.

It uses press advertising, placed in specialist trade press and business titles such as The Director, as well as credit and marketing magazines. This is supplemented by direct mail, promoting the full range of D&B products and services. Public relations work is boosted by well-respected publications, such as D&B's Quarterly Business Expectations and Business Failures. These surveys generate considerable media interest and D&B's spokespeople are regularly invited to participate in television and radio interviews.

The brand is also promoted at exhibitions – large and small – including the annual Online exhibition at Olympia, London, and the International Direct Marketing Fair. D&B also fields speakers at conferences which are attended by business leaders and important prospects.

D&B's website, which offers online ordering facilities, is another important tool, as are partnership deals, such as those with Oracle, SAP and Siebel.

Corporate hospitality is also used for key customers. Sporting events including the Monaco Grand Prix, Henley Regatta, Ascot, and the Prix de l'Arc d'Triomphe are some of the events D&B targets.

Over the years, the tone of D&B's advertising has changed. Since 1995 there have been four major campaigns. Between 1995 and 1996, the 'Worst nightmare' campaign highlighted the risks to business of not using intelligent information. Concepts included: 'Is this your next position in the City?', with a photo of a businessman fallen on bad times sitting tramp-like on the steps of a large city office block. The message of these ads was, 'Come to us and you won't end up in this position'.

Between 1996 and 1998, the 'Talking heads' campaign featured real D&B customers quoting their reasons for choosing D&B business information. Customers including BT and People's Phone were used. The rationale of the campaign was to highlight the benefits of following best practice and the value of choosing D&B to support a range of business processes. D&B interviewed the customers and used their feedback as the basis for the advertising copy. Headlines were direct quotes from these interviews.

Between 1998 and 2000, the 'Partnerships' campaign used enigmatic photos featuring famously successful partnerships, such as Bang and Olufsen, the Wright brothers, Hilary and Tensing, Armitage Shanks and Gilbert and Sullivan. Research showed that customers saw D&B more as a partner than a supplier and the campaign was developed to promote this. D&B also wanted to reflect a different visual image of the company, communicating the image of an approachable, friendly partner. The campaign started by promoting D&B's credit services, before expanding into D&B's business marketing products and services. The same concept was also used in direct mail campaigns.

The 2000 campaign highlighted the D&B online brand, dnb.com. The colour press ads promote D&B's products and services and reflect D&B's status as a high-tech, web-enabled organisation. The first series of ads included 'biggernbetter', promoting D&B as an unrivalled source of business names and addresses, whilst 'Tensnhundredsnthousandsnmillions' communicated the idea that no one can match D&B's wealth of in-depth business data.

Brand Values

In 1994, D&B underwent a brand audit, which resulted in the creation of a new brand identity. D&B's values are based on the clarity, accuracy and reliability of its information, the rapid and flexible delivery of data and the strength of its global reputation. Research into the brand revealed that people saw D&B as a global organisation with extensive resources and a provider of information that helps managers make more informed business decisions. D&B also wants its brand to reflect its web-enabled services and development of products suited for the online world.

Things you didn't know about Dun & Bradstreet

Four US presidents worked for Dun & Bradstreet, including Abraham Lincoln, Ulysses Grant, Grover Cleveland and William McKinley.

In 1874 R.G Dun placed the first major commercial order for typewriters in the US, ordering 100 Remington machines at $55 each. This order allowed Remington to start making typewriters on a major scale.

R.H Donnelley's idea of inserting business ads into telephone directories was a direct predecessor of today's Yellow Pages.

In 1967 D&B announced it would convert its information on three million companies to an electronic database. It was one of the earliest companies to do this and the project took three years to complete.

Market

easyJet operates in one of the world's most competitive air travel markets – the European short-haul sector. Dominated for years by the big airlines, which kept prices artificially high, European air travel has been transformed by an influx of low-cost competitors. As a result, passenger volumes have soared and prices tumbled.

Having been one of the only budget carriers when it launched in 1995, easyJet now has several direct competitors, including Ryanair, Virgin Express and the off shoots of a couple of the 'flag carriers' British Airways/Go and KLM/Buzz. Together, they fly to around 80 European destinations, carrying over fifteen million passengers per year.

easyJet and the other budget carriers have introduced fares that would have been impossible to contemplate ten years ago and, as they begin to fight over routes, prices are getting even lower. Margins are too tight for some to sustain, as Debonair and AB Airlines discovered when they went bust in 1999.

The effect of price-cutting on European routes has also hit some of the major carriers hard, contributing to a sharp dip in British Airways' overall profits in 1999 and leading it to focus on the more profitable business sector. However, the cut-price concept is beginning to find favour in this market too, with easyJet beating established names like Lufthansa, United Airlines and American Airlines in a survey recently conducted among business travellers by Barclaycard.

easyJet will continue to target the business traveller as it rapidly expands its European flight network.

Achievements

The airline's biggest achievement has been to survive and prosper in a market in which it is all too easy to crash land. While Debonair went bust and Go continues to make heavy losses, easyJet is constantly expanding its operations.

Founder Stelios Haji-Ioannou put easyJet into profit in its third financial year, and with the airline set to float on the stock market by the end of 2000, financial experts are predicting an impressive valuation.

As well as building a network of 28 European routes served by 150 flights a day, easyJet has won plaudits for operating one of the youngest fleets in the airline industry. It buys all its 737's brand new from Boeing in Seattle.

Like Richard Branson did with Virgin, Stelios has made easyJet a 'people's brand' – a champion to take on the giants and break the mould of conventional business practices. He has succeeded by showing other airlines that you don't need to offer tickets, travel agents, free drinks and lunches and flights from hub airports to survive. Consumers will gladly forgo these to save money, as long as reliability and safety standards are up to scratch. The fact that more business travellers think the same way is a major breakthrough.

easyJet has also taught the industry what is possible with direct sales over the phone and the internet. Not paying commission to travel agents is one of its biggest cost-savings and allows it to sell seats at prices other airlines could not afford. It tapped into the telemarketing revolution of the mid-90s with perfect timing, blazoning its telephone number on the fuselage of its aircraft. And then it got into the internet at the right point, offering online seat sales, which now account for well over 70% of all seats sold.

Most of all, easyJet has shown the airline industry that the no-frills business model not only works but is extremely popular with all types of travellers. The fact that it was voted the fifth most popular airline used by business travellers in Barclaycard's Travel in Business survey, is a significant achievement, as it shows that cost-cutting does not mean compromising on reliability. According to the same survey, 38% of business travellers used budget airlines in 1999, compared to 28% the year before. Much of that growth is thanks to easyJet.

History

Stelios Haji-Ioannou, son of a Greek shipping tycoon, launched easyJet in 1995. He launched easyJet with £5 million, beginning with a headline-grabbing fare of £29 from Luton to Glasgow. Stelios got the idea for easyJet from Southwest Airlines in the US – which also prospered by introducing a no-frills, low-price service on short-haul routes. Stelios was also an admirer of Virgin's 'consumer champion' strategy and met with Richard Branson before setting up easyJet to get some advice.

At first, easyJet operated without too much competition from other budget carriers – who stuck to different routes – or from the major airlines. But then, after only a year in business, British Airways made a discreet attempt to buy the airline. This initially friendly approach soon turned sour when the global giant launched its own budget carrier, Go, in 1998. easyJet accused BA of unfairly cross-subsidising Go and took its case to the High Court in February 1998.

The launch of Go was a massive threat to easyJet, which interpreted the move as a thinly disguised attempt by BA to put the budget carriers out of business. Stelios and his team went to war, initially fighting Go in the media, and then in the air, as its rival launched a service to Edinburgh, one of easyJet's most important routes.

However, since Go's launch, easyJet has had to deal with competition on other fronts. Ryanair has rapidly expanded its fleet and KLM has launched Buzz as yet another budget brand in an increasingly crowded market.

Product

easyJet flies 28 routes between eighteen key European leisure and business destinations. It flies from bases in London Luton, Liverpool and Geneva to Barcelona, Nice, Madrid, Zurich, Amsterdam, Athens, Malaga and Palma. In the UK, it flies to Aberdeen, Edinburgh, Inverness, Glasgow, and Belfast. The easyJet fleet now comprises eighteen Boeing 737-300s and 32 additional firm orders for new Boeing 737-700s are in the pipeline until 2004.

As businesses seek to cut down

on their travel budgets, easyJet is winning a bigger slice of the business traveller market. As such, the network of destinations and timetables are designed to suit business and leisure customers' needs. easyJet calculates that companies could save up to 89% on their travel budgets by using low-cost airlines.

easyJet employs a 'yield management' strategy, meaning that prices are closely linked to demand and the amount of time in advance that the ticket is booked. A ticket booked three months in advance will be significantly cheaper than one booked a week before the flight. Equally, peak-time tickets, like 6pm on a Friday, will cost more than one at a less busy time. The idea behind this strategy is to maximise seat sales for every flight.

easyJet's product relies not only on cost effectiveness, but also punctuality. Central to this is the ability to turn the aircraft around quickly on the ground. Compared to the hour and a half that it takes on average to turn a 737 around at Heathrow, easyJet's target time on the ground between flights is just twenty minutes.

All tickets are booked direct, either on the internet or the telephone. Buying a ticket involves being given a reference number, which is used in place of a ticket. The direct-sales approach is a prime example of how easyJet seeks to simplify business processes to maximise efficiency and reduce costs to itself and its customers.

As well as the airline, Stelios has launched a car rental company, a chain of internet cafes and is planning to enter the financial sector at the end of 2000 with easyMoney and easy.com – an online price comparitor.

Recent Developments

easyJet was recently voted Low Cost Airline of the Year by Business Traveller Magazine and Stelios himself has won a clutch of prestigious awards, including New Media Marketer of the Year by Revolution Magazine and Businessman of the Year by the Liverpool Daily Post.

The March 2000 launch of easyRentacar.com – the group's new car rental brand – has added value for the airline's customers. A fleet of Mercedes A-Class cars is available for rental at all easyJet destinations for as little as £9 per day.

Promotion

Given its margins – it barely makes £2 profit on each seat – easyJet has not got much to spend on advertising. Consequently, its marketing relies for the most part on public relations and sales promotion.

Like his mentor, Richard Branson, Stelios has proved a skilled PR operator, building easyJet into a powerful brand with the minimum of marketing expenditure.

He is a master of the publicity stunt, such as 'hi-jacking' Go's maiden flight by booking onto it with a team wearing boiler suits in easyJet orange. More recently, the airline landed the starring role in ITV's 'Airline' docu-soap. This strategy has attracted a level of media coverage a lot of companies can only dream about.

Stelios also generates publicity by positioning easyJet as the David against the airline industry's Goliaths. The company occasionally uses press advertisements to attack giants like BA and Swissair, including one which compared BA chief executive Bob Ayling and Go managing director Barbara Cassani, to Disney's Beauty and the Beast. In another dig at BA, easyJet uses the catchphrase 'The Web's Favourite Airline' to mock its competitor's 'World's Favourite' tag. No expensive advertising agencies are used to produce the ads – Stelios and his marketing team design the ads themselves.

More of these ads are being used to target the business traveller, with easyJet positioning itself as a huge saving for companies with large travel budgets. In 1998, it used a press campaign showing closed down factories and offices to warn that companies have to cut costs to survive.

Promotions, offering special deals on selected routes, are a vital marketing tool. In the past, these used to run primarily in the tabloid press, but now

Brand Values

Stelios sums up the easyJet brand as "the no bullshit approach". As the name suggests, the company's mission is to take the complexity and hidden costs out of every sector it enters. Whether it is car rental, internet cafes, airlines or financial services, the idea is to offer high quality products at the lowest possible price by selling them with the least number of costly overheads.

The company balances its cost-cutting image with an emphasis on safety, security, punctuality and in-flight service. It beat BA in these latter two areas in a recent survey amongst business travellers.

The company believes in demonstrating its commitment to low prices by keeping its own costs to a minimum. While British Airways spent millions on identity consultants to design its range of 'ethnic tailfins', easyJet's look is deliberately cheap and cheerful. Stelios does not sit in a huge penthouse office – he sits anywhere in any of his companies, working elbow to elbow with his employees.

As Richard Branson has done with Virgin, Stelios has made himself the personification of the easyJet brand. He appears in many of the advertisements, conducts numerous PR stunts and enjoys playing the part of 'consumer champion'.

The airline is making itself increasingly internet-based, offering £5 discounts on all seats sold on the web. Currently, all bookings made two months prior to departure will have to be made online.

easyJet continues to invest heavily in state-of-the-art hardware. The 32 new aircraft – the latest 737-700 from Boeing – will primarily build frequency on existing routes. This will lead to greater frequency on business routes as the airline looks to further build its profile with business travellers.

they are predominantly internet-based – reflecting the airline's sophisticated use of the internet.

However, the most prominent marketing tools for easyJet are its own aircraft. The company utilises them as airborne billboards, using them not only to advertise the phone number and internet address, but also to convey messages attacking competitors like Go. The plane which operated on easyJet's first flight to Athens had 'No Travel Agents' written in Greek on its side – a message that spawned a mini-riot among the local holiday companies.

Things you didn't know about easyJet

Before starting the airline, Stelios was already a successful businessman, helping to run his father's shipping empire and setting up his own tanker business (Stelmar) before his 26th birthday.

easyJet cabin crew enjoy injecting some humour into their intercom messages. On a recent flight, the steward said: "We hope you enjoyed your flight as much as we enjoyed taking you for a ride."

easyJet's Luton headquarters is a paperless office. All memos and letters are scanned into the computer system and, to do away with office secrecy, everyone in the company can read them.

In 1996, easyJet invited BA into its Luton offices to study how they ran the business. Months later, BA announced the launch of its own budget carrier, Go, based on a remarkably similar model to easyJet's.

easyJet came up with the cheapest ever European air fare with a £6 single fare between Liverpool and Belfast.

Equitable

Market

The UK pensions industry is entering a period of dramatic change. Historically, pensions have been complex products, hard for many investors to understand. As a consequence, few individuals have saved for their own retirement, increasing the government's burden. In an effort to bring the costs of saving for retirement down and make pensions more attractive, the Government said in its white paper 'Partnership in Pensions' that pension providers must make simple, good-value stakeholder pensions available by April 2001. These new plans must have low annual management charges and allow penalty-free transfers. The Government hopes that by switching regulation and control away from the sales process to the products themselves, they will bring about a rapid increase in the number of people and businesses holding and offering personal pension plans.

The low costs of these plans will make the market intensely competitive. The companies that prosper will be those with the economies of scale and brand strength to offset the narrower margins with large volumes of new business.

The new plans will affect businesses too as the Government has made the provision of the new plans a legal requirement for employers.

The strong economy is encouraging people to save more and investors' preferences have shifted from traditional vehicles such as bank deposits to higher return options such as mutual funds. According to Datamonitor, the European mutual funds industry – in which The Equitable is an important player – is growing dramatically, with net mutual fund assets growing from €1,412 billion (£893 billion) in 1993 to €2,940 (£1,860 billion) in 1998. Annually, these assets are growing at a rate of 16%.

Being an established player in this market is not enough to survive in this ultra-competitive environment. The internet has spawned a host of new players in the financial services market and has put further downward pressure on prices. Also, well-known brands from outside the financial world – such as Marks & Spencer and Virgin – have entered the market and, with the arrival of stakeholder plans in 2001, more are sure to follow.

All of these factors combine to make industry observers bullish about the sector's future. For example, Keynote Research anticipates that the total annual premium income from all forms of pensions in the UK will reach £30 billion in 2001. This represents a growth of 30% since 1998.

Achievements

The Equitable is highly unusual in that it has never paid commission to third parties, instead dealing directly through a salesforce of around 400 nationwide representatives. This salesforce is one of the most highly productive in the UK, bringing £6.4 million of new business per representative per year.

The Equitable's pension funds are some of the best value and best performing on the market. In February 2000, The Equitable was voted Best Personal Pension Provider in the Consumer Finance Awards, sponsored by The Guardian, The Observer and Money Observer. In addition, The Equitable's pension funds have been recognised as some of the best performing over time. The industry journal, Planned Savings, has monitored the performance of with-profits pension plans since 1974. In the 60 tables published, The Equitable has appeared in the top ten a total of 47 times – more than any of its competitors.

The company has also won plaudits with Money Management magazine, being one of only two companies to have won a five-star 'best buy personal pension' in each of its pension surveys.

History

The Equitable was founded in 1762, trading under the name of 'The Society for Equitable Assurances on Lives and Survivorships'. The initiative and drive behind the Society came from its actuary, James Dodson, who devised a new scientific system for calculating life assurance premiums based on life expectancy. It was the first life assurance society ever to be based on such a carefully calculated, logical approach and broke new ground in the nascent financial services industry. This approach of basing members' premiums on how long they could be expected to live was much fairer than that offered by the life assurance policies available at the time and was central to the Society's 'equitable' approach.

For many years, The Equitable was the largest life company in England, and, in 1799, it had over 5,000 contracts and sums of around £4 million. In order to compete, rival life companies began paying commission for the introduction of new business – a practice which was fiercely criticised in the press at the time. In complete contrast, The Equitable introduced a waiting list for new members, placing strict limitations on the number of people who could be in the Society at one time. Although the waiting list has not been retained, the Society remains true to its original non-commission paying stance.

In 1893 'The Society for Equitable Assurances on Lives and Survivorships' became 'The Equitable Life Assurance Society' under the Companies Act. This allowed the Society to grow in size significantly over the years and, it now has funds under management in excess of £32 billion.

Products

The Equitable is best known for its pensions, for which it has an excellent reputation for combining low cost with strong financial performance. First introduced in the 1950s, The Equitable's pension plans set the standard for other companies to follow, with their low charges, high performance and unprecedented flexibility. Whilst other companies levied high and hard-to-understand charges, The Equitable offered simple, good value plans.

The Equitable also offers one of the broadest and most innovative range of

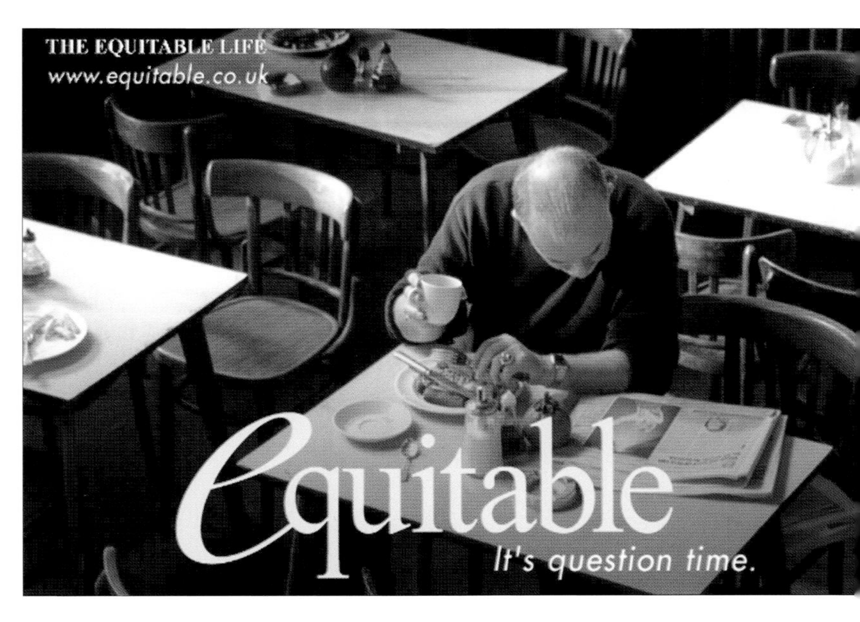

annuities on the market – an increasingly important factor for clients facing the lower rates paid on traditional compulsory annuities. As well as linking their retirement income to the performance of the stockmarket or a with-profits fund, The Equitable allows pensioners to draw income from a proportion of their pension fund, leaving the rest to grow for the future.

The Equitable is not limited to providing pensions or annuities. Under its investment arm, Equitable Unit Trust Managers, the Society offers twenty unit-linked funds covering different geographical areas, risk profiles and investment types. These include a managed fund, Japanese, European and North American funds, an ethical fund as well as two tracking funds and a trust of investment trusts.

The Equitable also offers a with-profits fund, which invests in a basket of stocks, shares, gilts and property. Each year the Society allocates a rate of return to the fund which smoothes its returns, so investors can benefit from stockmarket growth potential without wide fluctuations in returns.

These funds can be used to invest in a range of tax-efficient plans including ISAs, maximum investment plans and personal investment plans. In addition to its broad product range, The Equitable offers its clients an unprecedented level of service. Clients are able to deal with the Society however and whenever they wish – face-to-face with representatives in any of its 32 branch offices, directly over the telephone with Equitable Direct or in real time over the internet. In addition, all documents coming into the Society are stored on an imaging system which means they can be called up on screen anywhere within The Equitable, vastly speeding up the time taken to answer clients' questions and resolve problems.

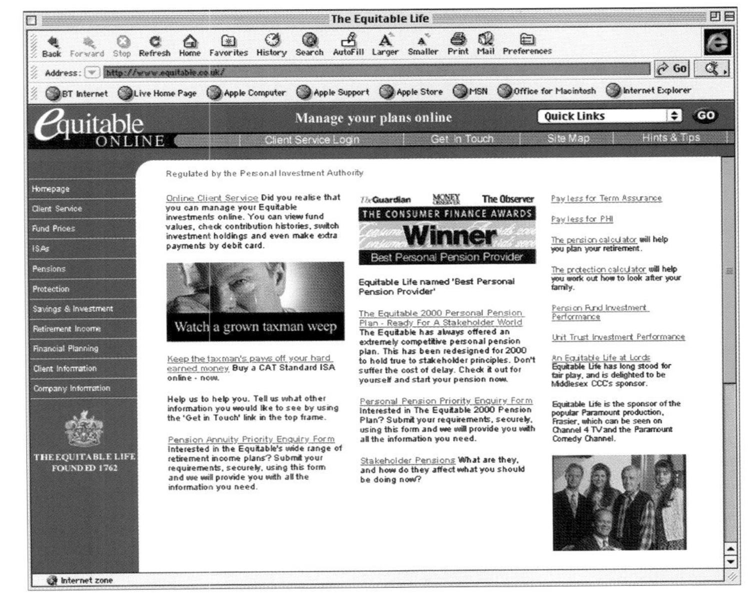

Recent Developments

The Equitable launched a personal pension which fits many of the charging and flexibility criteria of the new stakeholder friendly plans, long before the 2001 product offering. The annual management charge is among the lowest on the market, offering an attractive package for private investors and for companies wanting to offer their employees an affordable pension package.

A key feature of The Equitable pensions is that they are supported by a powerful and innovative internet presence. The Equitable is one of the few companies in its sector to allow investors to track the performance of their funds online at www.equitable.co.uk.

The Equitable also offers individual savings accounts (ISAs), giving investors the chance to invest their money in the wide range of shares making up the UK all-share index. Investors can buy an ISA online as well as check the value of their funds, change their personal details or vary the level of their investments – all at no additional charge.

Promotion

The Equitable recently overhauled its promotional strategy and image, investing in a new corporate identity as well as television and press advertising campaigns plus sponsorship of the hit TV series, Frasier.

All of these help it reach a broad business and consumer audience. The television sponsorship deal is aimed at an upmarket demographic with money to invest. The television campaign, through TBWA GGT Simons Palmer is one of the most ground-breaking in the financial services sector. Featuring a range of celebrities, such as John Peel and Tom Bell, who encourage investors to ask questions of their pension provider, playing on The Equitable's image as a fair company for whom integrity is a central watchword.

The company also sponsors a number of events targeted specifically at the business community, such as a deal backing a major squash tournament held in the heart of the City and, in a broader perspective, its sponsorship of Middlesex County Cricket Club.

In order to both build The Equitable brand and generate short, medium and long-term business the Society invests heavily in a series of advanced direct marketing programmes, mailing a series of carefully targeted prospects with information about its pension, annuity and investment products.

Brand Values

The key values of The Equitable brand are integrity and fairness. The Equitable's overriding philosophy is to maximise the benefits and service it provides to its clients. As it does not pay commission, it is also committed to keeping costs to a minimum. As the 'it's question time' line suggests in its advertising, it is also a brand that wants to show it has nothing to hide and aims to be honest and transparent to its customers and investors.

Things you didn't know about The Equitable Life

The Equitable invented scientific life assurance.

John Ware Stephenson, actuary of the Society 1870-1888 was also a fellow of The Royal Microscopical Society and invented the binocular microscope.

Past policyholders have included Charles Babbage, Samuel Taylor Coleridge, WG Grace, William Wilberforce and Sir Walter Scott.

The Equitable has never paid commission for the introduction of new business.

The motto of The Equitable is 'sic nos non nobis' (Thus do we, but not for ourselves'). This reflects the principle that members of the Society join in order to provide for their dependants.

The Equitable's £32 billion funds under management is overseen by just 28 fund managers.

Market

The world's largest express transportation company can justifiably claim to have revolutionised the way people live and do business. FedEx invented overnight delivery in 1973 and has continued to connect people across the globe ever since. It handles everything from urgent medical supplies and fragile scientific equipment to last minute gifts, time-sensitive documents and bulky freight.

FedEx's business customers have come to regard its aircraft fleet as their 500 mile an hour warehouses. The economy built around the old business model of trying to predict customer demand in advance, which requires costly inventories of finished and unfinished goods, is being replaced by a model of information and transportation system networks. Networks, such as FedEx, mean products can be built and shipped within days from the time consumers, anywhere in the world, place orders electronically. The company's skill in transportation and logistics enables major corporations and small businesses alike to maximise profit and efficiency by eliminating expensive inventories from the business equation.

The business environment is becoming ever more global as borders and barriers to trade continue to come down. Roughly 20% of manufactured items are sold across borders, but by 2020 some 80% of all production will be distributed globally (Source: McKinsey). E-commerce, in particular, has and will continue to drive globalisation and is in itself changing the way the world does business.

FedEx was a pioneer of e-commerce in the 1980s - before the internet was opened for commercial use - through a proprietary network of computers in its customers' offices. Since its inception, it has invested heavily in information technology and is now ideally placed to help its customers take advantage of the exponential growth of e-commerce, the increasing

globalisation of business and the growing need for fast cycle logistics.

Today FedEx delivers over 3.3 million items a day to 210 countries with a fleet of 663 aircraft and over 45,000 vehicles.

Achievements

Few people can claim to have invented a global industry, yet Frederick Smith did exactly that. The idea that Smith came up with while at university has grown into a global empire employing over 150,000 and generating revenues of almost $14 billion in 1999. FedEx's proudest claim is that it connects to markets that generate 90% of the world's GDP (gross national product) within 24-48 hours.

FedEx firsts are numerous. Having invented the overnight delivery in the early 1970s, it has constantly sought to make transportation and shipping easier, faster and more flexible. It invented the 'hub and spoke' system, which was subsequently adopted throughout the airline industry, where shipments from 'spokes' all over the world are flown to a central hub to be sorted, loaded onto planes and despatched to their final destinations.

It was the first air express company to offer overnight letters, guaranteed 10.30 am next-day delivery, Saturday delivery and time-definite services for freight. It was first to offer money-back guarantees and free proof of performance and to offer real-time package tracking over the phone. It developed barcode technology in the 1980s to track packages on every step of their journey and it introduced a dedicated computer network for use in its customers' offices when PCs were rarely sighted. It now operates the planet's largest civilian network of computers linked to satellites.

A pioneer of e-commerce when the internet was unknown to most, FedEx has constantly sought to anticipate the technology its customers will need tomorrow and introduce it today.

History

The FedEx story began in the 1960s when a political science and economics student at Yale wrote a paper on the logistical challenges facing the pioneers of the IT industry. Fred Smith concluded that a new system to move parts overnight and door-to-door had to replace physical inventory. Smith returned from a tour of duty as a Vietnam pilot and made his idea a reality in 1973.

FedEx was the most heavily financed start up in US history and it became the first US company to reach $1 billion in revenues without any mergers or acquisitions within ten years of its launch.

In the mid 1970s it lobbied hard for deregulation of the US market and won. It has since campaigned ceaselessly for 'open skies' policies around the world. Its international expansion began in 1984 with the launch into Europe and Asia. In 1988 it began scheduled flights to Japan and the following year acquired Tiger International Inc, which operated routes to over 21 countries.

While FedEx's physical network has grown, its information-based network is, if anything, more impressive. In 1979 it opened the first automated call centre and gave couriers handheld computers to log shipment information. In 1980 it put computers in vans to guide couriers to their next pick-up and the following year established a central computer system managing vehicles, people, packages and routes and tracking weather systems. In 1984 it introduced the world's first automated shipping service. In 1986 it developed barcode technology to provide even more accurate and accessible tracking information and a year later it took the then radical step of giving customers dedicated computer terminals on which to track their shipments. In 1992 it introduced free tracking

software to enable customers to track packages from their PCs and in 1994 FedEx scored yet another industry first with the launch of its website – www.fedex.com.

Its acquisition of Caliber System in 1998 created a global transportation and logistics powerhouse. FedEx shortened its name from Federal Express in 1994 to make better use of the brand across its many discrete services. In January 2000 it further strengthened the brand by adopting the FedEx name across its entire operation to provide the ultimate one stop shop for total supply chain solutions.

Product

FedEx offers global transportation, logistics, e-commerce and supply chain management solutions. Products are engineered to constantly improve FedEx's service to customers and to its customers' customers. FedEx offers a door-to-door, customs-cleared, money-back guaranteed delivery service backed by the most extensive flight and vehicle network in express delivery and the best in information resources. Its products cover express document, package, freight and bulk delivery through to full supply chain management.

Each shipment is scanned seven times on average to ensure that the customer can track its precise location by email, on the internet or by telephone, 24 hours a day.

Dedicated technology consultants design and implement e-commerce and electronic data exchange systems to enable customers to join the electronic revolution and to save them time and money. FedEx simplifies and speeds the shipping process by providing online ordering

and processing facilities, free packaging, straightforward shipping documentation and bespoke e-business facilities.

Recent Developments

In September 1999 FedEx opened its European super-hub at Roissy-Charles de Gaulle in Paris. The $200 million project, which was funded jointly by FedEx and Aeroports de Paris, is the principal sorting and distribution centre for Europe capable of processing 60,000 packages and documents an hour. At the same time it launched FedEx EuroOne, a network offering next business-day deliveries to major European cities, with pick-up capabilities as late as 7pm. In April 2000 it extended the network to connect 40,000 European postcodes.

In August, responding to the growing demand for reduced transit times, later customer pick-ups and early deliveries, FedEx made further improvements to their European and Asian services – enhancing the speed, reliability and customer service that have made FedEx the worldwide leader in express transportation.

In 1999 FedEx chalked up yet another first when it introduced a single European tariff. All packages within the 'euro zone' are charged at the same rate (assuming that they are the same weight) and customers can be billed in either euros or their local currencies.

As the driving force in the introduction of new technology to the industry, FedEx has continually sought new ways to harness the power of information. It now enables customers to track up to 25 shipments simultaneously, order a pick up, calculate costs and transit times, prepare all necessary shipping documentation, review shipping history and store up to 300

names and addresses online. In April 1999 it extended its tracking service to handheld devices, such as the PalmPilot.

FedEx can provide the infrastructure for e-commerce needs. In October 1999 two new internet-based tools designed to boost e-commerce were launched in Europe, the Middle East and Africa. FedEx ShipAPI and FedEx TrackAPI enable companies to automate shipping, streamline their supply chains and improve customer service by giving their customers access to accurate online tracking. Effectively it means that FedEx can become their logistics and fulfilment operations offering on time delivery to over 210 countries worldwide.

Promotion

FedEx was the first cargo carrier to advertise on television and in the consumer press in 1975 announcing itself with the line: 'America, you've got a new airline'.

Since its first campaigns, FedEx has set the industry standard with classic commercials such as the 'Absolutely, positively, overnight' series by legendary American director Joe Sedelmaier in 1979.

Whilst ingrained in the American psyche, FedEx is less well known in Europe and its latest advertising, launched in 1999, is designed to help build its brand personality and raise awareness of what FedEx fundamentally stands for: reliability, efficiency and the absolute dedication of its staff. The 'Whatever it takes' campaign, which appears on television, press, posters and radio, is the result of in-depth planning and research among FedEx customers and non-customers in the UK, France and Germany.

Ultimately people want the business of sending a package to be straightforward, but problems can happen and denying that could make the company appear unrealistic. FedEx's most valuable assets are by far its employees, who have a dynamic, 'can-do' attitude in dealing with the problems which make or break customer relationships.

FedEx wanted a campaign that would stand out from its competitors' advertising, which remains dominated by pictures of planes, packages and globes and claims of 100% perfect service. Customers want to rely on people not faceless organisations. Hence its brand idea was born: 'FedEx people take it on better than anyone else'. That translates as staff acknowledging their responsibility to customers, always problem solving, showing initiative and doing whatever they can to help. The strapline 'Whatever it takes' encapsulates the FedEx mentality and demonstrates the lengths to which its couriers will go to get packages delivered – on time. The fun, humorous ads show couriers trekking through head-high snow, walking through sewers and doing 'whatever it takes' to get it there.

Equally in 1999 FedEx commenced its sponsorship programme with the Ferrari Formula One racing team. By teaming up with this legend of the motor world, FedEx is maintaining its prominence in the international transportation business. The important values of speed, reliability, sophisticated technology and teamwork are indeed determining factors of success for both FedEx and Ferrari.

Brand Values

In its broadest sense FedEx is selling peace of mind: the surety of knowing that your goods are safe in its hands and that they will be delivered on time. Its culture is built on a simple philosophy - People, Service, Profits (PSP). It believes that only committed and satisfied staff can deliver the impeccable service standards expected of FedEx, which in turn produce its profits. It recognises staff as its most valuable asset, a belief echoed time and again by its customers. Its history is littered with tales of staff quite literally going that extra mile to get the job done. Without that sort of commitment its brand values – excellent customer service, reliability, efficiency, security and innovation – would be meaningless.

FedEx is now far more than a delivery company and in recent years has sought to communicate the vastness and power of its network and the breadth of its expertise as a global solutions provider. However, PSP remains at its heart. In the words of Fred Smith: "FedEx is not a logo or its advertising or its salesforce. To the customer, FedEx is the person who comes to your door and doesn't let you down."

Things you didn't know about **FedEx Express**

During Desert Storm FedEx flew 576 missions, equalling a third of the war effort's total cargo tonnage.

Each month 14,000 FedEx employees take advantage of the company's free flights offer to work in another part of the world.

Each FedEx plane is named after an employee's child.

A FedEx jet can be unloaded of its cargo in just seventeen minutes.

FedEx kept the Rolling Stones rolling during their 1995 Voodoo Lounge tour, which made 120 stops across six continents. FedEx moved all the production materials for the show, including 300 tons of fragile sound and lighting equipment.

THE GALLUP ORGANIZATION

PRINCETON

Market

Gallup competes in a fiercely competitive market. There are a staggering 6000 companies, operating in 100 countries, which compete in the research and opinion polling sector. There is huge demand for this type of information, as businesses, political parties and other organisations become increasingly responsive to public opinion. With the rise of consumer power and the stakeholder economy, those that are responsible for forming political and corporate policy ignore public opinion at their peril. As such, opinion polls play an increasingly important part in our lives. In the US last year, some 72 million people were asked their views in opinion or market research surveys.

However, this is not the only market in which Gallup operates. It is also active in the management consultancy sector, helping companies sustain profitability by providing them with crucial information about their customers and employees. As such Gallup offers a research-based service to improve management practice. Companies spend billions on intelligence that will help them compete more effectively. In the UK, the Management Consultants' Association says that in 1999 its members' sales exceeded £6 billion, with exports approaching £1 billion.

Achievements

Gallup is the world's largest, best-known and most trusted opinion polling firm. For over 60 years, it has been the world leader in the measurement and analysis of peoples' attitudes, opinions, and behaviour. Over that time, it has built up a formidable international network, with subsidiary operations in more than 25 countries, covering 75% of the world's gross national product. More than 3000 research, consulting and teaching professionals work at Gallup to provide services that stretch across geographical, linguistic and cultural boundaries.

The Gallup Poll is a legend, dating back to 1935. People the world over associate this with authoritative, trustworthy information, often pertaining to crucial events and outcomes of intense interest. For example, it has an outstanding record of predicting general election results and, at the 1997 UK general election, achieved the most accurate result of any polling organisation.

These strengths have led to Gallup not only being trusted by the public at large but also by influential media organisations who want to have the most authoritative, up to date information. In the US, its insight regularly informs debate on CNN and in USA Today. In the UK, Gallup has an extremely long-standing relationship with the Daily Telegraph.

But, although Gallup is best known for the Gallup Poll, most of its work nowadays is in providing measurement, consulting and education to many of the world's leading companies. Its long history of measuring and analysing human attitudes and behaviour has made it one of the most trusted sources of information on the dynamics of companies and the factors that create success. For over twenty years, it has been working to identify the core characteristics of great managers and workplaces, resulting in the development of a unique and highly valuable process, The Gallup Path. This unique system of measuring the factors that contribute towards profitable growth – The Gallup Path – helps companies maximise the potential of the 'human side' of their business. It is based on the world's largest research base into the factors surrounding individual talent and success and it provides unique insight into how these drive productivity, profitability, customer satisfaction and employee retention.

Some of the world's best known companies – such as Standard Life, Glaxo Wellcome, Toyota, Intel and the Volkswagen Group – work with Gallup to take advantage of its insight. Gallup has also found considerable success sharing its findings through publications like 'First, Break All the Rules', which has sold over 225,000 copies and has been on the Wall Street Journal best seller list for over a year.

FIRST, BREAK ALL THE RULES
WHAT THE WORLD'S GREATEST MANAGERS DO DIFFERENTLY
MARCUS BUCKINGHAM & CURT COFFMAN

History

The father of the Gallup Organization is George Horace Gallup, an American public opinion analyst and statistician. In 1935 he founded the Gallup Organization and also became president of the American Institute for Public Opinion. In September of that year, Gallup asked its first official question in a US opinion poll. That question, testing approval ratings for US president, Franklin Roosevelt, was, 'Do you approve or disapprove of the way (the president) is handling his job as president?'

Since then, The Gallup Poll has tested public opinion on a wide range of issues. In the 1940s, Gallup interviewers were asking about wartime rations, in the 1950s about the Korean War, in the 1960s about civil rights riots, in the 1970s about Watergate and, more recently, about news-grabbing events like the OJ Simpson trial. The Gallup Poll has also been used to test public opinion on vital issues such as approval for the death penalty, abortion and levels of taxation.

Internationally, Gallup's development has been complicated by the fact that George Gallup allowed his famous name to be used by research organisations around the world in return for sharing the insights of their findings. This led to a loose confederation of independent companies, all using the Gallup name but few of which were formally owned or connected to the parent company. In the mid 1980s, this issue was addressed when a Nebraska-based research company, SRI (Selection Research Inc), acquired The Gallup Organization in the US and set about trying to regain control of the Gallup name.

SRI was founded by Dr Donald O Clifton, Professor of Educational Psychology at the University of Nebraska. Now one of the most prominent occupational psychologists, Don Clifton's lifelong work has been the study of individual success. He has created the unique structured interview processes which identify the relevant talents for specific roles. These form the essential foundations of The Gallup Path.

In the UK, an independent company, Social Surveys Ltd, had been using the Gallup name for many years. In 1994, Gallup – now owned by SRI – acquired Social Surveys and so officially made the UK Gallup a wholly owned subsidiary of the parent company. This marked a new phase in the global development of the brand, as The Gallup Organization brought more and more international offices under its direct control.

Product

Gallup's product is mainly divided between the two distinct sides of its business: polling and consultancy. The former comes under the name of The Gallup Poll, while the latter is known as The Gallup Path.

Famous as The Gallup Poll is, it should be remembered that this side of Gallup's activities only represents 5% of its turnover. The vast majority – 90% – of its business is now in the area of consultancy.

Nonetheless, Gallup's polling remains extremely influential and a trusted source of information. All of its surveys are conducted by phone, replacing the previous technique of polling in face to face interviews. A crucial element of the polling service is in the care given to ensuring the quality and consistency of the interview sample. Gallup uses highly advanced technology to gather, analyse and interpret the data, such as automated telephone interviews and the use of specialist statistics software.

The Gallup Path is the unique selling point for Gallup's consultancy services. It forms the basis of Gallup's rapidly growing business, which has recently reported annual revenue growths of 25% over the last decade. The Gallup Path is a model which describes the path between the individual contribution of every employee and the company's ultimate business outcome – namely an increase in its value.

THE GALLUP PATH

Enter Here
Identify Strengths
The Right Fit
Great Managers
Engaged Employees
Loyal Customers
Sustainable Growth
Real Profit Increase
Stock Increase

For publicly traded companies, this is best measured by increases in stock price and market valuation.

The actual path begins with identifying employees' individual strengths. Relevant 'talents' are the key to excellent performance, supported by appropriate skills, knowledge and experience. Next is finding the right fit – a position that capitalises on that talent in the most appropriate way. Having taken these steps, the Path reaches a critical point, highlighting the importance of 'Great Managers'. Gallup's research has shown that the only way to truly engage talented employees is to select great managers who can create a great work environment. It is on these foundations that companies can build customer loyalty over the long term. These 'bottom five' steps of the Path link together to drive the top three steps, namely, sustainable growth, profit increase and enhanced market value.

For each of the bottom five steps, Gallup has developed a range of tools to help companies achieve these goals. An example is its Q12 Workplace Survey – a 12-point questionnaire which correlates employee attitude to four measures of business performance: employee retention, productivity, customer satisfaction and profitability. Overall, Gallup has accumulated evidence worldwide covering 200,000 employees in nearly 8000 business units, which show the strong links between employee engagement and business outcomes.

Recent Developments

A major new addition to Gallup's consultancy offering is the StrengthsFinder™ created by Don Clifton from Gallup's extensive research base. This is a product of Gallup's Strength Management Practice – a division of the company which is devoted to helping companies identify and capitalise on the strongest characteristics of their employees.

The StrengthsFinder is a web-based measurement tool which helps people identify in themselves which of 34 different 'strength themes' are most prominent. Managers can use the StrengthsFinder to learn more about their employees' strengths so that they can help them leverage them to best effect. They can use Gallup's StrengthsInventory™ to compare divisions, workgroups and units.

This strength-based approach lies at the heart of Gallup's latest publication, co-authored by Don Clifton, published in the UK in Spring 2001.

Promotion

Gallup does very little advertising to attract business clients, instead relying on a powerful use of PR and written publications. Some of its best publicity has been derived from its hugely successful books, most notably 'First, Break All the Rules', which was written by two senior Gallup executives. The book, which provides insight into what the world's greatest managers do differently, is based on interviews with 80,000 managers at 400 companies and has been widely acclaimed as a seminal management text.

Gallup derives great PR value from the success of these books – another on individual strengths is published in 2001 – and its experts are widely sought after for media interviews on management and workplace issues. It also regularly publishes other material on its website, www.gallup.com.

Its people also write regularly on these subjects in respected industry journals like People Management and The Director. In all cases, these provide opportunities for Gallup to draw attention to The Gallup Path and its consultancy services.

Its polling activities are also amply promoted through media partnerships, such as those with the Daily Telegraph in the UK and CNN in the US, where Gallup presents regular analysis of social and political trends.

Seminars and conferences are another valuable promotional channel. For example, in 2000, it held a summit in New York based on The Gallup Path, with over 270 senior executives in attendance to hear the authors of 'First, Break All the Rules.'

Brand Values

Unlike many consultancy firms, Gallup is committed to helping companies understand the human side of their business. As such, it is committed to providing clients with 'solutions, not data'.

On the polling side of the business, it places great emphasis on the responsibility and professionalism of its opinion surveys. Gallup is a brand that enables peoples' opinions to be heard, making them and the Gallup name a significant and informed contributor to the democratic process.

Things you didn't know about The Gallup Organization

Gallup's Q12 Workplace Survey is based on feedback from millions of employees around the world. Companies that audit their employees using Q12 can find dramatic results. For example, applied to a group of retail companies, it found that the 25% of stores with the highest employee satisfaction had productivity levels 22% above the average for all stores. They also had 22% less employee turnover and 27% higher than average profit. Customer satisfaction was 39% above average.

George Gallup was a pioneer in the use of statistical methods for measuring the interest of readers in the features and advertisements of magazines and later extended his research to include the reactions of radio audiences, founding the Audience Research Institute in 1939.

Don Clifton, now Chairman of Gallup's International Research and Education Centre, has been instrumental in helping establish a 'Positive Psychology' group of prominent psychologists dedicated to research and education on the components of well-being and fulfilment.

Gallup has a structured interview to measure the talents of NHL ice hockey players. One of the attributes that the best hockey players have is something Gallup calls 'Elapsed Time'. Simply put, the best NHL players have an ability to see the puck in slow motion – time seems to slow down for them at pressure moments.

GlaxoWellcome

Market

Healthcare giant Glaxo Wellcome is one of the world's largest pharmaceutical companies, with a 4.4% market share of the £180 billion global market. By market capitalisation, it is the fourth largest company in the UK behind Vodafone Airtouch, BP and BT. It has global sales of £8.5 billion.

It supplies 150 international markets, employs 60,000 people and has 76 operating companies in some 57 countries worldwide. Its biggest areas for making prescription drugs are respiratory ailments, viral and bacterial infections, central nervous system and gastro-intestinal disorders. Its biggest market by sales volume is North America, which accounts for 42% of sales (£3.6 billion), followed by Europe with 34% (£2.9 billion).

Research into unmet medical needs and development of medicines to combat them (as well as innovative new delivery techniques) is central to Glaxo Wellcome's business. In 1999, it spent £1.27 billion on R&D and 10,000 of its employees work exclusively in this area. The 'molecule to marketplace' process can often take up to twelve years, as scientists move from identifying the right target to treat a disease through drug discovery into periods of exhaustive safety studies and clinical trials.

The biggest share of its R&D budget goes into combating viral infections, including HIV treatment – in which field Glaxo Wellcome is the market leader. In terms of sales, the respiratory market is the group's biggest sector, supplying a range of asthma treatment medicines.

The strongest brands in Glaxo Wellcome's portfolio are its five 'lead' products: Serevent (asthma), Flixotide (asthma), Combivir (HIV), Imigran (migraine) and Zantac (peptic ulcers). These are bolstered by new products that Glaxo Wellcome has high hopes for: Seretide (asthma), Zeffix (Hepatitis B), Relenza (influenza), Ziagen (HIV) and Agenerase (HIV). In addition to these it has just launched a treatment for irritable bowel syndrome in the United States and plans to introduce new compounds to treat diabetes and prostate disease.

Achievements

The group's many achievements are best illustrated by the string of awards and honours heaped on it over the years.

Since 1973 its medicines have been awarded no less than ten Queen's Awards for Technical Achievement. These include: Ventolin (1973), Zantac (1985), Zovirax (1985), Imigran (1994), Lamictal (1996) and the Diskus/Accuhaler in 1999. This innovative inhaler has won numerous other awards, including the Design Council's Millennium Product Award in 1998. Glaxo Wellcome has also won a Queen's Award for Technical Innovation, for the Becotide inhaler, which was the first inhaled steroid.

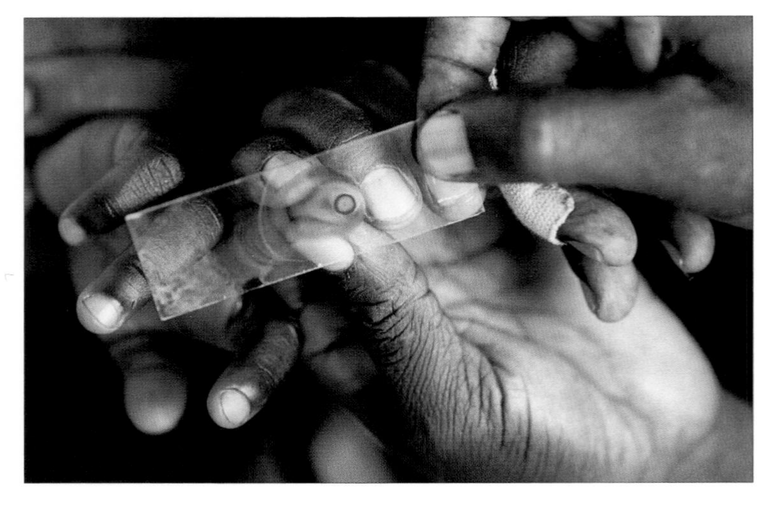

Glaxo Wellcome is also consistently recognised as one of the world's best companies, ranking third in Management Today's Most Admired Company Award in 1999 and topping a February 2000 Sunday Times ranking of companies delivering best value to shareholders. It has also been honoured for its work in HIV/AIDS research.

However, its greatest achievement has been to develop the many medicines and treatments that have contributed so greatly to health in the modern world. Its work in the treatment of HIV/AIDS, cancer, asthma, hepatitis and malaria, as well as its ground-breaking work in genetics have put it at the forefront of medical care and research. In the process, it has put UK science on the international map and helped make this country a respected centre of excellence in the field of pharmaceuticals research.

History

Glaxo was founded in New Zealand by an Englishman, Joseph Nathan, in 1873. Initially specialising in powdered baby milk, Glaxo expanded into Britain in the early 1900s, whereupon it became a well-known name in the baby care market. After the First World War, the company continued expanding with baby milk distribution in India and South America.

It entered the pharmaceutical business in 1927 with the launch of Ostelin, a liquid Vitamin D formulation. This was followed by a Vitamin D-fortified milk, Ostermilk, which further fuelled Glaxo's international distribution.

In 1936, with a new laboratory at Greenford, West London, the company's product range grew; by 1944 it was making 80% of Britain's penicillin. Demand grew dramatically during World War Two.

In 1947, Glaxo was listed on the London Stock Exchange and during the 1950s it started to diversify, acquiring veterinary, medical instrument and drug distribution companies.

In 1969 it launched its well-known asthma treatment, Ventolin, and in 1978, entered the US, the world's largest pharmaceutical market. It consolidated this move with the launch of its most successful drug, Zantac, in 1981. This massive launch rewarded Glaxo with leadership of the US anti-ulcer drug sector and, by 1986, Zantac was the world's top selling medicine.

In January 1995, Glaxo launched its take-over bid for UK competitor, Wellcome. Burroughs Wellcome was established in London in 1880 by two American pharmacists – Henry Wellcome and Silas Burroughs. In 1884 they coined the word 'tabloid' to describe their compressed tablets. Wellcome did not become a public company until 1985 by which time the company's reputation was firmly founded on its success with anti-virus and tropical medicines. This company was a world leader in anti-viral medicines and boasted Nobel prizes for two of its scientists. The research foundation, The Wellcome Trust, which was Wellcome's biggest shareholder, agreed with the takeover, and integration of the two giants eventually began in March. In September 1995, the new Glaxo Wellcome launched worldwide. At the same time it bought the Californian high-tech combinatorial chemistry company Affymax.

Product

Glaxo Wellcome makes seven of the world's 50 best-selling medicines, including Zantac, Imigran, Flixotide, Serevent and Zovirax.

Its product areas are split into: viral infections, respiratory, bacterial infections, gastro-intestinal, oncology, pain, endocrine, metabolic, cardiovascular and dermatology.

Within viral infections, Glaxo Wellcome is the market leader in drugs to combat HIV, such as Epivir and Retrovir. These drugs form the basis of a triple combination therapy regimen, while Combivir, combines these two agents into a single tablet formulation. Glaxo Wellcome has introduced two new medicines into this area, Ziagen and Agenerase. Another important drug in the field of viral infections is Zeffix, used to treat Hepatitis B.

Influenza is one of the most common and disruptive of all viral infections, affecting 10-15% of the world's population in any given year. In 1918, between 20 and 40 million were killed by flu – more than the death toll of the First World War. In 1999 Glaxo Wellcome made a major breakthrough in the treatment of flu with the introduction of Relenza, an inhaler-based flu drug that is now treating patients in markets around the world.

This drug complements the company's wide range of other respiratory medicines, an area in which Glaxo Wellcome is the world's leading supplier. The incidence of asthma is increasing worldwide, boosting demand for medicines like Ventolin, Serevent, Flixotide, Becotide and a new treatment, Seretide.

Treatment of gastro-intestinal disorders – such as peptic ulcer – has been the foundation of Glaxo Wellcome's growth over the years. The main product in this area is Zantac, which treats a wide range of acid-related problems. Now that the patent for Zantac has expired in the US, several other competing products have come onto the market. However Glaxo Wellcome remains committed to the area with the launch of Lotronex to treat irritable bowel syndrome.

Imigran is the group's best known brand in the central nervous system (CNS) treatment area. This treatment for migraine sufferers is one of Glaxo Wellcome's biggest sellers – not surprising given that up to 12% of the population can suffer from migraine. Other CNS medicines include an award-winning anti-epilepsy treatment called Lamictal, the anti-depressant Wellbutrin and the first non-nicotine, prescription, smoking cessation aid, Zyban.

Finally, the 6-10% of the population that suffer from eczema will be familiar with the anti-inflammatory skin preparations Dermovate, Betnovate, Cutivate and Eumovate.

Recent Developments

The biggest story affecting Glaxo Wellcome is the proposed merger with SmithKline Beecham. If approved, the merger will create a group with combined sales of approximately £16 billion and an estimated 7.3% share of the global pharmaceutical market. Its combined R&D budget will be approximately £2.3 billion. The merger will make Glaxo SmithKline the market leader in four of the five largest therapeutic categories in the pharmaceutical industry: anti-infectives, CNS, respiratory and alimentary & metabolic. It will also give it a leading position in the vaccines market and a strong position in consumer healthcare and over-the-counter medicines.

However, this is not the only big story Glaxo Wellcome has been involved in. It has made several major drug and product launches recently. In 1994, it introduced the Diskus/Accuhaler – a futuristic dry powder asthma inhaler. The award-winning device was designed by asthma sufferers for asthma sufferers and includes a range of innovative features, such as a dose counter. The inhaler was designed to be used with a variety of asthma treatments, including Glaxo Wellcome's latest asthma treatment, Seretide which combines ongoing immediate relief and protection in a single dose.

The anti-flu drug, Relenza, is another of the company's recent high-profile launches. Although a UK government institute recently advised against prescribing the inhaler-based medicine to patients on the NHS, over one million patients in other parts of the world have already received treatment with it.

Zeffix, the new drug for Hepatitis B was launched in September 1999. This international launch was held in Hong Kong because the drug is targeted primarily at the Asian Pacific market, where Hepatitis B is most prevalent. The disease is the ninth deadliest in the world and 75% of its carriers live in Asia and the Western Pacific. Zeffix is said to be the first effective oral treatment for chronic sufferers and is Glaxo Wellcome's most important drug in the Asia Pacific region.

Another major new drug is Malarone, an anti-malarial treatment which is of particular value in areas of multi-drug resistance. Malaria kills over one million people every year. Glaxo Wellcome has established a donation programme for Malarone in developing countries.

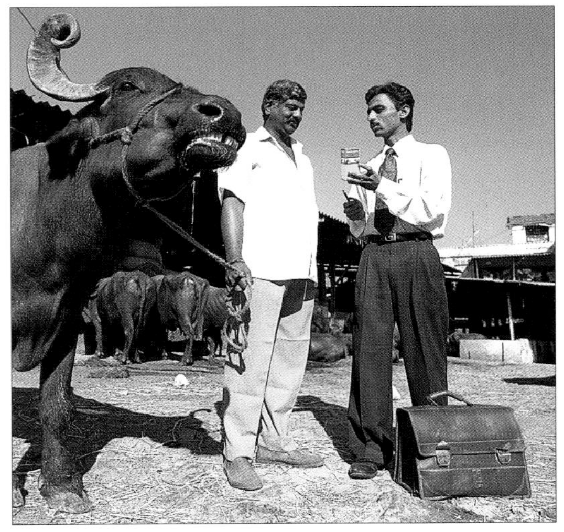

Promotion

The group's products are primarily sold to wholesale drug distributors and hospitals. In some markets, drugs are sold direct to pharmacies to health maintenance organisations. Many of the group's products are marketed directly by its subsidiaries and associates. Glaxo Wellcome has also entered into co-marketing agreements with other pharmaceutical companies.

Most of this promotion is inevitably business-to-business activity and on an individual product level. However, the group also conducts direct to consumer advertising in those markets where it is permitted. This activity is biggest in the US, where the pharmaceutical industry spends

$1billion a year on consumer advertising. Glaxo Wellcome's own expenditure in this area in the US increased by 16% in 1998.

A major launch for Glaxo Wellcome took place in the United States in March 2000. Lotronex has been developed to treat multiple symptoms of irritable bowel syndrome. IBS affects three times as many women as men, and the US sales force has been named in honour of Gertrude Elion – a Nobel prize winning scientist who worked at the company. Thus the company's mission of finding treatments for unmet medical needs on the basis of the best science is being recognised.

Brand Values

Glaxo Wellcome positions itself as a research-based company, whose people are committed to fighting disease by bringing innovative medicines and services to patient and healthcare providers around the world. It is this balance between cutting edge technology and human care that underpins the brand, with all marketing communications striving to show the human benefits of its medicines and research.

Things you didn't know about Glaxo Wellcome

Every year, Glaxo Wellcome donates £30 million to the worldwide community.

Glaxo Wellcome is the world's 23rd largest company by market capitalisation. Microsoft and General Electric are the two biggest.

It can take twelve years to get a new drug through research & development and onto the market.

During the Second World War, Glaxo was one of the leading suppliers of penicillin. By D-Day on June 6, 1944, over 80% of penicillin in Britain's field and base hospitals was supplied by Glaxo from Greenford.

The £2,474,655,000 handed over by Glaxo plc to Wellcome Trust Nominees Ltd. on March 30, 1995 for the Trust's share in Wellcome plc is said to be the largest amount paid by a single cheque in the history of banking. The amount was so large that it couldn't be generated by the Lloyds Bank computer system, so the cheque had to be typed by a Lloyd's employee. She was so overawed by the task that it took her three attempts to get right.

Market

Goldman Sachs is a giant among giants. With global net revenues in 1999 of £13.3 billion, over 17,000 employees and 48 offices in 23 countries, the Goldman Sachs Group is one of the best-known and most successful investment banking and securities firms in the world.

It competes across a wide range of areas, providing services to corporations, financial institutions, governments and wealthy individuals. Its core areas of activity are investment banking, trading, asset management and securities.

As a specialist in mergers and acquisitions and equity offerings, the current business climate provides rich pickings for Goldman Sachs and its competitors. Seeking global power, companies are undertaking increasingly ambitious mergers and acquisitions – such as Vodafone merging with Airtouch to become the world's biggest mobile phone company in 1999. In addition, more companies are seeking to raise money for such activity by issuing equity on the world's stock markets.

Goldman Sachs is competing in an increasingly crowded sector. Strong global rivals plus the internet changing business practices and blurring lines between investment and commercial banking have combined to make Goldman Sachs' market more competitive than ever.

Achievements

Although Goldman Sachs is a global company, it is also the UK's leading investment bank – a position reflected in consistent praise from customers and opinion formers. In an influential survey of investment banks published by Reuters in 1999, Goldman Sachs was voted Best Investment Bank by 350 UK finance directors – a score higher than any of its rivals. The same survey also revealed that UK finance directors rated Goldman Sachs the best investment bank in six out of seven different categories, such as quality of financial advice and execution of transactions.

The bank has been honoured in numerous other awards, such as Euromoney's third annual Credit Research Poll. In that, investors gave Goldman Sachs more first place rankings than any other investment bank – 21 in all.

The bank was also honoured in the 1999 IFR Awards, winning Equity-Linked House and US Equity-Linked House of the Year. These awards are testament to Goldman Sachs' excellent performance during uncertain and volatile conditions in the global convertible market in 1999. The company also won the IFR's US High-Yield Bond House Award in 1999, a year in which it made its most pronounced push into the high-yield bond business.

The bank has been voted Best Bank in Mergers and Acquisitions in North America and also in Europe in Global Finance magazine's 1999 Best Banks Awards. In Europe, this achievement was driven by it advising on the merger of Vodafone with Airtouch Communications of the US. The deal created the world's largest telecommunications company with a market value of approximately £78 billion.

Goldman Sachs' marketing has also been honoured, most recently scooping several prizes at the 1999 Mercury Awards in New York. This is a prestigious competition recognising outstanding achievement in professional communications, taking entries from around the world. In the most recent awards, Goldman Sachs won Gold awards in four categories: Best Print Advertising, Best Video under ten minutes, Best Design for Bound Publications and Best Print Media Campaign. This latter campaign, a recruitment ad using the line, 'Minds. Wide Open', was the overall Best of Show Award Winner.

History

Goldman Sachs traces its origins back to New York in 1869, when Marcus Goldman, a European immigrant and budding entrepreneur, specialised in finding financing for North America's fast-growing companies. His son-in-law Samuel Sachs soon joined him, and the two helped turn the firm into a major source of short-term finance for American companies in the late nineteenth century.

By the turn of the century, Goldman Sachs was at the heart of developments in the domestic capital markets, introducing major new innovations to the way in which debt and equity capital was raised. During this time it started to forge relationships with companies that have since grown into industry giants – such as Sears, Ford, Woolworth and General Electric.

As for most of Wall Street, the Great Depression of the 1930s was a testing time for Goldman Sachs. Thanks to the far-sighted leadership of Sidney Weinberg and Gus Levy, the firm weathered the storm. Weinberg – known as 'Mr Wall Street' – was legendary for his financing expertise and unsurpassed commitment to clients. Levy was a key architect of modern equity trading, helping to expand the firm into market-making and securities arbitrage activities.

The 1950s saw rapid expansion of industrial and consumer markets and Goldman Sachs introduced several key innovations, such as pioneering the buying and selling of large blocks of stock and setting up a separate group dedicated to serving institutional investors. It was also the first Wall Street firm to establish a specialised Mergers and Acquisitions advisory office, founding what would become a central discipline of today's investment banking industry.

In 1956, the bank oversaw the £438 million IPO for the Ford Motor Company – the largest-ever stock offering at that time and a harbinger of Goldman Sachs' future strength in managing large financing.

During the 1950s and 1960s, Goldman Sachs set about its international expansion, building a network with the aim of providing services for the increasingly global activities of its clients. The first international office opened in London in 1970, followed in 1974 by Tokyo. It opened in Hong Kong in 1983 and soon after followed a string of other offices across Asia, including Singapore, Sydney and Seoul. In 1998, it opened offices in Moscow and Johannesburg.

The group's European activities have grown rapidly, from five people in 1970 to 3500 in Europe by the end of 1999. From London, the firm has spread out to Paris, Zurich, Madrid, Frankfurt and Milan.

In May 1999, Goldman Sachs passed an important milestone in its history when it became a public company.

Product

Goldman Sachs' core business activities are divided into two principal areas, Global Capital Markets and Securities Services. Global Capital Markets includes Investment Banking and Trading and Principal Investments businesses.

Investment Banking services are divided into two categories: Financial Advisory which includes advisory assignments with respect to mergers and acquisitions, divestitures, corporate defence activities, restructurings and spin-offs; and Underwriting which includes public offerings and private placements of equity and debt securities.

Trading and Principal Investments comprises: The Fixed Income, Currency and Commodities Department which makes markets in and trades fixed income, currencies and commodities, structures and enters into a wide variety of derivative transactions and engages in proprietary trading and arbitrage activities.

The Equities Department makes markets in and trades equities and equity-related products, structures and enters into equity derivative transactions and engages in proprietary trading and equity arbitrage; and Principal Investments.

The Asset Management and Securities Services part of the business sees the firm providing a broad array of investment advisory services to a diverse client base. Securities Services includes prime brokerage, financing services, securities lending and a matched book business. This area also includes commissions-based businesses, including agency transactions for clients on major stock and futures exchanges.

Recent Developments

In May 1999, Goldman Sachs became a public company, after more than a century as a private partnership. As such, it completed its own initial public offering. Raising a total of £2.43 billion on the New York Stock Exchange, the offering was second in size only to the oil giant Conoco's £2.93 billion IPO in 1998.

The move coincided with the launch of the company's first ever global marketing campaign. As well as helping to define Goldman Sachs' distinctive brand positioning in the market as a high quality superior service brand, the campaign communicates important new areas of focus in the group's activities.

For example, Goldman Sachs is currently focusing on technology as being one of the driving forces of its business. Some of the new ads highlight the fact that the firm is a leading investor in the technology industry and a force in promoting technology's role in reshaping financial markets. Goldman Sachs is rapidly building a profile as one of Europe's leading investors in hi-tech ventures, and in 1999 was number one in internet IPO's, with a 30% market share in Europe. These activities fit in with the development of its European technology business, which aims to be at the centre of hi-tech entrepreneurial activity in the EU, which Goldman Sachs has called the €-Valley℠.

Promotion

Goldman Sachs actively promotes its corporate brand and individual products in a wide range of activities. Its marketing is principally aimed at existing and prospective clients, shareholders, employees and recruits.

In May 1999, the group launched its first-ever global corporate advertising campaign, reinforcing its values among its key target audience. All the executions are united around the central theme of 'Unrelenting Thinking'.

The campaign makes extensive use of print advertising in business and professional publications, such as The Financial Times, The Economist, and the Wall Street Journal. These promote individual offerings, such as leveraged finance or investment research, as well as the corporate brand. The ads feature the firm's distinctive way of thinking and wide range of services. For example one advertisement, demonstrates the firms skill in financing with the line: 'Inside every risky, under-capitalised company is a blue-chip multinational waiting to get out.' Another says: 'If ever we find two companies that are exactly alike, we'll offer two recommendations that are exactly alike.'

The aim of the campaign was to differentiate the Goldman Sachs brand in what has become an increasingly crowded market. The campaign has been adapted into seven languages.

Brand Values

The two most recognised strengths of Goldman Sachs are intellectual strength and executional prowess. The tagline 'Unrelenting Thinking' was born from these qualities as well as from the pillars of the brand's positioning of seamless integration, inclusive working relationships and fresh thinking.

The firm has an eleven point set of business principles that direct its overall positioning, culture and outlook. Client focus, creativity, imagination, professionalism and teamwork are just some of the values which feature in the map of the Goldman Sachs brand.

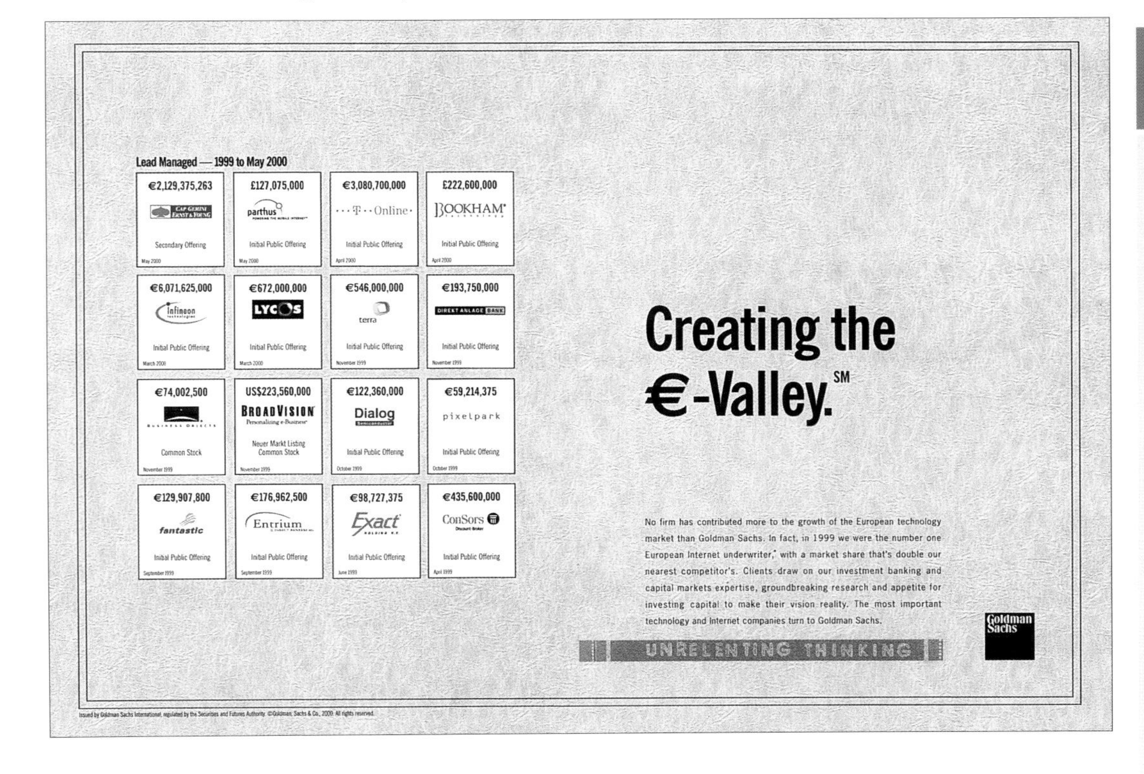

Things you didn't know about Goldman Sachs

In 1999 Goldman Sachs strengthened its commitment to charitable initiatives in the field of education by making a contribution of $200 million to The Goldman Sachs Foundation. The foundation makes grants to high-quality organisations to enhance secondary school students' academic achievements, and to generate interest and educational opportunities worldwide in business and entrepreneurship.

Goldman Sachs has a long-term commitment to serving communities and supports volunteerism globally through its Community Teamworks program. During 2000 over 15,000 people participated in mentoring and other community service activities.

Goldman Sachs has launched a for profit urban initiative program, run by a former New York City housing expert that will promote investment, to generate urban renewal.

invent

Market

The IT industry has never been more dynamic or competitive. The pace of change is exponential as the new 'internet economy' becomes a reality. The internet has revolutionised the way the world does business, creating entirely new industries, challenging accepted business models and processes and connecting organisations internally and externally in a way that was unimaginable five years ago. E-commerce is in its infancy and while the shock waves from its explosive birth have rippled throughout industry, the IT sector has been at ground zero.

Hewlett-Packard is focussed on capitalising on the opportunities presented by the internet and the proliferation of electronic services. It is uniquely positioned to offer integrated solutions covering applications, e-services and the infrastructure needed. Its ethos is accessibility for all and it is at the cutting edge of 'open' technologies for the internet that make it faster, smarter and easier to use.

In Hewlett-Packard's vision of the future everyone and everything – printers, photocopiers, cameras, alarm clocks, vending machines, buses – will be connected to the web. How, why and where we use the internet will change with the emphasis on smart, personalised services rather than 'browsing and buying'. It believes that the second internet revolution will make the first look like cosmetic change. It intends to help its customers exploit the internet's potential and shape its future by developing the software, security, systems and devices needed to access the always-on infrastructure.

Achievements

From a workshop in a one car garage in 1938, Hewlett-Packard has grown into a global giant with net revenues of $42.2 billion (1999), 86,200 staff and operations in 120 countries. It is a world leader in computing, printing and imaging solutions for businesses and the home.

It is synonymous with innovation. The company that created the world's first pocket calculator and the first programmable calculator, that set a new standard in printers and portable computers, is also one of the leading medical equipment and instrumentation developers and suppliers. Over 60 years it has kept up an astonishing pace of technological development. World-class technicians working in a vast variety of fields staff its laboratories. In the last five years alone it has spent $10.4 billion on research and development.

Hewlett-Packard was considered a late starter in the home PC market, launching the multi-media Pavilion range in 1995. However, even a somewhat late entry has not stopped it becoming the fastest growing retail PC brand in the world and the number one selling retail PC brand in the US.

Hewlett-Packard has built an enviable reputation for quality, reliability, technical innovation and value for money in professional and business markets over the years and is consistently ranked as one of the world's most highly admired companies in numerous surveys. It is respected as much for the way it treats its staff as it is for its profitability and efficiency.

History

Dave Packard and Bill Hewlett met on a two-week camping and fishing trip in the Colorado mountains shortly after graduating as electrical engineers. In 1938 they began work in a one car garage in Palo Alto, California with start-up capital of $538 making all sorts of electrical gadgets. Their first 'big' sale was of eight electronic test instruments to Walt Disney Studios for use in the film Fantasia.

The company grew steadily through the 1940s and by halfway through the decade it was acknowledged as the leader in microwave test and signal products. The 1950s were a period of maturation: how the company grew was as hotly debated as how much it should grow and in 1957 it hammered out its corporate objectives, enshrined in 'the HP way'.

Hewlett-Packard continued to grow throughout the 1960s, branching out into medical electronics and analytical instrumentation. By 1965 it had achieved net revenue of $165 million and employed 9,000 people. In 1968 its introduction of the first desktop scientific calculator presaged the company's development of high performance workstations.

Hewlett-Packard pioneered the era of personal computing in 1972 with the world's first hand-held calculator, which made the engineer's slide rule obsolete. The same year it moved into business computing.

The 1980s were arguably the most significant in the company's history. At the beginning it introduced its first personal computer, by the end it had established itself as a major player with a product range encompassing everything from desktop machines to powerful minicomputers. During a decade of non-stop innovation, it introduced the first electronic mail system in 1982 and in 1984 entered the printer market with the InkJet and LaserJet series, which set a new standard in print quality and value for money.

By 1985 net revenue had grown to $6.5 billion and the pay roll ran to 85,000 employees. The following year saw the introduction of an innovative new computer architecture, code-named Spectrum, which cost over $250 million in research and development over five years and was the company's most expensive R&D effort ever.

The 1990s saw Hewlett-Packard strengthen its dominance in the medical test equipment and printer markets, while branching out into personal organisers, notebook computers and, in 1995, its first consumer PC. A series of strategic acquisitions, such as electronic payment systems leader VeriFone in 1997, helped increase the company's impressive capabilities in e-commerce.

Product

Hewlett-Packard's product range is all but impossible to detail as it changes so fast – any attempt at committing absolute numbers to print is doomed to obsolescence before the ink is dry. The company is currently being granted patents at the rate of five a day. Hewlett-Packard offers the full gamut of information and communications products including hardware, software, peripherals, services and support and some of its most exciting developments have been in the field of e-services, designed to make the most of the web.

Broadly, Hewlett-Packard's areas of product interest span personal information appliances, including its award-winning handheld devices. Notebook PCs, such as the HP Omnibook family, which boasts some of the lightest full-function models on the market. Home PCs under the phenomenally successful Pavilion line, commercial PCs, which boast four of the world's top selling desktop models as well as technical works stations designed for demanding technical and computing-intensive environments, and networking products. In addition it leads the field with a full range of printing and digital imaging products for home or commercial use.

Recent Developments

In recent years Hewlett-Packard has developed a vision of the future that is nothing short of radical, where people, places and things are all connected to the web. It believes that the web will become fully integrated into our everyday lives and embedded into everyday appliances from fridges to faxes. This all pervasive web will deliver personalised services to individuals and businesses that will transform our relationships with each other, organisations and technology itself.

Hewlett-Packard is working on a plethora of technologies to make this vision a reality. In November 1999 it unveiled CoolTown, a massive research project designed to create information appliances, software and services for

When you need a ride, you don't pay for the whole cab. That's the philosophy behind hp's inventive applications-on-tap. Instead of investing big in software you only need from time to time, you rent the latest versions online and pay only for the time you use them. Or you can make your own applications or services available for other businesses to use, creating new revenue streams. And those applications are always available, running on hp hardware, software and solutions. It's another way hp is reinventing business as you know it. www.hp.com/e-services or www.hp.com/uk

Why own when you can rent? e-services solutions from hp.

hp invent

a fully connected world. In CoolTown your alarm clock is hooked up to an e-service traffic report through the internet and wakes you early if there are traffic snarl ups on your route to work. Ordering a cup of coffee to pick up on the way in is done electronically and cashlessly. The presentations you give to clients no longer involve any equipment except for your handheld computer as they are stored on the web and accessed via any device that can display rich multi-media content or is networked to the web.

CoolTown is part vision, part reality. Many of the tools and techniques it uses already exist but are not as yet interconnected or fully enabled. However, some of the new elements are already being made available. The concept relies on an IT and internet infrastructure that is always on, meaning an end to the 'worldwide wait' and tedious booting up procedures. Hewlett-Packard already has a range of 'always on' products covering PCs, notebooks, network servers and support.

It's because they're not afraid to get their hands filthy. To eat the glue. To use a hammer as a brush. To break something just to see how it works. And to start with the impossible, which is where grownups usually stop. Just a few of the things we're keeping in mind as we invent the new hp. Want to come along?
www.hp.com or www.hp.com/uk

hp invent

Another fundamental strand is the end of proprietary systems, distinct architecture and incompatibility. Hewlett-Packard believes that any digital device should and will be able to connect to the internet, which will operate on a completely open standards-based system. It is at the forefront of the democratisation of the web and is working with a vast array of partners from Cisco and Vodafone to Kodak, Disney and Swatch. Some CoolTown software has already been launched on the web, free of charge.

Other research initiatives are just as impressive: it is working on digital photography that yields better results than film, molecular computing, ink chemistry, atomic resolution storage and quantum devices.

At the end of 1999 it spun off Agilent Technologies as a separate company. The move coincided with a fundamental re-engineering of the brand under the 'Invent' campaign.

Promotion

The $200 million Invent campaign unveiled at the end of 1999 is far more than just advertising, direct marketing or any other promotional discipline. It is an attempt to take the company back to its ideological roots, return it to the one car garage of invention set up by Bill and Dave to invent cool, useful stuff. Hewlett-Packard believes that it is vital to return to its original mentality in order to prepare itself for the future of IT.

Invent is remarkably brave. Aside from baring its corporate soul, it is a rallying cry to its staff, partners and customers to re-evaluate their perceptions of what Hewlett-Packard is and what it can be. At its heart are 'the rules of the garage'. Those rules are: Believe you can change the world. Work quickly, keep the tools unlocked, work whenever. Know when to work alone and when to work together. Share – tools, ideas. Trust your colleagues. No politics. No bureaucracy (these are ridiculous in a garage). The customer defines a job well done. Radical ideas are not bad ideas. Invent different ways of working. Make a contribution every day. If it doesn't contribute, it doesn't leave the garage. Believe that together we can do anything. Invent.

In addition to its sponsorship of Formula One and Tottenham Football Club, Hewlett-Packard was the official IT hardware and maintenance supplier to the organising committee of the 1998 World Cup. Some 37 billion viewers watched the tournament worldwide. Equally important are its 'thought-leading' initiatives, such as sponsoring the Confederation of British Industries conference since 1989, which sets the agenda for business.

Brand Values

Founder Dave Packard believed that you don't advertise your brand values you live them. In today's fast-paced, marketing savvy global economy such fine sentiments are not enough by themselves, although they continue to underpin the corporate philosophy. Hewlett-Packard has increasingly realised the crucial role of branding and brand management, particularly in an industry that has historically been technology-driven not marketing-led and has sought to bring its underlying values to life both for staff and customers.

At the heart of its communications and the very heart of the company are 'the rules of the garage' which fundamentally define how employees operate within the context of the Hewlett-Packard organisation. The HP way is not so much corporate policy as corporate ideology and the company readily owns to the fact that to succeed in Hewlett-Packard you have to buy into the values that inform this ethos.

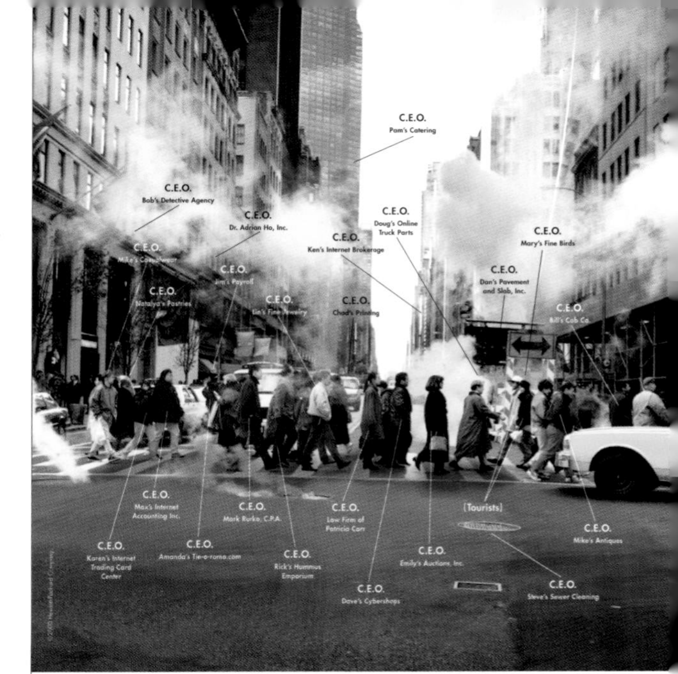

Create a new business in the e-services marketplace. Launch your great idea into a world of millions of other great ideas to spark even greater ideas.
No matter what you dream up, hp hardware, software and consulting will connect it all together, and get you up and running.
Invent your business here: www.hp.com/e-services or www.hp.com/uk
And don't take orders from anyone. (Except your customers.)

The IPO of everyone. e-services solutions from hp.

hp invent

Hewlett-Packard's fundamental proposition is to invent the useful and significant for the common good. That translates into six brand values, which are quality-conscious, trustworthy, optimistic, inclusive, human and, of course, inventive.

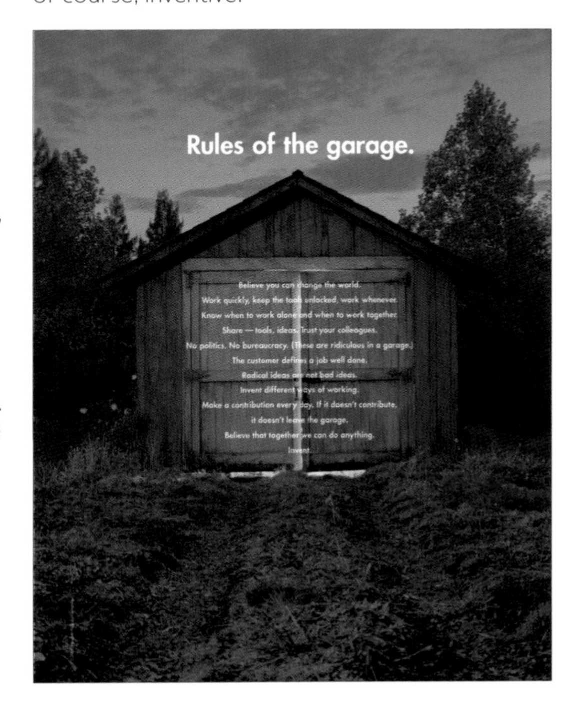

Things you didn't know about Hewlett-Packard

The name Hewlett-Packard was decided on the toss of a coin.

Hewlett-Packard's first building in 1942 was designed so that it could be converted to a grocery store if the company failed.

Founder Dave Packard served as US deputy secretary of defence from 1969-71.

Hewlett-Packard gave $80 million in cash and equipment to non-profit agencies and educational institutions around the world in 1999. It also supports the arts, health and human services, civic groups and environmental organisations.

Hewlett-Packard sold over 100 million Inkjet printers since it entered the market in 1985.

HSBC

Market

HSBC operates in the fiercely competitive world financial services market. It is a truly international brand, and operates some 6,000 offices in 81 countries and territories, and has over 170,000 staff. With assets of over $580 billion, it is one of the world's largest banking and financial services organisations.

The London-based Group is active in personal banking and other financial services, business banking, asset management, investment banking, securities trading, insurance, finance and leasing.

HSBC operates in Europe, the Asia-Pacific region, the Americas, the Middle East and Africa. In the UK, it owns HSBC Bank plc, while in continental Europe, Crédit Commercial de France has recently become a member of the Group. In Asia it owns The Hongkong and Shanghai Banking Corporation Limited and has a 62.14% equity interest in Hang Seng Bank Limited. In the US it owns HSBC Bank USA and operates a joint venture trade bank with Wells Fargo Bank. It also owns banks in Brazil, Argentina and the United Arab Emirates.

Over the last few years, the financial services sector has become even more competitive with the arrival of new low-cost entrants, especially the new breed of 'virtual' brands offering branchless banking over the internet. Without the costs of a 'bricks and mortar' network to support, these brands are competing fiercely on price and cherry-picking high margin business. The internet is also underlining the fact that modern banking is a borderless, worldwide business. As HSBC now operates its international businesses under one brand, the Group is well positioned to be a leading player.

Achievements

Key to its many achievements in the financial marketplace is HSBC's commitment to building one of the banking world's most recognisable brands. In November 1998, a plan was implemented to create a universal brand for the entire organisation, uniting all elements of the business under a single identity. As a result, it has replaced corporate signatures and names around the world with 'HSBC' and the hexagon symbol. This decision demonstrates the Group's realisation that it needs a strong, internationally recognisable brand in a worldwide market.

The Group is pursuing its aim to be the world's leading financial services company. It was recently rated the 'world's strongest bank' by The Banker magazine and the 'Best bank in Asia' by Euromoney. Forbes rated HSBC second in its 'Super 50' league of international companies.

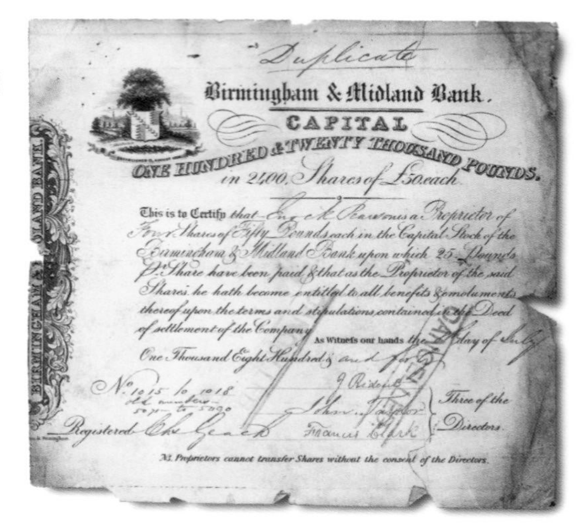

Duplicate

Birmingham & Midland Bank.

CAPITAL

ONE HUNDRED & TWENTY THOUSAND POUNDS.

in 2400, Shares of £50 each

This is to Certify that [illegible] is a Proprietor of Four Shares of Fifty Pounds each in the Capital Stock of the Birmingham & Midland Bank upon which 25 Pounds Pr Share have been paid & that as the Proprietor of the said Shares he hath become entitled to all benefits & emoluments thereof upon the terms and stipulations contained in the Deed of settlement of the Company. As Witness our hands the [illegible] day of July One Thousand Eight Hundred & [illegible]

No. 1015 to 1018

Registered [illegible]

Three of the Directors

NB. Proprietors cannot transfer Shares without the consent of the Directors.

History

Whilst the Group's holding company, HSBC Holdings plc, was formed in 1991, most of its principal members have been in operation for over a century. For example, The Hongkong and Shanghai Banking Corporation Limited opened for business in 1865, and in the UK, HSBC Bank plc (formerly Midland Bank) dates back to 1836. The Hongkong and Shanghai Banking Corporation was the founding member of the Group and from which HSBC derives its name. It was founded by Thomas Sutherland, then the Hong Kong superintendent of the P&O Company, who saw the need for a local bank to handle the increasing amount of trade occurring around the China coast in the 1860s.

Initially, HSBC expanded by establishing new offices in its own name. However, this changed in the 1950s, when it began to create or acquire subsidiaries. In 1992, HSBC made one of the largest cross-border acquisitions in banking history at that time, when it took over Midland Bank, firmly placing the HSBC name on the map in the UK.

Midland's origins were in Birmingham, where it opened its first office in 1836. Here, in the heartland of the Industrial Revolution, the bank was established in a thriving local economy. Over the years, it expanded and acquired other banks, eventually moving to London in 1891.

In 1967, Midland moved into merchant banking, taking a share in Montagu Trust. Samuel Montagu & Co. Limited became a wholly owned subsidiary in 1974 and in 1993 was transferred to HSBC Investment Bank plc.

In 1980, HSBC acquired a 51% share in New York State's Marine Midland Bank, which became wholly owned in 1987. By now, HSBC had also established a prominent presence in the Middle East, acquiring The British Bank of the Middle East in 1959, taking a 40% shareholding in The Saudi British Bank in 1978, and a 40% interest in Egyptian British Bank SAE in 1982.

In 1986, it further extended its merchant banking operations, buying James Capel, a leading London-based securities company. Following the purchase of Midland Bank in 1992, HSBC moved its Group Head Office to London in 1993. In 1994 The Hongkong and Shanghai Banking Corporation was the first foreign bank to incorporate locally in Malaysia, forming Hongkong Bank Malaysia Berhad – now HSBC Bank Malaysia Berhad. In 1997, Banco HSBC Bamerindus SA was established in Brazil and the acquisition of Roberts SA de Inversiones was completed. The banks were subsequently renamed HSBC Bank Brasil SA-Banco Múltiplo and HSBC Bank Argentina SA, respectively.

Product

The Group's two principal lines of business are commercial banking (90% of pre-tax profit in 1999) and investment banking (10%).

HSBC aims to become one of the world's leading providers of financial services through its international network of personal, commercial, corporate and investment banking and insurance businesses.

Trade finance and related services, provided through HSBC Trade Services, are a long-standing core business of the HSBC Group, whose office network in the Asia-Pacific region, Europe, the Americas and the Middle East is well placed to facilitate and finance the world's primary trade flows. The Group's distribution network and specialised non-recourse export financing such as forfaiting, factoring and general trade expertise – coupled with a highly automated trade systems capability, including electronic documentary credit services – make it one of the largest trade finance organisations in the world. As its customers make increasing use of the internet for trading, the Group is well positioned to support this vital market place.

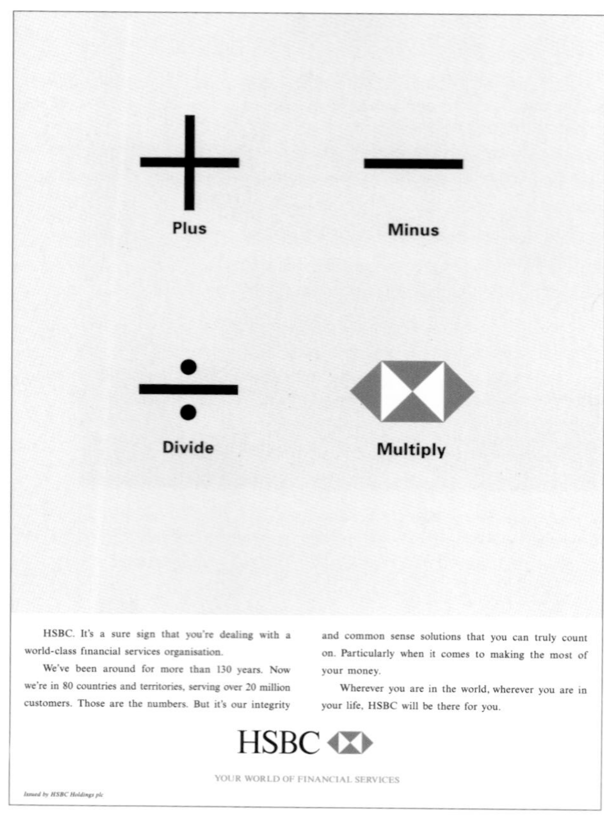

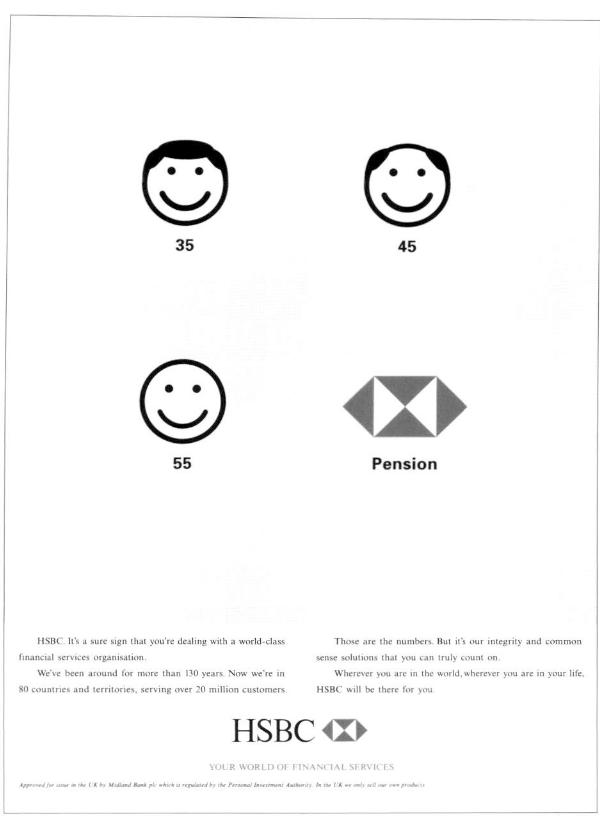

Securities Services in HSBC is a leading player in international securities and custody markets, offering services to domestic and cross-border investors in eighteen Asia-Pacific centres and thirteen in Europe. Custody and Clearing is the largest custodian in Asia-Pacific and the Middle East, and Global Investor Services is one of the largest UK-based international custodians.

Payments and Cash Management assists both corporates and institutions to manage and optimise their cash flows and associated liquidity. The Group provides expertise on a local, regional and international basis to meet clients' cash management needs, and also to assist with major regulatory and environmental changes in the market.

Investment Banking and Markets brings together the advisory, financing, investment and dealing services for the HSBC Group's corporate, institutional and retail clients. Operating through dedicated offices and via the Group's network of commercial banks, this division employs around 13,000 staff. Major services include advice and finance, research, sales and trading, risk management and private banking and asset management.

Recent Developments

HSBC maintains one of the world's largest private data communication networks and is now reconfiguring its business for the e-business age. It has a growing e-commerce capability, including the UK's first banking service to be available on interactive television, 'Open....'.

Other deals reflect HSBC's commitment to this area. For example, in April 2000, it joined forces with Merrill Lynch to invest $1 billion in a new internet bank targeting private investors. The service has research, equity dealing, planning and profiling tools, targeting those customers with between $100,000 and $500,000 in assets.

Promotion

To raise awareness of its brand, HSBC is investing heavily in a range of promotional activities. Commercial sponsorship is a vital element of this.

For example, HSBC recently announced a £40 million sponsorship deal in London with the British Airports Authority, the London Tourist Board and the City of Westminster. The four-year deal is part of a wider scheme called Partners for London, which is the world's first commercial capital city sponsorship programme.

The initiative sees the HSBC brand featured on street furniture in the City of Westminster – including lamp posts, signposts and hanging baskets – as well as on 201 passenger jetties at Heathrow, Gatwick and Stansted airports. The deal will help market the brand to up to 100 million people per year, building awareness among Londoners and international travellers. The revenue will be invested in enhancing customer services at the airports; in Westminster, it will be used to 'clean and green' the borough's streets, raising awareness of HSBC's community activities. This is an important element of all the Group's marketing, with subsidiary companies also investing in their own local community and educational initiatives.

HSBC's other major sponsorships include a £3 million deal backing drama premières on ITV and a £25 million, five-year sponsorship of the Jaguar Racing Formula One team. HSBC also sponsors Britain's number one tennis player, Tim Henman.

HSBC undertook a phased approach to advertising following the announcement of its rebranding. Immediately following the announcement, the imperative was the need to communicate the name change and pass the equity from the old brand names to the new, unified brand.

The objective of the first phase was to build brand awareness recognition for the newly unified, international HSBC brand, communicate a differentiated positioning, as well as reassure and educate customers and followers of HSBC. This phase focused on who HSBC are and what it can offer, as well as promoting its values, such as trust, integrity and excellent customer service.

The initial promise was: 'We can be sure that HSBC will always bring the benefits of its international network and worldwide experience to you, our customer.' HSBC is positioned as straight talking, founded on common sense and integrity. Stating that it is international, secure, accessible (81 countries and territories, over 500,000 ATMs and 6,000 offices), multi-cultural

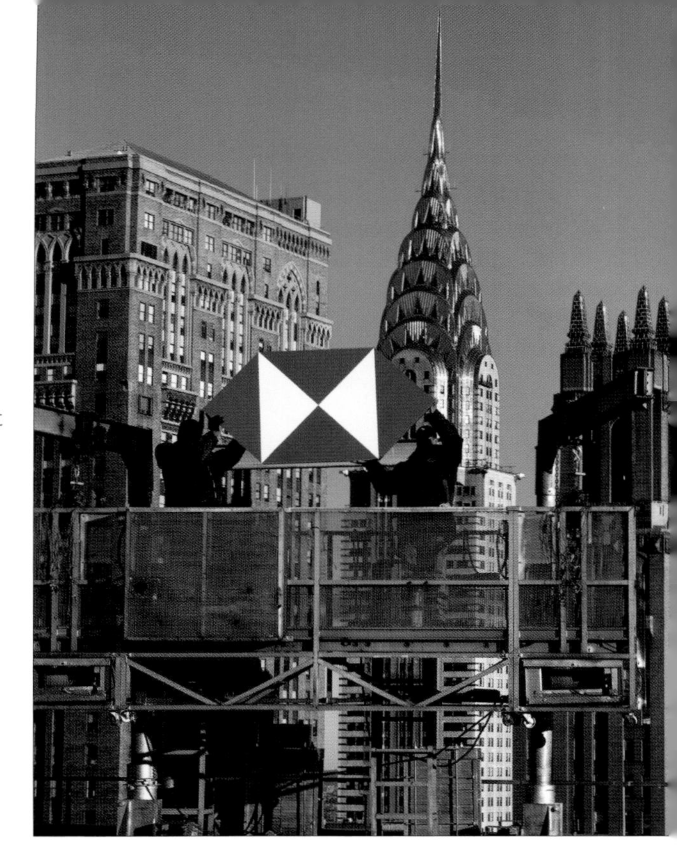

(rooted in the development of many diverse economies) and committed to excellence.

The tone of the advertising is friendly and straightforward. The symbols were chosen as an international language, understandable in all its markets. The Group was able, through this creative approach, to run the same campaign around the world with only minor cultural adaptation. The symbols also communicate clarity, integrity and performance. Associating the hexagon logo with internationally recognised symbols, for example, eat or sleep, indicates that the hexagon is the internationally recognised symbol for banking. It also indicates that banking is an integral part of life, just like eating and sleeping.

The campaign was created in 1999 by Lowe Lintas and Partners Worldwide, the international advertising agency for the HSBC Group. Zenith Media, the Group's lead media agency, booked the media and the Group campaign was seen in over 100 countries and territories.

Brand Values

HSBC's 'cultural values' are those of a responsible, prudent, cost-conscious, ethically grounded, conservative, trustworthy, international builder of long-term customer relationships. The Group aspires to be highly productive, team-oriented, creative and customer focused. Its vision is to be the world's leading financial services company. In short, its brand is built on integrity, trust and excellent customer service.

Things you didn't know about HSBC

HSBC Bank is responsible for many banking innovations. These include personal loans (1958), personal cheque accounts (1958) and cheque cards (1966). In 1988 it was a leader in the introduction of the 'Switch' paperless cheque and, in 1989 it launched the UK's first telephone bank, First Direct.

HSBC printed Thailand's first ever banknotes, in 1888.

HSBC's head office in the Hong Kong SAR is one of the territory's most famous buildings, designed by Sir Norman Foster and officially opened in 1986.

HSBC was the first UK bank to offer personal banking via interactive television.

ICL

Market

Characterised by a range of initiatives which are pushing back the boundaries of innovation, and with online trade set to grow at twice the rate of the US, Europe is the heartland of e-business.

Four key trends underline the growing importance of Europe. According to Forrester Research, more than 200 million Europeans will be connected to the internet by 2004, spending an average of $1,774 per year and driving a total online trade of $1,600 billion. Forrester have also identified that the shift towards the mobile internet is gathering pace. While the US remains wedded to the PC as an access device, Europe is moving rapidly towards a new way of thinking - with net phone users expected to amount to more than 50% of the continent's population by 2004.

The European market for designing, operating and building websites is expected to be worth over $15 billion in 2003, split between business-to-consumer ($5.8 billion), business-to-business ($5 billion) and corporate intranets ($3.5 billion) (Source: IDC 1999). While Jupiter Communications reports that households with digital TV access will more than quadruple to over 50 million by 2003, with the UK leading the way.

Centred on Europe, ICL is well positioned to help European-based organisations exploit these trends. The company has a major presence in Finland, the most online country in the world, as well as in the UK, which is taking up digital TV faster than anywhere else. So ICL is very well placed to fully harness and exploit new technology in the most buoyant market in the world.

However, increasing globalisation has meant that country borders are no barriers to commerce. From multinational retailers to agile dot.coms, many organisations trade globally, and ICL, with a truly global service, is ideally suited to support them all.

Achievements

Today, the technology at the customer interface - whether it is smart cards, interactive TV sets or mobile phones that send emails - is compelling, inspiring and immensely liberating. With easy to use technology at the fingertips, access to banks and retail organisations is just a click away. However, this technology can only fulfil its true potential if it is supported by a proven infrastructure and long-term support - mortar to hold the clicks in place.

It is not difficult to imagine the consequences for an e-business if the system crashes for an hour or a whole day. The financial losses would only be part of the story - the loss of credibility and trust would simply tear apart the customer relationship.

Committed to being a European leading e-business services company, ICL has a

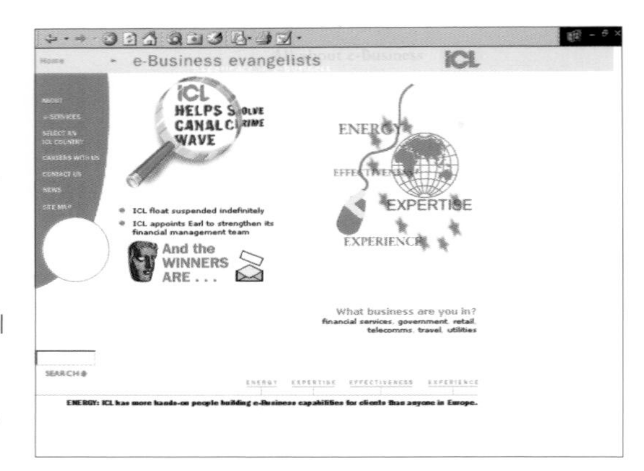

long-standing and loyal customer base. Through its knowledge of industry, IT and the digital economy, the company helps them to exploit the e-world for competitive advantage in three distinct ways.

Creating leading edge e-business solutions that enable customers to transform their businesses. ICL has experienced business transformation itself and understands how to navigate through times of change. Implementing those solutions at speed, helping customers gain maximum benefit in the minimum timeframe. Plus supporting those solutions with a deep and thorough understanding of mission critical systems that is based on over 30 years of working with some of the world's most demanding organisations.

In the fifteen months to 31 March 1999, ICL reported a group operating profit of £40.9 million on a turnover of £3356.1 million.

History

ICL was formed in 1968 by merging the UK's leading indigenous computer suppliers, English Electric Computers and International Computers and Tabulators (ICT).

In 1984, ICL was acquired by STC (Standard Telephones and Cables) for approximately £430 million to form one of Europe's leading communications and information systems groups. 1984 was the year in which ICL was last listed on the London Stock Exchange.

At the end of November 1990, Fujitsu Limited acquired an 80% shareholding in the company for £743 million and Nortel Networks (formerly known as Northern Telecom) held the 20% balance. By virtue of two rights issues in 1993-4 and 1996, Fujitsu increased its stake to 90.1% before acquiring the remaining 9.9% from Nortel Networks in September 1998.

Product

ICL designs, builds and operates e-business services which significantly improve the performance of its customers' businesses. The company also aims to unlock the full potential of the 'knowledge society' for its customers.

Banks, retailers, communities, telcos, major utilities, travel companies and governments all work with ICL to help build and maintain their reputations. The company meets their expectations in three key areas: e-innovation, e-applications and e-infrastructure.

In the area of e-innovation ICL works with leading edge, innovative customers to deliver services including interactive TV, PC banking and websites. Relationship Applications help ICL customers build profitable and long-term relationships with their customers via projects such as retail websites and online loyalty schemes, as well as banking.

Its e-applications involves business-to-business solutions which include services such as the creation and operation of branded internet access which organisations provide to their own customers. Business-to-consumer solutions include interactive retail systems, which allow retailers to reduce costs and build a marketing database by selling goods over the internet. Internal-to-business solutions, such as ICL's focus on citizen centric government help governments and government agencies deliver and gather information in a way which meets the needs of citizens.

Finally e-infrastructure sees ICL design, build and operate scalable and resilient applications and the mission-critical infrastructure on which e-businesses rely. Enterprise Outsourcing, involves ICL managing infrastructure services including web hosting, portal access and firewall management for customers, allowing them to focus on their core business. IT Lifecycle Services, is a single source for the building, deployment and financing of integrated office infrastructures designed to allow customers to maximise their e-business capability. Enterprise Systems Solutions, supplies enterprise systems infrastructures which are robust and flexible. As business needs change, the ICL infrastructure intends to evolve to meet the new requirements.

Recent Developments

There is a popular misconception that e-business hit the ground running in the final months of the last

We're turning the Internet into a plaything.

ICL designed, built and operates Sega's online games community 'Dreamarena' which is accessed by its Dreamcast games console. While functioning as a standalone games machine, the Dreamcast has the added advantage of allowing users to play games against people anywhere in the world in real-time. E-mail, chatting and online games facilities will also be available.

Sega couldn't work with just any organisation in developing this service but ICL has a true passion for bringing the benefits of interactive technology to customers everywhere. Perhaps that's why they and so many other blue-chip clients continue to ask us to handle major e-Business projects. We're already a total solutions organisation, and we fully intend to become the pre-eminent e-Business services company in Europe.

Call 017 53 53 23 23
Or visit us at http://www.icl.com

ICL

millennium. This is not strictly true, because although e-business is now transforming the corporate landscape forever, the momentum has been apparent for some time.

It was evident in 1996 when ICL launched the world's first high street online loyalty card for WH Smith. In 1997 ICL worked with First Direct to introduce their first PC banking service. And in 1998 ICL created an online community in the remote Kuusamo district of Finland. In fact before the century turned ICL had already implemented over 500 e-business solutions around the globe - many of them world firsts.

What is new is that the drivers for e-business have now reached critical mass. Today, the tremendous innovation demonstrated by technologies such as interactive digital TV and the mobile internet is complemented by an equally seismic shift in how organisations view their customers. The customer has been officially crowned king.

As an acknowledged European leader in e-business, ICL is uniquely positioned to help its customers step forwards into the e-world. With ICL's input, organisations will be able to transform the world for their customers.

In 1996 ICL implemented Buckingham Gate, the first multi-currency internet shopping mall. The next year ICL implemented TradeUK, the first internet export directory for worldwide trade and proposed the UK National Grid for Learning, which aims to connect all schools to the internet.

In 1998 ICL became a key partner in Affinity, the major provider of free branded internet access. That same year ICL innovated a multi-currency internet payment system to help gather more than £400,000 for the Comic Relief charity.

In 1999 ICL helped Affinity become the biggest supplier of branded internet access, with 120 organisations serving over 800,000 consumers. ICL was also behind the launch of the world's first net access through a games console for Sega. By the end of the year ICL had implemented the world's first national secure ID infrastructure for the Finnish Government.

As Forrester Research reports, "ICL has begun to grasp how process-oriented solutions must realign for e-business effectiveness. He (ICL's Director of e-business) gets a qualified cheer from Forrester for taking just one small step toward the e-business integration that companies will require."

Promotion

ICL is one of the most widely-known IT services brands in Europe. Research places ICL as one of a very select number of companies in its market with a high instantaneous re-call of the brand.

The well recognised brand name of International Computers Limited, denoted by the distinctive three letter ICL mark, has become synonymous with quality, reliability and trust. ICL is a brand that has been built through customer interaction.

As a member of the Fujitsu group of companies, the ICL brand is seen by millions of people each day. TV advertising and full page press advertising in the European business and computing press, ensures that ICL is communicating its expertise to a select class of business and IT executives.

ICL also communicates its brand messages through targeted and high profile corporate sponsorships. Over the past years, this has included major events such as Formula One, Rally motor sports events, golf and football.

ICL

Designs, builds and operates e-Business services

Unlocking the full potential of the knowledge society for our customers

Brand Values

ICL applies e-business experience and expertise to help organisations build high value, personalised relationships with their customers. Specifically, ICL designs builds and operates e-business services that significantly improve the performance and productivity of those organisations.

ICL has established itself as one of Europe's leading e-business service companies through a direct result of developing innovative solutions that fulfil the needs of organisations operating in the connected world.

This capability is driven by the core values and ethos of the company: ICL aims to continually improve the lives of people, throughout the world, by developing and delivering innovative solutions. Supported by a proven heritage of delivering mission critical solutions, ICL is able to deliver a full end-to-end solution.

Things you didn't know about ICL

ICL touches the lives of over 100 million people a week as they live, work, learn and shop.

ICL has won seven Queen's Awards for technological achievements and export sales.

ICL is the UK's leading IT training organisation and trains 100,000 people each year.

ICL was the first western company to be accredited to trade in the former Soviet Union in 1968 and has been operating in central and Eastern Europe ever since.

ICL has 347 offices worldwide, is represented in over 40 countries and employs 22,500 people.

Nine of the top ten UK banks rely on IT systems supplied by ICL.

ICL services over 60 million internet hits every month in the UK.

ICL is the leading supplier of retail IT systems in the UK and the third largest worldwide.

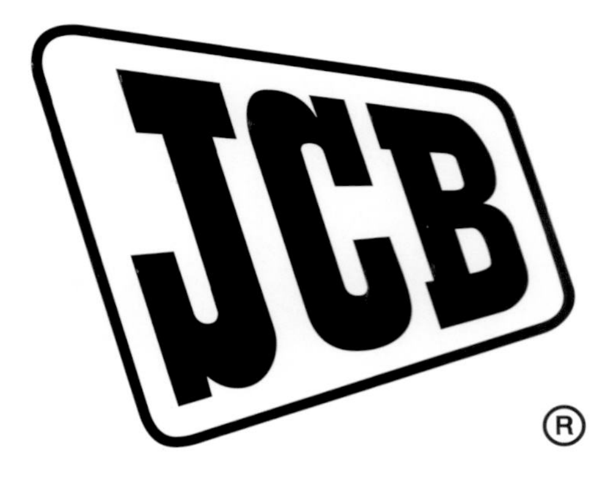

Market

There's no reason why the average man on the street should be familiar with the brand of an industrial equipment manufacturer, but this is not the case with JCB, as it is one of the UK's best known brands and business success stories.

JCB is Europe's premier manufacturer of construction equipment. It enjoys a 7% share of the international construction equipment sector. The market for this equipment stands at around 400,000 machines worldwide per year. Europe and North America – JCB's major markets – account for 250,000 of these.

JCB exports more than 70% of the 28,000 machines it produces each year, selling around 40% to Europe, where it commands a 16% market share. It is aiming to build a 10% share of the US market and, thanks to a joint venture factory in India, Escorts JCB, it has a clear lead in the construction equipment sector, with an 80% share.

In the UK, the construction equipment market is relatively buoyant thanks to an upturn in post-recession construction. The spate of building projects in the run-up to the Millennium further boosted demand for equipment in the UK and elsewhere in the world. An indication of this growth can be seen in the health of the plant hire market, which stood at £1.85 billion in 1998 and is expected to reach £2.5 billion by 2003 (Source: Keynote).

Achievements

JCB has become a generic name for construction equipment. When people think of a digger, they invariably call it a JCB, whichever brand it is. The proper name for this 'digger' is a backhoe loader, first introduced by JCB in 1953. Since then, it has become the brand leader virtually the world over and its yellow machines are a familiar part of the landscape and language. The JCB name even appears in the Oxford English Dictionary.

The backhoe loader is part of a rich heritage of innovation. Another major achievement was the introduction of the Loadall machine in 1978. This revolutionised aspects of the building industry, allowing bricks to be lifted in pallets instead of being carried in a hod by a labourer. JCB also developed the first and still the only high-speed tractor, the Fastrac. Designed to combine all the benefits of a normal tractor with road versatility, the Fastrac won numerous awards, including the Prince of Wales Award for Innovation in 1995. Another design classic was the Teletruk – the only forklift truck not to use cumbersome double masts at the front. Instead, it employs a single lifting arm which gives the driver greater flexibility.

Altogether, JCB has been awarded over 50 major awards for engineering excellence, exports, design, marketing, management and care for the environment. Among them are fifteen Queen's Awards for Technology and Export Achievement. JCB has a particularly impressive record in this latter area, exporting to 140 countries around the world. The company reports sales of around £833 million with profits of £91.2 million.

History

JCB started business in October 1945, when Joseph Cyril Bamford manufactured a tipping trailer with a £1 welding set in a lock-up garage he rented in Uttoxeter. He sold it at the local market for £45 and a great British engineering enterprise was born.

In 1948, with Joe now employing six people, the company produced its first hydraulic machine – Europe's first hydraulic tipping trailer. It then developed a hydraulic arm kit for tractors – the Si-draulic – which was a world first and one of JCB's earliest commercial hits.

The first product to carry the recognisable JCB logo was the Loadover, a machine with front-loading shovel. Launched in 1953, the machine was not a commercial success, but is remembered still for giving birth to the brand as we know it today.

The road to the dramatic success began when JCB developed its first backhoe loader machine in 1953. Joe had spotted a machine with

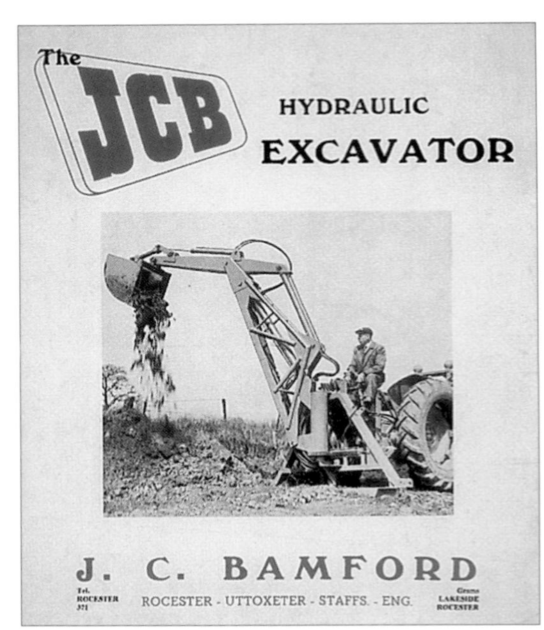

a rear digging arm in Norway and brought a unit back to the UK to see if he could improve the design. Called the MkI Hydraulic Excavator, the backhoe could be combined with a front loading arm to create the first true ancestor of today's familiar machine. This evolved into the Hydra-Digga of 1957 – a much more powerful front and rear hydraulic shovel machine which many regard as the true commercial beginning of JCB.

In the 1960s, JCB introduced the legendary 3C machine. This was a massive success, selling over 3,000 units in 1964. Around this time, Joe Bamford demonstrated his marketing skills with a touch of brilliance which is still quoted today. For the 3D, he designed the cab so that the operator could make a cup of tea in it and promised that for the first 100 3Ds sold he would visit the purchaser and personally give them an in-cab kettle. Joe's visits in his Rolls-Royce (number plate JCB1) became legendary and the 3D was an overnight success.

Joe's publicity skills were also evident when he began the tradition of JCB 'stunts' in the 1960s. Elaborate manoeuvres performed for the TV cameras – such as driving a car under a machine raised up on its hydraulic arms – showed the versatility and power of the machines and began the tradition of the famous 'Dancing Digger' shows which continue to this day.

JCB's attention to detail has greatly contributed to its export success. In the 1960s it began flying foreign buyers into the UK on a

'Robot skid steers'. This revolutionary vehicle – designed for small loading operations – sets new standards in safety and performance.

Another division of JCB – JCB Landpower – makes the Fastrac tractor for the agricultural market.

specially acquired, JCB-branded aircraft. Passengers were ferried from the plane to the factory in a special customer limousine. The company still operates its own 'Exporter' aircraft under the name of JCB Aviation. This name itself is now older than many of Europe's best-known airlines.

In the 1970s the company began expanding its product range, such as the hugely successful Loadall telescopic handler. Later, JCB expanded into wheeled and tracked excavators and, in 1991, signed a joint venture with Japan's Sumitomo Construction Machinery and has since gone onto produce its own range of excavators. By 1994, JCB's product diversification had paid off, with £140 million of its £565 million sales coming from products launched in the previous five years.

Product

Nowadays, JCB has nine subsidiary companies in Europe, the US and Singapore and manufactures at nine factories in the UK. Its wide range of equipment now comprises construction machines of all shapes and sizes. Including all the different models, there are more than 100 different products in the JCB range.

These include the world-beating backhoe loaders, which range from the smallest 1CX to the heavy duty 4CX Super. Tracked excavators comprise fifteen models with over 20 boom and undercarriage variations. JCB also makes mini and midi excavators, designed for use in urban and confined areas.

JCB makes seventeen different wheeled loader models, with power ranging from 60 to 200 horsepower. Telescopic handlers – the world-leading Loadall range – go from ultra-compact to heavy duty models. There are also rough terrain fork lift trucks and single loader arm

Recent Developments

In January 2000 JCB opened its first manufacturing plant in the US, sited in Savannah Georgia. The $62 million factory is part of a $100 million investment in the US and is on a 1064 acre site. This is now JCB's North America HQ.

The company is also investing in its Indian subsidiary, Escorts JCB, based near Dehli, where it produces 3,000 backhoe loaders per year, as well as Loadalls and wheeled loading shovels. JCB has announced a £20 million investment plan to build another factory in India and introduce additional products to the market.

In the UK, JCB recently opened a new business, JCB Earthmovers, manufacturing from a 250,000 square foot factory. It makes a brand new range of dump trucks as well as wheeled loading shovels. The new articulated dump trucks take JCB into a new sector. Another new factory, at Wrexham has also opened, making axles and a state-of-the-art new JCB World Parts Centre has opened at Waterloo Park, Uttoxeter.

The company has not only invested in factories and equipment. It has also concentrated on improving its design and development expertise, helping its Heavy Products division to recently record record sales and win another Queen's Award for Export Achievement.

Promotion

JCB has a rich promotional heritage, with the company's founder, Joe Bamford, setting the standard. He instilled a culture of showmanship, which has famously set JCB apart from the competition over the years. The best-known example of this eccentric approach of using fun to sell, is the JCB Dancing Diggers formation team. Following calls in 1962 from Mr Bamford for ideas that would attract interest from TV, an employee came up with the idea of raising the entire chassis of a backhoe loader off the ground by pressing down on the front and rear shovels. More and more tricks were developed and a specialist demonstration team formed

to perform ballet-like routines. More than 35 years later, these routines – known as the JCB Circus – are still a firm favourite at exhibitions around the world.

Other famous stunts include the development of the JCB GT – a backhoe digger customised with a V8 Chevrolet 7440cc engine. Capable of 100 mph, the JCB GT attracted huge media attention and made popular appearances at major events from 1988 to 1990.

The company's PR brilliance is also demonstrated by its 'flying digger' strategy of deploying customer jets and helicopters. These help the company offer a highly personalised service for valued customers, flying them to its factories and maximising selling time.

The company has also invested heavily in advertising over the years. Many of the techniques now familiar in consumer advertising were being used by JCB's ad agency, Brookes and Vernons, in the technical press over 25 years ago. The lavishly photographed ads have won the agency and manufacturer many awards over the years and set new standards in heavy equipment marketing.

Brand Values

Now under the guidance of Joe Bamford's son, Sir Anthony Bamford, JCB is one of the UK's most famous family businesses. Family is in the DNA of the JCB brand, not only because its name is made from the initials of its founder, but also because of how the family has stamped its personality on the company. Inventiveness, enthusiasm and eschewing convention have been guiding principles through JCB's history, influencing its adventurous approach to design, marketing and expansion.

Things you didn't know about JCB

From the earliest days JCB wanted to harness the power of its logo. From 1960, the company fitted its typewriters with special keys to accurately render the logo. This practice continues to this day, with all desktop PCs pre-formatted so that JCB logos can be selected for use on faxes, letters or memos.

In 1958. Joe Bamford bought ten scooters with the proviso that they must have registration plates from JCB 1 to JCB 10. The company still acquires additional JCB plates whenever possible and owns 1-14 and 17-20. Numbers 15 and 16 are still missing.

JCB has released its own single, called 'JCB and Me' by Lenny Green in 1965. The country and western single was promoted with a picture of a lone backhoe loader digging in Monument Valley, Utah.

JCB's 100 mph digger – the JCB GT – was road-tested in a 1988 edition of Autocar & Motor.

JCB is one of the UK's last great manufacturing companies. Whilst since 1975, UK national manufacturing employment has fallen from 7.7 to 4.2 million, and in the West Midlands from 1.1 million to 562,000, in the same period, JCB's workforce has doubled.

Knight Frank

Market

Knight Frank has grown to become one of the world's leading property advisory groups. Operating as a private partnership, Knight Frank is a formidable presence in the residential and commercial property sectors.

The UK property market is one of the most competitive in the world and Knight Frank's long history at the top of the UK property market has served it well through the years. In London, where prices have recently soared higher than anywhere in the country, the firm is involved in around 80% of all residential properties bought and sold at the top end of the market.

Although Knight Frank's reputation has been built handling ancestral castles, country estates and the homes of the rich and famous, the scope of the modern business is much wider. With 7,000 staff working in 27 countries, Knight Frank provides the complete range of real estate services (consultancy, brokerage, management) across multiple markets.

Today, more than half of its business is in the commercial property sector, working for clients including JP Morgan, PricewaterhouseCoopers, Citibank and Prudential. It is now the largest and longest established multi-disciplinary practice in London's booming Docklands area, handling properties like Canary Wharf, Harbour Exchange and East India Dock.

Thanks to the recovery in the UK economy towards the end of 1998, commercial property is buoyant. Strong rental growth and the availability of cheap financing have underpinned the sector, with bank lending to UK property companies up 11.4% in the year to September 1999.

Achievements

One of the firm's greatest achievements is its resilience. Thanks to shrewd expansion and the ability to change with the times, Knight Frank can boast the rare distinction of turning a profit for each and every year of its long history.

Given the current desirability of globalisation, the firm gains a lot of its strength from its long established international network. Built up over the years, this 27-country reach makes Knight Frank a powerful player in the global property market.

Also worth mentioning is Knight Frank's impeccable pedigree. Not many real estate companies can claim to have been entrusted with many of the UK's most famous landmarks, like the BBC's Broadcasting House, The Royal Naval College at Greenwich, Wembley Stadium, Crystal Palace and Stonehenge.

On top of its enviable reputation for handling country estates and historical property, some of the world's landmark real estate – like the Pan Am building in New York and the Bank of China Tower in Hong Kong – have passed through its hands.

As well as celebrities like Mick Jagger and historical giants like Winston Churchill, the firm has acted for multi-national corporations, national governments and major landowners. Nowadays, it reports an annual revenue approaching $200 million.

History

Knight Frank and Rutley opened for business in 1896. The founders were John Frank, an auctioneer, Howard Frank, an estate agent and William Rutley, an antiques valuation expert. To begin with, the bulk of its business was auctioning antiques and objets d'art from its galleries in Conduit Street, London.

By 1902 property became the largest part of the business and grew quickly thanks to Howard Frank's expert handling of large country estates. This speciality saw it through some property recessions early in the century and, while others suffered, Knight Frank and Rutley's business prospered.

In 1910 the firm moved into the offices at 20 Hanover Square that it still occupies today and in 1912 opened offices in Edinburgh to serve its rapidly growing country estate business in Scotland.

By the 1920s the firm was large enough to be handling the sale of the entire town of Reigate – a bizarre task that saw many of the town's houses, shops and pubs sold at auction. In 1922 the firm's reputation was sufficient to attract the interest of Winston Churchill, whom it assisted with the purchase of Chartwell Manor in Kent. The house, with 80 acres, cost £5000. During the 'twenties the firm was involved in development projects that changed the face of London, including the BBC's Broadcasting House in 1928.

During World War II the company was kept busy conducting valuations of property flattened in the blitz and for looking after clients' properties while they were away at war. In 1945, Knight Frank was charged with selling the contents of the German Embassy, including a bust of Hitler and German flags intended to fly from buildings in conquered London. Unexpectedly out of his job after the war, Knight Frank also had to find a London home for its old client, Winston Churchill.

The 1950s saw more significant property deals in London, including acquiring the land for the American Embassy in Grosvenor Square, and the sale of Piccadilly Arcade. In the 1960s it started acting on behalf of the new breed of pop star millionaires seeking homes – the Beatles and Adam Faith were just two who came to Knight Frank. In 1961, Knight Frank was appointed joint letting agent for the Pan Am building in New York. At the time, this was the largest single letting in the world. One of its biggest and most complex tasks in the 1960s was moving the Covent Garden market to its current site at Nine Elms. The move took eleven years.

Around this time Knight Frank's international work started to increase, especially in Africa, where the firm started doing a lot of valuation work for British companies that led to it becoming a major force, particularly in Nigeria. It also began working in Australia, forging relationships with local firms that laid the foundation for future growth. It now handles more property in Australia than any other agent.

The 1970s saw the beginning of Knight Frank's expansion into Europe, opening offices in Brussels, Amsterdam and Paris. It also opened its City of London office – a move that helped Knight Frank become a major player in the UK commercial property market. The firm was also beginning to prosper from an upturn in the UK residential market as overseas buyers bought up luxury homes. In 1979, the firm opened an office in New York. Its involvement in selling the Warner building in the Rockefeller Centre helped establish the firm's reputation in the New York market.

By the 1980s, the firm was growing steadily at home and abroad. A highlight was the sale of the Pan-American World Airways Intercontinental Hotels Corporation to Grand Metropolitan for $500 million – hailed at the time as the largest ever real estate transaction. At this time the group filled a gap in its international portfolio by opening offices in Hong Kong and Singapore. In Hong Kong, it acted as agents for another prestigious development, the Bank of Shanghai.

Now, over a century after it first opened for business, Knight Frank is a multinational business, with over 200 offices in 27 countries, employing 7,000 people worldwide. During its long history, the firm has adapted its activities and profile to suit the needs of a twenty-first century business.

Product

Knight Frank's geographical diversity is supported by multiple service and product lines that are designed to support any organisation with exposure to the property market.

Its business is primarily divided into residential, agricultural and commercial services. Within the residential and agricultural sector, its extensive services include London Residential, Country Houses, Farms and Estates, International Residential, Residential Development, Residential Lettings and Management, Rural Consultancy, Planning and Building Consultancy. Buying services are also offered to purchasers who need an expert to make purchasing residential property an easy and enjoyable experience.

The Commercial Services offered by Knight Frank cover all areas of the business property sector, with departments devoted to office, industrial retail, leisure, investments and hotels. Knight Frank offers a full range of consultancy and management services to help clients make the most of their property. The company deals with some of the most sought-after commercial property in the UK, including Canary Wharf and Harbour Exchange in Docklands. Knight Frank is also well known for its expertise in the UK retail market, advising names like Marks & Spencer, J Sainsbury, John Lewis, Woolworths, HMV, Waterstones, Boots, BHS, Tesco and WH Smith.

Knight Frank manages over £3 billion worth of UK property with an annual rent of over £170 million. Its building consultancy department regularly undertakes work for names as famous as Lord's Cricket Ground and the All England Tennis Club.

As well as these core activities, the firm also offers financial services and corporate finance to assist in all types of property transactions.

Recent Developments

Today Knight Frank seeks to meet the challenges, which arise from the powerful and dynamic forces shaping both the business economy and the property sector. Recent and important areas of expansion include the residential development and investment markets, the provision of integrated pan-continental services, particularly in Europe. These developments led Knight Frank to sign a strategic alliance with US firm, Grubb & Ellis. It has also been expanding its activities in the corporate finance and corporate real estate sectors and has created a network of offices in the Caribbean.

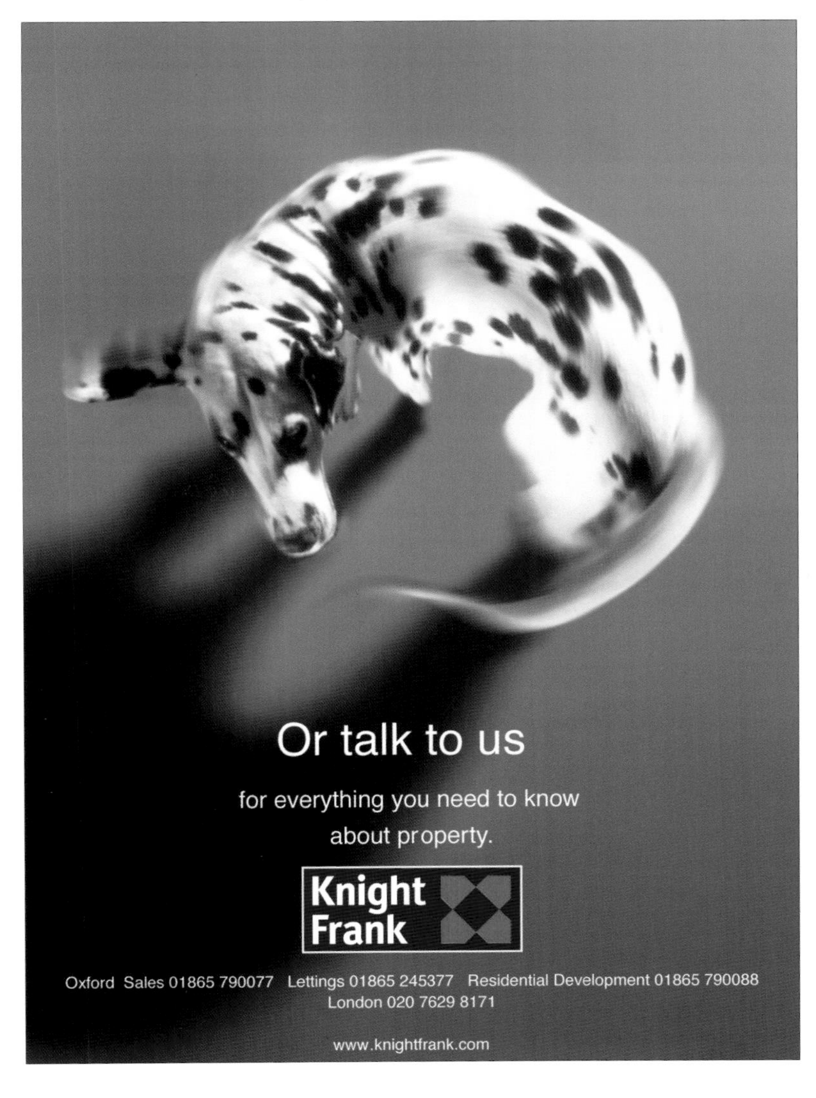

Promotion

The company has always appreciated the value of brand building, spending £1,800 on advertising in its first year of operation – a third of its annual turnover and a huge amount in 1897. In 1912, this bullish approach was illustrated when Knight Frank and Rutley acquired another estate agent, Walton & Lee, just so that it could take over its front-page advertising position on Country Life. It has held this prime position ever since, spending over £20 million on advertising in this magazine alone.

Whilst Knight Frank's advertisements have evolved and developed over the years the quality of advertising remains as important today as always and no expense is spared on professional photography. It is famous for its lavishly produced brochures, particularly The Catalogue – an annually produced publication detailing the best Knight Frank has to sell in the residential market. Most of the firm's promotional activity is linked with properties it is selling, which explains why brochures and magazine advertising is so important.

Other promotional tools include the Book of 100 Facts. First produced to mark the firm's centenary in 1996, it was followed by a second edition in 2000. This entertaining and interesting booklet is mailed to existing and potential clients and is useful not only for communicating information about the firm, but also strengthening the brand.

On top of this, the firm holds two key commercial presentations per year, each attended by 300 property professionals. The sessions are an opportunity for the firm to share some of its research with the property market – intelligence for which Knight Frank is highly respected. It produces over 35 research reports into the domestic and international property market every year.

Knight Frank also makes extensive use of sponsorship, backing various sporting events from point to point meetings, horse trails and racing to rugby clubs and tennis tournaments.

Brand Values

Knight Frank has its own place in British history, however, the firm is not all about ancestral castles and country estates. It is now a diverse international business and its brand has to combine the best aspects of tradition with a forward-thinking modern approach.

The history of the firm as a family business is kept alive through an emphasis on teamwork and loyalty to the firm. The firm's brand positioning, translates into a powerful sense of independence and employee pride. Customers receive personalised service and peace of mind that comes from working with a firm who value trust so highly. Balancing these values in the context of an aggressive and highly dynamic global property business is the key challenge successfully faced by the Knight Frank brand.

Things you didn't know about Knight Frank

In 1999, the firm marketed one of London's most expensive houses, an eleven-bedroom mansion next to Kensington Palace in London. The house went on the market for £35 million.

Knight Frank has sold art collections by Raphael, Rubens, Turner and Van Dyck.

In 1911, Knight Frank sold Crystal Palace to Lord Plymouth for £210,000.

The Earl of Lucan, who gave the order that led to the Charge of the Light Brigade, used to live at Knight Frank's headquarters at 20 Hanover Square.

In 1921, Knight Frank sold the entire town of Reigate – including pubs, shops and the castle – for £203,840.

In 1915, Knight Frank helped Cecil Chubb buy Stonehenge for £6,600 as a present for his wife. She gave it to the nation three years later.

Knight Frank was appointed by the Ministry of Defence to advise on the future of the Royal Naval College in Greenwich and to seek alternative occupiers.

Market

One of the best-known brands in the insurance business, Legal & General operates in a wide-ranging and fast-changing market.

The insurance industry is being transformed by giant mergers, Government policy and the emergence of new internet brands introducing low-cost, simplified products. Traditional insurance companies find themselves under increased pressure from nimble-footed e-business brands, forcing them to invest heavily in technology in order to meet ever-higher levels of customer expectation.

The wider business trend towards globalisation and the need to reduce costs in the face of intense competition has sparked a round of consolidation amongst the UK's biggest insurance brands. It began in 1997, when Royal Insurance and Sun Alliance merged to create Royal & SunAlliance. In 1998, Commercial Union merged with General Accident to form CGU, and, in 2000, CGU and Norwich Union announced their plan to wed.

Pressure on costs has been further intensified by the UK Government's introduction of Stakeholder Pensions in 2001. Cheaper, simpler pensions are popular with consumers. The popularity of products like this, and the new Individual Savings Account (ISA) are attracting a raft of new players into the financial services industry, like Marks & Spencer and Virgin. Banks are also increasingly looking to enter the insurance market, and many have been on the hunt to buy well-known life assurance brands. Lloyds TSB has already done so, buying Scottish Widows, and NatWest was close to joining with Legal & General before it was taken over itself.

The interest shown in the insurance sector by banks, internet start-ups and non-financial brands is understandable. As governments around Europe move away from traditional welfare systems, the market for private pensions and savings is booming, with some analysts predicting it will be one of the fastest growing industries in the twenty-first century.

In 1999, new insurance business in the UK totalled £40 billion, a 21% increase on the previous year. However, this has to be balanced against the high investment costs necessary to compete in the internet age. In 1999, UK insurers were estimated to have spent £2 billion on new technology.

Achievements

Over its long history, Legal & General has built an excellent reputation and a leading position in the UK financial services industry. Indeed, it is widely viewed in the City to be the UK's leading life insurance company. This position is illustrated by the fact that, in 1998 and 1999, Legal & General was voted the UK's most admired insurance company by the readers of Management Today magazine.

Its track record of providing low-cost, innovative products has helped it attract over 2.5 million policyholders and manage investments for the pension schemes of 33 companies in the FTSE 100. It has £107 billion in worldwide funds under management.

As one of the best-known and trusted names in business, Legal & General is one of the UK's Top 50 quoted companies, and its financial strength has been recognised by the world's leading credit rating agencies. In 1988, it became the first UK insurer to be awarded the coveted Standard & Poor's AAA rating for financial strength. It has maintained the rating ever since. No other company has held the AAA rating for this length of time.

As the insurance industry has been transformed by the internet, Legal & General has responded by ensuring it is a force to be reckoned with in the new media age. It has one of the best online services in the business, and, in 1999, won numerous industry awards for its use of the internet. One of these was for 'Electronic Commerce Product of the Year', at the Exchange Electronic Service Awards.

Other awards recently won by Legal & General, include Life Insurer of the Year in June 2000, Specialist Unit Trust Company in 1999, by What Investment magazine, Best Centralised Lender 1999 by What Mortgage magazine and Electronic Company 1999, by Financial Adviser magazine and the Golden Star award for excellence from Professional Pensions magazine.

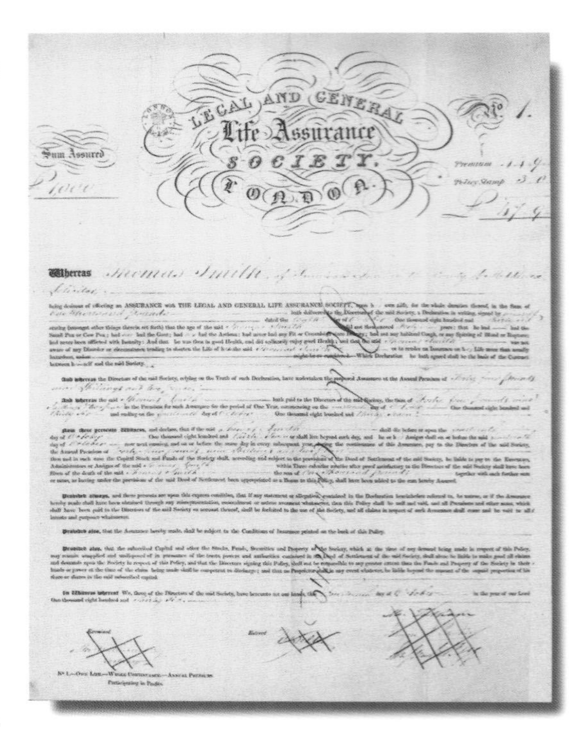

History

The Legal & General Life Assurance Society – the forerunner of today's group – was formed 164 years ago by six London lawyers. The venture soon prospered, combining a constantly expanding life assurance business with far-sighted fund management.

Until 1919, the company was only involved in life assurance, but, in that year, it changed its name to the present form when it expanded into all other types of insurance. The company

began to attract a reputation for innovation, underlined in 1930 when it introduced the first company pension scheme, devising a plan for the Gramophone Company (which later became part of EMI).

During the 1940s the company began expanding overseas, entering Australia in 1948. By the end of the 1960s, the Society's assets had grown to over £1 billion and, thanks to its size, the company re-organised into five operating divisions, covering administration, investment, operations, planning and actuarial. During the 1970s, the group also diversified into unit trusts, launched a pensions managed fund subsidiary and linked up with several European insurance companies to further raise its international profile. By 1979, its total assets exceeded £4 billion and it was active in most areas of the insurance business and the world.

In 1981, the group made its largest-ever transaction, buying the US-based Government Employees Life Insurance Company (which later became Banner Life) for nearly £90 million. This put Legal & General on the map in the US and made it the first company of its kind to take such a major step out of Europe. In 1989, it made another US acquisition, buying William Penn Insurance.

Some of the most recent milestones to affect Legal & General include the launch of deposit accounts by Legal & General Bank in 1997 and the sale of Legal & General Australia in 1998.

Product

The Legal & General Group is one of the UK's largest pension providers and the largest ISA provider in the insurance sector, with multi-channel distribution. It is also leading the market in launching new low-cost Stakeholder personal pensions.

For the business market, Legal & General is an important provider of group risk insurance cover and employee pension schemes. Employee benefit schemes are designed to help businesses protect their workforce in a variety of ways, such as paying their salaries when they fall ill, or providing life assurance when an employee dies. Principal products in this area include Group Death in Service Benefits and Group Long Term Disability Income. Legal & General also offers a wide range of options for Group Critical Illness Cover and Health Care Cover, providing further options for protecting employees and employers. Benefit packages like this are important for increasing workforce loyalty and morale and in helping companies to recruit on the job market.

As a leading brand in the pensions market, Legal & General also offers a wide range of services to help employers operate pension schemes for their workforce. New government legislation will require companies with five employees or more to provide access to a stakeholder pension scheme from October 2001 and requires employers to designate a registered pension provider. This is an important market for Legal & General, which has led the way developing one of the most competitive pre-stakeholder pension schemes.

Recent Developments

Legal & General's Pre-Stakeholder Pension is one of the best on the market, coming top of a recent value-for-money league compiled by Life & Pension Money Facts.

A vital element of this new product is Legal & General's guarantee which promises anyone taking one of its personal pensions since March 31, 1999 the opportunity to transfer to a Stakeholder product from April 2001 without any reduction in the value of their transferred fund. This means it promises that the transfer value will be worth at least as much as if it had been a Stakeholder pension all along.

This 'Full Stakeholder Transferability' guarantee was the first to be offered by any UK pension provider and remains a key advantage for Legal & General in the competitive pension marketplace.

The strength of its offering in this sector helped Legal & General win over £13 billion in new pension fund management business in 1999.

Promotion

Part of Legal & General's £10 million annual marketing spend targets the independent financial adviser (IFA) market which, ultimately, sells many of Legal & General's products. To target IFAs, Legal & General advertises in the specialist financial titles which include Money Marketing.

The company also does a great deal of direct response advertising in the national press for individual products, like ISAs, mortgages and term assurance.

Legal & General has, historically, made significant use of sponsorship. In the mid-1990s, it was one of the first major sponsors of the ITV weather, finding a perfect fit with its umbrella logo. More recently, it sponsored a national debate about pensions. This 'Millennium Debate of the Age' was held in association with Age Concern and, thanks to the highly topical nature of the discussion, gained Legal & General a lot of positive media coverage. The company has also recently sponsored members of the British Athletics Team competing in the Sydney 2000 Olympics.

Brand Values

The firm's core brand proposition is that it is a company which offers value for money to its customers - 'Legal & General makes financial security easier to achieve.'

In addition it defines its differentiating brand values, or character as being accessible, involving, responsive and credible.

Given the complexity and daunting nature of the financial services industry, Legal & General is keen to be seen as the brand that brings simplicity and personality to financial planning. The attributes of its personality are key to achieving the other values of the brand. These demand that the company is 'assured and approachable', 'intelligent and professional' and 'warm and understanding'.

Things you didn't know about Legal & General

During World War Two, Legal & General evacuated its London offices and relocated to Chessington Zoo. However, it also had to leave there because, from the viewpoint of German bombers the zoo resembled a military camp.

One in eleven UK housing transactions involve Legal & General products.

There are over 500 visits to Legal & General's web site every day.

Legal & General collects over 1.5 million direct debits every month.

Legal & General processed around 150,000 claims from General Insurance policy holders in 1998.

Legal & General's call centres receive 15,000 calls per month.

THE LONDON SCHOOL OF ECONOMICS AND POLITICAL SCIENCE

Market

The London School of Economics and Political Science is the pre-eminent social science institution in Europe. As a specialist institution concentrating on political and economic sciences, it has long had a reputation as an intellectual powerhouse with an enviable international standing. In the most recent national research assessment, it was ranked second (after Cambridge) out of 200 universities and colleges for quality.

LSE has a reputation for having the ears of governments and leaders around the world. Its former directors include William Beveridge, founder of the UK social security system, and Ralf Dahrendorf, prominent in Anglo-German academic and political life. The current director, Professor Anthony Giddens, is one of Tony Blair's key advisors. Giddens is credited as the architect of the 'third way' school of thought which is now influencing not just the British, but other governments in Europe and around the world. Professor Giddens has helped to maintain the tradition of placing LSE at the very centre of political debate. He was also one of the first people to try to identify a trend affecting all business people today – globalisation – in the late 1980s.

LSE staff actively engage in policy development, through advice to government departments, and representation on governmental advisory bodies including the Monetary Policy Committee, Urban Task Force, National Consumer Council and the Press Complaints Commission, and also as members of the House of Lords.

For the business community, LSE is invaluable, turning out some of the best business thinkers of any learning institution and providing intelligence and insight on the latest macro and micro trends affecting all companies. As a result, it attracts many millions of pounds in funding from the private sector.

LSE has 6,340 full-time and 790 part-time students. Of these 40% are from the UK, 18% from the European Union and 42% from 130 other countries around the world. The School has an enormously cosmopolitan and diverse student community.

Achievements

Seven Nobel Prize winners for economics have been LSE staff or alumni. These are: Sir John Hicks (1972), FA von Hayek (1974), James Meade (1977), Sir Arthur Lewis (1979), Ronald Coase (1991), Amartya Sen (1998) and Robert Mundell (1999). Furthermore, the School has educated around 28 past or present heads of state, including ex-US president John F Kennedy, the president of the European Commission, Romano Prodi and the prime minister of Greece. Other famous alumni include Cherie Booth, and international financier, George Soros.

LSE's Library is one of the world's largest modern libraries, with international recognition for its social science collection comprising over four million titles.

History

LSE was founded in 1895 by Sidney and Beatrice Webb. They founded LSE because they and others saw a need for a British centre to study political and social problems as deeply as institutions in Europe and the US were doing at the time. From the beginning, LSE's stated aim was to improve society by promoting the impartial study of its problems and to train those who, in the future, would translate policy into action, making a real difference to the world they lived in. Also from these earliest days, the School has opened its doors to women and men, and encouraged older students to attend. It attracted many from the worlds of business and administration – something that remains true today.

The School became part of the University of London in 1900, and in 1922 adopted the motto 'To understand the causes of things.' Since then it has pioneered the development of the social sciences in this country, including founding the study of sociology, social anthropology, social policy, criminology and international relations as subjects of university study in the UK.

Product

LSE's product is its academic excellence, delivered through its courses, research, events and publications.

There are eighteen academic departments and 30 research centres. These include areas as diverse as accounting, cities and urban development, economics, environment, government, human rights, international relations, industrial relations, IT, law, management, media and communications, operational research, philosophy, social policy, social psychology, and statistics.

For undergraduates and postgraduates there is a wide range of courses. At postgraduate level, LSE offers over 80 taught master's programmes leading to the award of MSc, MA, MPhil, LLM and various diplomas, which students can take over a year full time, or two years part-time. Research programmes for MPhil or PhD degrees are offered by all departments and institutes.

LSE's world renowned and influential research centres and institutes include: the Asia Research Centre; Centre for the Study of Global Governance; Centre for Economic Performance; Computer Security Research Centre; the European Institute; Financial Markets Group; Interdisciplinary Institute of Management; and the Suntory and Toyota International Centres for Economics and Related Disciplines (STICERD).

LSE's Library is an important part of its 'product'. Internationally recognised, the Library is particularly rich in items on economics, transport, statistics, international law and economic history. It also holds some of the most important texts in the history of economics, including a 1776 first edition of Adam Smith's seminal work, The Wealth of Nations.

Large collections of government publications from around the world are held in the Library and these and other materials can be accessed via a substantial electronic information resource.

LSE's public lectures are another important element of its offering. World thinkers and leaders come to speak at events, including the presidents of Poland and Brazil, Gordon Brown, JK Galbraith, Susie Orbach and the former US Treasury Secretary Robert Rubin.

An important pillar of LSE's product for business is Enterprise LSE – an arm of the School that undertakes consultancy services using the expertise of academics. Enterprise LSE offers team and individual consultancy, providing insights into political, economic and financial aspects of world markets (including Eastern Europe, Latin America and Asia Pacific); customised professional education and training; facilitation and decision support; and research. Enterprise LSE can build interdisciplinary teams to tackle complex projects, matching LSE's skills with that of individual clients and their business requirements. For example the LSE Public Policy Group carried out research for the National Audit Office, as part of the modernising government agenda, focusing on government on the web, a landmark for the NAO as it was the first value for money report to be fully contracted out.

LSE staff are also prolific authors, and each year produce many books, articles and other publications, often based on their research.

Recent Developments

In April 2000, LSE joined five other world-leading institutions to create Fathom.com – a new portal and destination internet site providing the best of knowledge and education on the web. The site amalgamates learning content from universities, museums and libraries for a worldwide audience of business and individual users. Much of the information has never been available outside of the participating organisations before. Fellow founding partners are Columbia University, the British Library, the Smithsonian Institution's National Museum of Natural History, New York Public Library and Cambridge University Press.

In 1998-99 external funding for LSE research reached record levels, with nearly £12 million of new research contracts secured. LSE now leads other UK higher education institutions in the cost efficiency of its research. Many well-known businesses invest in LSE's research, including Deutsche Bank and BP. In March 2000, Deutsche Bank announced plans to fund a chair and teaching programme in risk management based within LSE's newest research centre, the Centre for the Analysis of Risk and Regulation (CARR).

CARR has received £10 million in private and public centre funding since its launch in December 1999. The idea of CARR is to investigate ways in which managers and shareholders can protect themselves against unforeseen crises.

LSE has strategic alliances with some of the world's great universities. The School is a partner in UNext – a distance learning, technology based project delivering learning on the web, involving the universities of Carnegie Mellon, Columbia, Chicago, and Stanford. UNext dot com delivers a world class education curriculum directly to businesses.

The Lionel Robbins Building, which houses the Library and five of the LSE's research centres, is being redeveloped by architects Foster and Partners. The £24 million scheme will modernise facilities for students, staff and the public and will be completed in 2001.

Promotion

LSE's promotion comes from its recognition as a world-class centre of expertise. Thanks to its reputation, the media often go to LSE staff for comment or analysis on whatever social or political issues happen to be in the news. It provides a reference book of experts for the media, guiding them to staff who can comment authoritatively on a wide range of issues. At times, staff field up to twenty media calls per day. This strategy pays handsome dividends for the School, which, according to media monitoring, gets over 8,000 print, radio and TV mentions every year.

In addition to this, LSE's director, Professor Anthony Giddens, is a tireless ambassador for the brand. As a world-renowned social theorist, Professor Giddens is in high demand to speak all over the world. The intense interest in the 'third way' has made him an essential spokesman whenever the issue is discussed.

LSE also gains valuable publicity from the numerous debates it holds featuring prominent speakers. With names like, Benazir Bhutto, Nelson Mandela, Ken Livingstone and David Puttnam speaking recently, its debates are often in the news.

As valuable as these are for attracting students and funding, LSE also has the weapons of its information-rich website and prospectuses, which results in fifteen student applications for every place.

Brand Values

LSE's core values are that it is a research-driven teaching institution, an intellectual powerhouse with a strong social commitment. It wants to be where ideas for social betterment and change are developed and the place where 'socially engaged' leaders of the future – in business and politics – form their views. It is also resolutely internationalist, continually playing a key role in world affairs, but, at the same time, aware of its links with London.

LSE insists that the brand stays true to the original core value 'to understand the causes of things'. It is well-known for its atmosphere of

vigorous intellectual argument and critical debate, and sees part of its role, as to understand the forces shaping society and then disseminate information about these forces to the wider public.

Things you didn't know about LSE

Rolling Stone Mick Jagger studied at LSE between 1961 and 1963. Other graduates from the music world include Matt Osman, bass player with Suede and Radio One DJ, Judge Jules.

Writers Pat Barker and Mary Wesley both studied there.

32 current UK members of parliament and 32 current members of the House of Lords have either studied or taught at LSE.

LSE is situated on a campus of inter-linking buildings just off the Aldwych in the heart of central London.

LSE is a mainly postgraduate institution.

Most students come from outside the UK.

Market

LYCRA® is one of the best-known names in the clothing industry. As the company's uniquely flexible fibre is used in such a wide variety of garments, the market for LYCRA® is correspondingly broad.

LYCRA® is one of those few brands whose name has become synonymous with the sector it operates in. When people think of fabrics that stretch and recover, of comfort, fit and freedom of movement, the name LYCRA® automatically comes into their minds. This only happens with brands that have not only invented the category they work in, but have developed products that keep them at the top of that sector. LYCRA® has achieved this.

As LYCRA® is an 'ingredient', as opposed to a fabric in its own right, its market is primarily clothing manufacturers and designers for use in their garments. Nowadays, people have much higher expectations about the 'performance' of their fabrics – they want them to stretch, to breathe, and to 'wash and wear'. As such, they want 'super-fabrics', so designers and clothing brands are looking to ingredients such as LYCRA® to meet that demand.

Already, LYCRA® is one of the world's top ten textile brands and in the top five ingredient brands. As well as having high awareness with the manufacturer, LYCRA® wants its brand to have high consumer awareness so that shoppers seek out its name in garments. Consequently, its brand needs to work on two levels – the trade market of retailers, manufacturers and designers, and the consumer market of the end-user.

LYCRA® looks like it now has the right product at the right time. In a new book, called 'Millennium Mode', acclaimed designers like Donna Karan, Calvin Klein, and Kenzo say fabric technology is the most important factor shaping their visions for the twenty-first century. With this in mind, LYCRA® looks set to be in demand for some time to come.

Achievements

With over 90% global awareness, LYCRA® is one of the best-known brands in the world. Research by Interbrand ranks it among the top ten clothing and textile brands in the world – along with Levi's and Armani – while the Council of Fashion Designers of America rates it as one of the twentieth century's most important fashion innovations.

One of its success stories has been the development of Wool plus LYCRA® – the result of a strategic alliance between DuPont and The Woolmark Company which launched in 1996. The addition of LYCRA® to woollen garments greatly enhances their washability and ease of care – making wool a more popular material for designers and clothing manufacturers. Before LYCRA®, the industry had been achieving easy care performance by blending untreated wool with polyester, but this only worked if the wool content was kept below 60%. Using LYCRA® can give strong washability with up to 98% wool content.

NEXT plc was one of the first high-street chains to buy clothes made with the mixture in 1998. Strong sales and consumer enthusiasm led them to extend the range in 1999. The Wool plus LYCRA® programme now extends across fifteen international markets, making it one of the clothing industry's biggest success stories.

History

Before LYCRA® was invented in 1960, consumers took saggy, baggy, stretched and bunched clothes for granted. But when the DuPont scientist Joe Shriver perfected a revolutionary new fibre – code named K – that all changed.

The fibre had been in research for a decade and was originally intended to replace rubber in underwear. But then wider applications for the fibre quickly became apparent and a fashion phenomenon was born.

In the 1960s LYCRA® revolutionised beachwear, replacing thick and heavy swimsuits with light, quick-drying garments like the bikini. In 1968, the medal-winning French Olympic ski team became the first high-profile sports personalities to wear ski suits with LYCRA® – a trend that soon spread to other sports. By 1972 Olympic swimmers swore by the sleek, lightweight suits contoured with LYCRA®. The fibre soon became an integral part of performance wear for millions of amateur and professional athletes.

In the 1970s, the brand started to make an impact on the fashion scene, as disco fever and interest in fitness made leggings and figure-hugging leotards the look of the moment. Leggings and stretch jeans with LYCRA® are among the defining looks of the decade. By the mid-1980s, over half of all women's hosiery and underwear relied on LYCRA® for a close, comfortable fit.

During the 1990s, the position of LYCRA® in the sports market strengthened, developing hi-tech fibres, including LYCRA® Power compression shorts, which help reduce athletes' muscle fatigue. Active lifestyles took off with consumers, creating demand for flexible, comfortable, fabrics. This decade also saw the rising popularity of the fabric among men, with President Clinton giving the brand an important endorsement by sporting a suit made with LYCRA®.

Product

When 'fibre K' was invented in 1960, its genius was that it could stretch up to 600% and then retain its original length. Normal fabrics tend to have a small amount of 'give' and yet the skin can stretch up to 50% around the joints. This discrepancy between the flexibility of the skin compared to clothes lies at the heart of the success of LYCRA®. Its revolutionary stretchability has made it an indispensable product.

Never used alone, but blended with other fibres, LYCRA® is a man-made elastic fibre which adds movement, comfort, drape, shape retention

and wrinkle resistance. There are no natural or man-made clothing fibres that it cannot be mixed with. Very small amounts of it can transform the performance of a fabric – the amount of LYCRA® in a material can be as little as 2%. As it is invisible when used in clothing, designers have the freedom to build elasticity into clothes without compromising on appearance.

There are various ways of integrating LYCRA® with other fibres, depending on the function of the fabric. The degree and direction of elasticity depend on how much LYCRA® is used and how it is knitted or woven into the fabric. LYCRA® can be used in women's, men's and children's clothes, and even leather shoes.

DuPont has continued to innovate to keep LYCRA® at the cutting edge of sports and fashion technology. LYCRA® with Chlorine Resistance helps keep swimwear in peak condition for longer, and LYCRA® Power is specially designed to reduce muscle fatigue and increase endurance. LYCRA® Soft offers improved comfort for hosiery garments and LYCRA® 3D is a knitting technique that further improves appearance, comfort and fit. And for the ultimate in fashion watch out for Leather plus LYCRA®.

As a global brand, LYCRA® is in a good position to pick up information from a vast variety of end-user and manufacturer sources around the world to constantly improve the product.

Recent Developments

DuPont is constantly developing new LYCRA® propositions to expand its audience. Recently, notable developments include Denim with LYCRA®, which is being used by designers at Levi's, Mudd, Girbaud and Parasuco. LYCRA® Soft is a new type of LYCRA®, designed for body-shaping underwear that combines softness with comfort and strength. LYCRA® has even found a use in combination with leather, adding flexibility and comfort to shoes.

2001 sees DuPont pushing LYCRA® even more into the knitwear market, emphasising the benefits of combining it with cotton, linen and silk. New technology has allowed a much wider range of methods of knitting LYCRA® into fashion fibres than before, making it possible for designers to use it more creatively.

With this extended range of fibre solutions, LYCRA® has been progressively raising its profile among new audiences. Retailers like H&M and Marks & Spencer have been stocking more lines using LYCRA® targeting the children's and teen market, while NEXT plc, Armani, Marks & Spencer and Jeff Banks are among the names which have been successfully selling garments with LYCRA® to men. Overall, DuPont wants LYCRA® to become a brand name that consumers seek as part of their clothes buying.

Promotion

The promotional strategy of LYCRA® is essentially two-pronged. Its most important audience is the business partners who include the fibre in their clothes. But to do this, designers and retailers have to be convinced that there is strong consumer demand for clothes with LYCRA®. Consequently, it often uses consumer advertising to increase the penetration of its brand among trade partners.

In mid-1999, DuPont launched its biggest ever advertising push behind LYCRA®, investing $30 million in a campaign devised by Saatchi & Saatchi.

The global campaign is based on an 'enjoy the difference' positioning that market research revealed to be the key attraction of wearing clothes with LYCRA®. The fibre is marketed as a 'magic' ingredient which has functional and emotional benefits. The global campaign targets men, women and teens – a much broader audience than LYCRA® has attempted to target to date.

The objective is to dramatically extend the use of LYCRA® with new brand partners by growing demand for the fibre among trade users and consumers. For example, the brand has never actively targeted men before, who have a high awareness of the fibre through sports, but may not have considered it for their casual or fashion wear. For women, the ads attempt to shift association with LYCRA® away from its dominant position in the intimate apparel sector and build its profile in outerwear. For the trade, the ads communicate the benefits of marketing and product support offered by linking with DuPont.

The campaign is print-based, targeting every significant fashion community. However, TV, point of sale and the internet all play a part in the 2000 campaign and beyond. All executions show the carefree element that LYCRA® can bring to all types of clothing, showcasing the difference it makes in men's and women's ready to wear, sportswear, intimate apparel, hosiery and shoes. A smiling face logo is used to communicate the small levels of LYCRA® content that are needed to improve the performance and comfort of a garment. Compared to previous marketing, this campaign's target audience is 250% larger.

Brand Values

The LYCRA® brand has enviable levels of awareness among global consumers. Among the key market of upper-income fashion-conscious 18-54 year old women, research shows that it scores awareness levels of over 80%. The same data says that the brand is preferred to generic 'stretch' products like spandex, is looked for at point of sale and is associated with benefits across a wide range of fibres and garments.

The essence of the brand is defined as 'look better, feel better' – summing up the mixture of functional and emotional benefits of wearing LYCRA®. The benefits of feeling better about yourself because you can move more freely, look better and make a statement of individuality are extremely important elements of the brand's positioning. These characteristics are central to fashion becoming a part of the broad personal care market, as clothing is seen as an extension of the consumer's personality and sense of wellbeing.

As an 'ingredient brand' LYCRA® has to communicate its value to host products across a wide variety of sectors. Its strategy is to build value in a way that complements the host brands of designers and garment manufacturers, as opposed to interfering with their communication. The brand promise is that 'a touch of LYCRA®' makes clothes better and gives the wearer an emotional lift.

Things you didn't know about LYCRA®

LYCRA® is never used alone – it is always mixed with other fibres.

Pound for pound, LYCRA® has more holding power than rubber.

LYCRA® was originally designed to replace uncomfortable rubber elastic in underwear.

LYCRA® can stretch up to six times its original length and then revert to its normal size.

Madonna personified the 1980s fashion for wearing innerwear as outerwear, driving millions of women towards figure-hugging LYCRA®.

LYCRA® has played a key part in other fashion high points – Donna Karan used it to advocate stretch for working women and in the design classic, the bodysuit shirt.

Clint Eastwood wore a suit with LYCRA® on his wedding day.

MERCURY
ASSET MANAGEMENT

Market

The last three decades have witnessed an explosion in the market place for investment management services. Fund management has become glamorous and lucrative and the significant amount of merger and acquisition activity in this sector during the last five years is testament to the attractions of this growing business characterised by stable and growing fee income. As recently as the 1960s, an asset manager rarely had discretion over a client's investments and his role was more akin to that of a stockbroker. Companies and private individuals today are increasingly entrusting their investments to professionals whose success is measured against a mountain of benchmarks, indices and the performance of their competitors.

Providers of financial services were not renowned for their marketing skills. Undoubtedly, things have changed. The stock market has become increasingly accessible to retail investors. In consequence, institutions associated with it have become more marketing literate. And, slowly but surely, they are becoming aware of the value of branding.

This process has been accelerated since the 'Big Bang' of 1987 and globalisation of financial products. This meant open competition. And competition has convinced firms of the need to differentiate themselves.

Mercury managed successfully to ride this wave of change. It stuck to the underlying principle that the brand must truly reflect everything about an organisation.

Despite a succession of significant changes to its ownership and market place, it has remained true to its roots. It has now been entirely integrated into the newly branded Merrill Lynch Investment Managers (MLIM) which sits at the peak of the global asset management market.

Achievements

There can be no surer way to disengage a reader than to quote a plethora of financial statistics. Performance figures have become manipulated by marketing men. And the financial supplements have become battlegrounds for the performance-obsessed providers of mutual funds.

Out of the many achievements Mercury could boast, three simple ones follow. By 1993 Mercury had become the tenth most profitable quoted company in the UK. By 1995 it owned for its clients 5% of the entire London Stock Exchange. Combined with Merrill Lynch's various asset management arms, the integrated entity Merrill Lynch Investment Managers now manage over $560 billion globally. It is fast approaching its ultimate goal – becoming the world's leading asset manager.

History

Despite roots that are deeply imbedded in the City of London, Mercury only became an independent entity in 1987 when 25% of its shares were floated on the London Stock Exchange.

Its people had previously been working within SG Warburg, the merchant bank that had built up an asset management arm in the 1960s and 1970s. Until 1987, the business was called Warburg Investment Management. This incorporated Mercury Fund Managers.

The origin of the Mercury name within the business has been the subject of much conjecture. 'Mercury' is an emotive word. Those with Classical leanings have argued ferociously that in Roman legend, Mercury originated as a god of commerce – an ideal image for a financial firm. His name came from the Latin word 'mercari' meaning to deal or trade.

Later he came to be associated with the Greek god Hermes, adding responsibility for messages to his duties. The Classical school has augmented its case by pointing to Roman coins where he is often depicted holding a moneybag – another contender as the reason for the choice of name.

The Scientists present an entirely different argument. They point to the planet Mercury that sits close to the sun and is associated with heat and light. Furthermore, they explain that Project Mercury launched the first American into space in 1961 – an innovative, technologically advanced, exciting venture.

The truth is, perhaps, stranger than these well-worn theories. Siegmund Warburg, the fabled mastermind behind the development of the Warburg empire, had a deep respect for his chief executive, Henry Grunfeld. The two worked together over decades. Warburg found the perfect way to acknowledge his debt to Grunfeld. He noticed that his initials also denote the chemical name for Mercury. And so the name was born – owing less to rocket science and classical legend than to a particularly talented and dedicated employee.

In 1995 SG Warburg was brought by Swiss Bank Corporation. In November 1997, Merrill Lynch, the leading global finance services provider and the largest securities firm, (see Merrill Lynch entry) acquired the then fully independent Mercury Asset Management. By 1997, Merrill Lynch Chairman Dave Komansky had described Mercury as a jewel in his business' crown.

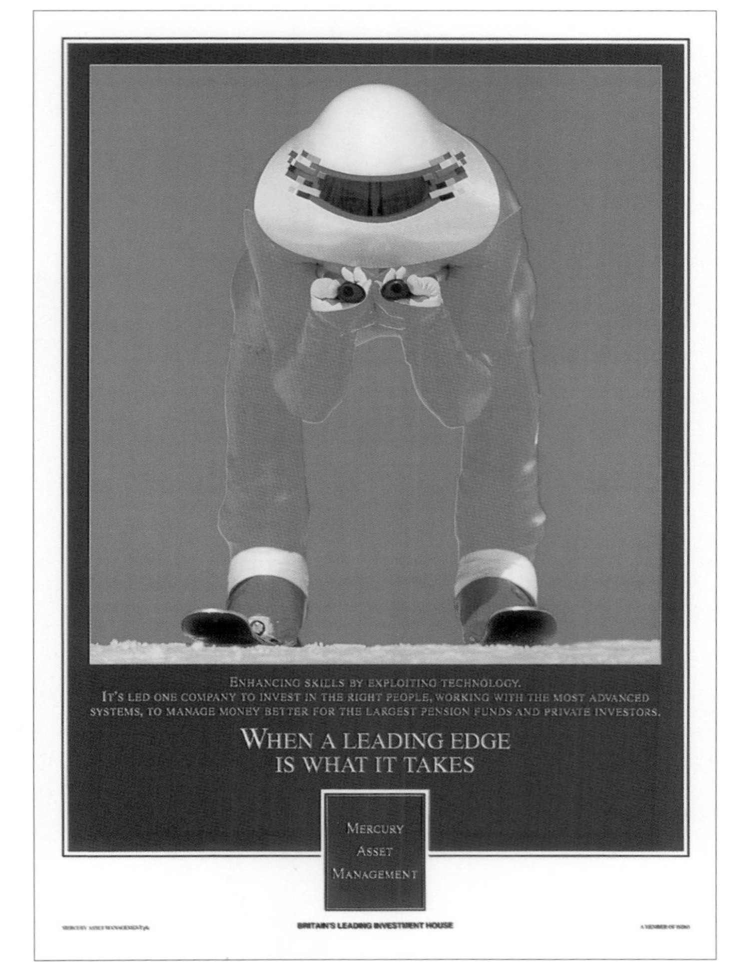

Product

Mercury is now a product label within the integrated Merrill Lynch Investment Managers. As a stand-alone company it has stood for rigorous and 'active' fund management processes. And it inherited from Warburg a reputation for an 'intellectual' approach to business.

As the last century drew to a close, it was growing at a phenomenal rate. And it fostered a burgeoning product range. It managed funds on behalf of governments, companies and private individuals around the world. It developed a range of mutual funds that made its expertise available to small investors.

The acquisition by Merrill Lynch created a

magnificent opportunity. Mercury's outstanding fund management capability and Merrill Lynch's distribution outlets globally were a perfect match. The two businesses complimented each other perfectly. Merrill Lynch's asset management strengths were in money-market funds and US mutual funds. Mercury's strengths were in active global equity and fixed income management but it had yet to develop its capability in the huge and rapidly growing US fund management market. The combination was transforming.

The newly integrated Merrill Lynch Investment Managers employing over 4,000 employees worldwide has drawn these strengths together. And so, although Mercury is now a product label rather than a business name, it comprises a fundamental part of the new business.

Recent Developments

The newly integrated division is one of four within Merrill Lynch & Co. Its relationship with its parent enables Merrill Lynch Investment Managers to leverage off its world class distribution capabilities and global reputation, whilst developing its own distinctive approach to investment services.

Merrill Lynch Investment Managers is committed to fulfilling its clients' investment and service goals. It has asked hundreds of its clients how it can move closer to their vision of the 'ideal' asset management company.

Clients responded by saying that they wanted to be managed locally, by people who understood their specific market needs. This is how the new division has been structured – regional teams have been drawn together by a common culture, global management, and shared resources.

The philosophy that draws the division together is that Merrill Lynch Investment Managers should use its expertise across the investment spectrum to provide its clients with an intelligent and comprehensive approach to their every investment need. So its experienced professionals manage passive, active or fixed income, cash, equity, hedge funds and private equity. This means that clients can choose the right investment solutions to meet their needs. And they can be confident that they are being offered the very best investment advice.

Promotion

Mercury's advertising has historically taken place at a product level. And within the new brand architecture, there remains scope for creative product campaigns.

Although Mercury has been best known for its relationships with institutions, its promotional activities have tended to focus on its retail clients within the UK.

Over the past fifteen years, Mercury's work has been developed with award winning subtlety and creative flair. As a general rule, executions have attempted to appeal to its clients' desire for high performing funds. But within an increasingly cynical and informed market place, the days of selling funds through performance graphs and tables are over.

The 'Cat and the Cream' campaign won wide acclaim for its subtlety and simple imagery. The idea that any client of the company could expect the best of both worlds highlighted the company's intelligence and client focus. The campaign was mainly carried out on posters and was followed by, among others, the 'PEPamint' and 'AppetISA' executions.

As Mercury expanded into Europe in the 1990s, its range of funds grew significantly. These were marketed under the 'Mercury Selected Trusts' banner. The key to their promotion has been the strapline 'Investing with Intelligence'.

This has been translated into a campaign that shows various pursuits where intelligence is required to achieve success. 'Intelligence' is a key attribute within the Merrill Lynch Investment Managers brand. So these advertisements fit perfectly within the divisional personality.

Brand Values

During the 1960s and 1970s, branding was an alien concept for many banks and investment management companies. In the past few years, this lack of understanding has been addressed. Mutual funds bearing the company name have featured in some innovative and catchy advertising campaigns highlighting Mercury's intelligence and high performance record.

The newly integrated Merrill Lynch Investment Managers' essence, and that of its Mercury products is clear cut and draws heavily on Merrill Lynch and Mercury's tradition and strength. The business inspires confidence in its clients. They are able to embrace the future with optimism, knowing that Merrill Lynch Investment Managers has the most informed view of the world's financial markets. And this is backed up by its integrity. It is rigorous and client focused.

It believes that to play in the asset management business, a company requires good performance, research capabilities, insight and experience. And Merrill Lynch Investment Managers stands out in a crowded marketplace because of its integrity, client focus, innovation, passion and quality of communication.

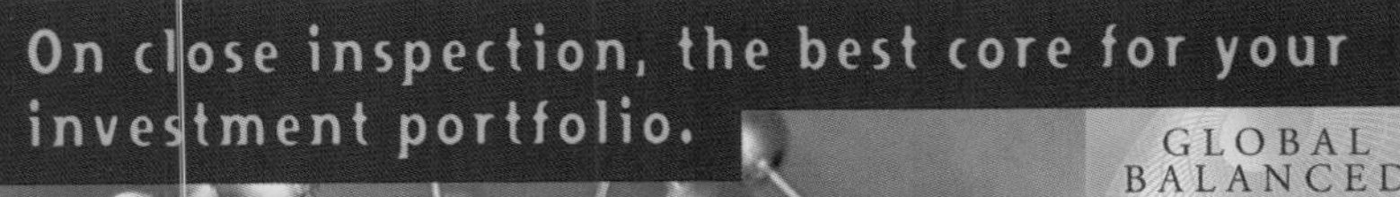

Things you didn't know about Mercury Asset Management

The merger of Mercury Asset Management and Merrill Lynch Asset Management in February 1998, at a stroke created the third biggest asset management firm on the planet.

The business has grown fast in Asia Pacific in recent years. Fortuitously, in Mandarin Chinese, the word 'Mercury' means 'Rising Star'. Phonetically, it can also mean 'Rising Wealth'.

Merrill Lynch Investment managers now manage over $560 billion globally.

Mercury was named after Henry Grunfeld, whose initials create the chemical symbol for mercury.

Merrill Lynch

Market

Merrill Lynch is a leader in global financial services, serving the needs of institutional and individual investors, corporations and governments in 43 countries around the world.

It is the world's largest securities firm with over 19,000 financial consultants and stock exchange memberships in 28 countries. It is the top-rated research firm in the world, with over 800 debt and equity analysts in 26 countries monitoring the performance of over 3,700 international companies.

Merrill Lynch has ranked as the largest underwriter of stocks and bonds for the past eleven years. It is among the top three investment banking advisory groups, and, with client assets of around $1.8 trillion, it is the undisputed leader in planning-based financial advice and management. The firm is active in all the world's major financial markets, and to cover this geography, Merrill Lynch has 950 offices and 67,200 employees. Total net revenues are nearly $22 billion (1999), of which around 20% is generated in Europe, Middle East and Africa.

Achievements

Despite being a pioneer of twentieth century financial services, Merrill Lynch remained, effectively, a US retail brokerage firm until the mid-1970s. A quarter of a century ago, the company launched an ambitious growth strategy which succeeded in transforming the group from a primarily US business to a global enterprise, with strong capabilities across all key financial markets: debt; equity; investment banking; private client and asset management.

Reflecting the success of this strategy, the company has won many awards. These include IFR Financial Bond House of the Year 1999 and IFR Equity House of the Year 1999. The firm was also voted 'Best Investment Bank' by the Finance Directors of Europe's largest 350 companies in The Reuters Survey 2000, originated by Tempest Consultants.

A key plank of the company's growth has been the development of a world-class research capability. In the past year alone, the research team won five out of six Institutional Investor awards – an unprecedented feat - and collected the most awards in the annual Wall Street Journal All Star Analysts Survey (1999), for the third year in a row.

Merrill Lynch has brought more equity and equity-linked issues to market than any other firm over the past 25 years, raising $275 billion since 1974. Some of the landmark transactions it has managed include Walt Disney's $927 million issue in 1990 – the largest ever convertible bond issue at that time. In 1993, it completed a $782 million issue for Time Warner in a single day. Last year, it oversaw the 15.6 billion Lira IPO for Italy's Enel, the largest initial offering ever for a European firm, and the second largest ever in the world at that time.

History

Charles Merrill linked his name to Wall Street, irrevocably, when he started his own firm in January 1914 after working in New York's financial markets for eleven years. Months later, a friend Edmund Lynch joined him in the business.

From the start, Merrill established his name by making stocks and bonds accessible to middle-class customers. As he said at the time, his intention was to "bring Wall Street to Main Street". In the years directly following the Depression, Merrill Lynch executives strove to re-build the public's faith in the capital markets, selling stocks and shares as other salesmen would sell household accessories. This image earned them the nickname 'The Thundering Herd' – a label which stays with it to this day and was inspired by the firm's famous bull logo.

Although it took until after his death in 1956 for stock ownership to take off among the general public, Merrill is credited with starting the mass stock market ball rolling. This irresistible trend has culminated in millions of ordinary people who today own stock as part of their routine personal financial management.

During the late 1940s and early 1950s, Merrill Lynch soon became the best known brokerage firm in America. In 1958, this status was recognised when the firm was admitted to the New York Stock Exchange. At that stage, the firm had 126 branch offices, and $43 million in capital.

Up until the mid 1970s, Merrill Lynch remained primarily involved in the US retail brokerage business it had been so influential in creating. However, in the 1970s, it started to diversify. In 1976, it launched Merrill Lynch Asset Management, and in 1978, it acquired White, Weld & Co – an international investment banking firm. This marked its first step towards becoming a global capital markets player.

In 1982, recognising the potential of the Asia Pacific region, it opened a Hong Kong Office and in 1985 it became the first foreign securities firm to become a regular member of the Tokyo Stock Exchange. By 1988, it reached the top of the global debt and equity underwriting charts for the first time.

Between 1974 and 1998, the firm made twenty significant acquisitions, boosting its market shares around the world. For example, when it bought the leading UK broker, Smith New Court, in 1995, it became a leader in UK, European and South East Asian equity markets.

It is no coincidence that many of the strategic investments were made in Europe. Merrill Lynch's Europe, Middle East and Africa geographic region is one of the largest and fastest growing parts of the business. To capitalise on the extraordinary opportunities emerging in Europe with the advent of the euro and overall strong economic growth prospects, Merrill Lynch has rapidly grown its regional capabilities in recent years. In 1994, the company had 28 offices in sixteen countries – by 1999 this had grown to 51 offices in twenty countries. It has also increased the number of currencies it does business in from 39 to 73 even after the introduction of the euro.

Product

Merrill Lynch's investment banking division provides financing and strategic advisory services to corporations, institutions and governments around the world. With its powerful research resources and global reach, the firm can bring formidable intelligence to its client relationships. It has more analysts covering more companies than any other house.

Its investment banking services are widely used by corporations to advise on mergers and acquisitions. Recent deals Merrill Lynch has been involved in include the Royal Bank of Scotland's takeover of NatWest; and Vodafone's

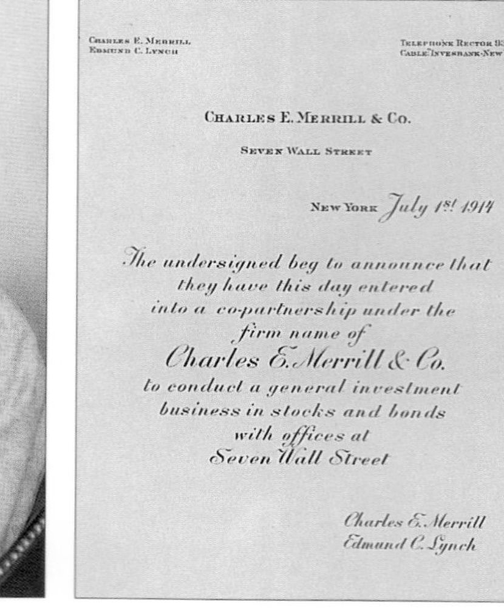

Charles E. Merrill
Edmund C. Lynch

Telephone Rector 9377
Cable "Invesbank-New York"

Charles E. Merrill & Co.

Seven Wall Street

New York July 1st 1914

The undersigned beg to announce that they have this day entered into a co-partnership under the firm name of

Charles E. Merrill & Co.

to conduct a general investment business in stocks and bonds with offices at Seven Wall Street

Charles E. Merrill
Edmund C. Lynch

acquisition of Mannesmann - Europe's largest ever.

The Debt and Equity groups provide issuers and investors with access to world markets through the global underwriting, trading and distribution of stocks, bonds, government securities, municipal securities, convertibles, derivatives and interest rate swaps. Merrill Lynch's global footprint makes it the biggest equity trader in many markets, including the UK and the US. Approximately 55% of its equity revenue is now derived from outside the US.

For US and international private clients, including individual households, small to mid-size businesses and regional financial institutions, Merrill Lynch provides financial planning, private banking and investment services through its network of financial consultants and private bankers around the world.

Merrill Lynch Investment Managers (MLIM) is one of the world's largest active asset managers and mutual fund providers, offering over 200 fixed-income, equity and money market mutual funds.

Merrill Lynch's asset management division, significantly enhanced by the 1997 acquisition of Mercury Asset Management, now has a pre-eminent asset management capability in Europe and across the world, managing assets exceeding $557 billion for clients including 103 of the Fortune 200 companies, 54 FTSE-100 companies, and 25 of the top Japanese corporates. The group offers 259 mutual funds to over 500,000 retail investors, and is one of the world's largest active managers.

The Global Securities Research and Economics Group offers equity, fixed income and economic research services to institutional and private clients worldwide. Last year, Merrill Lynch came out on top of nearly every major poll and ranking of research teams, making it unquestionably the world's leading research house among financial services firms.

Recent Developments

The internet represents one of the biggest challenges and opportunities for Merrill Lynch and the group is in the midst of a major overhaul of its online services. Like many financial institutions, Merrill Lynch faces both challenges and opportunities from the internet – online trading for private investors is already a massive market, which the firm simply had to get involved in.

In July 1999, Merrill Lynch announced a new model for its internet-based activities for US private clients. Combining its advisory and research capabilities with a powerful technology platform, its new Unlimited Advantage product gives US clients access to information, advice and guidance, financial planning, cash management, investment, asset and liability management, and e-commerce services, as well as online trading of stocks, bonds and mutual funds. It also provides real-time positions and pricing, enhanced access to Merrill Lynch research, and portfolio management tools. The new service is intended to make Merrill Lynch a one-stop financial services portal, also offering a range of e-commerce services through third-party partnerships. In addition, in December last year it launched ML Direct, an online trading product for US investors who prefer to develop their own investment strategies. Within a short rollout period ML Direct has already been rated number two by Forrester, and is one of only three US brokerages to receive four stars by Barron's. While both products are based in the US, Merrill Lynch is also in the process of launching similar products abroad.

On 18th April 2000, Merrill Lynch and HSBC announced that they were to create a new company, forming the first global online banking and investment service. The new company serves individual customers across the world except in the US, providing the industry's most comprehensive and innovative range of online banking and brokerage services for consumers who prefer to make informed investment decisions for themselves. The company is co-branded 'Merrill Lynch HSBC' as a 50:50 partnership.

Ultimately, Merrill Lynch is quickly becoming as strong in the online financial world as it is in the offline environment. It intends to re-engineer all of its businesses to leverage its wealth of core skills and knowledge into an extensive online product offering.

Promotion

As early as the 1940s and 1950s, when Charles Merrill was trying to re-establish the public's faith in the capital markets after the Wall Street Crash, the company has had an imaginative approach to promotion. Then, it held conferences, published reports and literature designed to educate the public in the workings of the financial markets. It even took to the roads in 'campaign buses' spreading the word of stock market investing all over America. It invested heavily in advertising. In 1947, when Merrill Lynch was already the US's largest retailer of stocks, the firm spent $400,000 on advertising. One ad, in The New York Times, was typical of the approach. It read: 'What Everybody Ought to Know About This Stock and Bond Business.'

Nowadays, the firm continues to invest heavily in the support of its brand, with the identity of the bull always playing a prominent part. Thanks to its major re-engineering to increase its online services, the firm will be advertising much more to raise its profile as a financial web portal. This will include a lot of internet-based activity as well as mass media TV campaigns and high-profile sponsorships.

An example is a recent TV ad campaign for www.ml.com which aired during the 2000 Oscars ceremony. The campaign positions ml.com as 'The smartest place to invest online.'

Recently, Merrill Lynch was also the lead sponsor of the Art Nouveau 1890-1914 exhibition at the Victoria and Albert Museum (V&A) in London, which ran from 6 April-30 July 2000 – the exhibition was chosen because it tied in so well with Merrill Lynch's own brand values.

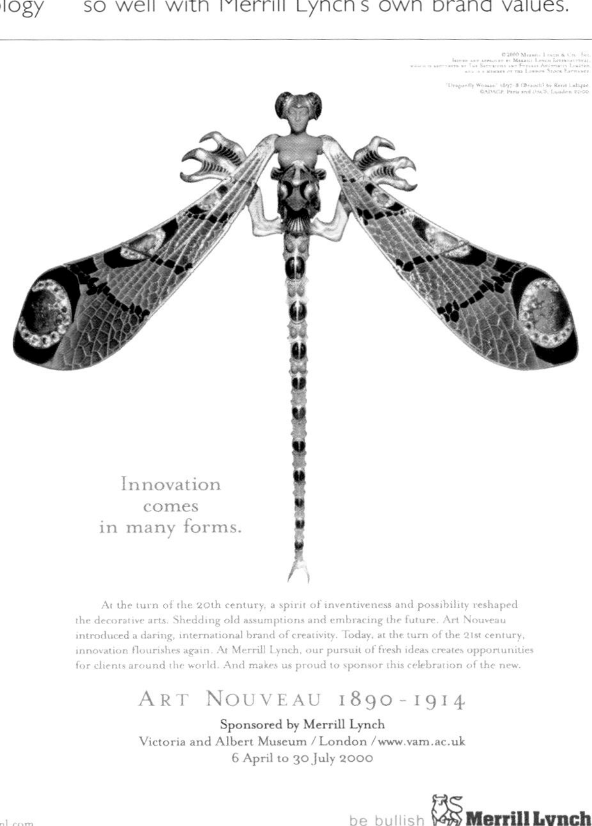

Brand Values

Merrill Lynch's operation is founded on five key principles: Client Focus; Respect For The Individual; Teamwork; Responsible Citizenship and Integrity. The firm's founder, Charles Merrill, remains a big influence on its brand values. Charlie Merrill insisted that clients' interests should always come first. He also had a pioneering populist view of financial services – as evidenced by his promotional roadshows – and this respect for the individual remains the firm's 'Golden Rule', both for customers and employees.

Merrill's aim of 'Bringing Wall Street to Main Street' is still relevant through the firm's commitment to Responsible Citizenship. Merrill Lynch is an advocate of employee volunteer schemes and community involvement. This guides its commitment to sponsorship and support of the arts, education and the community.

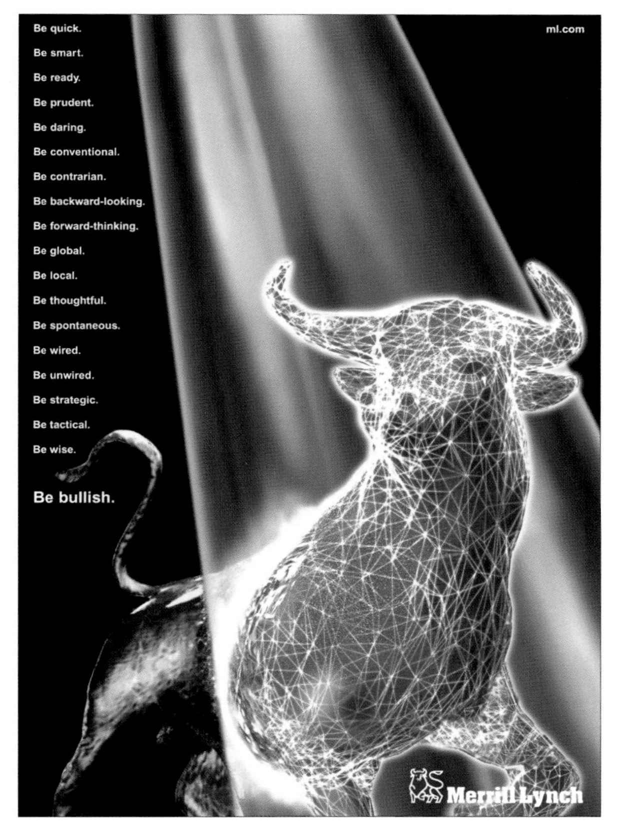

However, its most important brand value is its overwhelming sense of optimism, highlighted by the 'Be Bullish' campaign. Having brought Wall Street to Main Street to the World, the electronic bull symbol and its inherent values of optimism and intelligence define the company in the twenty-first century. The company defines its core-brand values as: Intelligence, Inventiveness, Client-focus, and Essential (i.e. essential to the global markets). Bullishness, and the informed optimism it represents, differentiates the Merrill Lynch brand.

Things you didn't know about Merrill Lynch

Charles E. Merrill played semi-professional baseball in Mississippi before finding his true talent on Wall Street, while Edmund C. Lynch was selling soda fountain equipment.

In 1951 Merrill Lynch opened its first European office in Geneva, Switzerland.

Merrill Lynch was the first US securities firm to open an office in China, in 1994.

Merrill Lynch was the first Wall St firm to issue an annual report, in 1941. At the time, in the cloak and dagger world of New York finance houses, such financial transparency was unheard of.

Michael Page

INTERNATIONAL

Market

Even discounting the astounding growth of recruitment services on the internet, the traditional office-based terrestrial recruitment industry is a multi billion pound market worldwide. Its growth rate over the last ten years has been phenomenal, variously calculated at between 8-15% per annum.

As part of this global marketplace, Michael Page International is a world brand leader in the recruitment of highly qualified and skilled management for organisations and businesses across nearly every sector of industry, commerce, public bodies and the professions.

The rapid reduction of labour market controls and regulations has fuelled the market and led to the movement of labour at all levels across national and international borders. As a result, Michael Page International is competing in an extremely dynamic and increasingly global marketplace.

Achievements

Specialising in very specific and narrow markets has been the key factor in the company's exceptional growth from a small London based consultancy to an international group with offices in every continent. This specialisation means that clients and job applicants can directly access their relevant markets and receive the same standards of professionalism and corporate philosophy from one location to another and from one discipline to another. There is also the added value of specialist knowledge of local situations. This policy of specialisation, created and developed by Michael Page International, established a new level of expertise and service which revolutionised the conduct of recruitment assignments worldwide.

The company's specialist knowledge and record of building strong client relationships has been enhanced by its state of art computerised recruitment systems. Michael Page International has invested heavily in the development of these systems which are accepted to be amongst the most innovative in the business. For example, Michael Page International was the first in the recruitment industry to develop a computerised international applicant network, providing an instantaneously accessible consultant database of job vacancies and applicants the world over.

With over 1500 consultants working in 50 offices worldwide and a leading internet recruitment service, Michael Page International has achieved brand leadership in serving the recruitment markets in which it operates. It also became the first recruitment and selection group to have its shares listed on the London Stock Exchange.

The company has achieved some other notable firsts. It was the first to develop a pan-European network exclusively using nationals of the specific countries into which it was expanding. It was also the first recruitment and selection company to establish a bespoke consultant training programme covering all operational and management aspects of the selection business.

History

The Michael Page recruitment business was established in 1976 by its eponymous founder who came from the oil industry, and Bill McGregor from the brewing industry. Bill McGregor remains part of the management team.

The company was founded in London principally to recruit accountants for industrial clients. Within ten years it had built a network of offices throughout the UK and continental Europe, and had expanded to cover recruitment in the legal, marketing, sales, information technology and banking sectors. Further expansion soon followed in Australia, the Far East and the United States of America.

Product

The Michael Page International brand has been developed along two central and connected fronts. Firstly, the creation of specialist consultancy teams to recruit in the disciplines in which they themselves are qualified. Thus the company has bankers recruiting for banks, salesmen recruiting sales professionals, accountants recruiting accountants and so on. Secondly, the business operates on a global network to facilitate the international movement of skilled management.

Michael Page International has developed its brand to signify efficiency and quality in recruitment services. Working with the most important assets an organisation possesses – its people – Michael Page International's recruitment service provides an unrivalled level of expertise and market penetration. It operates at a personal level where consultants get to know both clients and applicants. Those personal relationships are enhanced by the company's specially-designed IT systems which provide instantaneous access to information on applicants and job vacancies worldwide. The advantages of this network recruitment system to job applicants is obvious. However another factor is the assistance to multi-national clients whose global recruitment requirements can be catered for through one point of contact, wherever that may be.

Recent Developments

Although the company continues to expand its terrestrial office network with new offices recently opened in Italy, Spain, Portugal and Brazil, the most exciting and important recent development has been the establishment of www.michaelpage.net, the company's online recruitment website. The world knows that the e-business arena offers tremendous potential and Michael Page International has long been active in developing a website which would provide job information, in addition to advice, guidance and information to both active and passive job seekers. Employers can also take advantage of the global information available on the site on positions and salaries throughout the world. Other offerings in certain niche markets include tools to help candidates create CVs online and news for the individual professions.

Although essentially a transactional tool for promoting business over the internet, www.michaelpage.net, in its application concentrates on the information sharing potential of the net which directly and indirectly presents opportunities in its various specialist market places.

Since www.michaelpage.net was launched, traffic has increased even faster than the company's anticipated projections and this enormous success has established the site within the top fifty most visited in the UK alone.

Consequently, the internet and the new technologies such as Wireless Application Protocol (WAP) and interactive digital TV are enabling Michael Page International and other players in the industry to add innovative value in its service to clients and applicants.

Promotion

The recruitment industry, which is rapidly coming to terms with the digital and internet revolution, also continues to use the more traditional methods of search and selection. The main element of this is recruitment advertising in the press and other printed media. Michael Page International is a market leader in the classified advertising pages of national and trade press worldwide. For example, in the UK it is the industry's biggest advertiser, significantly ahead of its nearest rival. Similarly it holds a leading position in France, The Netherlands and Australia.

The quality and creative content of the company's advertising and other recruitment publications has been an important factor in promoting the company and its over-riding objective of excellence of service. The critical acclaim that its work has received reflects the professionalism and innovation in an area in which it is frankly difficult to achieve these qualities.

The company's global offices, where close links and relationships have been established with local organisations, is another significant factor in promoting the recruitment services of Michael Page International to a wide audience. This local presence also greatly assists the company achieve an extremely high level of local market penetration.

The internet has also become a major promotional channel. The development of online recruitment services has considerably increased the opportunities for promoting the Michael Page International brand to approximately ten million people around the world who use the web to seek job information. The company has used the popularity of the internet to its advantage. A good example of online brand promotion was the Michael Page International sponsorship of the 1999 Rugby World Cup. Its involvement with the event saw recruitment registrations increase by over 64% throughout the first ten days of the tournament. As www.michaelpage,net grows, the company will forge further alliances with other high quality brands to ensure Michael Page International continues to be promoted to a well-targeted international audience.

The internet also helps the company target new clients, especially in places where it does not have an office – such as South Africa. For candidates in those countries looking for international job opportunities, the website is an extremely useful resource.

Brand Values

The Michael Page International brand value is reflected primarily in the quality and expertise of its consultancy and support staff. The company's policy is to recruit and train its staff to be the best in the business. Secondly, the Michael Page International brand is identified as a specialist brand with its individual businesses operating in specific markets and disciplines. Thirdly, the Michael Page International brand is a global brand which sets common standards of excellence of service together with continuity and certainty of operational effectiveness throughout its global operations.

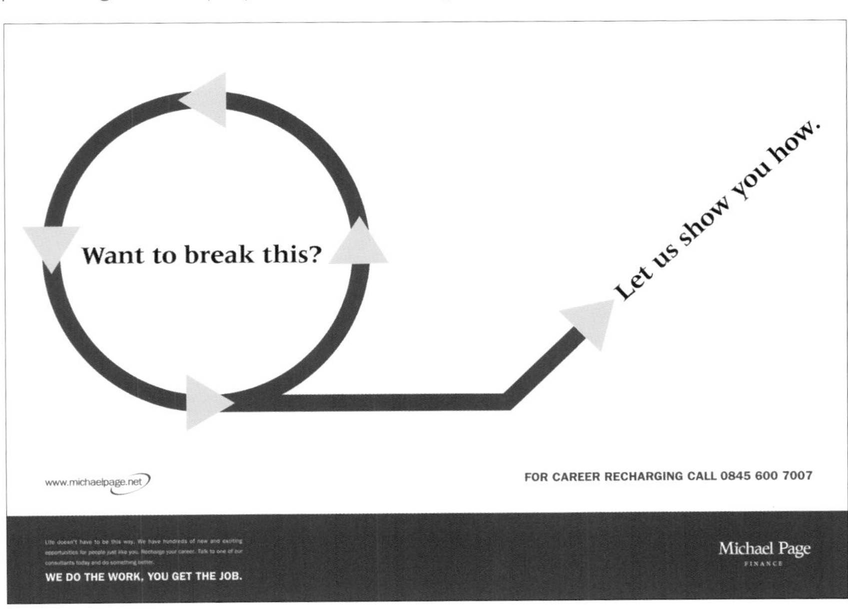

Things you didn't know about Michael Page International

Michael Page International's Chief Executive, Terry Benson, has twice been in the Winners Enclosure at the famous Cheltenham National Hunt Festival. His horses Kissair and Tiutchev have both been festival winners.

In 1978 the company's first office outside London was opened in Manchester. The board minute states "it was decided to open an office in Manchester solely on the basis that if we can be successful there, we can be successful anywhere."

Michael Page International receives an estimated 100,000 unsolicited applications every year from would be job seekers.

In pre-internet days, the fastest piece of recruitment carried out in Michael Page International's London office was when a candidate was interviewed at 8.30am, sent to the client for interview at 11.00am and accepted the position at 12.00 noon, commencing work the following Monday.

An applicant who was interviewed after lunch by a panel of three at a famous FMCG (fast moving consumer goods) company suddenly woke up with a start and found himself alone in the interview room. His interviewers had all tiptoed out when he fell asleep. He didn't get the job.

One London-based chartered accountant was offered 34 positions within six months. He turned them all down.

Microsoft®

Market

As technology continues to change at a breakneck pace, Microsoft's market is mushrooming. Although the personal computer will undoubtedly remain at the heart of computing at home, in education and business, other devices and appliances – from handheld computers to WAP phones – are heralding the dawn of the 'PC Plus' world.

Increasingly, software will be delivered via the internet and the boundaries between software products and online services are likely to blur. Microsoft is supremely positioned to take advantage of this trend, by providing the dedicated software and tools which make accessing this global database easier.

Just a handful of figures indicating the growth of the networked economy show how dynamic a market this is. In March 2000, there were an estimated 300 million people in the world hooked up to the internet, mainly connecting via conventional PCs. But that figure will soar as people access it via different devices. For example, Yankee Group forecasts that there will be one billion mobile internet devices in use around the world by 2003. And that's not including internet access via the TV. According to Forrester Research, 80 million European households will be using interactive TV to go online by 2005.

Achievements

In a little over 25 years, Microsoft has risen to become arguably the most influential company in the world. When he founded his company, Bill Gates articulated a vision that there would be "a PC on every desk and in every home". Already, he has almost achieved that dream. Nearly every business certainly has a PC on most desks and home computer usage is rising all the time. Currently, around 60% of homes have PCs. What's more, a high percentage of them run on Microsoft's Windows operating system and run Microsoft software.

According to Interbrand, Microsoft is now the world's second biggest brand behind Coca-Cola. Its brand value is calculated to be £35.4 billion, compared to £52.4 billion for Coke. But Microsoft's brand is worth significantly more than names as famous as IBM, General Electric, Ford, Disney and McDonald's.

However, Microsoft's most important achievements have been to make software that has enabled everyone to benefit from computers. It made the operating system for the first PC: the now ancient-sounding MS-DOS. It introduced the first ever computer mouse and the most widely used word-processing programme, Microsoft Word. And, of course, it gave us the now ubiquitous graphical interface that made it possible for anyone to use a computer – Microsoft Windows. With Windows, Microsoft truly put the 'personal' into the PC, making IT accessible to billions of people around the world.

Its innovations have constantly made computers easier to use. It was the first to exploit the concept of 'wizards' and 'toolbars' in its applications to simplify complex tasks. The integration of internet protocols, HTML and DHTML into Microsoft Windows 95 and 98 was another major innovation in operating systems and design.

In the UK, Microsoft has grown from a company of only five employees in 1980 to an organisation employing over 1000 people in 2000. Worldwide, Microsoft now employs over 35,000 people.

History

Microsoft was formed in 1975, in Albuquerque, New Mexico, by Bill Gates and Paul Allen. Together, they developed the first computer language programme written for a personal computer. The language was called BASIC and the computer was an Altair 8800.

The Microsoft trade name was registered in 1976, when Gates was still only twenty years old. At the time, he was still studying at Harvard and running the new business part-time. Meanwhile, BASIC became the language of choice for the burgeoning computer industry.

A milestone was reached in 1981, when IBM launched its first personal computer. It was based on Microsoft's 16-bit disk operating system, MS-DOS 1.0. This became the hardware standard for PCs, with nine out of ten of the world's 140 million computers using it.

1983 was a momentous year for Microsoft. It launched the Microsoft Mouse – the now ubiquitous hand-held pointing device. In this year it also launched its famous word-processing software, Microsoft Word, and the operating system that, arguably, lies at the root of the company's success – Microsoft Windows. Microsoft windows was an extension of MS-DOS, providing a graphical operating environment which is far more flexible and easy to use.

In 1986, Microsoft went public, issuing stock at $21 per share. At the same time, the company moved to its new corporate campus surrounding 'Lake Bill' in Washington. At this very early stage, Microsoft held its first international conference on CD-Rom technology.

1987 saw the launch of Operating System/2 – the result of a new joint venture with IBM. It also introduced Microsoft windows 2.0 and the first version of the hugely popular spreadsheet package, Excel for Windows. By the following year, Microsoft became the world's biggest software vendor, overtaking Lotus Development Corporation.

In 1990 Microsoft launched Windows 3.0 with a $10 million marketing campaign. 100,000 copies were sold in six weeks and company revenues reached $1.18 billion. This was the time that PC users started to take Microsoft Windows to heart. In 1991 four million copies of Windows 3.0 were shipped to 24 countries in twelve languages. By 1993, there were 25 million Microsoft Windows users in the world.

In 1994, the company launched a $100 million marketing campaign, coining the phrase, 'Where do you want to go today?'. The launch of Microsoft Windows 95 in August 1995 was the most successful Microsoft launch to date, with over one million units sold in the first four days. Soon after, the company heralded the dawn of the internet age with the launch of Internet Explorer 2.0. These were fitting milestones for the company's twentieth anniversary.

By 1996, Microsoft had reinvented itself to respond to the fast-growing popularity of the internet, launching MSNBC – an internet news and information network in conjunction with NBC. The following year, the US Justice Department filed the anti-trust motion against Microsoft which, in June 2000, eventually led to a judge decreeing that the Microsoft company should be split into two separate businesses. Microsoft is appealing that ruling and remains confident that at the end of the day the American legal system will rule in Microsoft's favour.

Product

Microsoft now has around 200 products and services. The principal brand in the stable is still Microsoft Windows. Windows 2000 has already sold over 1.5 million copies. The Microsoft Windows family of operating systems spans the complete range of computing needs, from handheld devices to network servers.

The Microsoft Office range of suites brings together the world's best-selling productivity applications used by business and personal users the world over. It includes the presentation software, Microsoft Powerpoint, the messaging and collaboration package, Microsoft Exchange and the spreadsheet programme, Microsoft Excel.

Microsoft BackOffice is a family of server applications and suites spanning email, database management, intranets, e-commerce and security. It includes the Small Business Server – a network solution providing essential tools to help businesses manage information and customers – and Site Server, a powerful intranet application. Site Server Commerce Edition is an enhanced version which allows businesses to conduct online transactions and set up channels for dealing with distributors and partners. Proxy Server is a firewall and web-cache application which provides secure internet access.

Microsoft Visual Studio is a suite of tools for creating enterprise and web-based applications. Nearly all world-class software, from the leading web browsers to mission-critical corporate applications is built using the Visual C++ development system. Visual FoxPro is used to create and manage high performance database applications.

Microsoft's online presence is organised under the umbrella of the Microsoft Network (MSN) portal. MSN helps consumers get the most from the web, with services and localised content for users around the world in 33 countries and regions and in seventeen languages. Services such as email, instant messaging, search, personal finance, news and weather information bring the everyday web to users worldwide, allowing them to stay in touch and personalise the web around what's important to them.

Recent Developments

After several years of development, Microsoft Windows 2000 Professional, Windows 2000 Server and Windows 2000 Advanced Server operating systems were launched in February 2000. From notebooks to high-end servers, the Microsoft Windows 2000 platform is the business operating system for the next generation of PC computing. Built on NT technology it is the best operating system for doing business on the internet. The combination of Microsoft Windows 2000 Professional and Microsoft Windows 2000 Server provides businesses with more complete end-to-end desktop management and distributed networking. This can be achieved by running them separately or with other operating systems.

In April 2000, Microsoft and its partners launched the Pocket PC powered by Microsoft Windows. This enables people to do more than just organise personal information – it allows them to keep in touch with their offices and daily lives when they are on the move. It is the first Microsoft product to feature ClearType technology, which enables easy reading of e-books with improved LCD screen clarity.

Microsoft's vision for the future is centred on the Internet User Experience (IUE) and Next Generation Windows Services (NGWS). Whereas some of Microsoft's competitors talk of a single technology helping a single website, Microsoft's vision is one of opportunity and interaction for many players – consumers, businesses and developers – all linked by a variety of devices, online and offline. This is the frontier where the next generation of user value will be added.

Promotion

Microsoft invests heavily in the support of its brand. In 1999, Microsoft UK was the 11th biggest computing advertiser.

On a business-to-business level, Microsoft has done some award-winning work. Its recent Direct Access Business Critical campaign promoted Microsoft's telephone support services for channel partners who need urgent help with their customers' IT problems. The campaign used cover-wraps on key industry magazines (Microscope and PC Dealer) personalised with the name of the subscriber in the text of the advert itself. This personalisation required the use of cutting edge technology, tailoring 30,000 individual magazines. This was followed up by a CD Rom and email newsletters directing channel partners to the Direct Access website. The campaign won an award for the most Innovative use of Media at the Business-to-Business Advertising Excellence Awards.

Another example of its business-to-business work was a campaign for Microsoft Passport, a tool to help businesses improve their websites through easier online registration and purchasing processes for customers. The campaign used the line, 'Make your website a commercial hit, not a financial miss' and used ads on the internet and in computing press. It also employed cover-wraps in titles like Revolution and New Media Age and sponsorship of online newsletters.

The company also regularly advertises other products in business magazines, promoting its different business-related services, such as building e-commerce and knowledge management solutions.

Brand Values

As the IT landscape is quickly changing, Microsoft is moving away from PC-centric usage to embrace a wider variety of devices and more networked solutions. To fit in with this, Microsoft has a new vision for the future: 'Empower people through great software – any time, any place and on any device.' This new vision is a re-invention of the Microsoft business, an overarching statement that directs its strategy from now on.

The brand has always been about how software makes life easier, encompassed in the famous question, 'Where do you want to go today?'. The central values of the Microsoft brand are innovation, diversity, partners, people and entrepreneurialism. Most importantly, it is a brand which is passionate about the exciting future of technology.

Things you didn't know about Microsoft

There are over 255 million users of Windows in the world.

Bill Gates is also a successful author. His 1995 book, 'The Road Ahead', held the number one spot on the New York Times bestseller list for seven weeks. His latest work, 'Business @ the Speed of Thought' has been published in 25 languages and is available in 60 countries.

Bill Gates started programming computers at the age of thirteen.

In 1997 pollsters Hart and Teeter ranked Microsoft as the most admired company in America.

More than 100 million PCs were sold in 2000.

MINTeL

Market

The explosion in the information industry has been brought about by the acknowledgement of the power of market research. It is now widely recognized that objective, independent analysis allows an unblinkered assessment of the current state and future potential of any given market.

The development of the internet has had a dramatic effect on the information industry. Predictions about the impact of internet technology have finally materialised, stimulating unabated growth for the sector. The launch of mintel.com has catapulted the Mintel brand globally. With immediate online access to the information purchased, reports are available 24 hours a day. Throughout the industry, the internet acts as both a threat and an opportunity. Organisations are no longer competing solely against UK-based companies, but a

multitude of concerns in an increasingly fragmented marketplace. Speed and ease of delivery are now the key differentiators, combined with the essential requirements for a seamless transition of brand values onto electronic media.

Achievements

Mintel is a rapidly expanding company. In the past five years the number of employees has doubled, as has the number of UK reports published. The company has also taken its Global New Products Database (GNPD) to the US, opening up an office in Chicago. The US operation has grown rapidly and now employs over fifty people, with the GNPD service company spearheading Mintel Group's entry into the US.

Collectively, the Mintel Group has over 2000 clients globally. Supplying the majority of the UK's blue-chip companies and an increasing number of global players.

With almost 30 years of market presence, Mintel has become both a business and a household name. The company is in the enviable position of achieving constant daily press coverage, with the press office receiving an ever-ending stream of enquiries. Furthermore, the company boasts a number of prominent speakers and consultants with regular media exposure.

Referred to in innumerable company brochures, Mintel is used as a source in presentations and government and trade publications. Frequently cited for PR purposes, the company provides an objective assessment of a market, guaranteeing trade credibility. Furthermore, Mintel has also assisted the flotation prospects of several companies, with data included in prospectuses and statement of accounts.

The latest company achievement is perhaps the most significant yet, Mintel being the first research organisation to offer reports instantly over the internet, permitting immediate online access to the product. The result – instant access 24 hours a day.

Mintel has played a crucial role in business lives for almost three decades, defining the consumer marketplace and providing an important benchmark for future industry growth.

History

Established in 1972, Mintel has earned itself the status as one of Britain's leading analyst of consumer markets. The company was the first to introduce reputable commissioned market research on a multi-client basis. In addition, it was also the first to produce computer-based statistical forecasts for mass-market research publication.

Mintel reports focus on consumer markets and topical issues, reacting to ever changing market conditions. The list of 500 reports has become progressively more specialised through the decades, with report titles ranging from red meat to teenage and cult magazines. Originally a provider of fmcg (fast moving consumer goods) and food and drink reports, the company has expanded into leisure, retail, financial, Ireland and, most recently, European markets. Perhaps the most famous of Mintel's reports is the annual British Lifestyles 'flagship report', the year 2000 seeing the 16th launch of this ever-popular compendium of consumer lifestyles – now the industry bible.

For over 25 years Mintel has also monitored the global fmcg market, supplying product

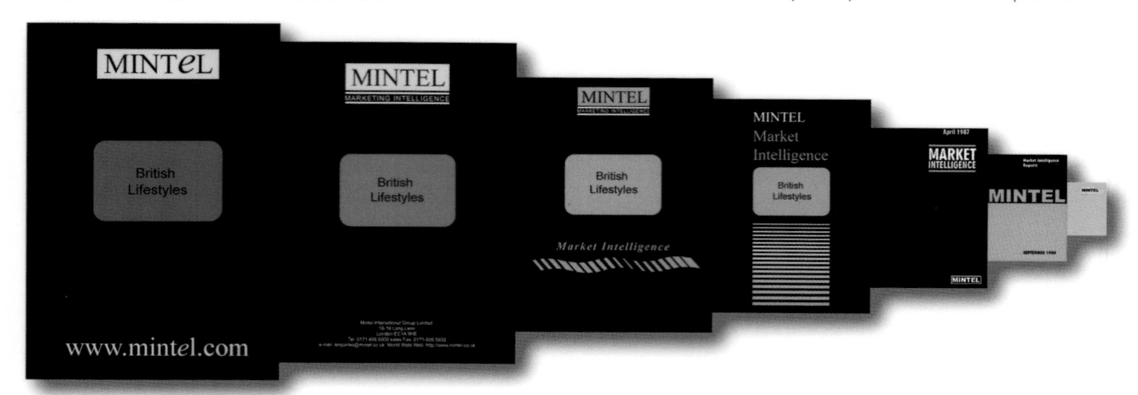

intelligence to companies across the world – culminating in the Global New Products Database or GNPD. The GNPD looks at worldwide new product developments as they happen, tracking over 41 food and non-food sectors in all key global markets across over 130 different countries, using a network of more than 500 country-based field researchers. Last year the database tracked some 50,000 new products globally. The monitoring of fmcg markets led to the development of POS+, the UK's premiere database tracking sales promotion activity throughout Britain. Two years ago, the company decided to focus on the US market, and has successfully expanded its product intelligence sector across the Atlantic.

Mintel's employees are all key components of its success – flexibility, creativity and drive have underpinned its success. A unique combination of market expertise, long-standing experience and youthful creativity ensures that the company remains the most dynamic among its peers.

Product

The bedrock of the Mintel brand is the Mintel market report. Every month, Mintel publishes 25 reports covering a wide range of consumer markets. Each report includes analysis of market sizes and trends, market segmentation, consumer attitudes and purchasing habits as well as assessing future and forecast data, which are converted into actionable marketing information. Mintel is renowned for its unique consumer research, commissioned exclusively for individual reports. It is this research, which brings an up-to-date and unique insight into topical issues of importance. The company virtually coined the word 'lifestyles', and was one of the first to realise that conventional ways of classifying consumers do not provide enough insight into behaviour and attitudes. Consequently, hundreds of special marketing-orientated groups have been created, from the 'hedonist' to the 'hearty & healthy', typifying consumer habits of the new century.

Mintel's Information Centre – MIC –

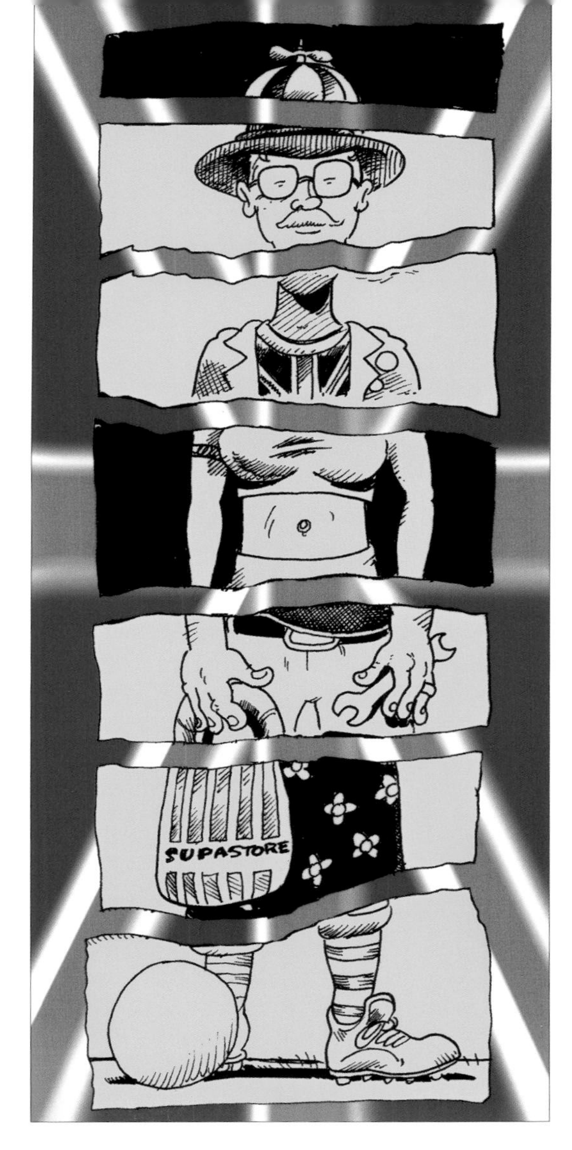

undertakes bespoke research and further analysis of consumer information. The MIC contains virtually all the raw material for the desk research work, comprising government statistics, consumer and trade association statistics, manufacturer-sponsored reports, annual company accounts directories and press articles. The latter are culled from over 200 publications, both British and overseas. All Mintel analysts have access to customised Market Size and Economic Database – a computerised database containing all areas of consumer spend as well as macro-economic and demographic factors which impinge on consumer spending patterns going back some twenty years.

Further services have been developed to meet the needs of the fast-moving product intelligence sector. In-house team researchers continually study trends in packaged consumer goods sectors. Global consumer products are analysed and sourced, and new products can be picked up and placed in the hands of clients if desired. Stores are monitored from Aruba to Zanzibar and Burkina Faso to Tahiti.

An extension to new product monitoring is the analysis of in-store sales promotion. POS+ allows manufacturers, retailers and marketing/advertising agencies alike to determine on-pack and on-shelf promotional activity adopted throughout Britain's retail stores. The entire food and non-food fmcg market is analysed – all 41 categories – and the results are presented by 30 different promotion types.

All Mintel services, from the range of reports to the GNPD and POS+, are supplied electronically and all clients are offered daily news updates on their specific industries.

Recent Developments

Launching mintel.com has proved to be more than a new revenue opportunity, it represents a refocus for the entire company. Business professionals do not have time to search for market data – they want it instantly, wherever they may be, at any time of day. By incorporating an e-commerce facility in mintel.com, the company has provided just that – market intelligence in e-seconds. The traditional battleground of price has been superseded as the speed of delivery or 'instant gratification' fuels demand. Browsing, choosing, purchasing and viewing immediately is the only way to satisfy this desire – all websites contain a contact form. Mintel is currently the only research company to process the order instantly and permit immediate online access to the product.

Key to the success of mintel.com is an internal infrastructure which enables effective management of online relationships. For any web-based company this is a unique challenge – email is an 'emotionless' medium – and Mintel expects traditional, more personal contact methods to survive significantly longer as companies strive to translate their core brand values onto this new media.

Indeed, the technological solution used by Mintel has potential across a number of industries, creating diversification opportunities and a number of 'spin-offs' for clients. Mintel is concentrating on strategic online relationships with key suppliers that can complement the brand.

As online relationships grow, customer relationship management increases in importance. Mintel has made this a core focus for the next year. Incoming enquiries have doubled, as has the size of the customer service department. Clients are regularly contacted for constructive comment and direct input into the product development process.

Promotion

Known for distinct yellow and black corporate colours, Mintel's internet development has been emphasised by its use of the electronic 'e',

in the brand name, together with the strapline 'market intelligence in e-seconds.' The launch of mintel.com was accompanied by an ongoing advertising campaign in key marketing and information press. All marketing and PR is carried out in-house by an established integrated team enjoying a wealth of experience across many industries. All Mintel employees are ambassadors for the brand, focusing on supplying more than just an information solution, but also the tools and instructions required for successful implementation within client companies. Mintel's marketing team regularly works with clients of internal communication teams to ensure effective usage of the Mintel Group products.

A sponsor of The Chartered Institute of Marketing's (CIM) national conferences for the last two years, Mintel also works with the CIM to promote the importance of market intelligence in any industry and enjoys the status of being the 'preferred information supplier' for all CIM members. On a lighter note, the company has worked in conjunction with several community projects and currently sponsors an up-and coming motorbike racer.

This year, the company has joined forces with the trade magazine Supermarketing as a sponsor of the retail Lunch Club, encouraging strategic business planning among senior business management in the retail sector.

Brand Values

What does the future hold for your business? What do your consumers want? What strategies are your competitors employing? What is likely to happen over the next few years?

The future of a company's market depends upon answering these questions effectively, questions which Mintel is able to answer.

The Mintel name provides reassurance and peace of mind – an independent and dependable view of a market or product gives a reliable benchmark upon which companies can measure their performance.

With dedicated editorial teams working solely with industry experts to ensure essential specialist sector knowledge, Mintel's links with manufacturers and retailers are unrivalled.

Mintel's aim is to help its customers achieve sustainable competitive advantage by providing the highest-quality content and widest coverage of consumer markets.

So established is the Mintel brand that its research is now used as a basis for marketing courses providing a marketing framework. A visit to a business/university library will reveal well-thumbed report copies and often a queue at the Mintel shelf.

Things you didn't know about **Mintel**

Since 1972 Mintel has asked almost two million consumers about their consumption attitudes and habits.

Mintel asks around 200,000 adults a year 1,500 consumer research questions.

Readers of Mintel research include Prince Charles and David Mellor.

You can submit business questions each day to Mintel's website.

Mintel has researchers in over 130 different countries worldwide.

When Mintel's World in a Shopping Basket was published in 1992, it was revealed that Iceland was by far the most expensive country of the fifteen surveyed - as a result, questions were asked in the Icelandic parliament.

Mintel research has revealed that: 15% of men don't use a deodorant; the Scottish are Britain's most charitable people; the British spend more than France, Italy and Spain collectively on fast food; and only 16% of British women are natural blondes.

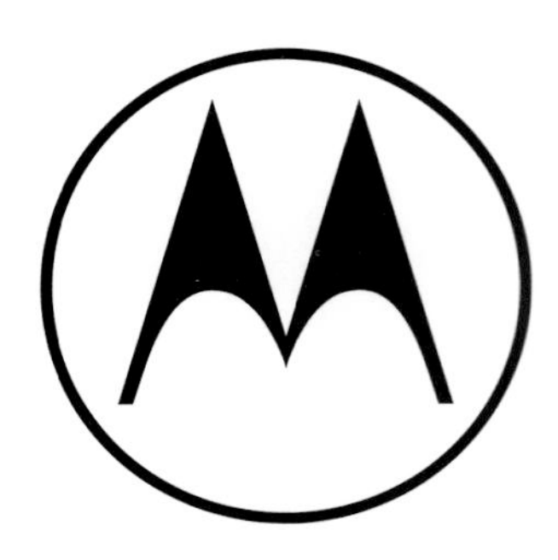

MOTOROLA

Market

The mobile phone market has grown almost ten fold over the past five years – a dynamic growth pattern that is expected to continue well into the new century. During 1999 sales of mobile phones hit 84 million units in Europe (Source: Dataquest) with the highest growth area coming from business and corporate users. 2000 saw sales reach approximately 100 million in Europe (Source: Dataquest) with 15% of new subscribers being business users.

Several factors have affected the rapid growth in this industry including the ready availability and affordability of pre-pay packs and internet access via mobile devices. Technological advances also means that a mobile phone is no longer used just for making calls. Consumers today can play games, listen to the radio, download and listen to music from the internet or even buy goods online – all via a mobile phone.

History

The beginnings of the company can be traced back to 25 September 1928, when two brothers, Paul V and Joseph E Galvin purchased a battery eliminator business and renamed it the Galvin Manufacturing Corporation.

Over many decades, the corporation expanded from the battery eliminator business into other areas such as the production of car radios – eventually supplying car radios for Ford, Chrysler and General Motors. In fact, this area of the business was so successful that in the 1930s Paul Galvin changed the company name to Motorola in order to link together the ideas of motion and radio. The now famous 'batwing M' corporate logo was not developed until 1955.

In 1948 Motorola entered the television industry, producing the first television to sell for under $200. More than 100,000 of these sets were sold in one year, catapulting Motorola into

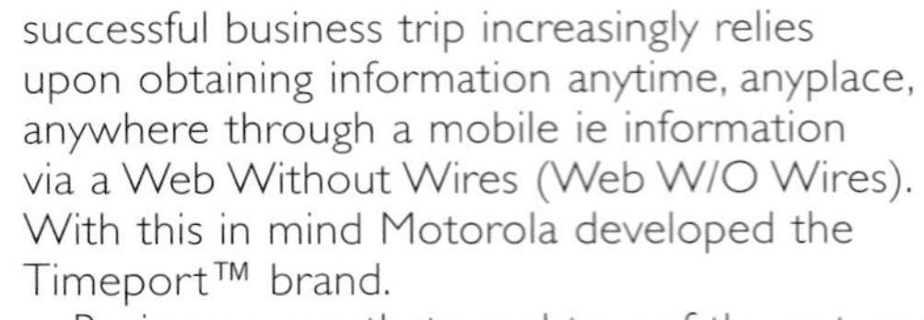

fourth place in the television sector. By 1964, in a joint venture with National Video, Motorola developed the first rectangular picture tube for colour television. The tube quickly became the standard for the industry.

In 1956 Motorola developed a new radio communications product – a small radio receiver called a pager. Hospitals were among the first to use pagers. As the Official Radio Communications Sponsor of the Olympic Games in 1984, Motorola provided a radio network comprising more than 10,000 pieces of equipment for the Summer Games in Los Angeles.

In 1987 Motorola said goodbye to its old business and produced its last car radio. Instead the company concentrated on its mobile phone business, developing a low cost secure telephone terminal to protect sensitive information relayed in voice and data telecommunications. Called the Secure Telephone Unit (STU-III), it is still used by governmental agencies and defence contractors.

Achievements

Motorola is a global leader in providing integrated communications solutions and embedded electronic solutions. Throughout more than 70 years of operation, Motorola has time and time again been first to bring new technology-led products onto the market place. These firsts include the development of the first portable FM two-way radio, the 'walkie-talkie' backpack radio. The creation of the first hand-held two-way AM radio for the US Army Signal Corps – a vital piece of equipment which enabled battlefield communications throughout Europe and the South Pacific during World War II.

As well as developing the first practical and affordable car radio, Motorola was also responsible for the innovation and launch of the first dual-band GSM 900/1800MHz mobile phone allowing greater coverage across Europe.

More recently Motorola's introduction of the world's first tri-band GPRS handset – the Timeport™ P7389i means that consumers benefit from high-speed connection to the internet or intranets.

Product

In the business world today, effective communication is no longer limited to the office. Instead, a successful business trip increasingly relies upon obtaining information anytime, anyplace, anywhere through a mobile ie information via a Web Without Wires (Web W/O Wires). With this in mind Motorola developed the Timeport™ brand.

Business users that need to surf the net need look no further than the Motorola Timeport™ P7389 – the first tri-band GSM (Global System for Mobile Communication) phone with web access. With a Motorola Timeport™ P7389 phone, information can be accessed from the internet while travelling the world. In addition, the Timeport™ P7389 phone gives business users secure access to company intranets – helping users to stay connected even when out of the office. Composing emails and other text messages on a numeric keypad is also easy, thanks to intelligent iTAP software used in the phone. The 'one key, one letter' software predicts the word that the user is trying to spell. Furthermore the Motorola Timeport™ P7389 phone's key features – such as placing calls and retrieving voice mails – can even be accessed by voice, thanks to a speaker dependent voice activation feature. A VoiceNote™ digital voice recorder allows up to three minutes of conversation to be recorded – perfect for 'noting' vital phone numbers or addresses.

Introduced to the market during the summer of 2000, the Motorola Timeport™ 250 combines stylish design together with hard core functionality. Offering all the normal features of Timeport™ P7389, this WAP enabled (Wireless Application Protocol) phone boasts an increased display size – a feature that makes it the ideal tool for business users who need to be able to surf the net while on the move.

The versatile Timeport™ P7389e combines internet access, mobile commerce and globetrotting capability in a single GSM tri-band compact handset. A third party electronic banking card allows users to buy tickets, trade stocks, or even bank on the move, as well as access information from the internet.

Finally the Timeport™ P7389i phone is the world's first tri-band GPRS (General Packet Radio Services) handset. Using GPRS technology, it gives consumers high-speed connection to the internet or corporate intranets and the benefit of being almost always on, always connected.

Recent Developments

GPRS technology is the next significant step after GSM – providing consumers with a fast and effective new way of transmitting data on GSM networks.

Once again proving its leadership in the development and implementation of new technology Motorola used this technology to conduct a world first demonstration of mobile e-commerce using WAP over a live GPRS network.

Subscribers are able to enter their preferences, credit card details and personal tastes for an evening at the theatre, cinema or any other social event of their choice via Motorola's concept solution and have tickets delivered directly to them. The system simply requires the user to enter particular preferences on the portal, such as number of seats, preferred location, type of entertainment, costs and even seating plans if required and allows instant booking confirmation, via the mobile handset and secure e-commerce technology.

The system gives consumers the freedom to enter in their preferences and personal information on a web-based portal and personalisation engine, and then to be informed when a solution matching those requirements is identified by the intelligent system. Details are sent straight to the mobile terminal for confirmation giving consumers the ultimate in control and information flow.

In the future, consumers will be able to update event information directly from Motorola's WAP-enabled wireless devices and even receive personalised alerts on their phones from their favourite venues to remind them about an event they have booked or bookmarked, all at the touch of a button.

Promotion

Motorola positions itself as a twenty-first century company which delivers wireless communication devices designed for individual consumers. However, getting this message across is not easy as consumers are being constantly bombarded with a mass of information regarding mobile phone communication. In order to try and differentiate themselves from this advertising clutter all Motorola advertising has a quirky, irreverent and humorous tone that brings the benefit of the feature to life for the user.

The overall communication strategy for the Motorola Timeport™ P7389 has been two-fold. Firstly, to communicate that the user can access the internet directly from the handset and secondly to communicate that this handset is the first truly global GSM phone (an important brand positioning statement for Motorola as they were the first manufacturer to launch a tri-band GSM mobile phone).

The benefits of internet access were communicated via a campaign known as 'Snake'. A television advertisement showed a hiker in a forest who stops for a drink of water. While resting, a snake climbs up his trouser leg. Despite being in shock, the hiker has enough presence of mind to pick up his phone and access the internet in order to search for 'venomous snakes'. Luckily he discovers that the snake that has climbed up his trouser leg is non-venomous. This campaign ran for a six-month period across Europe, Middle East and Africa and was supported by heavy weight print, outdoor poster and point of sale campaign.

The print executions depicted a long arm holding the phone and were produced with two different straplines, namely 'Pocket Internet' and 'Internet Unplugged'. This print advertising also launched the term Web W/O Wires to describe the fact that the internet can now be reached via a mobile phone ie with no wires involved.

To support the second key user feature in this handset namely the tri-band or Global GSM feature, Motorola developed a television advertisement that showed a businessman in three airports around the world desperately trying to locate his lost luggage by using his mobile phone. At each airport he is looking more and more tired and unshaven. At the last airport he sees his baggage on the aeroplane runway just as a truck drives over it.

Motorola firmly believe in an integrated marketing strategy. Therefore, strategic media campaigns which encompass TV, print, outdoor, point of purchase and direct mail elements are always supported by extensive public relations and trade marketing activity to customers and the sales force respectively.

Brand Values

The Motorola brand strives to link people's dreams with technology's promise. The Timeport™ brand has been designed with time aware, time efficient business users in mind. Time is scarce, schedules are full and being in control is a top priority.

To address these concerns, Timeport™ communications are built around the idea that a Motorola Timeport™ is a business tool that gives its users 'rights' – right time, right information, right decisions.

By using a Motorola Timeport™, business users can make sure that they are always up to date for informed decision-making – so that they can get the right things done at the right time.

Things you didn't know about Motorola

Motorola haven't always produced phones, – in 1930 'Motorola' invented the world's first car radio.

In a joint program with Ford and RCA, Motorola designed and manufactured the first 8-track tape players for the automotive market.

On its flight to Venus, Mariner II carried a Motorola transponder that provided a radio link spanning 54 million miles. Images of Mars were relayed back to Earth by similar equipment aboard Mariner IV in 1964.

In 1972 Motorola began to manufacture components for battery powered quartz watches.

Neil Armstrong communicated with the earth from the Moon using Motorola equipment.

NOKIA

Market

There's probably no hotter, hipper industry to be in at the moment than mobile communications. At the last count – guaranteed to be out of date by the time you read this – there were 450 million mobile phone users in the world. By the end of 2002, that number is predicted to reach one billion. It is estimated that of the 275 million phones sold in 1999, 78.5 million were Nokia units. That makes it easily the world's largest mobile phone manufacturer.

On top of this, Nokia Networks is a leading supplier of data, video and voice networks that form the backbone of the Mobile Information Society, meeting the needs of operator customers and internet service providers. As such, it sells its products and services to a broad consumer and business audience.

The next few years will see the telecommunications industry facing a period of fundamental change. The way we interact and communicate will be revolutionised in the era of the Mobile Information Society, as a number of technological enablers take hold. These are: Wireless Application Protocol (WAP), Symbian, Bluetooth and Wireless Imaging.

WAP is a global standard that specifies how internet content needs to be transformed in order to be accessible over mobile phones and other wireless devices. Symbian is a joint venture between Nokia and other companies to develop and licence the EPOC operating system for mobile information devices. Bluetooth is a short range radio interface that enables interconnectivity between different types of electronic devices like mobile phones, digital cameras and PCs. Wireless imaging will allow not just voice but visual content to be exchanged between terminals.

Beneath all of this is the arrival of third generation (3G) mobile communication standards. 3G allows huge increases in the amount and quality of data which can be carried over networks, with the first 3G terminals set to hit the market around 2001-2002.

Achievements

In 1998, Nokia became the world's leading supplier of mobile phones. However, this milestone was no more than the end result of nearly a decade of achievement under the guidance of Jorma Ollila, Nokia's chairman and CEO.

If there is one technical achievement that stands out for Nokia, it was in being first into GSM – the leading digital standard for mobile phones. Nokia developed the first GSM phone in 1991 and, predicting that GSM would generate huge demand for compliant handsets and networks, focused its resources in that direction. When digital mobile phones took off, Nokia was in prime position, while many competitors were still making analogue handsets.

Nokia is also credited with making the mobile phone a mass market item. It was one of the first to recognise that mobiles would eventually become more than expensive toys and regarded as essential business and consumer accessories.

History

Nokia was founded in 1865 by Fredrik Idestam. In those days it was a wood pulp mill on the banks of a river in Tampere, but Idestam soon moved it to a new position where a town slowly grew up around it. The town was given the name it still holds today – Nokia.

Initially, the company prospered as demand for paper and card in the newly industrial Europe spiralled. However, by the end of the century, the company's business changed as it joined forces with the Finnish Rubber Company, which opened a plant near the pulp mill. It took the Nokia name and the company soon became best known for making galoshes.

In the 1920s Nokia's activities spread even broader as it took over the Finnish Cable Works in Helsinki. This saw the start of the industrial conglomerate that survived until the 1990s, with the three companies making anything from rubber tyres and cables to boats and raincoats. They formally merged in 1967 to form the Nokia Corporation. Nokia Plastics began operations in the early 1970s, and in 1982, the group acquired Finnish Chemicals.

At the beginning of the 1980s, Nokia strengthened its position in the telecommunications and consumer electronics markets by acquiring Mobira, Salora, Telenokia and Luxor of Sweden.

In 1984 its Mobira Talkman was the world's first transportable phone (complete with a 22lb charging box the size of a suitcase) and in 1987 it launched the Cityman, the first hand-held mobile phone (about the same size as a loaf of bread). The company scored a PR coup when Mikhail Gorbachev was filmed using one, leading to it being nicknamed, the 'Gorba'.

Since the beginning of the 1990s Nokia has concentrated on its core business, telecommunications, by divesting its information technology and basic industry operations.

Product

Today, Nokia comprises two business groups: Nokia Networks and Nokia Mobile Phones. It also has a separate Nokia Ventures Organisation (NVO). By the end of 1999, Nokia had sales to over 130 countries, research and development in fourteen countries and production in eleven. It employs more than 55,000 people.

Nokia is best-known for its mobile phones, selling one in four of all the phones purchased around the world in 1999. Beautifully styled products combined with cutting edge technology are extremely important to Nokia, which launched eighteen new mobile phone models in 1999 alone. It makes some of the smallest and sleekest models on the market, like the super-small Nokia 8850, the chrome-plated Nokia 8810 and the immensely popular Nokia 3210. It was also the first manufacturer to launch a fully WAP-compliant phone, the Nokia 7110 in 1999, as well as the Nokia 9110 Communicator – a combined phone, fax, e-mail, web browser and personal organiser.

As well as making mobile phones, Nokia is a leading supplier of data, video and voice network solutions. In addition, it is a world-leading supplier of mobile and fixed access solutions, and broadband and IP network solutions. It also supplies digital multimedia terminals for digital TV and interactive services via satellite, cable and terrestrial networks.

Recent Developments

In February 2000, Nokia Ventures expanded its operations into Europe by opening a headquarters in London. This move highlights the importance of the growing wireless internet sector in Europe and Nokia's leading role in developing it. Formed in 1998, Nokia Ventures invests in early stage ventures in the internet, wireless, e-commerce and new media sectors. To date, it has invested in around fifteen start-up companies, such as eVoice, Pogo.com and FusionOne.

Promotion

Nokia Mobile Phones underpins its 'Connecting People' message. As well as highlighting the technological advances of its phones, Nokia's advertising is also very innovative and portrays its products as lifestyle accessories as well as cutting edge phones. TV advertisements created by its ad agency Grey exemplify this approach – in one a fisherman uses his Nokia 9110 Communicator to show his friend a digital photo of the biggest fish he has caught. Another, for the Nokia 3210, shows friends using the picture messaging feature to arrange to meet at a fancy dress party. Once they are there, the interchangeable Nokia Xpress-on™ coloured covers come in handy to match their outlandish costumes.

As well as TV, Nokia makes imaginative use of other media. The company struck a high profile product placement deal to have its phones featured in the hit Keanu Reeves film, The Matrix. And for the ultra-trendy, chrome-plated 8810, a fashion show was chosen as a suitable venue for its launch. A series of press ads presenting the phone in a variety of packaging more usually associated with luxury products, like Belgian chocolates and designer perfume, underlined its credentials as an object of desire.

Brand Values

According to a 2000 survey by Interbrand, Nokia is now the fifth most valuable brand in the world. Nokia's overriding concern is to deliver what the brand promises.

The cornerstones of its brand values are: Human Technology, Enduring Quality, Individuality and Freedom.

You cannot underestimate the importance of design to the Nokia brand. It is fundamental to the phones being seen as devices that support a lifestyle, as opposed to fulfilling a merely technical function. Nokia's aim is to combine the user-friendliness of good ergonomics and design with technology that makes the phones perform better than any on the market. For its networks business, it wants to emphasise that it supplies the infrastructure that makes the Mobile Information Society function.

These values will become ever more important as wireless internet access transforms the mobile market. A personal device that is technically capable of embracing the power of the internet, as well as being a style statement for the owner, is territory that Nokia is well-placed to own.

Things you didn't know about Nokia

For 100 years of its history, Nokia had nothing to do with telecommunications. Its core business was making paper and rubber.

Mikhail Gorbachev was televised making a call on the first true mobile phone, the Nokia Cityman, in 1989. The phone became known as 'The Gorba'.

In 1999, Nokia made one in four of the 275 million mobile phones sold world-wide.

Nokia phones played a key role in the plot of The Matrix, starring Keanu Reeves. So good was his Nokia, that Keanu was able to communicate with beings from another world.

95% of Finns aged 18 to 21 have a mobile phone. Most don't install a landline when they leave home.

Nokia's research shows that people who are annoyed by mobile phone users in public are actually irritated because they can only hear half the conversation, not because of the noise.

one 2 one

Market

The mobile phone market is now about much more than voice traffic alone. This is the age of wireless communications and mobile networks are increasingly carrying data, fax, multimedia and internet traffic. Operators like One 2 One have to move quickly in order to keep up in this most competitive of business sectors.

With over five million customers, One 2 One has an 18.5% share of the UK mobile phone market. The sector is growing incredibly fast. According to Key Note Research, there were 3.9 million UK subscribers to mobile phone services in 1995, growing to 21.8 million in December 1999 – an increase of 453%. In terms of value, Key Note estimates the UK cellular market to be worth £7.16 billion – an increase of 232% since 1995.

By 2004, the market is set to be worth £15.94 billion. A lot of this growth will be fuelled by the move towards broadband data networks, and WAP (Wireless Application Protocol) internet traffic. Technology will transform handsets into mini-computers, capable of handling multimedia services which will greatly increase usage of the operators' networks. For example, Vodafone predicts its average user revenue will increase by 25% by 2004 because of the increase in data services.

As with its major UK competitors – Vodafone Airtouch, Orange and BT Cellnet – One 2 One has secured a licence to operate third generation (3G) services which will have the capacity to handle this type of traffic. The high cost of securing the licences and the continuous need to invest in their networks has led to significant pan-European rationalisation in the mobile market. Following its acquisition of Mannesman, Vodafone Airtouch is now a major international player. Orange also has added muscle following its £27 billion take-over by France Telecom. One 2 One is at the cutting edge of this trend, thanks to its £8.4 billion acquisition by Europe's largest telecom provider, Deutsche Telekom.

Achievements

When it launched, One 2 One was the world's first Personal Communication Network (PCN) operating at 1800 MHz frequency. This, combined with a string of pricing and service innovations means that the brand is credited with leading the development of the mass market for mobile phones in the UK.

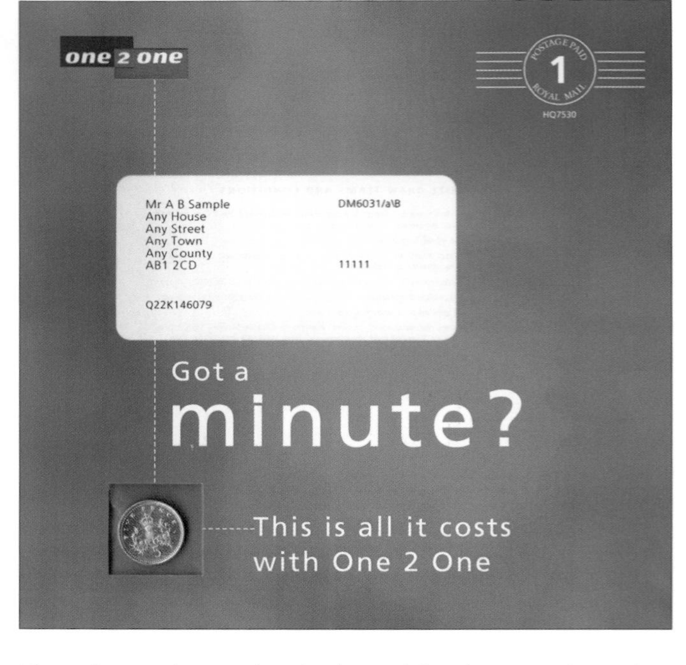

Some of these innovations include being the first to introduce digital pre-payment in the UK, a move which proved to be a catalyst for the now widespread pay-as-you-go services. This, combined with ground-breaking new time plans which cut the cost of mobile calls by 25%, helped drive usage of mobile phones across the market. It was the first UK mobile operator to offer a daytime service with comparable rates to a fixed line. It was also the first to offer free voicemail to all its customers retrieving messages in the UK.

Technologically, it has been at the cutting edge of the industry, being the first UK mobile operator to join the Bluetooth Special Interest Group – a body which is developing wireless communication solutions between mobile phones, computers and electronic equipment.

One 2 One has also led the field with its imaginative tie-ups with business partners. The most significant of these was its deal with Virgin in 1999, leading to the launch of Virgin Mobile. This ground-breaking deal saw One 2 One allow a rival operator to rent capacity on its network.

The success of its service and highly acclaimed marketing recently helped it achieve a massive 161% year on year increase in its customer base, rising to a total of just over five million.

Thanks to its ongoing investment programme, One 2 One's network is one of the best-performing on the UK market. This was confirmed recently when it came second in an Oftel survey measuring service quality. One 2 One beat both Vodafone and Cellnet to take second place in overall successful call rates. It came first for the number of calls connected. The survey shows that 98% of calls made on the network are connected. Overall the One 2 One network handles over 200 million calls per week.

Excellent value for
business
one 2 one

History

Mercury One 2 One – as it was known then – was launched on 7th September 1993. Initially confined to an area inside the M25, the service was closely associated with London. But in 1996 this all changed, when it took the decision to cut loose from Mercury and become a national network in direct competition with Orange, Vodafone and Cellnet.

Changing its name to One 2 One, the company launched one of the best-known and most acclaimed TV ad campaigns in the mobile phone market, using the famous end line, 'Who would you like to have a One 2 One with?'

This was a period of massive change for One 2 One, with its coverage increasing from just Birmingham and London to full national scale. By December 1997 it already had achieved coverage of 97% of the population and by January 1998, it had notched up one million customers.

An important innovation was the September 1997 launch of Up 2 You, the UK's first digital pay as you go service. This was designed to kick-start the then sluggish UK mobile phone market and it worked well.

In June 1998, it targeted the business user with the launch of the Precept business package. This included enhanced digital sound technology, known as EFR. Another important business innovation – also popular with private users – was the launch of mobile email in April 1999.

In August 1999, the company was acquired by Deutsche Telekom, and, in the same month, One 2 One struck a deal with Virgin on a new 50:50 joint venture, Virgin Mobile.

Product

The basis of One 2 One's product – the spine of its service – is its network. Over £2 billion has been invested in One 2 One's infrastructure, including £300 million in the network during 1999. This investment has created a network which is ideally suited to the high performance requirements of business users. With the greatest capacity per customer of any UK operator, the One 2 One network is ultra reliable.

This helps One 2 One deliver a wide range of services to business customers. Companies can hold Business Accounts with One 2 One, providing employees with mobile communication solutions tailored to their needs. Large and small business can benefit from One 2 One's service – overall, the company has over 800,000 small business customers.

One 2 One has specialists to help business customers with technical support – including advice on how to get the best out of fax, data and SMS text messaging and how to implement more complex solutions. Specialists can also advise on how to migrate a fleet of phones to One 2 One or on how to integrate different mobile data services. The business support team also offers 24-hour handset replacement for business users who lose their phone or find it does not work.

One 2 One offers a range of additional business services, like Business Voicemail. This enhanced package allows users to store more messages and for longer than the standard consumer service. Other features for business users include Call Transfer – allowing the phone to be used like a mini-switchboard – and Call Waiting. Priority Line is a service which provides a second telephone number which can be given to selected contacts. One 2 One is the only operator to be able to offer companies Freephone 0800 numbers that connect to mobiles – an effective way of improving customer service and generating new business.

Further business services include Corporate Time Plans designed to meet the needs of corporate customers, such as reduced daytime call charges and lower fax and data call charges.

International roaming is an important service for any travelling business user. One 2 One offers one of the best packages in this area too, offering roaming in over 80 countries on five continents. This involves agreements with 160 operators around the world.

Recent Developments

The sale of the One 2 One partnership by Cable and Wireless and MediaOne International to Deutsche Telekom was completed on 1 October 1999. Deutsche Telekom is Europe's largest telecommunications company and the third largest carrier worldwide. The deal is crucial in helping One 2 One further invest in its network and third generation mobile services.

To keep ahead in this market, investment is an ongoing requirement. For example, One 2 One announced its investment of £600 million in enhancing the quality and depth of its network in 2000.

The company is striking some major deals that will help it offer relevant, innovative and easy-to-use services across its high capacity, high quality network. For example, One 2 One and Sun Microsystems announced an alliance to work together to develop innovative new data services. Using Java technology for mobile devices, this agreement ensures that One 2 One can offer its customers the latest, state-of-the art data applications. Enhanced graphics, superior interactivity and increased security are just three of the major benefits that One 2 One customers have following this collaboration with Sun.

The two companies work together with selected handset vendors to introduce a range of WAP phones and personal digital assistants which provide the best interface and user experience for these enhanced services.

Promotion

The use of celebrities in the much acclaimed 'Who would you most like to have a One 2 One with?' and the more recent 'Welcome 2 Your World' campaign has almost become a One 2 One property. The core of these campaigns is to show how One 2 One helps customers connect and interact with the people that make up their 'world'. For example, a recent TV campaign featured Zoe Ball using her mobile to interact with friends and family.

As well as extensive use of TV advertising – which is mainly consumer focused – the brand also invests in sponsorship, particularly football. Over 30 million people in Britain follow football and this audience is targeted with a variety of sponsorship programmes. For example, the brand sponsors Everton Football Club, Rotherham United and is the chosen mobile phone of the England Football Team and the Football Association. It also sponsors the FA Charity Shield. All of these deals help it reach a business audience, not least through hospitality at major matches and events.

The brand also reaches business audiences by sponsoring a competition to find the most innovative and effective initiatives supporting UK businesses. This, the One 2 One Best 4 Business awards, helps the brand position itself as one which is eager to support business users and recognises the importance of entrepreneurial initiative and innovation.

Brand Values

One 2 One's branding has always clearly differentiated it from the competition. The brand's defining value is its humanity. Research has shown that every network has its own characteristics in the minds of its customers and One 2 One's values are consistently and uniquely recognised to be humanity and emotion.

But in order to move forward with the market, One 2 One needs much more than these values alone. It needs a vision. One 2 One's new business vision is a world of connections – a world where One 2 One seamlessly connects people, devices and services to help customers build their own networks.

To achieve this, One 2 One has a mission 'to connect more people, in more ways, for more time'. This is a combination of building its customer base by offering more connection possibilities – such as email – and making it cheap enough for people to make more use of its services.

Helping customers build their own world of connections – by whatever means they desire – is at the heart of the new One 2 One brand. As such its core values are now defined as 'enabling, closeness and connectivity'. Crucially, its brand is positioned in the new world of the internet and its multi-connections, and not in the old days of single line communication.

Things you didn't know about One 2 One

Each year more than 9.9 billion calls are handled on the One 2 One network.

Some 500,000 miles are covered each year by One 2 One network testers.

Each working day, One 2 One invests £2 million in improving the network.

Up to December 1999, a total of £1.6 billion had been invested in the One 2 One network.

One 2 One has the greatest capacity per customer of any operator, with the network handling 200 million calls each week.

Notes

Market

3M created an entirely new market when it launched Post-it Notes in 1980. It is hard to know how offices survived before 'Repositionable notes' were invented. Go into any office today and computer terminals, doors, desks and folders will be dotted with the familiar brightly coloured notes. They have become an essential element of our working – and home – lives. Whether they are reminding us of the address for the next meeting or to 'Call Dave at 5pm', the Post-it Note is an example of a product we didn't realise we needed until it was invented.

Doing away with the need to scribble on pieces of paper and attaching notes with paper clips, the target market for Post-it Notes is any business which needs to remember, communicate and organise information. In other words, every business. According to 3M's research, secretarial is the largest slice of the Post-it Note market, with other big users including education, management training and the small office/home office (SOHO) sector.

Despite what everyone says about e-mail doing away with the hand-written word, 75% of adults are described as 'note writers' or 'messagers'. Of these, 56% are heavy users of repositionable notes, 30% are light users and 14% don't use them at all. Curiously, 71% of heavy repositionable note users are women. Women also go for the brighter coloured notes more than men, which partly explains why Post-it Notes are now available in many more colours than the original canary yellow.

Achievements

The Post-it Note was a genuinely important invention. Fortune Magazine recently recognised this when, in November 1999, it ranked the Post-it Note in its Products of the Century League. Alongside the paper clip, the Xerox photocopier and fax machine, the Intel microprocessor and the Apple Macintosh, 3M's sticky note was judged to be a product which has helped to revolutionise the workplace.

As with other brand names in the Fortune league – like Xerox and Hoover – Post-it is one of those rare trademarks which has gained fame the world over and is immediately identified with 3M's innovative repositionable yellow notes. That in itself is an enviable achievement and a formidable marketing position for any brand.

Not surprisingly, brand awareness is very high, with 62% spontaneous and 95% prompted awareness.

The Post-it Note, and its inventor, Art Fry, have been suitably honoured over the years. Fry received the Outstanding Alumni Award from the University of Minnesota, the Premio Smau Industrial Design Award from the Italian Design Association and was voted one of the best 100 people in the world by Esquire Magazine. The product has even been celebrated in a book, called 'Rapid Problem Solving with Post-it Notes'.

History

In the 1970s, 3M scientist Art Fry used to sing in a church choir on Sundays. His idea for the Post-it Note came when he was looking for a way of organising musical scores and song sheets for the service. Making do with marks made from small slips of paper, he began to think of how he ideally needed a bookmark that would attach and detach lightly, stick without falling off and not damage the paper.

Remembering an adhesive discovered a few years earlier by another 3M scientist, Dr Spencer Silver, Fry started to form his idea. Silver had been working on a project to create an extra strong adhesive, but, in the process, had inadvertently discovered a new 'low tack' glue. It had the peculiar characteristics of having a low adhesive capacity, yet was able to stick paper perfectly and could be stuck and re-stuck without leaving a trace of adhesive behind.

Fry ordered some of the adhesive and experimented putting some on the edge of a paper to make bookmarks. During the early stages of development, Fry stuck one of his new marks to a document, wrote a message on it, and sent it to his boss. His boss wrote a reply and sent it back, attached to some other work. Later, the two realised they had inadvertently invented a new communication tool.

Thanks to a 3M policy of encouraging its employees to spend up to 15% of their time working on personal projects, Fry was able to concentrate on developing his idea, and, after eighteen months, presented it to the marketing department. As he had come up with a product that nobody realised they needed, the marketers needed some persuading. For a start, they had no idea how to test market it. Indeed, when it was test marketed in four US cities in 1977, the results were not good. However, some stores had seen extremely high sales. It turned out these were at places where samples had been given away free – allowing people to try the product first.

This persuaded 3M to launch a heavy consumer sampling campaign. The results showed that 90% of consumers who had tried Post-it Notes said they would buy them. Soon after, in 1980, 3M launched the product nationwide in the US and followed with a launch into Europe.

Product

Nowadays, there is a lot more to the Post-It Brand than yellow squares of sticky paper. There is now an entire product portfolio under the Post-it Brand name, offering a range of time saving solutions to meet various needs in the office and home.

The original Post-it Notes now come in square or rectangle-shaped, large or small format, pastel or neon colours, in pads, printed cubes or dispensers.

Post-it Index are repositionable book marks of various colours and shapes, designed for marking, ranking and classifying information.

Post-it Memoboards are designed to keep documents within handy reach and important information within view without needing drawing pins or magnets to position them.

Post-it Meeting Charts turn walls into writing surfaces. They are giant sheets which can be stuck and re-stuck on walls without leaving traces, and are ideally used in group work sessions and brainstorms.

Post-it Cover-up and Labelling Tapes are white repositionable adhesive tape, used for correcting documents or to cover sections before photocopying.

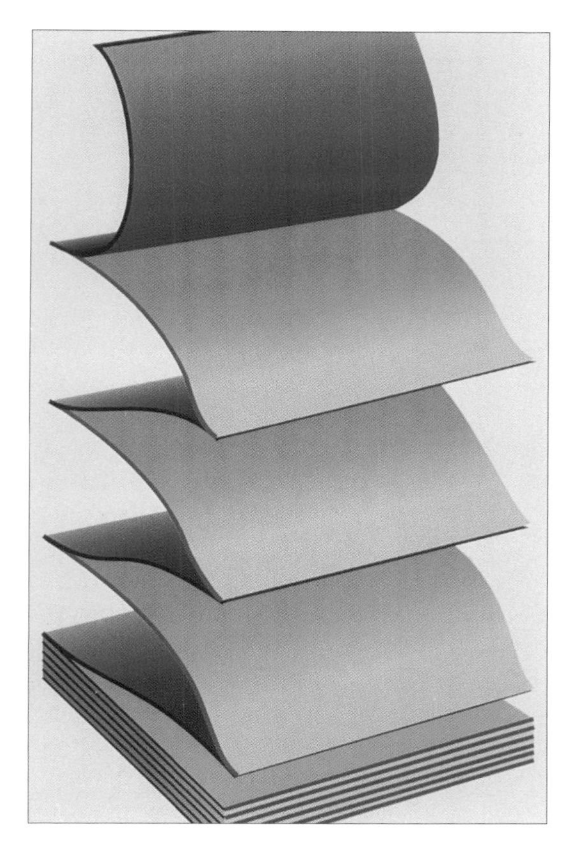

Although the core business in the original canary yellow coloured note remains strong, 3M is seeing a lot of growth with other Post-it Products.

Recent Developments

The introduction of Post-it Z-Notes is the biggest development of the Post-it concept in recent years. Z-Notes are easy to use with one hand. When a single note is pulled out, another pops up ready for use. They come in a variety of dispensers, including a sturdy, weighted design that is less likely to 'walk' from the desktop than a normal pad of Post-it Notes.

To mark the recent 20th Anniversary of the Post-it Note, 3M launched a new palette of colours. Four new rainbow packs and five new colour-themed cubes were launched, building on the popularity of bright colours in the range. Research shows that customers use at least two different palettes of colour from the Post-it Note range, with half of all secretaries using brightly coloured notes.

New rainbow packs include the Sunflower Cube, Ice Blue Cube and the Ultra Intense Rainbow Pack. Post-it Notes are now available in over 30 colours.

Promotion

When Post-it Notes were first launched, the dilemma of how to market a product nobody knew they needed was to turn to sampling. That way, people could see the benefits for themselves. After the success of large-scale sampling in the US, the UK was used as a test market in 1981, with Post-it Notes flooding London's business districts. They were received just as enthusiastically and the initiative spring-boarded the product's launch across Europe, Asia and South America.

More recently, 3M has used advertising in bold campaigns positioning Post-it Brand as the brand of preference in terms of quality, leadership and emotional value to the end user. Now that there are several other repositionable note competitor brands, 3M aims to invest in the integrity and 'original leader' position of its Post-it Brand.

The latest print advertising campaign draws attention to the wide range of colours in which Post-it Notes are now available. Using the line, 'Stand out from the Crowd', the ads are based on a fashion theme, showing people dressed in vibrant outfits made from multi-coloured Post-it Notes. Four executions each carry a different coloured note, with the message, 'Be loud, be seen, be heard'.

Targeting18-45 year-olds, the campaign's objective was to maintain the brand's market leading position, increase coloured note usage and to build preference and loyalty for the Post-it Brand.

Following the fashion theme, 3M also uses sponsorship, recently sponsoring Maria Grachvogel's show at London Fashion Week.

Backing campaigns like this and product innovations such as the bright colour range, is 3M's extensive use of market research. User interviews and focus groups are used to shed light on how people use the product. Recent research commissioned to gather information about colour preferences, for example, told 3M how hundreds of users rated and used different colour palettes.

Brand Values

The Post-it Brand promise is to provide products which are fast, friendly, repositionable communication and organisation tools to help get the job done.

They are designed to meet specific needs, such as not forgetting anything, accessing information, communicating quickly and managing the paper trail.

As the original brand in the repositionable notes sector, 3M attaches great importance to the integrity of its Post-it Brand. The brand watermark that appears on the reverse of every Post-it Note is a symbol of reliability, quality and innovation. 3M has a tradition of innovation which is second to none and this value is strongly reflected in its most famous brand.

Things you didn't know about **Post-it Notes**

The formula for making the adhesive on Post-it Notes is a closely guarded secret at 3M. Only a handful of scientists at the company know it.

Over 400 Post-it Note products are now sold in over 200 countries.

Post-it Notes feature in the millennium Dome, in the Work Zone, where a wall is made up of messages that sum up twentieth century working life.

The most common place to find a Post-it Note in an office is on a computer.

A Post-it Note travelled 3,000 miles, through all weathers, attached to the back of a van.

The original test marketing name of Post-it Notes was the less catchy 'Press and Peel Notes'.

In Japan and China, Post-it Notes are made in narrow downward strips, to accommodate the writing styles.

The most popular Post-it Note colour is currently neon pink.

Market

Few industries have undergone such fundamental changes in such a short period as the UK's energy markets. Just a few years ago the UK's electricity came from local regional suppliers and gas came from British Gas. Nowadays, consumer and business users are all free to choose which company (or companies) they want to supply two of the most basic and essential commodities.

The sector is not just about keeping the lights lit and the cookers cooking anymore. The major players in the energy market are now offering a complete package deal for gas, electricity and telecom services. Powergen has managed to position itself as one of the leading lights in this burgeoning market.

Powergen is also competing in the energy solutions market, working with business customers to help reduce their costs and their impact on the environment. Through long-term partnerships, the company can help customers manage their energy consumption and offer a wide range of energy efficiency measures.

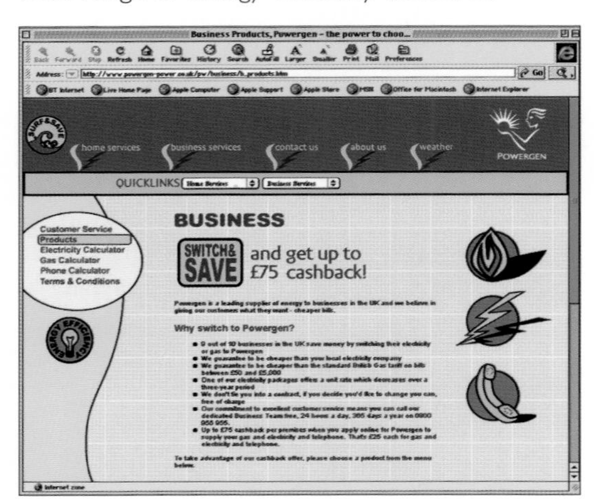

It is a far cry from the days when Powergen only owned power stations and generated electricity. In those days, the only customers to whom Powergen as a generator was allowed to sell directly were large industrial concerns whose energy consumption was far in excess of an ordinary household.

A gradual move to full competition began in 1994 and meant Powergen could compete to sell its electricity directly to a wider range of industrial and commercial customers. But still, the domestic market, comprising some 26 million households, remained the province of the regional electricity companies (RECs).

That all changed in September 1998 when full competition was introduced and allowed energy companies like Powergen to offer their wares directly to consumer and business users alike.

According to Datamonitor, more than three million UK domestic customers – nearly one in eight – have so far taken the plunge. It is estimated that the domestic energy retail market of customers who have switched supplier will be worth £1.8 billion by 2005.

Achievements

Powergen made history in 1990 as the first company in the UK to sponsor a TV programme – the national weather bulletins on ITV. Now, the sponsorship deal is hailed as farsighted. Powergen's Ergon logo became a familiar sight in millions of households and research shows that Powergen now has the best known national brand name in the electricity sector. Effectively, the company gave itself a head start over all of its rivals when the market opened to full competition in September 1998 and millions of new customers could decide which supplier to choose.

It is typical of the kind of innovative thinking that has established Powergen as the UK's leading integrated electricity and gas company with a growing presence in international markets.

Over the years the company has stayed ahead of its competitors through a willingness to innovate. It was the first in the UK to invest in a new breed of environmentally-friendly and technologically-advanced gas-fired power stations on a large scale. It has established itself as the leading supplier of electricity to the UK's major industrial concerns and has built up a portfolio of blue-chip companies for whom it supplies a total energy needs package through its subsidiary Combined Heat and Power business. It was also the first UK energy company to offer domestic customers the chance to sign up for electricity and gas over the internet.

History

In 1831, Michael Faraday discovered that if you rotate a magnet through a coil of wire, it will produce an electric current – and a whole new industry was born.

Powergen came into being nearly 160 years later, born out of the privatisation of the Central Electricity Generating Board (CEGB) in 1991. The move to privatisation was the first step in establishing a fully liberalised market, where electricity would be traded like any other commodity.

The company was one of three generators established in direct competition in England and Wales, the others being National Power and Nuclear Electric. They vied to sell power into an electricity 'pool' from which twelve RECs would supply domestic customers. The equation was relatively simple: the cheaper you could supply your energy into the pool, the more you were likely to sell. Competition gradually increased as more independent generating companies joined the market.

Powergen also realised the benefits from being able to offer 'dual fuel' packages of gas and electricity to its industrial customers. In fact, Powergen was one of the first companies to challenge the monopoly of British Gas through its joint venture company, Kinetica.

In 1998, with the move to full competition imminent, another milestone in the Powergen's history was achieved when it purchased East Midlands Electricity, one of the RECs. At a stroke, Powergen became a fully integrated energy company, with an electricity distribution network and direct access to 2.3 million customers to enable it to become a major force in the domestic retail sector.

In February 2000, Powergen fulfilled its ambition of entering the US market with an agreement to acquire LG&E Energy Corp. of Louisville, Kentucky, for $3.2 billion. The move fulfilled Powergen's strategic objective of gaining a major platform for growth in the US, which is the world's largest energy market.

Product

Powergen's power stations produce electricity from three fossil fuel sources: gas, coal and oil. In each case, the fuel is burned to heat water, which is converted to steam to drive a turbine. The company is also committed to producing electricity from renewable sources and owns, or co-owns a number of windfarms. In total, Powergen supplies around 14% of the electricity consumed in England and Wales each year.

However, 'product' no longer simply means selling electricity or gas. Powergen now offers a whole range of services to its customers, as witnessed by its move into the telecoms sector at the end of 1999 through a joint venture with Affinity Internet Holdings. It means Powergen now offers telecoms and internet products.

The company has always been quick to respond to its customers' needs and can offer a total energy management service for its industrial and commercial customers through Powergen Energy Solutions. This helps the customer to cut energy bills and take measures to increase energy efficiency.

Recent Developments

The current Powergen is far removed from the company that was first set up at privatisation. It has evolved from an electricity generator to a company providing home and business services and operating in a highly competitive market.

That is where the company's strong brand image has come into its own in persuading customers to switch to Powergen. But like companies, brands can not stand still and to help it remain at the forefront of its sector, Powergen undertook a thorough review of its brand and brand values to ensure they retained their relevance to the new business areas the company had moved into.

Powergen's brand and visual identity has been refreshed in a way that ensures it communicates clearly exactly what the company does and what it stands for. It is also appropriate for use in electronic media like the internet - something that obviously wasn't relevant when the original identity was designed.

The strength of Powergen's brand has also made the company a desirable partner for other companies with equally strong brands looking to offer other services to the energy sector. This has enabled Powergen to launch a number of affinity deals offering benefits for its customers. A strategic alliance with Legal & General gives Powergen's 250,000 business customers access to stakeholder pensions. Through the alliance, Powergen is also able to offer its electricity, gas and telephone package through Legal & General's estate agency relationships.

Similarly, top brands in the financial sector have been keen to join forces with Powergen. Alliance & Leicester customers, who use one of the company's credit cards, can save money on their electricity and gas bills when they switch supplier to Powergen and pay by credit card. Details of the offer were sent to around 600,000 card holders.

A similar scheme is run in conjunction with the Halifax, the country's leading mortgage lender. Around one million of their customers who qualify for the top two levels on its reward card have been offered cash back if they switch to Powergen for their energy supplies.

Promotion

Powergen managed to revolutionise the public perception of electricity through an innovative national advertising campaign in 1998.

The TV and national newspaper campaign centred on Powergen's 'box of electricity', designed to appear like a soap powder box and emphasising that the company's product is a fundamental part of everyday life. Building on the long-established ITV weather sponsorship, it was a campaign that captured the public imagination and cemented Powergen's position as the best-known brand in the market.

To capitalise on the strength of its brand, Powergen has developed strong marketing campaigns aimed at winning customers in the domestic retail sector and targeted through TV, radio and newspaper advertising. The company has also pioneered promotional advertising on the internet and has also established its own internet service provider, which allows customers to collect discounts on their energy bills for every minute they spend online.

The company also uses direct mail and face-to-face sales to offer business customers tailored corporate products. It also publishes a regular business magazine to keep its customers and prospective customers up to date on happenings in the marketplace.

Brand Values

During a recent brand evaluation Powergen asked its employees at all levels: 'What is it that distinguishes Powergen differently from other companies in the sector?'. The words that occurred most frequently and that have been adopted as the Powergen brand attributes are: inspiration, freedom and vitality.

Powergen believes it makes a difference to its customers' lives by providing the services that are vital to their wellbeing and allow them the freedom to concentrate on their lifestyle – this is reflected in the attributes.

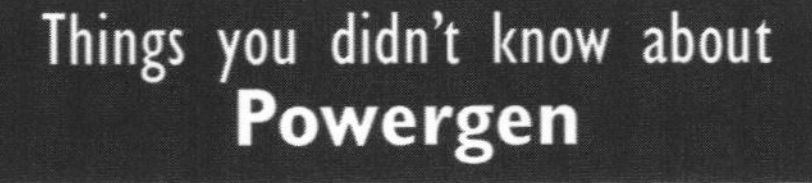

Powergen's UK power stations produce enough electricity to supply the homes of more than eight million people.

Through East Midlands Electricity, Powergen owns and operates 67,000 kilometres of overhead lines and underground cables in a 16,000 square kilometre area stretching from Chesterfield to Milton Keynes and Tamworth to the Lincolnshire coast.

The Government set UK electricity targets for helping customers to use less energy. The initiatives Powergen has launched to date are set to cut the amount of electricity used in the East Midlands by 830 gigawatts. That's more than the average amount of electricity used by a city the size of Nottingham in four months.

Powergen Renewables, with its twelve operational windfarms, is one of the UK's leading developers of windfarms, which generate electricity in an environmentally beneficial way.

Powergen was the first UK energy company to offer domestic customers the opportunity to sign up for gas and electricity over the internet. Customers receive a £30 cash-back incentive when they sign up on-line.

PSION

Market

The mobile computing and wireless communication market is exploding. Miniaturisation means that palm-top size computers are now as powerful as cumbersome desktops used to be just a few years ago. What's more, the coming arrival of broadband wireless telecommunications (3G and GPRS) technologies, means that mobile devices can be used for much more than personal computing alone. Internet access and data delivery at broadband speeds are set to transform the mobile communications market and brands like Psion are at centre stage.

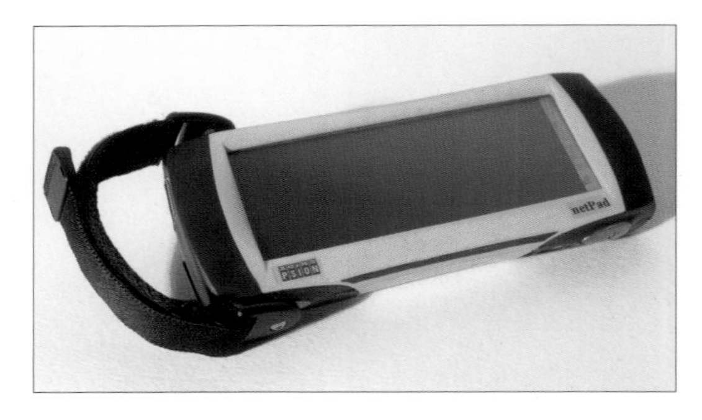

In the emerging age of mobile internet, increasing numbers of people will depend on personal, wireless access to the internet wherever they are. There are expected to be one billion mobile devices in the world by 2003 (Source: Gartner) and 41 million internet users in the UK by 2005. Mobile internet will empower people in their work and personal lives, with information, communications, services and entertainment. Psion is in a position to shape and lead the mobile internet age by delivering distinctive mobile internet solutions and devices to people and organisations.

Achievements

With revenues of £160 million and a market capitalisation of more than £3 billion, Psion Plc is recognised as one of the few companies worldwide to be pioneering convergence between computing and communications technologies. With a particular focus on mobile internet and network access devices and services, Psion's strengths are enhanced through partnerships with some of the world's leading technology companies, like IBM, Sun Microsystems, Vodafone Airtouch, Lotus, Citrix and Oracle.

The company has become a major exporter and commercial success. It has grown at a rate of over 35% per year since it was formed. In 1997, Management Today and WM Mercer rated it as the London Stock Exchange's leading company for total shareholder returns, and, in 1996 and 1997, it received the Exporter of the Year and Innovation in Export Awards. It has also won three Queen's Awards for Export and Technological Achievement.

The latest Series 5mx handheld computer has been acknowledged as delivering unprecedented computer power combined with cutting edge design. The Series 5mx was rewarded when the Design Council picked it as a 'Millennium Product', representing the best of British innovation and design. Psion Computers' product range has won numerous other international awards, including Comdex Asia Best Hardware award by Byte Magazine (US), Editor's Choice Award of Distinction, the Golden Globe and the Design Business Association's Best Consumer Design and Grand Prix awards.

Psion has blossomed from a twinkle in the eye of David Potter, founder and Chairman, in 1980 into one of the UK's most successful high-tech stars. Nor are its boundaries limited to the UK shores alone: Psion's current distribution tentacles extend to over 51 countries in the world, with over 50% of its turnover generated in continental Europe.

Psion is a company that according to Potter has been "dancing with elephants" since its inception. In other words jostling for market share with companies much bigger and with much more considerable sums to spend.

History

The company was founded in 1980, when it originally concentrated on software development for the Spectrum and the Commodore, early computer gaming consoles. Some of the programmes were extraordinarily successful, Flight Simulator for example, selling over one million copies. The revenue from this initial foray into the world of computing was to help finance the next major development for the company.

1984 was the first real turning point for Psion, with the invention of the world's first electronic organiser. The idea for the Psion Organiser emerged at a lunch in London in 1982 where Potter and Development Director Charles Davies were furiously scribbling on napkins. At the end of the lunch, they began to wonder if there could be a better portable medium to capture thoughts and ideas when on the move. After that conversation, they went back to work and two years later the Psion Organiser was born. In developing the Organiser, Psion pioneered the use of groundbreaking production methods and the device was based on Psion's own 8-bit operating system. But key to Psion's success was the excellent marketing for the Organiser, so much so that it achieved the ultimate accolade of the company becoming synonymous with the product category, in a similar vein to Kodak, Xerox or Hoover.

Despite the challenges, sales of the Organiser were high particularly with corporations and in 1987 Psion launched the Organiser II. Sales soared, and, in 1989, anticipating the convergence of communication technologies, Psion launched its Psion Dacom arm to specialise in portable data communications.

During the late 1980s, Psion invested to develop a new generation of 16-bit machines, including the Series 3, the HC and Workabout ranges. Soon the Series 3a was the world leader in palmtop computing and Psion Dacom was leading the European PC Card modem market. By 1996, the company's turnover exceeded £124 million and it had sales subsidiaries in the US, Holland and Germany, as well as sales to over 45 countries.

In 1997, Psion unveiled the EPOC operating system, a new 32-bit software platform that took over 100 man-years to complete. This was designed to provide a platform for the next generation of handheld devices that Psion predicted would integrate mobile computing and cellular communications. The first product based on EPOC was the Series 5, launched in 1997 to huge acclaim.

June 1998 was another significant landmark in the history of Psion. In a groundbreaking deal, it managed to persuade some of the fiercest rivals in the mobile phone industry to link up with Psion in a joint venture to establish EPOC as the standard platform for future mobile devices. The joint venture called Symbian, consists of Psion (28%), Nokia (21%), Motorola (21%), Ericsson (21%) and Panasonic (9%).

Like all good ideas, the rationale behind the company was simple. Licensees of the technology would pay between $5-$10 per unit depending upon the type of device produced. With industry analysts predicting an explosion in mobile phone sales of up to one billion units by 2003, the opportunities for Symbian are substantial. So far, apart from the shareholders, other significant licensees to sign up to Symbian include Qualcomm, Sony and Philips.

Product

Psion comprises four principal operating divisions, all based in the UK. Psion Computers is the market leader in enterprise and consumer mobile internet and computing solutions. The range includes products like the Psion Revo, Series 5mx and Series 7, as well as a wide range of peripherals and software applications.

Psion Connect Ltd (formerly Psion Dacom) designs, manufactures and markets a number of mobile communications and connectivity products. The company recently received the highest level of recognition available to British firms in the form of the Queens Award for Enterprise 2000.

Psion Enterprise Computing focuses on the growing global demand for commercial and industrial handheld computing and network access products. Psion Enterprise's product range includes the Psion netBook, Workabout, HC and Organiser brands.

In early 2000, Psion introduced its new InfoMedia Division. Psion InfoMedia focuses on product development, design and market understanding to develop a new range of groundbreaking appliances for mobile environments. Wavefinder, their first product facilitates digital radio by automatically detecting digital radio signals and allowing content to be broadcast and received over a PC.

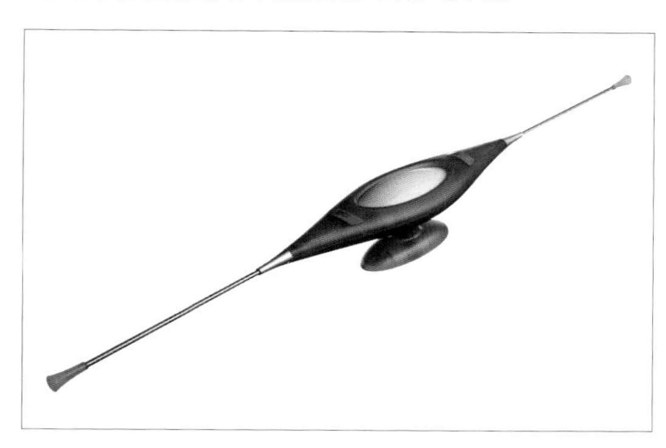

Recent Developments

Psion's commitment to exploring opportunities in mobile internet services and in wireless internet for mobile enterprise applications led to a number of key investments for the company in 1999/2000.

Firstly, Psion acquired Fonedata Ltd, one of the UK's leading WAP portals and corporate WAP and SMS services companies. It also acquired a 7.4% stake in RadioScape Ltd, a London-based software house specialising in digital radio technology. RadioScape develops software components for digital radio, and its technology forms part of Wavefinder.

Psion also agreed to acquire a 3.2% stake in WIDCOMM Inc, a privately owned San Diego, California-based wireless networking company and an emerging leader in Bluetooth™ technology. Furthermore, Psion signed an agreement to take a circa 3% stake in Quicknet Technologies, the US-based specialist in low-density internet telephony products.

Finally, Psion and United News and Media Plc have created a joint venture company to target the rapidly growing market for enriched mobile internet services across all device platforms. The company, Trivanti Ltd, will work in partnership with a range of mobile technology companies and media businesses to develop and market wireless internet services for business-to-business and business-to-consumer users.

Promotion

'The customer is king' could well be the motto of Psion's global marketing. From registration, each customer begins a journey which the company hopes will last a lifetime. Psion believes in regular communication with its users through a number of highly customised vehicles, such as online magazines, tailor-made e-communications and interactive web demonstrations in each individual market. It also actively encourages the communication to be two-way, seeking feedback on product improvements, design ideas and user experiences.

Advertising spend is targeted specifically at vertical market segments rather than at simple brand enhancement, while Psion's merchandising is designed to reflect the warm experience of becoming a member of the Psion family. Detail is everything, from the out-of-box experience right through to the after sales service. Sponsorships too are chosen to emphasise the Psion values of innovation, creativity and design, as are corporate exhibitions such as CeBIT in Hanover and Comdex in Las Vegas. Messages are kept consistent across the different sales regions, but taking into account local input and considerations. Psion's marketing is supplemented by a powerful public relations programme, recently ranked by Presswatch in the UK fourth out of 1600 international companies in terms of favourable coverage.

Psion's advertising in the business and consumer press targets corporate users of personal computing devices during their work and leisure hours. Advertisements for products like the Psion Revo organiser show a range of people benefiting from having access to the internet and to email while on the move. The advertising headline 'E-mail anywhere' perfectly fits Psion's aim to be at the centre of the mobile internet revolution.

Brand Values

Psion is the leading brand in the emerging age of the mobile internet. It is dedicated to providing innovative solutions addressing real customer needs. Psion aims to shape and lead the mobile internet age by delivering distinctive mobile internet solutions and devices to people and organisations.

The internet has moved to centre stage in the digital revolution whilst the frontier in communications technology has moved from fixed line to digital wireless systems. Psion is positioned at the heart of these developments in mobile data, mobile internet and software systems for cellular wireless systems. Psion's core purpose is to take advantage of the investment and market opportunities presented by its pivotal position in these fast growing markets.

Things you didn't know about Psion

The PSION initials stand for 'Potters Scientific Investments or Nothing'.

Psion's first offices were above an estate agents in North London.

Psion is a pioneer in the new Bluetooth wireless technology arena and will supply Dell and Compaq with their Bluetooth products.

Psion won the Best hardware Award at Comdex, Las Vegas for its newest organiser, the Psion Revo.

Psion has a division for new product development codenamed 'the Nursery'.

Alfred Yaghobzadeh, a French journalist, had his life saved by his Psion when reporting in Chechnia. His Psion deflected shrapnel from a bomb away from slicing a major artery. Remarkably his Psion still worked afterwards.

Famous people who use Psion include Jonathan Ross, Terry Waite, Kylie Minogue, Cher, Madonna and Michael Schumacher.

REED

Market

Reed enjoys a leading position in the UK recruitment sector at a time when the market is going through great and exciting changes. Valued at over £16 billion, the UK recruitment market is growing at over 12% a year and supports over 10,000 different recruitment companies. Today the market ranges from temporary staffing services, through outsourcing, training and assessment services to specialist recruitment services. Reed enjoys a position of leadership in every one of these areas.

The UK recruitment market is very large, second only to the United States in size. It is also fragmented, fiercely competitive and it moves very fast. Economists regularly cite the UK's flexible labour market as a primary driver of economic growth and national prosperity. Our flexible labour market increases the mobility of people and gives employers a broad range of options when considering their Human Resource strategies.

At a time when global competition is intense, labour market flexibility is a prerequisite for commercial success. People are the oxygen of business and organisations that seek to be world-class will only succeed in becoming so if they recruit and retain world-class talent. This means that the way an organisation chooses to approach the recruitment market will have a critical bearing on its future success. Reed is committed to ensuring that its clients gain an enduring competitive advantage as a result of the range of staffing services and solutions the company can deploy.

Most recently the UK recruitment market has seen an explosion in temporary work, a rapid rise in the use of the internet and other new technologies, together with a renewed recognition of the importance of identifying and attracting the most talented individuals. New ways of looking for work together with new ways of looking for people mean that the market is both more demanding and more adequately supported than ever before. This pace of change will only accelerate, to the benefit of employers and job seekers alike.

"Our market has changed more in the last five years than it did in the previous 35," says James Reed, Chief Executive. "Good ideas are quickly copied so our challenge as a company is to continually create and deliver a service for our clients that is different, difficult to copy and second to none."

Achievements

Reed began on 7th May 1960 when James Reed's father, Alec Reed, then aged 26, opened the first Reed branch in Hounslow, West London. He started with just £75 and worked alone for a year. Perhaps Reed's greatest achievement is that from these modest beginnings the company has grown organically, and not by acquisition, into a business with over 2000 Co-Members (staff) and 280 branches that generated sales of £293 million and profits of £20 million in 1999. The initial investment of £75 has grown into a business that is valued at well over £100 million and that is generally acknowledged to be worth at least double that if it were for sale.

Reed has grown by giving clients what they want – the right people – and has won a growing number of clients by continually innovating and improving the service it has to offer. Reed is committed to delivering The Intelligent Response, and this has been a consistent theme since the company began.

Thanks to Alec Reed's entrepreneurial flare the company quickly emerged from the pack, not least because it approached the market in new and original ways. Reed was the first recruitment company to offer specialist recruitment services. This began with the creation of Reed Executive, Reed Accountancy Personnel and Reed Nursing Personnel in the early 1960s. At least another dozen specialist niches have been developed since. Reed's move into specialisation fundamentally changed the UK recruitment market.

Following its first decade of success, the company was floated on the London Stock Exchange in 1971.

To this day the founder's entrepreneurial spirit is fundamental to the company's culture and to its approach to the market. Reed prides itself on being an organisation that continues to innovate, and to specialise and that will rise to meet any challenge, however great.

One memorable challenge was the Channel 5 'retuning project'. When Channel 5 needed to retune every video recorder in the country before going live in 1997, they chose Reed to organise the recruitment and payrolling of the retuners. At the time this was not without risk – the job required recruiting and vetting some 12,000 people, a huge number – and the retuning programme had been described by Greg Dyke who later became an Executive of the channel as a 'burglars charter'. The retuning project was an enormous challenge for Reed, but by working closely with the client and improving things as the project progressed, it was successfully completed and was acknowledged by Greg Dyke and the Board to be an outstanding success.

Another more recent achievement has been the company's emergence as the leading private sector provider of welfare to work services to the UK Government. The Labour Government's New Deal programme began soon after their election in 1997 and Reed was the first company to win a contract as private sector lead. This was in Hackney, East London, a challenging area with traditionally high unemployment. Since 1997 the company has won a number of other contracts across the country and has made substantial inroads into the problem of unemployment in the areas in which it operates. In Hackney, in 1999, over 3000 unemployed people were placed into work and unemployment in the original target 18-24 age group fell by over 50%.

Reed was the first major UK recruiter to recognise and harness the power of the internet. The company's website, reed.co.uk was established as long ago as 1995. It has been voted one of the top twenty sites in the world by the Sunday Times and has won numerous awards and received much critical acclaim. Today visitors can post details of their dream job on the site and when the job that they want comes in, the computer will match them to the job automatically and send a text message to their mobile phone. The message gives the job seeker details of the Reed consultant who is responsible for the vacancy so that they can then contact them at their convenience. This 'Jobsleuth' service was another Reed first and it means that at reed.co.uk the right job really does look for you.

Reed attributes its success to the quality of the Co-Members (staff) it attracts to work for the company. Reed has developed a unique programme of Co-Member training and development and offers all of its Consultants the opportunity to study for a Certificate in Professional Recruitment Services that is accredited by the University of London. This is unique in the recruitment industry. Trainees are also given the opportunity to gain prestigious industry qualifications with the Chartered

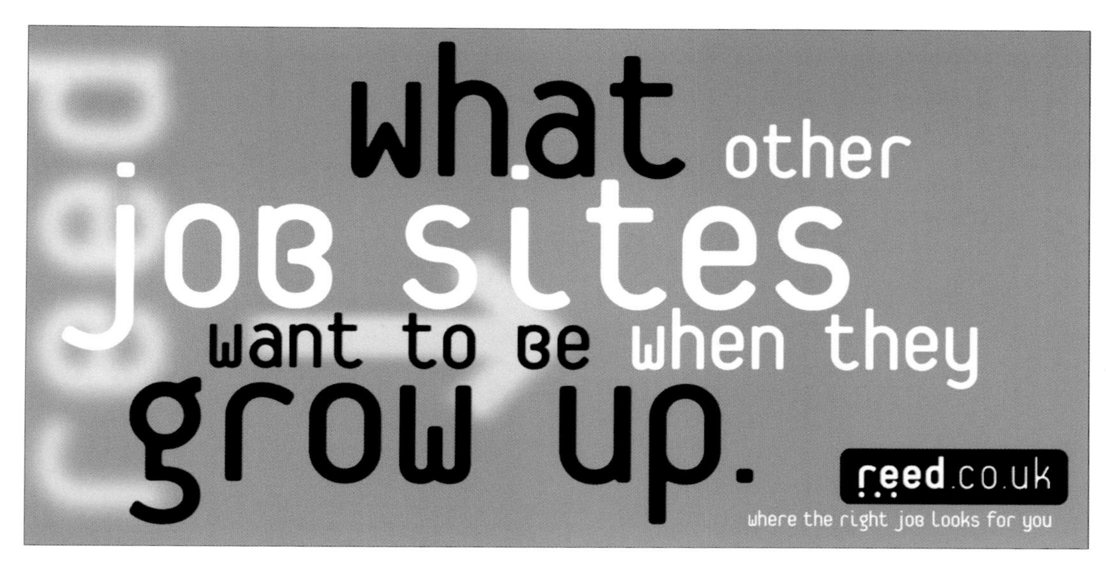

Institute of Personnel and Development. All these courses take place at the Reed Business School in the Cotswolds.

History

The company was founded by Alec Reed on the 7th May 1960, was floated in 1971 and celebrated its fortieth birthday on 7th May 2000. Most of its history is still to be written.

Product

Reed's growth has been dramatic and the company's stated ambition is to grow the business substantially in the future. Reed has been organised into five separate operating companies to make this happen. The five companies and the services they provide are: Reed Personnel Services PLC, which focuses on specialist recruitment services; Reed Solutions PLC, which delivers bespoke and general staffing solutions; Reed in Partnership PLC, which provides outsourced services to the public and private sectors; Reed Learning PLC, which supplies learning, training and education services, again to the public and private sectors; and Reed Connections Ltd, which delivers information technology solutions and financial and accounting services to both internal and external customers.

These businesses are pursuing opportunities that exist offline, online and through outsourcing. Company websites include: reed.co.uk; tempjobs.com; redmole.com; and reedon.net.

FREEDOM TO WORK OUT OF THE OFFICE

Don't get into a rut. Get into Reed.

Recent Developments

In early 2000, James Reed, Chief Executive, announced Reed's Starburst Strategy and the reorganisation of the company into smaller, more versatile business units. The reorganisation and the strategy that underpins it are designed to create an even more customer focused business that is capable of moving quickly to meet client needs and that is able not just to adapt to, but to lead, an ever changing market.

The Starburst Strategy will mean that there will be many more opportunities for people within Reed to take the initiative and develop their own areas of operation. The company also announced that in the future it would be pursuing a Venture Peoplist business model, which means that it will be investing in, and pursuing, new business opportunities that centre on people and people resourcing.

James Reed states: "At the very heart of the Starburst Strategy is the belief that we will deliver much more to our clients, candidates and Co-Members (or stars) if we create room for individual expression and for the development of distinctive client focused strategies in the different arenas in which we operate. The overall focus will continue to be the provision of business services centred on people. The ambition is to be the world's leading provider of human resource solutions."

Promotion

Reed's most consistently visible presence in the recruitment market comes from the physical locations of its 280 branches that operate across the UK and Ireland. This physical network is supported by an electronic network that is centred upon the website reed.co.uk. The website has almost as great a presence online as the physical network has offline and the two together make for a very strong market position that is unique to Reed.

To attract the best candidates for Reed clients, the company actively markets itself across all media. Reed utilises television, radio, press, posters, direct marketing, online advertising and specialist publications and journals. Over the years the weighting of the media mix and of the advertising spend has varied considerably, but care is taken to ensure that the brand always remains front of mind in the recruitment market. This investment means that Reed retains high awareness even at times when advertising has been relatively light.

Reed's advertising expenditure is supported by an active approach to public relations and the company's work is often featured in the national and regional press. The company regularly publishes information on the state of the labour market and frequently surveys the opinions of its clients and candidates. Reed is well positioned to provide a very up to date perspective on all that is happening in the world of work.

Word of mouth communications are especially important to Reed not least because the majority of the company's customers – candidates and clients – state that they first make contact with Reed as a direct result of a recommendation and what they know of the company's reputation. Reed is well aware that there is no better promotion than customer promotion and the company is determined to build on this bedrock of goodwill by continuing to improve its services to clients and candidates in the future.

Brand Values

Reed is and has always been passionate about people. The company's philosophy is that 'People Make the Difference,' its promise is to deliver The Intelligent Response and its purpose is to be First Choice for People. Reed wants to be first choice for clients, candidates, and Co-Members alike.

The Reed brand combines reliability and tradition with innovation and adaptability, but above all the Reed brand is about people, individuality, originality and eccentricity. Reed is about fulfilling individual and organisational potential; Reed is about rising to the challenge; Reed is about leading the market, not following it.

more positions than the kama sutra.

reed.co.uk

where the right job looks for you

Things you didn't know about Reed Executive

In the early days Alec Reed commissioned a new advertising agency Saatchi & Saatchi to work for the company, just after the agency had achieved some success with its 'pregnant man' ad. Maurice Saatchi, Charles Saatchi and Tim Bell all worked on the Reed account. The budget was £9,000. The campaign was a failure.

Reed Charity owns 13% of the company. This charitable trust has founded several new charities including Ethiopiaid, Women@Risk, Womankind and the Academy of Enterprise.

In 1994, the company established the Reed Restart project, which provides real work experience for inmates in Holloway prison before they are released into society.

Reed has unique links with several universities, one of which has asked the company to co-venture a Business School that will carry the Reed Brand.

REUTERS

Market

Reuters is in the business of information. Banks, brokers and other financial institutions rely on the authority of Reuters information to trade on markets, the media uses it to create the programmes and newspapers we consume every day and, increasingly, private investors are turning to it to help manage their personal finances online.

But Reuters is not just rich in content. It is one of the rare companies which combine a wealth of original content with a powerful communications capability and advanced technology enabling the information to be organised and used to best effect.

With the explosion of the internet, information has become accessible by far more people. As a result, Reuters is re-engineering its business to harness this new distribution channel and the related technologies in the distribution of news and information.

Currently, Reuters directly reaches over 521,000 users in 52,800 locations around the world, but with the internet, it is already attracting a far bigger audience. Reuters news and data is on over 900 websites, making it the leading provider of information to the internet. With plans to become a multi-functional portal, providing financial and information services to financial clients, corporations and private investors the world over, Reuters hopes to reach not just hundreds of thousands, but tens of millions. It has a target market of 65 million private investors buying stock on the internet and a total online audience potential of 125 million.

With offices in 212 cities in 97 countries, 16,500 staff, and annual revenues totalling £3,125 million, Reuters has the global muscle to achieve this transformation.

Achievements

Reuters has been at the forefront of innovation in information technology ever since it made some of the earliest use of telegraph cables in the late nineteenth century.

It pioneered the use of radio to transmit news around the world in 1923, the use of computers to transmit financial data internationally in 1964, and was the first to use computers to display real-time foreign exchange rates in 1973. It was also the first company in the private sector to send news via satellite.

In 1981 it launched the Reuters Monitor Dealing electronic broking service for international traders – a system with which around half of the world's spot foreign exchange is now traded. In 1992, its Dealing 2000-2 product became the first automatic, voice-free, broking service.

Its news reporting achievements are equally impressive. In 1900, it was the first to report the assassination of President Lincoln, in 1918, it was first with the news of the First World War Armistice, and in 1989 it broke the story that the Berlin Wall had fallen. It has built on this to become the world's leading news agency, providing news, film, pictures and graphics to media owners around the world.

History

Reuters was founded by Paul Julius Reuter, who began transmitting stock exchange prices and news from Aachen in Germany in 1849. He set it up as a news agency in London in 1851, taking advantage of the new telegraph technology.

By 1858, Reuter had opened offices all over Europe, following the wider installation of telegraph cable. The company quickly established a reputation for unbiased, speedy reporting of international news.

During the 1970s, Reuters was transformed when it pioneered a new range of electronic information products for the world's rapidly

growing financial markets. Its computer terminals providing real-time financial data revolutionised foreign exchange dealing, as did its introduction of electronic transactions in 1981. These developments made Reuters a force in the international financial information market. It now earns over 93% of its revenue from the financial markets.

Over the years, a number of strategic acquisitions have strengthened Reuters' position in key markets. In 1985, it acquired Visnews, the television news-film agency that later became Reuters Television, and in 1986 it bought Instinet, an electronic securities broking company which now accounts for much of the dealing on the NASDAQ market.

Product

Reuters' products are grouped into three divisions: Reuters Information, Reuters Trading Solutions and Reuterspace.

Reuters Information products are primarily designed for the financial markets, providing real time rates and prices, indices, economic indicators and historical data direct to subscribers' desktops. This is complemented by news services, including television news designed for financial professionals.

As well as these real-time services, Reuters Information also offers a large database of historical and background information, suitable for portfolio and investment fund managers. It includes data on over 940,000 shares, bonds and other instruments, as well as information on over 40,000 companies, and analysis to interpret the information.

Reuters' flagship information product bringing together all these services is the 3000 Xtra. Domestic information products have also been created for a wide range of specific markets, including Reuters Plus, which is marketed in the US.

In the Trading Solutions division, Reuters supplies Dealing 3000 for foreign exchange markets. This enables dealers to conduct electronic conversations, or automatically match bids and offers. This division also produces order routing systems, risk management systems and information management systems for dealing rooms. These solutions are all designed to give financial institutions best access to pools of trading liquidity, improve their efficiency and reduce costs.

Reuters Information products and Trading Solutions can be combined in a wide variety of ways to suit individual needs of market participants, and maximise their opportunities to trade profitably.

Media products are the original core of Reuters operations and what it is most famous for. Originally, it just provided textual news to media organisations, but now this has expanded into photographs, news graphics, televised news and packages of information specially designed for the internet. This latter market has grown particularly fast. This sector of the business is managed by the Reuterspace division, which is also responsible for developing retail products on the internet.

In the early 1990s, Reuters began supplying information to businesses outside of its core financial and media market with the Reuters Business Briefing – a comprehensive database about industry sectors and individual companies. In 1999, Reuters joined with Dow Jones to serve this growing corporate information market through a joint venture, Factiva. It gives access to over 7,000 information sources in twenty languages and had combined revenues of $225 million in 1998.

Reuters is using internet distribution technologies to help its banking and broking customers serve their own corporate and individual clients with market information more effectively. Reuters also set up a new joint venture with the business-to-business network provider, Equant, creating the world's largest secure Internet Protocol (IP) network. Besides operating Reuters' own communications network and converting it to internet protocols, the joint venture offers the financial services industry fast, secure, business-to-business services tailored to its various needs.

As well as its core divisions, Reuters has a computer systems subsidiary, TIBCO Software, which creates software linking together information systems operating on the internet. Reuters successfully floated part of TIBCO, for $2 billion, in 1999. Its electronic agency broking subsidiary, Instinet, is America's largest Electronic Communications Network, and is rapidly expanding into other key financial centres.

Recent Developments

One of the biggest recent challenges for Reuters has been to prepare for the internet age. When announcing its 1999 financial results on 8th February 2000, chief executive Peter Job, outlined a radical new plan to ensure Reuters was an internet-facing business. As he said at the time, "The internet has the critical mass to change our business model."

Overall, this means that Reuters is to offer more internet-based products and services to business and private customers. This will be a combination of building internet functionality into existing services and launching new internet-based products. Job called this a "breakthrough mission" for the brand, and said: "Our vision is that Reuters will make financial markets really work on the internet."

A key objective announced then is to aggregate Reuters' vast quantities of information into a consumer finance portal targeted at individuals who want to manage their finances online.

Besides the alliance with Equant, Reuters also announced two other joint ventures with Multex and Aether Systems. Multex is the leading supplier of equities research on the internet. Aether Systems specialises in WAP-based services, allowing Reuters to make its product available to mobile users. Reuters also plans to launch a new version of Instinet, designed for use by private traders.

Promotion

In 1999, Reuters' brand advertising campaign was based on the slogan, 'Reuters. The Truth. Deal with it,' targeted at professional financial market traders. It was decided to change this in 2000 to 'Reuters. Behind Every Decision.' This took the new brand proposition and made it relevant to the new ranks of private investors Reuters can reach through the internet.

This shift in the company's marketing strategy was backed by Reuters' first move into TV advertising. The company is also a growing user of business press, outdoor and online advertising. This use of mass marketing demonstrates the wider reach Reuters wants its brand to have in the internet age. Its sponsorship of the BMW Williams Team in Formula One motor racing is also part of this strategy.

Reuters also makes extensive use of PR. For example, a survey Reuters commissioned into the 'Information Overload' syndrome was extensively covered in the wider media. The company uses PR agencies in thirteen countries.

As part of this recent investment in marketing, a new corporate identity was launched, making the logo clearer and better suited to the TV and computer screen.

Brand Values

Reuters projects itself as the world's most authoritative first hand source of news and financial information. Its brand strength is founded on a bedrock of independence, integrity, impartiality and dependability. It also wants to be associated with leading edge innovation in information technology, constantly developing ways of getting information to those who need it as quickly as possible.

In December 1999, Reuters launched a Brand Revitalisation Programme, aiming to reflect how the brand is adapting in the faster paced, ultra-competitive new media market place. Because new media is putting the Reuters brand before a much wider audience than before, it recognised a need to make itself more meaningful to many people who may not have dealt with it before.

As such, its new 'Reuters. Where the Action is', brand proposition is designed to present a more upbeat, dynamic face for the organisation. It also allows it to integrate all of its services under one banner – equally as relevant to news reporting as to financial information and new technologies. As the company is now active in a much more competitive market, the positioning also aims to make Reuters a brand of preference. Part of this involves injecting more personality, making Reuters not just a trustworthy source of information, but also one with energy, confidence, intelligence and imagination.

Things you didn't know about **Reuters**

When Paul Julius Reuter first opened an office in Germany in 1849, he used pigeons to carry information between Aachen and Brussels, which were not yet linked by telegraph.

Although Reuters is best known as a news agency, over 93% of its revenue comes from its financial information activities.

Reuters news services are available in 23 languages.

To protect Reuters independence and integrity, no shareholder is allowed to own more than 15% of the company.

Reuters reaches an estimated 40 million viewers through the 900 internet websites it serves with news and data.

Reuters was an initial investor in Yahoo in 1995 as part of its "Greenhouse" programme of investments in internet start-ups.

Ryman

the stationer

Market

Ryman is the only specialist commercial stationery retailer operating in the high street. Others, including WH Smith, tend to compete in the wider personal, home and student sector. Direct mail companies, like Viking, and out of town office superstores, like Staples, further intensify the competition. However, none combines the local convenience service and speciality of Ryman and none can boast being the first self-service stationery shop.

According to Key Note research, the UK market for personal and office stationery is worth around £3 billion. Paper and board, writing instruments and filing and storage solutions are the core products in this area.

Changes in the way we work and the tools we use to do so all influence Ryman's market. Many predicted that the IT revolution and rise of the so-called 'paperless office' would torpedo demand for paper, pens and traditional office supplies. But, despite the growth of electronic information storage and trading, there seems to be as much demand for stationery as ever. The computer-based office has led to a surge in demand for consumables such as ink jet cartridges and particularly paper, which is now available in a wide variety of options to suit a proliferation of PC and printer led uses. Other factors keeping the sector buoyant include more students in higher education, lower unemployment and increasing numbers of people working from home.

But technological advances have also increased Ryman's scope of operations. Electronic developments – such as hand held PC's, organisers, fax machines and mobile phones – are now areas of significant growth. However, this has further increased the number of Ryman's competitors, setting it against retailers like Dixons and Argos.

Achievements

Ryman's has done especially well to continue to grow and prosper in a particularly difficult market. The high street has generally been under pressure from out of town shopping, mail order and, more recently, e-commerce, and, in addition, the market for paper products has been hit by high prices and IT-related uncertainty.

So, given that background, Ryman's is an impressive performer, with compound growth since 1995 of 80%. Nowadays, the business boasts a turnover of almost £50 million. The secret of its success has been to invest in the key areas of its business – its people, information technology and the warehouse and distribution function.

It has also continually invested in updating and improving the fabric of its stores and diversified into new product areas – like new electronic developments – to react to changes in market conditions. A significant achievement in its sector was to become the first stationery retailer to sell mobile phones. An important element of its success in putting service and product knowledge at the top of the agenda has been a policy of investing in people and promoting from within.

Most significantly, it has continually kept its brand at the top of its sector and at the forefront of people's minds. Ryman is as synonymous with stationery as fish is with chips and that, in itself, is a major achievement.

History

Ryman was founded in 1893 by Henry J Ryman, with the first store opening on Great Portland Street, London, where one of its major London stores still stands today. The first week's takings were £50.

Although it has since expanded to an empire of over 90 stores in the UK, Ryman's most concentrated area of business remains in the South East, with 60% of its stores situated within the M25.

The store chain was family owned until the 1960s, prior to acquisition, Ryman was part of two other retail companies and during a period in the 1970s it was Ryman Conran. In 1993 Ryman celebrated 100 years of history at The Park Lane Hotel, Piccadilly, where six small businesses were shortlisted for the Ryman small business award for outstanding enterprise and innovation.

Ryman was acquired in 1995 by Chancerealm Ltd, in which Theo Paphitis is the controlling shareholder. Since buying the company, some important developments have been made, such as the launch of the Ryman direct mail order catalogue in 1996 and the Ryman.co.uk e-commerce website in 1998.

Product

Ryman shops sell a range of over 2000 commercial stationery products from its chain of over 90 high street stores. Its products are mainly targeted at the small office and home office market.

It sells everything an office could

require, from writing equipment, paper and filing and storage solutions, to hi-tech items like mobile telephones, palmtop organisers and computers. It sells a full range of products needed to support most office machinery, like print cartridges and fax rolls. It also sells office furniture – desks, chairs, workstations and filing cabinets. Ryman has always been at the forefront of stationery innovation bringing a splash of life to what is traditionally a very conservative area by being the first to introduce colour to products such as box files, ring binders and filing cabinets.

As a specialist stationer Ryman carries all those products you don't find in a generalist such as WH Smith. Products are available with grades and sizings to suit specific needs. New product innovations are quickly embraced and Ryman strives to be ahead of the competition in all areas.

Ryman offers a full business service in a number of stores for photocopying, binding, laminating, faxing etc. Self service photocopying both black and white and colour are also available.

As well as the physical retail outlets, Ryman also sell these products via its website, www.ryman.co.uk and, its mail order catalogue, Ryman Direct, and a 650-page office supplies directory, covering over 600 extra lines.

Recent Developments

Building on its success in diversifying into selling personal communication products, the company has launched a new range of in-store Mobile Multi Media Centres. Ryman is the only retailer of its kind to offer this service, combining its wide range of communication devices with the expertise of its sales personnel. They are trained to advise customers on how best to integrate different devices in order to get the most from them. These mobile technology communications centres will focus on the ease of modern communications using mobile phones linked to palm PC's and desktops.

Another significant development is the launch of the Ryman e-commerce website, selling the full range of its products. This is designed to support the high street retail offering, providing an alternative channel of sales and communication to the Ryman business and home office customers.

Promotion

Ryman has become a household name over the last 100 years particularly in the South East but now throughout the country. The name is kept continually in front of the consumer by regular targeted promotion activity.

Ryman's promotional strategy is a combination of consistently offering value for money coupled with excellent service through ongoing multi-saver offers and regular price-led promotional activity. A typical Ryman promotion lasts between four to five weeks, however key selling time such as 'back to college' will last between eight to nine weeks. Ryman customers are continually offered selected price promoted products.

National and regional press advertising is used to promote the new technology ranges – mobile phones and palm top PC's. The Ryman Direct catalogue is mailed regularly to the business market and the Ryman telemarketing team are in contact with the large database of customers.

Ryman is also the sponsor of a major football league – the Isthmian League – which is a feeder league for the main National Football leagues. Ryman initially started its sponsorship in the 1997/98 season and its current contract is to sponsor through to the end of the 2002/3 season. This is an ideal linkup as all the Ryman League clubs are close to a Ryman store and close links are being built between clubs and local stores. Hardly a day goes by, particularly between August and May, when Ryman is not featured in all the National press, many local publications, TV and Ceefax/Teletext.

Brand Values

The Ryman brand is synonymous with quality, value, reliability and service. This has been developed and nurtured over 100 years and Ryman is an acknowledged specialist in its field.

The four pillars of quality, value, reliability and service have enabled Ryman to build and retain a loyal customer base. It is proud of its record for investing in its people, training them to be able to deliver the high standards of service, backed by expert knowledge in the range of products and their applications.

Things you didn't know about Ryman

Ryman sells annually: 100 million sheets of paper, eight million multi punch pockets, 200,000 lever arch files, 100,000 box files, 400,000 ring binders, 150,000 refill pads and two million pens with enough ink to draw round the circumference of the world 80 times or put another way you could draw round the M25 nearly 17,000 times (middle lane).

In 1947 Lord Tweedsmuir (Member of the House of Lords) wrote to Ryman, 'I would like to take this opportunity of expressing my appreciation of the very courteous assistant who usually deals with my requirements, and the way he always endeavours to help me. It is so refreshing to find such courtesy and willingness to help in these days when courtesy seems to be a 'back number'.'

All of Ryman's marketing activities are driven by a small marketing team based centrally. The vast majority of this work is done in-house and agencies are only out-sourced on an adhoc basis for specific projects when the work volume requires additional heads.

Market

Like JR Ewing's stetson hat, the oil industry is big, brash and hard to ignore. And, as corporate giants go, Shell is one of the biggest, being the world's second largest petroleum company.

Around 85% of the energy we consume comes from three principal sources – oil, natural gas and coal. Oil is the biggest energy source and this industry alone is worth over £500 billion in annual revenues. The recent series of mega-mergers has created two other giant corporations alongside Shell – ExxonMobil and BP. All operate exploration facilities, refineries, pipelines and retail outlets throughout the world.

These big players are not involved in oil alone. They are in the energy business, also exploring for, producing and marketing natural gas. This £30 billion industry is more competitive than ever thanks to the popularity of this clean-burning, environmentally friendlier fuel. Natural gas has become a major energy source in homes and businesses throughout Britain and now supplies around one-third of the UK's total energy needs. Gas demand is already growing rapidly – up 75% in just the last decade – due to its increasing use in electricity generation.

According to the World Energy Council, the world's demand for energy will be double current levels by 2020, driven by increased demand from the developing economies of Latin America and Asia. Oil and coal will inevitably play an important role in meeting this demand, but, as we enter the new millennium, other fuels are emerging as potential rivals. As well as natural gas, renewable energy sources including solar, biomass and wind power will be part of the long-term solution. In recognition of this, Shell has set up a dedicated Renewables business to bring these fuels to market as soon as possible.

Achievements

Shell has been a leader in developing Britain's oil and gas reserves for over 30 years. Since North Sea production began in the 1960s, Shell has invested over £10 billion locating and producing oil and gas, creating jobs and making a major contribution to British society. The development of the Brent oil field, the biggest discovery in the UK sector of the North Sea, is acknowledged to be one of the greatest ever technical feats of British private enterprise.

As well as its impressive achievements in oil and gas production, Shell has recently won plaudits for ground-breaking work in the area of ethical business. Since the dark days of 1995, when Shell was embroiled in its famous dispute with Greenpeace over the disposal of the Brent Spar platform, the company has undergone a top to bottom transformation.

In 1998, it published its ground-breaking report, 'Profits and Principles – does there have to be a choice?'. This saw the company radically changing its structure and reporting processes to create a 'triple bottom line'. This made Shell accountable not only on the basis of its financial performance, but also on its environmental and social performance – as illustrated by its ethical business achievements and commitment to sustainable development. The 3rd issue of the Shell Report, 'How do we stand?' was published in April 2000.

The restructure also aimed to make Shell a more open, less inwardly focused organisation. As a result, Shell does more than most companies in its field to safeguard the environment and local communities, investing around £60 million per year in these types of project.

Shell has also impressed the industry by the way it invites comment and debate on its actions. Its website features a discussion forum in which critics and supporters can air their views and includes links to the sites of its fiercest opponents, including Greenpeace and Friends of the Earth.

Its work in this area was recognised recently when the Royal Dutch/Shell Group of Companies was announced as the joint winner of the best social report category of the inaugural Association of Certified Chartered Accountants and Institute of Social and Ethical Accountability Social Reporting Awards. The 'Profits and Principles' advertising campaign that accompanied the business restructure has also been honoured, winning Business Week's Award for Excellence in Corporate Advertising.

History

Shell's origins can be traced back to 1833, when Marcus Samuel opened a small shop in London's East End dealing in antiques, curios and oriental sea shells. His trade in shells – a fashionable item in Victorian households – became so profitable that he set up regular shipments from the Far East. Before long this had turned into a general import-export business.

The connection with oil was not established until early 1890, when Marcus Samuel Jr visited the Black Sea coast, where Russian oil was exported into Asia. Samuel started exporting kerosene to the Far East, sending the world's first oil tanker through the Suez Canal. Samuel remembered his father's original business when he branded the kerosene 'Shell'.

In 1897, Samuel elevated the status of the Shell name, calling his enterprise the Shell Transport and Trading Company. A Pecten seashell emblem was chosen to give the name visual emphasis.

In 1907, Shell Transport merged with a Dutch rival which was also active in the Far East, Royal Dutch Petroleum, forming the Group of companies we still call Shell today. Rapid growth followed, leading to the development of an international network of oil exploration and production facilities. As with many other petroleum companies, the new motor car age literally fuelled their growth for decades to come.

By the late 1950s, oil had become the world's major energy resource. Supply and demand both boomed, and during this period, Shell supplied almost one seventh of the world's oil products. During the 1960s, there was a similar boom in the market for natural gas, leading to the exploration for and production of natural gas in the North Sea. Shell was a major player in these early years of North Sea operations, even more so when large oil fields were also discovered there in the early 1970s. The years ahead saw North Sea exploration and production become a major focus for Shell.

At this time, Shell also started diversifying into a new growth area – producing chemicals from petroleum products. Over the next twenty years, its chemical product range grew enormously, manufactured in 30 locations around the world.

Product

Operating in more than 135 countries around the world, Shell's core businesses are Exploration and Production, Oil Products, Chemicals, Gas and Power and Renewables.

Exploration and Production sees Shell searching for oil and gas fields in all manner of terrain, be it frozen tundra or arid desert. It also involves the creation of economically viable fields by drilling wells and building the infrastructure of pipelines and treatment plants which are needed to deliver the product to market. Shell is a leader in deepwater drilling and has developed oil reserves at record depths of over 3,000 feet in the Gulf of Mexico.

Shell's refining and processing facilities create a wide range of transportation fuel, lubricants, heating and fuel oil, liquefied petroleum gas and bitumen. Distributing and marketing these is a major business in itself, meeting the multiple demands of the vast array of commercial and private customers that use Shell products. In specialist businesses like Aviation fuels and lubricants or bitumen, Shell is an acknowledged market leader worldwide.

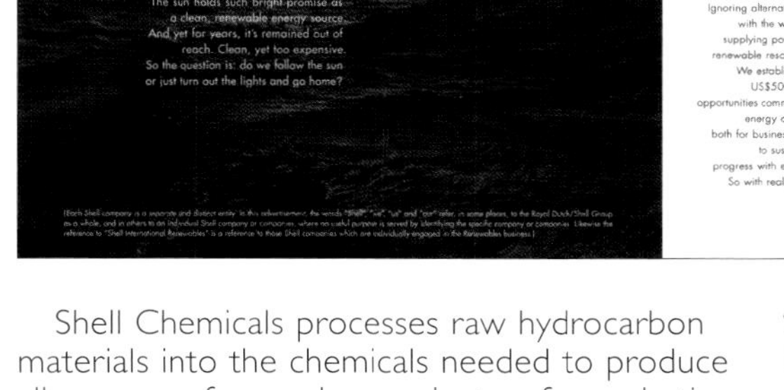

Shell Chemicals processes raw hydrocarbon materials into the chemicals needed to produce all manner of everyday products – from plastics and detergents to solvents and coatings. It also supplies chemicals needed by the oil refining and petrochemical industries.

In today's market, people are demanding cleaner, more sustainable methods of generating power and, increasingly, natural gas is the fuel of choice. As a result, Shell is not only involved in finding, extracting, processing, selling and delivering natural gas, but also in operating and developing gas-fuelled power plants to generate electricity. Shell led the world in the safe transportation of liquefied natural gas (LNG) from remote production fields to markets like Japan.

Renewable energy – such as solar, biomass and wind power – will be an increasingly important market for Shell in the future. It is cultivating sustainable, commercial hardwood forests and other environmentally responsible projects, like manufacturing and marketing solar panels and developing wind energy opportunities. It is also active in rural electrification projects in developing countries and converting wood fuel into marketable energy.

Recent Developments

As well as the 1998 restructure, Shell recently launched another major initiative to protect its brand, which is valued at over £3 billion. The 'One Brand' project aims to ensure the Shell brand and its values are consistently communicated all over the world. Using videos, the internet and literature detailing brand guidelines, the project provides the tools and products to ensure the Shell brand is consistently represented in all channels of communication and in all international markets.

Shell is embracing the internet as a communication medium and new sales channel. It has set up a European journey planner (www.shellgeostar.com) and has many initiatives and joint ventures in commercial marketing and procurement.

Operationally, an important development is the Shearwater oil and gas field in the central North Sea. This new investment for Shell lies 200km east of Aberdeen and is linked to Shell's gas terminal in Norfolk by a 463km pipeline.

The completion of the £876 million project will be the first major UK offshore development to come on stream in the new millennium. Shell UK Exploration and Production (Shell Expro), will operate the field on behalf of the co-venturers, Shell and Esso, ARCO British Limited and Mobil North Sea Limited.

Promotion

The fact that Shell's Pecten logo is one of the most famous brand symbols in the world is thanks to a great tradition of advertising. The famous 'You can be sure of Shell' ad line dates back to 1932.

1900

More recently, Shell's marketing has been focused on a different message. In 1999, it embarked on a ground-breaking corporate communications campaign, based around TV, print and new media advertising and public relations. The aim of the £15 million global 'Profits and Principles' marketing programme was to communicate Shell's new open, socially accountable structure to the world.

The TV advertising, devised by J Walter Thompson, features real Shell employees talking about their job and their work to protect the environment. Print ads in the campaign pose questions to show how Shell wants to stimulate debate about business, the environment and society. Questions like, 'Exploit... or Explore?', 'Cloud the issue... or clear the air?' and 'Wish upon a star... or make a dream come true?' formed the basis of the campaign.

The advertising is backed up by imaginative new media work which sees Shell constantly inviting discussion and seeking feedback on its performance. Its website (www.shell.com) is a forum for debate and includes links to environmental pressure groups like Greenpeace.

Building on a relationship with Ferrari motor racing that dates back to 1950, many of Shell's ads use Ferrari and Forumla One to promote products, like Shell Helix motor oil. It also ran a 'Waves of Change' advertising campaign around the world promoting the cleanliness and performance of its latest fuels, like Shell Pura.

In the area of sponsorship, Ferrari and Shell recently signed a deal to extend their successful Formula One partnership for another five years. The relationship also covers the close technological co-operation between the two companies, which has been an important part in their relationship so far.

Brand Values

Shell's 'One Brand' initiative is based on a philosophy and vision which reflects the brand's new positioning as an energy company committed to sustainable development. Recent communications from Shell show a company that cares about its customers and the world in which we live and demonstrates how Shell innovates to help build a better future.

Things you didn't know about **Shell**

Shell's network of 46,000 petrol stations around the world serves approximately twenty million fuel customers per day.

A 1998 survey revealed that Shell was the most preferred petrol brand in 40 out of 69 countries in the world.

The business of Shell's earliest founder, Marcus Samuel, had nothing to do with oil. In 1833, Samuel's London shop traded in oriental seashells, until his son expanded into oil trading in the 1890s.

Shell's distinctive red and yellow colours are thought to derive from the first service stations Shell built in California. It was decided to paint them red and yellow to appeal to the state's strong Spanish connections.

Shell produces over 500,000 barrels of oil a day.

Market

Sheraton is one of the best-known names in a truly massive industry. Most business people, at some point in their career, will have enjoyed the hospitality of one of Sheraton's 375 hotels in 68 countries.

Worldwide, the hotel industry makes revenues of around £30 billion per year. Globe-trotting business people greatly boost business and fuel competition amongst global premium brands like Sheraton. After a long period of industry losses, many of the world's big hotel groups are now enjoying sustained profits. For example, in the US, the industry made combined profits of nearly $18.9 billion in 1998, compared to $5.5 billion in 1994 (Source: Smith Travel Research).

Some of the strongest players on the global market are US chains. Sheraton, Marriot, Hyatt and Hilton – names like these dominate the industry and have an increasingly high profile on the European scene, where 75% of hotels are independent. In the US, around 60% of hotels are part of a national or regional chain.

Starwood, the holding company that owns Sheraton, is the biggest hotel operator in the world, by revenue, with Marriot coming in second. In terms of sheer number of rooms, then HFS, which, among others, owns the Ramada and Super 8 chains, is the world's biggest hotel operator.

Partly because it is far cheaper to buy an existing hotel than it is to build a new one, there is a lot of merger and acquisition activity in this sector. For example, in 1997, the value of hotel mergers and acquisitions was around £30 billion. Starwood has been particularly active in this area, buying Westin Hotels and Resorts in one of many deals that have helped to propel it to the top floor in the world hotel industry.

Achievements

Sheraton has built itself into one of the most recognisable and successful hotel brands in the world. It has been particularly successful in the business market being voted 'World's Best Hotel Chain for Business' by Business Traveller magazine. It won this award for the seventh consecutive year. It has also won plaudits from this magazine's sister title, Business Traveller International, winning an award for Best Hotel Chain in Latin America for Business Travel. Individual hotels in the Sheraton chain have also been singled out for awards, including the Royal Orchid in Bangkok, the Sheraton Towers in Singapore and the Sheraton Mirage Gold Coast in Australia.

As well as winning a clutch of prestigious awards, Sheraton has also notched up some impressive firsts in the hotel business. In the late 1940s, it became the first hotel chain to be listed on the New York Stock Exchange and, around the same time, the first to utilise a telex system for its room reservation network.

It has always been at the cutting edge of technology when it comes to making life easier for guests, installing a centralised, automated reservations system in 1958. Called 'Reservation', this was the first system of its kind in the hotel industry, followed in later years by Sheraton being the first to offer a toll-free 800 telephone number for direct consumer access.

In 1985, Sheraton became the first western hotel chain to operate a hotel in the People's Republic of China, opening The Great Wall Sheraton in Beijing in 1985.

History

Sheraton's origins date back to 1937 when the company's founders, Ernest Henderson and Robert Moore, acquired their first hotel in Springfield, Massachusetts. Within two years, they

purchased three hotels in Boston, including a hotel called the Sheraton. This property displayed its name with a handsome electric roof sign and Henderson and Moore decided to adopt the Sheraton name for all their hotels.

Soon, they expanded into further properties, stretching from Maine to Florida and, at the end of the 1940s, listed the company on the New York Stock Exchange. In 1949, the group began

expanding internationally with the purchase of two Canadian hotel chains. Rapid growth followed, with the company acquiring a further 33 hotels between 1954 and 1956. By the end of its first twenty years, Sheraton had grown to a network of 53 hotels across North America.

International expansion then began in earnest, with the group's first premises opening in the Middle East, in Tel Aviv, in 1961 and Latin America, with the Macuto Sheraton in Venezuela. By 1965, the Sheraton chain celebrated the opening of its 100th hotel with the Sheraton Boston.

The rate of expansion was unrelenting, with the group boasting 165 hotels by 1968 and 385 by 1976. At this time, the group also celebrated by taking its ten-millionth customer reservation. By now, it had hotels in Buenos Aires, Rio de Janeiro, London, Paris, Hong Kong and Guatemala City.

Sheraton's growth now continues under the stewardship of Starwood Hotels and Resorts Worldwide.

Product

Sheraton offers one of the most complete range of services for business travellers and the group places an emphasis on helping business travellers stay productive while they are away.

For example, all Sheraton Hotel guest rooms are equipped with desks and desk lamps, while most rooms also have as standard a telephone data port or in-wall jack allowing guests to plug in their lap-top computers to send and receive email and use the internet. Travellers can also take advantage of voice mail on their in-room phones, allowing them to record a personalised greeting and the ability to retrieve messages from inside or outside the hotel.

Another business service is ExpressPass, a free of charge benefit available to members of Starwood's loyalty scheme for frequent guests, Starwood Preferred. This virtually eliminates the check in and check out procedure, by storing guest billing and identification information in the Starwood reservation system. Arriving guests only have to show their Starwood Preferred Guest card and they are handed the key to their room.

Starwood Preferred Guest is one of the hotel industry's most rewarding frequent guest programmes and allows members to collect and redeem points at other hotels, including Westin, St Regis, W Hotels and Four Points. In all, members can benefit from using the scheme at 700 hotels in 76 countries.

Other business-focused services include Club Level and Smart Room accommodation, offering business travellers different types of room and service, depending on their requirements. For example, Club Level offers upgraded accommodation, extra services like free local phone calls, complimentary breakfast and the use of a Club Level lounge for meetings. These and other features are available for a small surcharge or can be used by redeeming points from the Starwood Preferred Guest loyalty scheme. Smart Rooms – available in more than 150 Sheraton hotels around the world – feature an enhanced workspace, with larger desk, additional electrical outlets, and a fax/copier/printer.

Sheraton has fourteen airport hotel locations in Europe, the US and Canada, and offers tailored services for travellers who stay there. These include four-hour express laundry and pressing, 24-hour business centre access, menus tailored to help travellers adapt to new time zones and a Day Break service which offers three or seven hour room rates for short stopovers.

Finally, Sheraton's Business Traveller Services Programme – introduced in 1995 – offers a complete package of additional business features. These include 24-hour self-serve business centres with facilities such as personal

computers, laser printers, photocopiers, stationery, fax machines and portable phones.

The programme also enables business equipment to be delivered to guests' rooms, including slide projectors, dictaphones, speakerphones and flipcharts. It also offers extended restaurant hours to 11pm and 24-hour room service.

Recent Developments

Sheraton is constantly leveraging the power of its brand to enter new markets and enhance its presence in well-developed areas. For example, it recently won a bid for a much sought-after convention hotel in the highly competitive Boston area, and opened all-suite hotels in Calgary and Vancouver. Further additions to its portfolio recently included new destinations such as Algiers, Davos, Montevideo and Sapporo.

Starwood continues to invest in Sheraton with an ongoing renovation programme. In 1999, more than $150 million was invested to renovate over 5,000 rooms in owned/managed hotels in North America alone. Part of this was $70 million spent on the company's flagship hotel in Boston.

This is part of a three-year $800 million renovation programme in North America, introducing a new look for guests' rooms, based on a cosy, residential style. Sleigh-style beds, comfortable chairs and oversized work areas feature in the renovation programme, which has been undertaken in response to customer feedback requesting rooms that felt more like a private home. The project has been billed the most extensive of its kind in the hotel industry's history. Already, some 6,000 Sheraton rooms have been renovated in the US and the company plans to add another 10,000 over the next two years.

Some of the biggest European hotels to be renovated in Europe include the Arabella Sheraton Grand Munchen, which recently re-opened after a $85 million overhaul.

Promotion

Customer service is central to Sheraton's promotional message. As long ago as the 1970s, when Sheraton launched its 800 toll-free telephone number and backed it up with a major advertising campaign to drive awareness of the number, Sheraton's marketing has been closely linked with customer service.

The latest marketing drive is no exception. The $30 million, international, multi-lingual campaign asks the question, 'Who's taking care of you?'. Featuring children as spokespeople for the brand, the campaign is designed to touch the heart of the business traveller. The idea is that children are the people who business leaders take care of and think of while they are away. The ads use lines like, "Please make sure my mother gets her faxes, especially the ones with my maths homework", and "Our dad is coming to America. Please give him a map. He hates to ask for directions."

The marketing drive is aimed to increase loyalty to the Sheraton brand amongst business travellers. Research shows that less than 10% of upscale business travellers are loyal to one hotel brand. Sheraton aims to have 10% loyalty for its brand alone. The Starwood Preferred Guest programme plays a vital role in boosting loyalty – it has been shown to increase occupancy growth from 13.4% to 20.4%.

Brand Values

Sheraton's brand is based on being the best hotel chain, with the most locations and complete range of services to suit travellers' needs. Providing peerless customer service is absolutely essential to its brand value and is reflected in its product offering and promotional activity. The advertising campaign adds another dimension to the brand, positioning Sheraton as the only hotel chain that provides an environment that makes travellers feel at home. Instead of saying 'there's no place like home', Sheraton aims to make its guests feel like 'there is a place like home'.

Things you didn't know about Sheraton

In the US, Sheraton was the first hotel chain to require in-room coffee makers in its upscale Sheraton hotels in 1992.

In 1986, Sheraton signed the first contract by a western hotel operator to open a site in the Eastern Bloc, located in Sofia, Bulgaria.

In 1959, when Hawaii officially became a US state, Sheraton opened four hotels on Waikiki Beach.

In the recent North American room renovation, the mattresses, if stacked one on top another, would reach 42,000 feet, or higher than the flight path of a Boeing 747 jet. The fabrics for bedspreads, chairs and drapery would cover 14.9 million square feet and reach from San Francisco to New York.

SIEMENS

Market

Siemens is one of the most diverse companies in the world. Operating in the energy, communications, healthcare, transportation, lighting and components sectors, Siemens is like a microcosm of industry itself.

It is hard to go through a day without Siemens' technology touching our lives. From supermarket checkouts, high street cashpoints and hospital equipment, to trains, lighting and mobile phones, Siemens technology is all around. Its expertise in IT and e-business spans all of the sectors it operates in, applying technological know-how as a common enabler.

Compared to its major competitors, Siemens is the third largest electronics group in the world, behind IBM and General Electric. The electrical and electronics market is one of the biggest in the world. In 1998, it was valued at £1.2 trillion and is growing at a rate of 6-7% per annum.

Information & Communications – including hardware, software and service solutions – is by far the biggest segment for Siemens, accounting for nearly 40% of revenue. This is one of the fastest moving and exciting sectors of business, driven by the internet revolution and the drive towards wireless communications. An eye on the future is essential to succeed in this cut-throat market and the winners are those that invest most in far-reaching research and development.

Investing 7.6% (just over £3 billion) of its revenue on R&D, Siemens spends more than any of its competitors on developing for the future. It is the business of companies competing at the leading edge of technology to devise applications of technology we do not even know we need yet.

Achievements

Siemens has one of the most enviable reputations for innovation in industry. Thanks to investing heavily in research and development, Siemens has been at the forefront of technological innovation for years. With more than 100,000 patents and 24,000 inventions to its name, Siemens can be proud of its track record and it is not letting up.

Over the years, some of the world's most influential inventions can be attributed to Siemens. From the early days, these include the first automatic-dial telegraph in 1847 and the first alarm bell system to warn railway workers of approaching trains, also in 1847. Siemens also introduced the first devices for measuring voltage and resistance in 1860, and its founder's measurement system for resistance – the Ohm – was adopted as the standard in 1884.

Siemens' discovery of dynamo-electric principle in 1866 was the starting point for electrical power engineering, giving us power generation and electric motors. Siemens built the world's first electric train for Bush Mills, Northern Ireland, in 1879, and, in 1883, the first public electric railway, designed by Siemens, was opened on Brighton sea front.

Siemens achieved numerous other firsts in Britain's technology history. It provided the first electric lighting for a theatre, in 1881 at the Savoy. Siemens also installed the world's first electric street lighting, in Godalming, Surrey, in the same year.

Siemens has also been at the forefront of radio and television technology, making some of the first mass-affordable receivers. The company also made some of the earliest engines for passenger-carrying aeroplanes (in 1922) and pioneered electric locomotive design in 1930.

More recently, it was behind the first 1Mb memory chip to go into production in 1988, the world's fastest neural computer, 'Synapse 1', in 1992, the first 256Mb chip in 1995 and the first GSM mobile phone with colour display in 1997.

Nowadays, the company is still at the cutting edge of technological innovation. In 1999 Siemens invented SIVIT, the world's first computer system that can be controlled by gestures, without the need for a mouse or keyboard. Scientists working at its research centre at Roke Manor in Hampshire are constantly working on technological solutions that sound like science fiction, not reality. The company predicts its work will lead to innovations like robot-powered public transport systems and identity chips embedded in the skin. Many of Siemens' ideas that sound bizarre today, will be commonplace in the future.

History

Werner Siemens established the company as a partnership – Siemens & Halkse – in 1847. Set up to take advantage of the latest advances in communications technology, Siemens quickly established a reputation as one of the leading innovators in the field. One of the biggest achievements of this period was Siemens' construction of a 500km telegraph line between Frankfurt and Berlin – the longest in Europe at that time. By 1870, Siemens had established the first intercontinental telegraph link, stretching 11,000km from England to India.

The company established an office in London as early as 1850, set up by Werner's brother, William. The company grew rapidly, opening three factories specialising in making submarine telegraph cables. Siemens in the UK has been extremely influential in this country's history of technical achievement. In 1873, it laid the first undersea cable linking Britain and the US, spawning an exciting new age of communication. As a result William Siemens, who had first arrived in Britain in 1843, was knighted by Queen Victoria in 1883 and played a vital role in the improvements of the age. By 1914, half of all cables connecting Europe and North America were laid by Siemens.

Thanks to its pioneering work in electricity generation, Siemens grew as quickly as the electrical industry and by the time the Second World War broke out, it was the world's largest electrical company, employing 187,000 people worldwide. However, by the end of the war, the company's operations – especially in Berlin – were in tatters. It lost 80% of its foreign assets and all of its patents and trademarks.

During the 1950s, the process of reconstruction saw Siemens shift its headquarters from Berlin to Munich and claw back its export business. In 1966, it concentrated its operations under one name – Siemens AG. At this stage, the company had recovered from the wartime damage, employing 257,000 people worldwide and with sales of £2.4 billion.

Nowadays, Siemens constantly reviews its wide portfolio, divesting its investments in some areas and expanding in others as market conditions dictate. For example, it has made several recent acquisitions which focus on two key trends driving the world economy – industrial process automation and internet technology.

Product

Information & Communications is by far the largest sector for Siemens, providing voice, data, and optical solutions for all kinds of communication products. As well as being a major supplier of networks, Siemens is a major provider of mobile telephones, wired, cordless and ISDN phones, server systems, personal computers, workstations and terminals.

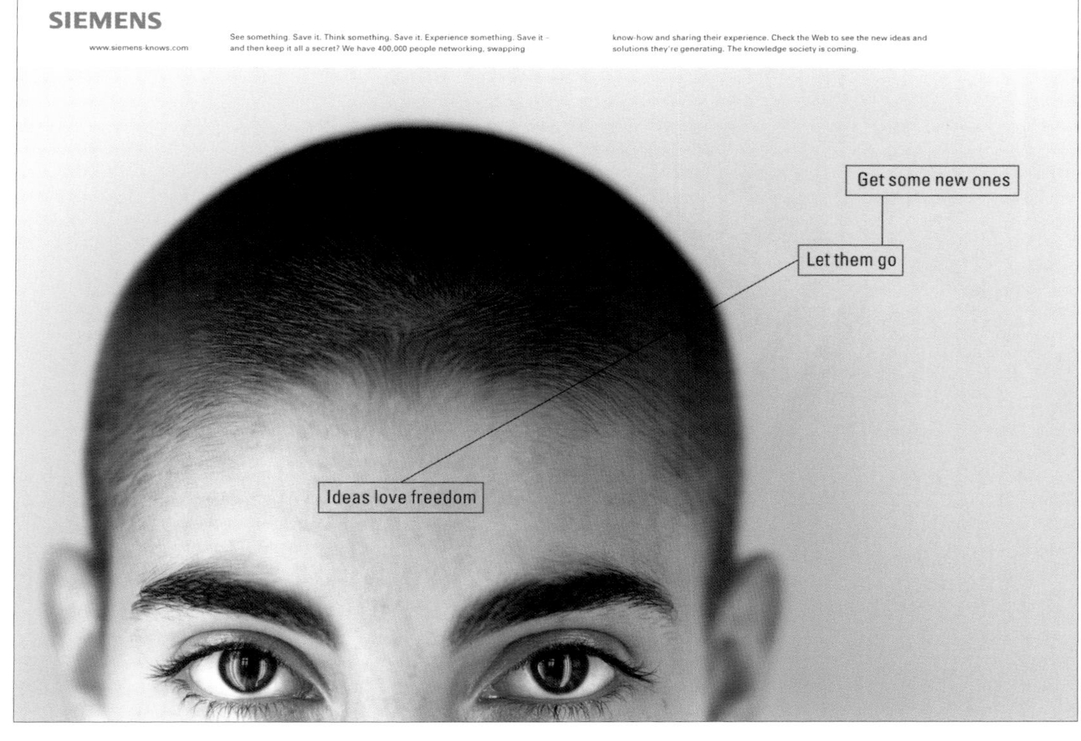

Siemens Information & Communications division also offers consultancy and systems implementation services via Siemens Business Services (SBS). This division provides a wide range of value-added services including staff training, outsourcing, customer relationship management and systems integration. In the UK, this division has been involved in some ground-breaking work, including a £1 billion contract with National Savings which involved the largest ever transfer of civil servants to a private employer. The contract essentially outsourced an entire UK Government Department.

Siemens' work in the energy sector has been an important aspect of its operations since the nineteenth century, when the company was at the forefront of the expansion of the electrical industry. Nowadays Siemens plans and builds fossil fuel and nuclear power plants and components and also provides instrumentation, control systems and fuel cells.

Automation is increasingly vital in all areas of industry, from manufacturing to cargo handling. Siemens is a leader in this field, making the automation and drive systems which power a multitude of specialist hi-tech machinery. This comprises electrical motors for industrial equipment, automation systems for manufacturing or goods handling plants, as well as the software and computer systems that control them.

Transportation is another important product area for Siemens, which provides crucial technology to help keep planes in the air, cars on the roads and trains on track. For the rail industry, Siemens manufactures and designs locomotives, electrifies railways, and takes care of signalling and safety systems. In the automotive sector, it provides electronic components which improve the efficiency and performance of vehicles, such as engine management systems, and also electronic messaging systems to improve safety on motorways.

In healthcare, Siemens supplies a wide range of products and solutions used in today's hi-tech hospitals. These include ultrasound, radiation therapy and angiography systems. In the Lighting area, Siemens' Osram subsidiary is a leading brand providing lamps and lighting solutions for an immense range of applications. The Components division focuses on micro-chip solutions for communications applications like the internet and mobile phones, as well as for smart card operations.

In the household goods sector, Siemens is also a well-known manufacturer of dishwashers, ovens and fridges. Many of these are made in a joint venture with another famous German brand name, Bosch.

Recent Developments

Responding to the demands of the new wireless information age, Siemens recently restructured in order to take full advantage of opportunities presented by the mobile internet. The change will ensure that Siemens is at the forefront of supplying WAP-compatible mobile phones and other products, as well as providing service to support the wireless communication society.

Many of the most recent projects undertaken by Siemens reflect the growing importance of service provision. For example, Siemens Business Services has signed a major contract with the Vehicle Inspectorate to computerise its national MOT network. The contract covers not only the computerisation of the system, but its management for the next twelve years.

In the UK, Siemens Business Services has recently been involved in some ground-breaking work for the National Assembly of Wales. It supplied the IT infrastructure for the newly inaugurated Assembly, designing, building and implementing a set of solutions in less than six months. Systems included touchscreens in the chamber, document management systems, intranets, video conferencing facilities, and automatic transcripts of the proceedings. Siemens Business Services is also responsible for training the Members and their staff to use the new technology.

In 1999, Siemens Automation & Drives worked with Peugeot to automate the Coventry production line of the 206 model.

In the healthcare arena, a consortium led by Siemens recently won a £64 million contract to build and run a 450-bed extension at Barnet General Hospital in North London. The contract includes the construction and maintenance of a new building and provision and maintenance of IT, communications and medical technology systems and all non-clinical services.

The company's impressive record in innovation was recently recognised when Siemens Communications won a Management Today award for being 'Britain's Best Innovator'.

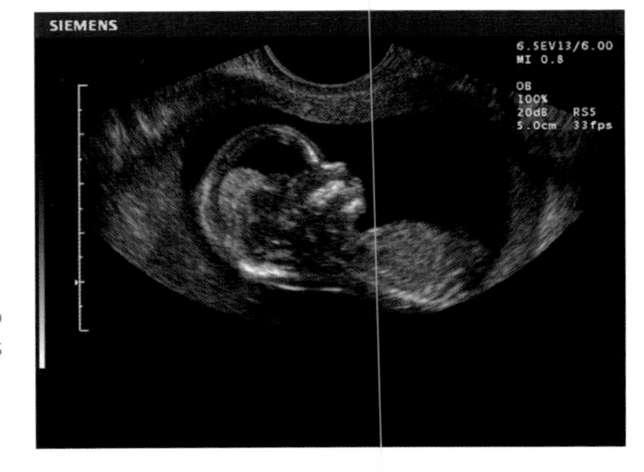

Promotion

Siemens does some promotion of its corporate brand, but mainly supports product-led advertising in the UK. It also sponsors the McClaren Formula One racing team.

Currently, corporate advertising for the brand focuses on Siemens' strength in networking knowledge from around the world and from within the group to find innovative solutions The ads emphasise the importance of linking different thoughts and ideas together to find solutions.

However, most of its advertising is undertaken by the business units individually. Information & Communications is the biggest advertiser, using ads in national press including the Financial Times. Others, like the Healthcare division, use specialist media in their sectors. Much of the creative work is developed for international customers and run on a pan-European basis.

Brand Values

Siemens encapsulates its values in a number of core principles: leadership; co-operation; learning; corporate citizenship; business success and customer focus.

Three additional pillars of values sit on top of this foundation: productivity, innovation and growth. Best practice sharing runs through each of these, ensuring that ideas and learning are shared throughout the group's divisions. At the top of these building blocks are the goals to create customer benefits and economic added value.

Things you didn't know about Siemens

Siemens built the world's first electric elevator, in 1880.

In 1879 Siemens presented the first electric railway, in which power was supplied through the rails, at the Berlin Trade Fair.

Siemens installed the world's first set of traffic lights at the Potsdamer Platz in Berlin, in 1926.

Siemens patents 28 inventions per day around the world.

More than 70% of Siemens products sold have been developed in the last five years.

Siemens invests £3 billion per year in research and development – more than any of its competitors.

Siemens made the first cardiac pacemaker to be implanted, performed in an operation in Sweden in 1958.

Siemens developed fully automated baggage handing systems for Hong Kong's new airport, with 18km of conveyors capable of handling 13,000 bags per hour.

SONY

Market

In today's hi-tech world, electronic goods feature in every aspect of our working and home lives. We seem to need an electronic gadget to help us with everything we do at home and at work. Sony has built a reputation as the premier supplier of the equipment that helps us function in this technology-led world.

As the pace of technological change becomes ever-faster, Sony's core electronics market is one of the most competitive in the business. Datamonitor predicts that 79% of Europeans will be 'interactive' by 2004, using an increasingly wide range of devices. We will live and work in totally 'connected' environments, leading to the rise of the digital workplace. According to Datamonitor, people will each have two or more digital devices by 2004 – Sony aims to be the leading company to supply these digital devices.

The line between conventional electronics, telecommunications, entertainment and the internet is increasingly blurred, which radically changes the market landscape for Sony and its closest competitors.

Sony's biggest sector is the consumer electronics market, of which it has a 21% share. However, its massive 5000-strong product portfolio also makes it a powerful player in the business market, supplying equipment across a wide range of sectors and for multiple applications. The strength of Sony's position is that it provides products which are all components in the digital network that businesses are plugging themselves into.

Business spend on technology is soaring, with a growing trend towards companies buying from third parties. According to Datamonitor, European financial markets will outsource £7 billion to external technology vendors by 2004.

Achievements

Sony has been at the cutting edge of technology ever since Masuru Ibuka and Akio Morita founded it in 1946. In that time, its products have had a major impact on the way we live our lives, introducing a stream of ground-breaking innovations.

It gave us the first Trinitron colour television in 1968, and the first colour video-cassette recorder in 1971. This, the Betamax VCR, was the world's first home use video system. In 1975, it introduced the Walkman which has since sold over 200 million units, making it one of the world's most successful products.

In 1979, Sony also introduced the 3.5 inch micro floppy disk, and, in 1981, the world's first CD player. In 1982, it launched the first consumer video camera and, in 1988, the first digital video tape recorder. In 1995 it revolutionised the video games market with the launch of PlayStation. This replaced the market's previous dominant player, Sega, and set new standards in home entertainment. Other inventions include the MiniDisc, and, most recently, the Memory Stick, which is the size of a piece of chewing gum and promises to be Sony's universal medium to make convergence a reality. It also launched the world's first laptop computer featuring a digital still camera and the world's first truly flat-screen television, FD Trinitron WEGA.

However, Sony's amazing track record has not only been in the consumer electronics market. Its inventions have led to great advancements in the worlds of professional broadcasting, telecommunications, and PC technology.

All this has resulted in Sony becoming a true global giant and one of the world's best-known brands. According to Interbrand, Sony is the world's 18th biggest brand, with a valuation of £9 billion. This is a sizeable share of the company's overall value, with sales of £63 billion in 1999/2000. Overall, the company employs 190,000 people around the world.

History

In 1946, Masaru Ibuka, an engineer, and Akio Morita, a physicist, invested the equivalent of £845 to start a company located in the basement of a bombed out Tokyo department store.

With twenty employees repairing electrical equipment and attempting to build their own products, the company was initially called Tokyo Tsuchin Kogyo. Its fortunes began to change in 1954, when it obtained a license to make transistors. The transistor had been invented in America but it had not been applied to radios, which were valve driven appliances. Sony made Japan's first transistor in May 1954 and the first all-transistor radio.

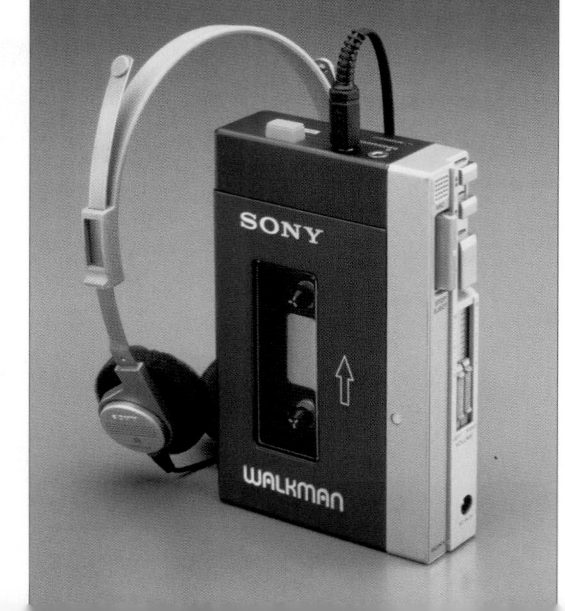

Akio Morita recognised from the beginning that his company needed to have global ambitions and not to restrict its activities to Japan alone. He was also a brand visionary, insisting that the Sony name be prominent on all the company's products. Guided by these principles, Sony quickly became an international force, with Sony Corporation of America formed in 1960 and Sony UK founded in 1968.

As Sony grew bigger, Akio Morita was determined to maintain the spirit of enterprise and innovation. His philosophy can be described as 'global localisation'. Operations were centred in small business groups which acted as self-sufficient companies designing and developing products which are 'sold' within the larger group. The corporate functions of research, strategic planning as well as the advertising and marketing activities bind the diversity of companies together.

Sony's most famous product – the Walkman – was launched in 1979. First described as the 'small stereo headphone cassette player', the Walkman introduced the concept of mobile entertainment. At first, retailers reacted badly to the Walkman, arguing that there was no future for a cassette player without a recording mechanism. However, the public thought differently and it sold 1.5 million units in its first two years on the market.

In line with its development in consumer electronic products, Sony has turned its attention to establishing a lead position in the software market as well. Consequently, in 1988 Sony bought CBS Records Inc to form Sony Music Entertainment, and in 1989 it purchased Columbia Pictures, to form Sony Pictures Entertainment. The launch of PlayStation in 1995 gave Sony a leading position in the burgeoning video games market.

Product

Sony's portfolio stretches over 5000 products. This vast range includes DVD players, professional and consumer cameras, personal computers, televisions, video recorders, hi-fi equipment and semiconductors. These are organised around a brand portfolio which includes Walkman personal audio, Trinitron televisions, VAIO personal computers, WEGA wide-screen TVs, Handycam camcorders, Mavica digital still cameras and the PlayStation games console.

For business customers, Sony is a large supplier of televisions, projectors, videoconference equipment, computer monitors, laptops, and peripherals like data storage systems. These can be used in a host of

applications such as business presentations and exhibitions. Many of its products are supplied by companies which provide equipment to major outdoor events, such as the Grand National and Stella Artois Tennis.

Sony's professional video and audio equipment such as videoconferencing and display equipment plus CCTV, digital photography and image sensing products makes it a leading supplier to all types of media companies. Sony Broadcast & Professional focuses on this market, providing high-spec cameras, audio equipment and production facilities to media professionals and broadcasters, like the BBC and Sky Sports.

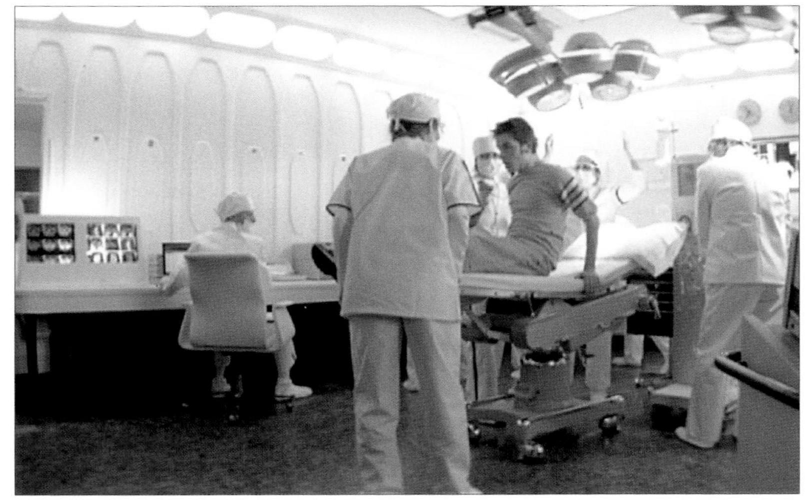

Sony's products will be increasingly designed to meet the demands of the digitally networked market. In the future, stand-alone products will not be enough – they will be designed for use with other multimedia devices. Sony's VAIO computers and Memory Stick are good examples of Sony's convergence strategy.

Recent Developments

Many of Sony's recent developments are linked to its efforts to integrate the internet and other network platforms with the company's core electronics businesses.

Sony's aim is to become the world's number one broadband network company and is changing its structure to achieve this. An example is a new unit dedicated to the broadband market, called eHQ. This oversees the company's strategy for the internet era, with the mobile communications sector being a key target.

In terms of its developments in its individual business units, Sony recently consolidated its position as leader of the LCD projector industry, thanks to strong sales of its VPL-CS1 product. This has increased its share of this important business-to-business market to 15%, rising from 8% the previous year.

Entering into the new millennium, Sony continued its record of innovation, launching in 1999 new formats such as Digital 8 – a digital video recording format. It also launched the next generation CD audio format, Super Audio Compact Disc. Furthermore a new product range, under the name CineAlta, is a new movie-making technology which is capable of delivering pictures akin to traditional 35mm film.

Promotion

Marketing is not just a function for Sony – it is a cornerstone of the company's business philosophy. As much attention is paid to innovation in marketing as it is within the development of Sony's new products. This strategy has helped keep the Sony brand at the top of its markets for over 50 years.

In the UK, Sony invests around £40 million per year in the marketing support of its brands, using a mixture of television, cinema, specialist and consumer magazine and public relations. It tends to employ a localised strategy for individual international markets, but passes everything through a centralised marketing committee to ensure consistency of look and feel.

It is a heavy user of TV advertising, running dramatic campaigns such as 'Armchair', which showed a man in an armchair free-falling from an aeroplane. As business customers also buy many of its products – such as televisions, video recorders, and cameras – many of these campaigns address a dual consumer/business audience.

In 1999 Sony launched a 'Power of Television' commercial to raise awareness in the UK of the possibilities of the digital TV future. This was broadcast on television and in cinema and is typical of Sony's strategy to promote not only its own products but the television industry as a whole.

Brand Values

Research by Millward Brown shows that Sony is one of the world's most respected brands, with 65% of people saying Sony makes products they like to be seen with and 57% of customers saying they would buy more Sony products in the future.

In order to maintain Sony's leading position in virtually all of its markets, the company works hard to ensure its marketing supports the Sony brand image of originality, uniqueness, high performance, ease of operation and cutting edge design.

In the digital network era, Sony's brand has embraced a new direction, summarised by the message of 'Go Create'. This embodies how Sony's products are at the forefront of technological change, opening up new possibilities at work, at home and at play. Sony's products invite and inspire people to do more and explore these new possibilities in their lives.

Things you didn't know about Sony

Sony's founder Akio Morita, coined the term 'Think global, act local'.

In 1986, the word Walkman was included in the Oxford English Dictionary.

Sony's first-ever product was a rice-cooker.

Before Sony called its personal music device the Walkman all over the world, it introduced it under other names, including the 'Soundabout' in the US, 'Stowaway' in the UK and 'Freestyle' in Australia.

We're the dot in .com™

Market

Sun Microsystems™ likes to say it is the company that is 'dot-comming the world'. The California-based corporation makes a lot of the computer hardware and software that paves the information superhighway. The $13 billion giant is particularly well known for making workstations and servers for the corporate market, and for Java™, the programming language which can run on any type of computer and enables computers to talk to one another and which helps bring the internet to billions of computers around the world. Its software, storage systems and servers help clients like AT&T, CNN, e-Bay, QXL.com and Yahoo! compete in the online economy.

The size of Sun's™ market is staggering. The world software industry alone is reckoned to be worth $122 billion and is expected to have reached $200 billion by 2002. The computer hardware market is worth $249 billion. As for the 'internet economy' – the world of e-commerce and the army of companies that supply the infrastructure to support it – that is said to generate over $300 billion in revenues and maintain nearly 1.5 million jobs. Between 1995 and 1998, the net economy grew by 175%. In the same time, the world economy grew by just 3.8%.

In 1999, consumers spent an estimated $12 billion online, while business-to-business purchases over the internet were estimated to be a staggering $100 billion.

Along with players like Microsoft, IBM, Cisco Systems, Oracle and Compaq, Sun Microsystems is in a select band of giants which is at the centre of the action. But Sun doesn't just want to be in this pack – it wants to be out in front.

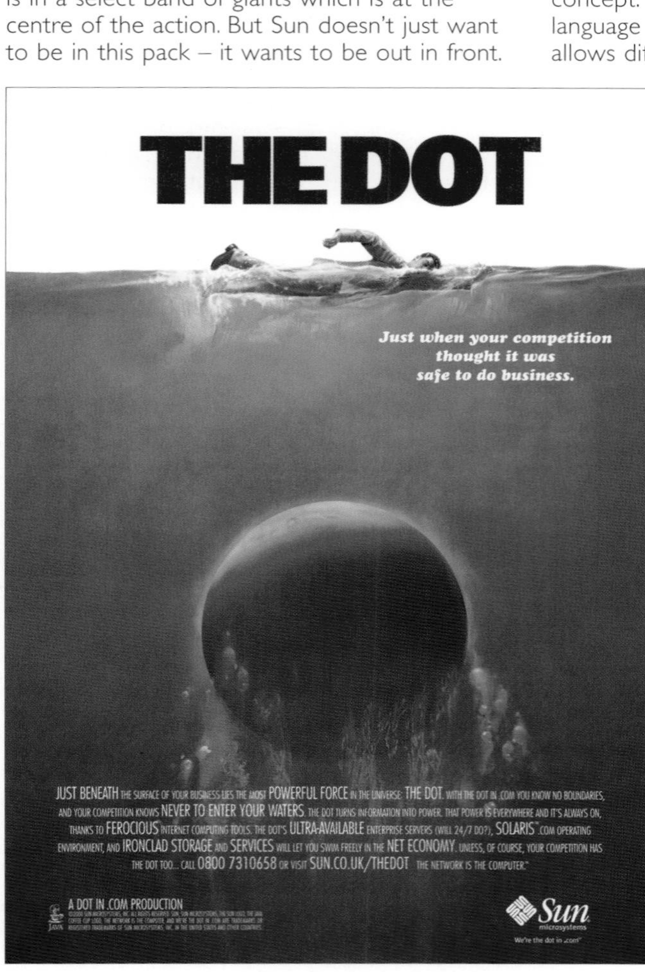

Achievements

Sun's technology has helped 500,000 companies the world over to get onto the internet, develop their websites and launch into e-commerce. Some of the household names it has helped do this are QXL.com, e-Bay, eSchwab, and Yahoo!. Amazingly, according to the respected new media research company, Forrester, 87% of internet traffic runs on Sun's technology. All top five online trading companies – eSchwab, Ameritrade, Dean Witter Discover Brokerage, eTrade and Fidelity – all run on Sun.
The company can boast with some justification that the internet revolves around Sun.

Getting to this position has been possible thanks to Sun's early realisation that the future was about networked computers. It's founding vision – 'The Network is the Computer™' – showed that it understood very early on that the future was going to be about computers talking to each other, not acting in isolation. While its competitors focused on developing proprietary systems, Sun's emphasis has always been on developing an open architecture. Its Java language is based on this concept. It is effectively a language for the internet that allows different computers – of whatever kind – to talk to each other. It is the key enabling technology of all network-centric applications and is now used in everything from smart cards to supercomputers.

Over the years, its pioneering work has given Sun leadership in all its major markets. For example, it is top of the UNIX workgroup server and UNIX midrange server markets. It is number one in UNIX storage and the top UNIX workstation vendor.

History

Sun Microsystems was founded in California by Scott McNealy, Bill Joy, Vinod Khosla, and Andreas Bechtolsheim, in 1982, today, both Joy and McNealy are still members of Sun's Executive Management Group. At the beginning, Sun was best known as a maker of engineering workstations, supplying high-performance networked computers for specialist users like scientists and engineers. At this time, in the mid to late 1980s, PCs did not have the power to perform this type of task, giving Sun a long head start in building a business client base and gaining experience in networks. From the beginning, every Sun workstation contained a network card, and further recognition of the importance of networking was evident as early as 1984, when it introduced NFS technology, which later became the industry standard for network file sharing. In 1986, this technology was adapted for the PC market – opening up a large new market for Sun. By this time, Sun was seen as a rising star, and had a very successful IPO (Initial Public Offering).

In 1987, a vital deal was struck with AT&T, developers of the UNIX operating system. UNIX was conceived as a powerful operating system, suitable for high-end uses like engineering, simulation and telecommunications. Sun had developed a popular version of UNIX, but the deal with AT&T paved the way for it to become the industry leader. However, there was stiff competition from a rival UNIX camp, the Open Software Foundation, and soon Sun was embroiled in the so-called 'UNIX Wars' of the late 1980s.

By 1992, Sun was the leading supplier of UNIX servers, shipping more in a single year than any other vendor. Its SPARC station desktop computers were also hugely popular, and Sun was among the first to combine power with compact size and affordability. By 1993 – after just over ten years in business – Sun recorded its one millionth system shipped and made its debut in the Fortune 500.

In 1995, Sun introduced the Java programming language – the first ever universal software platform and the technology that accelerated the internet revolution. This was fuelled further in 1996, when Java was licensed to all major hardware and software manufacturers. In 1997, NASA used Java to allow internet users all over the world see pictures of its ground breaking mission to Mars.

Product

Sun specialises in network computing-based systems including servers, workstations, storage, network computers, telecommunication systems and enterprise software.

In the workstations market, Sun offers a range of systems – including the entry level Ultra 5 to the high-powered Ultra 80 with 3D graphics – which are suitable for a variety of applications including technical design, engineering and software development.

Sun's servers are for workgroup and enterprise applications. Workgroup servers, such as the Ultra 5 and Ultra 10, are more economical and designed for smaller businesses. The higher end E250 and E450 are more powerful. Enterprise servers – like the E3500, E4500 and the top of the range E10000 – are designed for network-based business applications. They are used to support internet applications, data warehouse and decision support systems. The E10000 is a data centre class machine with up to 64 microprocessors.

Sun makes a specialist internet server range called Netra. These range from entry-level cost-effective systems to enterprise-ready models capable of supporting up to 350 gigabytes of data.

Sun is number one in the UNIX data storage market, offering back-up and storage systems for desktops to datacentres. The mainframe class StorEdge solutions offer up to 2.93 terabytes of raw storage capacity.

On the software side, Sun's Java™ platform-independent programming product is a write-once, read-anywhere language. Java can bring together different technologies and make them work together securely and quickly and is especially important for web-based applications. Solaris™ is Sun's UNIX®-based operating system, primarily designed as an internet platform. Solaris is used by internet service providers, e-commerce sites and other web-based enterprises.

Sun is also active in the microelectronics market, making microprocessors and processor boards based on Sun's SPARC™ and Java architecture. These are used in the telecommunications, computing, medical imaging and consumer electronics sectors.

All of these products are backed up by an extensive international support network, with 35 solution centres and more than 2,000 consultants. Sun also offers consultancy to advise clients on IT, networking and e-business solutions.

Recent Developments

In November 1998, Sun formed a joint venture with Netscape – the America Online owned internet company – called IPlanet™. This is designed to produce enterprise and e-commerce solutions for companies, combining Sun's expertise in supply chain integration with Netscape's speciality in e-commerce software. IPlanet develops and delivers a wide variety of e-commerce focused software applications and infrastructure, and is very actively involved in developing open technologies for the burgeoning mobile (or wireless) markets with companies like Motorola. The alliance also aims to develop Java-based mobile-internet devices. Sun has forged another alliance, with Motorola, to develop new open architecture wireless internet applications.

In August 1999, Sun acquired a private software developer, Star Division. This was an important deal as it allowed Sun to market Star Division's StarOffice™ software as a virtually identical rival to Microsoft's desktop tools suite, Office. Later, it shocked the market and threw down the gauntlet to Microsoft by making it free to download StarOffice direct from the internet or obtain it on CD-ROM for free from sun.co.uk/staroffice. The deal is also important in Sun's plan to offer end-to-end software solutions that drive network computing forward.

In January 1999, Sun launched Jini™ – a new technology that allows wireless networking between peripherals and servers. Ultimately, when combined with Java this could allow domestic appliances to be networked, so that they could be controlled remotely. It can also be used in wireless information devices, like mobile phones or palmtop computers. This new generation of small devices are called 'thin clients' which connect to 'fat servers'. Sun's vision is for easy to use mobile computers and digital devices to be as small and portable as possible, with all data stored remotely on servers.

Promotion

Sun promotes its brand and products extensively, using advertising, PR, sponsorship, direct mail, roadshows and special projects to raise its profile. The majority of its communications promote its dot-com expertise, targeting large and small businesses in specialist and business media.

A recent worldwide advertising campaign featured companies and individuals who have embraced the internet and realised its opportunities. As a spin-off of this campaign, Sun launched an initiative to look for new dot-com 'heroes'. Asking for internet entrepreneurs and visionaries to come forward, Sun pledged to feature them in its own publicity and PR activity.

Newspaper and magazine supplements covering internet issues are often sponsored by Sun to position itself as the 'owner' of the dot-com phenomenon. As such it has sponsored e-business supplements in The Guardian, Daily Telegraph and IT Week.

It also generates publicity from high-profile industry conventions, such as the annual JESS (Java Enterprise Solutions Symposium). This is where the latest technological innovations and discussions about the e-economy take place – attracting significant media interest and valuable column inches.

Sun uses specially produced magazines to highlight its strength in different areas, such as '.Com in Sport' and '.Com Your Business'. It also published handy internet pocket guides, such as the '.Com Guide to Life'. On top of this printed material, Sun uses its website, sun.co.uk, to promote its wide range of services and products.

Brand Values

Sun Microsystems' founding value was 'The Network is the Computer'. This simple but, at the time, revolutionary idea has guided its brand ever since. It always strives to improve and innovate in networking, bringing people and organisations together through the power of the internet. Thanks to it being into the internet possibly before any of its competitors, it strives to be seen as the 'father of dot-com', and the '.com' suffix has almost become synonymous with its brand. To illustrate its importance as the provider of the infrastructure that makes the internet economy tick, Sun refers to itself as 'the dot in dot com'.

Things you didn't know about Sun Microsystems

90% of e-commerce applications run on Sun technology.

Over 80% of internet service providers (ISPs) run their business on Sun.

Six of the world's ten most popular websites – such as Excite and Infoseek – run on Sun.

Sun spent $1.26 billion on R&D in 1999.

The value of European e-commerce is estimated to be worth over $64 billion in 2001, according to Forrester Research.

By 2003, the internet will become the predominant mechanism for conducting business.

Tarmac

Market

Tarmac is one of the world's largest building materials companies, and the largest in the UK. Its core activity is supplying aggregates (gravel, sand and crushed stone) and ready mixed concrete for all types of building and civil engineering projects.

In the broadest terms, Tarmac's market is the international construction industry, supplying the raw materials of aggregates and concrete. As well as being a big player in the UK construction sector, Tarmac is actively involved in selected worldwide markets including mainland Europe.

The company that pioneered modern roadbuilding now employs 11,000 people and has a turnover of £1.3 billion.

Achievements

Tarmac is most famous for inventing Tarmacadam, the 'metalled' road surface that it introduced in 1903 and took its name from. One of Tarmac's biggest achievements has been to build one of the best known brands in the construction industry. Starting from its original core business of making road surfacing material and supplying building materials, the company evolved into a premier group, providing a wide range of construction services and materials.

Following a demerger in July 1999, the construction services side of Tarmac's business now operates under the name of Carillion, with the building materials activities remaining as Tarmac. The financial strength of the group is underpinned by a minerals resource base of over four billion tonnes wordwide.

Tarmac's success at the forefront of UK industry can be measured by the leading role it has played in some of the best-known construction projects undertaken at home and abroad. It built the UK's very first stretch of motorway, the Preston by-pass, now part of the M6, and later the first concrete section of the M1. It also helped build a tunnel under the Suez Canal and was one of the main contractors working on the historic Channel Tunnel. It was on Tarmac's proposal for a twin-bore rail tunnel that the final design was based.

11 ADVERTISEMENTS.

1000 Vehicles per diem for Four Years-and—

—still in excellent condition

THIS is an actual recorded experience with "Tarmac." Under service tests "Tarmac" has proved itself the best and most reliable.

Write for Booklet:
"MODERN ROAD CONSTRUCTION"

Sole Manufacturers and Patentees,

"Tarmac" LD

Head Office:
ETTINGSHALL, Wolverhampton.
D. G. COMYN, *Manager and Secretary.*

Midland Office: A. W. MOORE, Carlton Ch., Wolverhampton.
London Office: H. WARD FOWLER, 20, Victoria St., S.W.

History

Tarmac began life as the brainchild of Nottingham's county surveyor, Mr E Purnell Hooley. He was passing a local ironworks when he noticed that a barrel of tar had spilled on to the road and, to prevent a sticky mess, the tar had been covered by waste slag. Unlike the surrounding dirt road, the patch of tar and slag was free of dust and wheel ruts. Hooley quickly realised the potential of the mixture as a new type of road surface, ideally suited to another revolutionary new invention, the motor car.

Hooley patented his new material under the name of Tarmac. The second half of the name is derived from John Loudon McAdam, who pioneered low cost nineteenth century road construction. Not being an overly skilled businessman, Hooley quickly sold the idea to the then Wolverhampton MP, Sir Alfred Hickman, who officially launched the company as Tarmac in 1905.

Tarmac became a public company in 1913. After the First World War, when demand for metalled roads in the UK started to take off, Tarmac acquired slag tips and roadstone quarries and set up works around the country.

Soon, Tarmac began to diversify into civil engineering. This saw the company become involved in building not only roads and bridges but, with the onset of the Second World War, defensive works, military-strength roads and airfields.

After the war, the building sector boomed and Tarmac invested £2 million in new plant and manufacturing sites. This served it well when the motorway construction programme began in the 1950s and Tarmac was awarded the prestigious contract to build Britain's first stretch of motorway in 1956. It continued to work heavily in the development of the UK motorway network from then on.

Spurred by this work, it expanded rapidly in the 1960s and 1970s, acquiring more quarries as well as buying up other leading construction firms. The 1980s saw another explosion in activity as Margaret Thatcher's capitalist boom went into overdrive. The construction of the M25 and the Channel Tunnel ensured that Tarmac stayed at the top of the tree in UK industry. During this time it also began diversifying into new areas, manufacturing bricks, tiles, building blocks and concrete products, with operations in the UK and the US. In 1987 this led to the formation of two new divisions, Building Materials and Tarmac America.

Having created a Housing Division in 1974, the property market began paying dividends for Tarmac, with a network of housing companies across the UK. The housing boom of the 1980s saw it become the nation's largest housebuilder. At its peak in the late 1980s, more than 12,000 homes were built in one year.

However, once the 1990s recession took hold, the construction and housebuilding industries were the first to slump. Tarmac was hit hard, with record profits of £390 million in 1988, plunging to a record loss of £350 million in 1992. This prompted a drastic overhaul of the company's operations and restructuring began.

In essence, this has involved Tarmac returning to its roots as a building materials supplier. It withdrew from property development and sold peripheral businesses, such as roofing products and brickmaking. In 1996, Tarmac exchanged its housebuilding division for Wimpey's quarrying and construction activities.

However, Tarmac still had a well-established construction services business. It was decided that this would perform better if allowed to operate independently from Tarmac. This resulted in the 1999 demerger to form two separately listed companies, Tarmac plc and Carillion plc.

Product

Tarmac's principal activities are the extraction, manufacture and supply of aggregates, asphalt, ready-mixed concrete, concrete blocks and pre-cast concrete products and cement. In the UK, it is the leading supplier of concrete building blocks, ready-mix concrete, and coated roadstone.

The company has three principal brands. Tarmac supplies aggregates and asphalt from a network of quarries and plants across the country. Tarmac Topmix is the biggest supplier of specialist concretes in the UK, and the second biggest of ready mixed concrete. Tarmac Concrete Products supplies building blocks, pre-cast concrete, concrete flooring and paving.

Tarmac America, focuses on the eastern seaboard of the US, supplies aggregates from a network of quarries, distribution facilities and recycling operations. It also operates 44 ready-mixed concrete plants and produces a range of concrete products. This business was offered for sale following the acquisition of Tarmac by Anglo American plc in March 2000.

Tarmac's overseas businesses operate in France and Belgium, making concrete blocks, pipes, kerbs and pavers, as well as further interests in Spain, Germany, the Czech Republic, Poland, United Arab Emirates, China and Hong Kong.

The company places an emphasis on innovation, developing products such as Mastershield – asphalt which is resistant to damage by fuel and other volatile liquids. It has also developed a range of coloured asphalts – the Mastertint range – which are designed to blend in with natural surroundings. This was recently used in the Peak District National Park, where buff-coloured asphalt was used for park roads.

Recent Developments

Tarmac has recently been involved in two major deals. In July 1999 the demerger of the old Tarmac Group into Tarmac and Carillion gave birth to a new corporate structure, and, in March 2000, Tarmac plc merged with the construction materials businesses of Anglo Industrial Minerals to form the new Tarmac Group. This followed the purchase of Tarmac's share capital by AIM's parent company, Anglo American plc.

The new Tarmac Group sees the merger of Tarmac Topmix and Tarmac Quarry Products. Together with these, the new group also comprises Tarmac Concrete Products and the overseas operations.

Operationally, the company has recently been winning plaudits for its environmental work. Last year Tarmac was awarded ISO 14001 certification – the internationally recognised standard for environmental management systems – for its quarrying and asphalt operations. The company was also praised by the Prince of Wales for a recent deal in which it helped to establish a new national nature reserve at one of its quarry sites in Wales.

Promotion

Tarmac's famous seven-T corporate identity – designed in 1964 – was updated in 1996 to reflect the multi-dimensional activities of the modern business. Designed by brand consultants Enterprise IG, the new identity also coincided with the long process of restructuring.

The group does some corporate advertising – including press work which carries the strapline, 'The Many Faces of Stone' and also sponsors the arts. However, for the most part, promotional activity is devolved to individual business units and products.

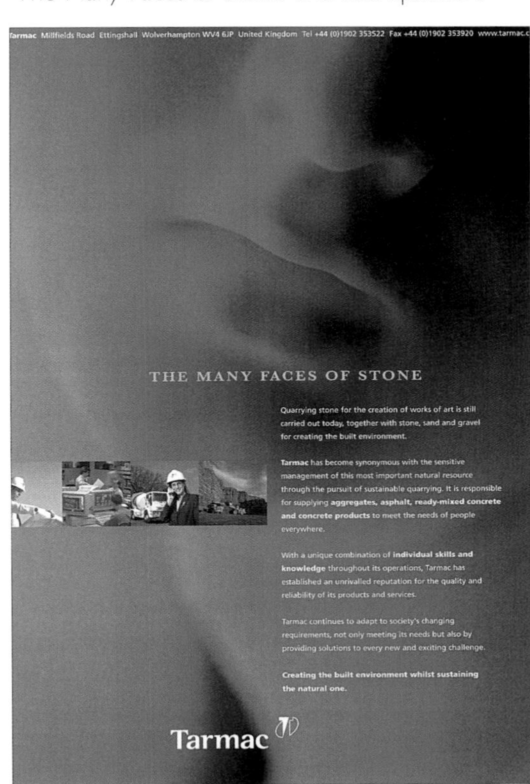

Brand Values

Tarmac has proved an enduring brand throughout the years, with an enviable reputation for the quality of its people, its products and services.

The demerger of the construction services business in 1999, leaving Tarmac as a pure building materials group, helped to bring even clearer focus to the name and its strengths. In an age where environmental responsibility has never been more important, Tarmac wants its brand to be synonymous with the sensitive management of natural resources through the pursuit of sustainable quarrying.

Tarmac's vision for the way forward is to consolidate its position as the most successful heavy buildings materials company, offering the best value in a safe working and sustainable environment.

Things you didn't know about Tarmac

Tarmac is named after its own invention – the road surfacing material Tarmacadam.

The word Tarmacadam is derived from the mixture of tar and slag which was first used to make it and the name of John Loudon McAdam, who pioneered low-cost roadbuilding in the nineteenth century.

Tarmac was 'called up' to widen and strengthen roads in the south of England to carry D-Day invasion traffic.

It built the first stretch of British motorway, in 1956, and its materials have been used, at one time or another, in the construction of all Britain's major roads.

The twin-bore design of the Channel Tunnel is based on an original Tarmac design. It was also part of a three-way consortium which constructed the Thames Flood barrier.

From the time of Dunkirk to the end of the war in Europe, Tarmac produced over five million tons of road and runway materials. This was occasionally a perilous undertaking, with one airfield bombed during construction and another machine gunned by German fighters.

TOYOTA

Market

The greatest challenge facing the car industry in the twenty-first century is limiting harmful emissions and damage to the environment. This has become a critical management issue and a key focus of corporate competition among manufacturers. Environmental issues have also gained status as a major topic with consumers across the world. Toyota is determined not just to respond to the challenge but to set the tone for the future. It is at the forefront of establishing greener technologies

and devotes half of its entire research and development effort in engine technology to finding alternative sources of fuel. Toyota is the third largest car manufacturer in the world with a richly deserved reputation for quality and reliability. It is a world leader in automotive innovation, investing over £2 billion a year – 5% of its annual net sales – in research and development.

The UK market is of major strategic importance for Toyota, as a key element of its plans to significantly increase market share in Europe. Historically this has been lower than in many other areas of the world, due largely to import quotas. Ambitious targets have been developed to significantly increase market share. Impressive growth in recent years has put the brand on course to achieve this.

The UK is one of Europe's largest, most mature and most competitive markets. Over two million new vehicles a year are sold in the UK and major manufacturers, such as Ford and Vauxhall, dominate the market. Fleet sales are crucial to all the main brands, with the fleet market accounting for around one million vehicles per year. Establishing strong links with corporate customers is crucial for Toyota and its competitors, especially given the size of some of

the largest fleets. Over 5,000 companies in the UK run fleets of 100 vehicles or more.

Achievements

From humble beginnings, Toyota has become the world's seventh largest company with interests in other areas, such as telecommunications, construction and boat-building, and a total net income of £2.74 billion (1999). It is the world's most respected engineering company, according to the Financial Times/PricewaterhouseCoopers World's Most Respected Companies survey (1998 and 1999), and ranked tenth overall. Its chairman Hiroshi Okuda was rated as the seventh most highly respected business leader in the world by the same study.

Toyota dominates its domestic car market with a 40% share and boasts the biggest selling car in the US, the Camry. The company manufactures over 4.7 million vehicles a year and now builds one vehicle every twenty seconds. Toyota is a truly global player with manufacturing sites in 26 nations and over 7,000 dealerships worldwide.

Toyota has achieved significant growth in the UK in recent years, in both the retail market and in the important fleet market. The Toyota brand is the choice of many highly respected corporate fleet operators, such as BT, Barclays, Granada, Tesco, CGU, IBM, NCR and Nortel. This success has been recognised by numerous awards, including the Fleet Industry Special Vehicle Award in 2000 for Prius. The model's extra low fuel consumption and carbon dioxide emissions helped it win the award, enabling companies to reduce their fuel bills and exposure to emissions-linked tax levies.

CAR OF THE YEAR
VI BILAGARE
AUTO
AUTOCAR
L'AUTOMOBILE MAGAZINE
STERN
AUTOPISTA
AUTOVISIE
2000

With its origins in innovation, Toyota has been at the forefront of technological advancement throughout its history and has led the automotive industry's environmental efforts since the launch of its 'Earth Charter' in 1992. It is the first company to mass-produce a car using a hybrid technology system, combining petrol and electric power. This has been introduced to the UK for the first time in 2000 with the launch of Prius. Prius has been on sale in Japan since 1997 and has sold over 35,000 units. It has won numerous awards including the US Environmental Protection Agency's Global Climate Protection Award in 1998. In 1999 Toyota became the first motor manufacturer to win the United Nations Environment Programme's Global 500 Award.

One of the first brands to offer a three year manufacturer's warranty on all new vehicles, Toyota is so confident of its vehicles' quality that it now offers a one year warranty on cars up to seven years old on its used car programme.

Toyota is now recognised as one of the leading car brands in Europe, shown most recently when Yaris was voted European Car of the Year 2000.

History

Established in 1918, the company's history actually dates back to 1902 when founder Sakichi Toyoda invented the world's first automatic loom. Toyoda's invention revolutionised the Japanese weaving industry and the sale of the machine's production rights to a British company enabled his son Kiichiro to spearhead the move into car manufacturing in the 1930s. Kiichiro laid the groundwork for 'just in time' production, a leaner, more efficient production system that had a dramatic effect on the entire motor industry. This has since been adopted by companies in every industry throughout the world.

The introduction of the discipline of Kaizen – continuous improvement – had an equally dramatic effect in the 1940s. The pursuit of continuous improvement in quality in every area drives Toyota now as it did then. Kaizen helped to create one of the most stable and productive workforces in the industry and an organisation that empowers individuals and recognises their worth: as an example, every member of Toyota's production staff can stop the production line.

In 1959 Toyota first exported and manufactured outside Japan. UK imports started in 1966/67 and the company now employs about 2,700 people at its car assembly plant in Derbyshire and its engine factory in Wales. Opened in 1992, the Derbyshire plant produces over 179,000 cars a year.

Product

With fifteen models on offer, Toyota offers the widest range of any vehicle manufacturer in the UK. It is also introducing new models at a faster rate than any of its competitors, launching seven new cars in 2000 alone. These were: Yaris Verso, Corolla, MR2 Roadster, RAV4, Previa, Avensis and Prius. These followed two hugely successful launches in 1999, Yaris and new Celica.

Its portfolio covers every category, from sports cars to multipurpose and commercial vehicles, all utilising innovative engineering and design. Toyota places a strong emphasis on being at the forefront of technology and on cutting-edge, imaginative design.

These priorities are evident in products like the RAV4, which created a new sector when it was launched in 1994. The new RAV4, launched this year, has now moved the industry benchmarks further forward for compact-off-road vehicles.

Yaris, the space defying small car launched in 1999, has similarly redefined its sector.

With class-leading levels of interior space, it combines power with economy and is one of the strongest and lightest compact cars. Toyota's passenger car portfolio boasts the world's best selling car, the Corolla, which continues to collect accolades for quality and reliability in every market, as well as the Avensis, which has taken the corporate sector by storm since its 1998 launch. The Celica, now in its seventh generation and with many World Rally Championship successes behind it, lines up alongside the MR2 Roadster, which has again become the class-leading sports car. And, of course at the cutting edge of environmental technology, Toyota has introduced the Prius.

Recent Developments

Toyota has always placed an emphasis on innovative engine technology and recently illustrated this with the introduction of Variable Valve Timing with Intelligence (VVT-i) across the range. Offering excellent performance and fuel economy, VVT-i represents a major step forward in engine technology. Another example of its ground-breaking work in engine design is hybrid technology. As car manufacturers seek to minimise fuel emissions, Toyota's hybrid power technology is leading the way in harnessing the power of electricity, gas and other alternative fuels. Unlike many of its competitors, Toyota's innovations in this area are not just on the drawing board – the Prius is the world's first production hybrid car, combining electrical power with a petrol engine. The car automatically switches between power sources and its electric cells recharge under braking, so it never has to be plugged in.

In Toyota's quest for greener technology, it is testing an electric version of its award-winning off-road RAV4 in Jersey. Toyota is also pioneering an electric vehicle commuter system that uses internet technology and satellite navigation. In addition it is developing intelligent transport systems which use navigation, automatic pilot and electronic toll collection schemes.

Not satisfied with its successful history in rallying, Toyota is developing a Formula One car and team for entry in the 2002 championship. Toyota launched seven new models in 2000, all featuring industry-leading technology as well as superb design.

Many of its new vehicles are now being designed in Europe for Europe, reflecting the company's determination to get closer to the market. Historically restricted by import quotas to niche areas, such as sports cars and off-road vehicles, Toyota is fast becoming a leading brand in Europe.

Promotion

Recent advertising has seen a shift away from model-focused commercials to a more heavily branded and image-based campaign, which is a significant change for Toyota. Its functional strengths are well known – the quality and reliability of its vehicles are legendary. Its new approach is designed to raise awareness of its brand values, and make it more aspirational and more emotionally appealing to a wider audience.

As well as extensive high-profile brand advertising, Toyota invests in business-to-business marketing support, including customer relationship marketing, the 'In Front' loyalty magazine, fleet advertising, direct mail and vehicle evaluation events.

Every facet of the marketing campaign, from press, posters and TV to customer loyalty programmes and direct marketing underpins its brand values. All activities use the strapline: 'The car in front is a Toyota', which is the most widely recognised in the automotive industry. Never slow to recognise the potential of technology, Toyota offers the facility to build your own car through its website (www.toyota.co.uk). It has invested heavily in the internet in recent years as a channel to reach younger customers. Meanwhile its customer relationship programme has become one of the most focused and highly respected in the business, with an ultimate aim to engender loyalty that creates customers for life.

Brand Values

Toyota's brand values can be summarised in a single word: imagination. Imagination is at the heart of the company, driving creativity, its understanding of customers and its new product development. The brand has five principal values, the first being quality, anchored in the discipline of Kaizen: it is always seeking to improve quality in every aspect of its products and services. The second principle is being responsive – anticipating, recognising and delivering its customers' needs and exceeding their expectations. Individuality is key: recognising the value of individuals, tailoring products and services to individuals' needs and finding opportunities to personalise them at every opportunity. The fourth value is creativity, where imagination and inspired thinking lead to an energetic, flexible culture where ideas are nurtured and encouraged. And finally it seeks to be engaging: attracting and captivating customers and identifying with them through a genuine interest in resolving their needs. Toyota wants customers to choose the brand not just for rational benefits, but because they want to be associated with what it stands for.

Toyota is committed to developing business partnerships with dealers, suppliers and customers around the world. This approach is one of the reasons the company is able to boast industry leading customer satisfaction ratings.

Toyota is leading other manufacturers in ecological awareness and responsibility. As well as developing new, greener, engine technologies, the company has created an 'Earth Charter' and has even cultivated a forest grown specifically to improve the environment.

The Land Cruiser is widely recognised as the most reliable off-road vehicle in the most extreme conditions. There is a sign in the Australian outback that reads 'No vehicles beyond this point except Toyota Land Cruisers'.

The Toyota Advanced Safety Vehicle programme (ASV) is leading the industry in the development of active and passive safety features, including pedestrian airbags fitted in the bonnet of the car.

A Toyota 2000GT was used in the James Bond film 'You Only Live Twice' in 1967.

Toyota has opened an automotive theme park in Japan, called Mega Web, which attracts 9.8 million visitors a year. Visitors are able to drive over 50 Toyota models, including electric vehicles, and participate on interactive rides.

UNITED AIRLINES

A STAR ALLIANCE MEMBER 

Market

The international aviation industry is notoriously cut-throat, with over 260 airlines fighting to win a slice of the estimated 1.5 billion passenger journeys that take place every year. There are few industries where customers have so much choice and in which brands compete so vigorously and on so many fronts.

Much of every major airline's attention is the business traveller. These high margin, globe-trotting executives are wooed with an arsenal of features to cater for their every need, including chauffeur pick-up services and 'beds in the sky'. This is where many airlines make their money. Prices have plummeted so much that competition on economy fares is often too fierce to provide meaningful returns.

Figures from the International Air Transport Association show the dynamics at work here. It says that the average air traveller is paying 70% less, in real terms than they were paying twenty years ago. It also says that slightly more than 14% of IATA member traffic was first and intermediate ('club' or 'business') class. However, this small percentage provided almost 32% of revenue.

Although this is a high-growth market – IATA estimates that passenger journeys by air could exceed 2.3 billion by 2010 – competition is becoming ever more intense.

De-regulation is the driving force encouraging competition. For example, the so-called 'Open Skies' discussions between American and British regulators, could greatly increase the number of carriers allowed to operate out of Heathrow Airport. Deregulation is happening across the world, ending the monopolies and protection enjoyed by certain airlines and exposing them to sharp-priced, fleet-footed rivals.

This has sparked a move towards seeking safety in numbers. Most large airlines nowadays are engaged in global alliances with other operators – allowing them to co-operate on marketing, ticket booking and frequent-flyer programmes. United Airlines and the Star Alliance – which also includes fourteen other airlines – is a prime example of this strategy.

This is a truly giant industry. In 1998 it provided at least 28 million jobs for the world's workforce, generating around £850 billion in gross annual output. By 2010, aviation's economic growth impact could exceed £1,200 billion and provide the basis for over 31 million jobs worldwide.

Achievements

During its long history, United has built itself into a world leader in the global aviation industry. It is now the largest airline in the world, when ranked by its $18 billion 1999 total revenue.

It has done this by expanding its brand outside of the domestic US market and making itself a player on the world stage. It has become one of the top brands for international business travellers, regularly winning awards amongst this important customer group. For example, it was recently voted 'Best Airline in North America' by Business Traveller International magazine.

Its formidable reputation in the business traveller market is backed by products and services designed to meet their needs. For example, it is one of a few transatlantic carriers to offer three cabin classes and has one of the most widely used and favoured frequent flyer programmes in the US – Mileage Plus. This programme, has 23 million members worldwide and was voted best frequent flyer programme by Business Traveller International magazine in 1999. Mileage Plus has won numerous other awards and is recognised to be one of the best in the airline business.

Other notable achievements include the fact that United was the first customer for Boeing's latest 777 wide-body jet. This – one of the newest and most advanced big jets flying today – was developed by Boeing in conjunction with United.

As well as this impressive record of working at the cutting edge of aircraft design, United is also a trailblazer in the business world. It was one of the founding members of the Star Alliance, which was the first global alliance between airlines and has now grown into the biggest. Its work in forming the alliance showed great foresight as airline alliances are now seen as one of the most important factors shaping the modern aviation industry.

Another impressive corporate achievement is the fact that it is the largest employee-owned company in the world, with 55-60% of its stock held by the United workforce. This dates back to 1993 when, in a cost-cutting exercise, the United board allowed employees to trade portions of salaries and benefits for stock in the company. This has grown into the Employee Stock Ownership Programme, creating a unique culture of employee involvement and pride in the company and the United brand.

History

United has a rich history in the airline industry, dating back to 1926. This was the year that Walter Varney initiated a contract airmail service from Pasco in Washington to Elko, Nevada. This marked the true beginning of commercial air transportation in the United States and the birth of United Airlines.

Varney was one of a handful of key pioneers in these earliest days of commercial air travel, along with William Boeing, the father of the giant aircraft manufacturer. He and Varney joined forces in the Boeing Airplane and Transport Corporation – a company which made aircraft and operated transport services. In 1929, the name United Airlines was adopted for the transport divisions of the company. In these early days, United built an unrivalled network of airmail contract routes.

During World War II United played a key part in the war effort, modifying aircraft for military use and training ground crew and airlifting personnel and freight around the country. The post-war boom that swept the US led to a surge in demand for air travel. It was around this time that the airline purchased its first jet aircraft and, when it merged with Capital Airlines in 1961, it became the world's largest commercial airline.

The 1960s heralded the dawn of the jet age proper and United began to spread its wings, with the launch of a lucrative route to Hawaii. By the early 1980s, United had opened a route to Tokyo and was competing in a newly de-regulated US air market.

In this ultra-competitive environment, United redefined itself, becoming a true global operator with the launch of services to Europe, South America and extended operations around the Pacific Rim. It made its ambitions clear with the placing in 1990 of the largest ever single aircraft order, totalling $22 billion. It also acquired Pan American's US routes to London and launched its now famous grey, navy and red livery to befit its global image.

In 1997 it helped launch the Star Alliance with Lufthansa, Air Canada, SAS and Thai Airways. This showed it was early to spot the trend towards global muscle in the airline industry. It was also fleet-footed in its home market, launching United Shuttle to compete against ever-more aggressive low-cost operators.

Product

United offers flights to 135 destinations in 26 countries. With its fleet of 600 aircraft, it offers 2,475 daily departures.

For the business traveller, a vital element of its product is its partnership with the fellow members of the Star Alliance and the benefits of its award-winning frequent flyer programme, Mileage Plus.

Mileage Plus members can earn miles towards travel awards when they fly United or a Star Alliance member airline. This gives travellers the opportunity to earn miles for free travel to more than 820 destinations around the world. These miles can also be earned against hotel stays, car rental and long-distance phone calls.

Business and First Class passengers have the added advantage of being able to use the airport lounge facilities of United and its partners. United's Red Carpet Club lounges offer premier facilities – such as conference rooms and complimentary food and drink – to frequent flyers.

The airline's first class service – United First – offers some of the best service on the market, including a dedicated concierge service in the airport terminal, Fast Track check-in and the United First Suite 'bed in the sky'. The First Suite reclines 180 degrees into a six-foot bed, complete with fine linens and a privacy screen. The business class service – United Business – offers similarly prestigious service levels, such as over-water satellite phones and early boarding.

An important element of all United's product is the introduction of more interactive services. These include an e-Ticket service, which does away with the need for a paper ticket and a telephone paging service which automatically alerts passengers to the status of their impending flights.

For business customers, United offers a comprehensive cargo service. It is one of the largest cargo carriers in the US, flying over 3.1 billion cargo tonne miles in 1999.

Recent Developments

On a service level, recent developments include the launch of Perks Plus. This is a service that targets small and medium sized businesses (SMEs) who are not big enough to negotiate the special corporate rate agreements United holds with large corporations. The service fills the gap between the benefits of having a corporate agreement and the regular perks enjoyed by members of Mileage Plus.

This target audience may also benefit from another recent introduction – Economy Plus. This is a premium seating area in the Economy cabin, offering five inches more legroom per seat. Over 21,000 Economy Plus seats are now available on US domestic flights.

Operationally, United launched a new service between London and Boston in summer 1999.

Promotion

United's promotion focuses mainly on the business and first class traveller as they make up the most lucrative part of its business. For UK executive travellers, often the two preferred airlines for flying to the US are the home carriers, British Airways and Virgin Atlantic. United's aim is to be the third preferred carrier, putting it above its US-based rivals American and Continental.

The airline has a rich history in advertising, having worked with Leo Burnett for 32 years before moving to Young & Rubicam. Its famous 'Fly the friendly skies' slogan dates back to 1965 and is still used today.

In 1998 United responded to growing evidence that business travellers were not satisfied with the airline industry's service standards with the 'Rising' campaign. This positioned United as the airline that was rising to the challenge of making business travel pleasurable.

This message was taken further in 2000 with a new campaign, based on the line: 'Life is a journey. Travel it well.' Utilising TV, radio, print and the internet, the campaign shows how United can help the business traveller throughout all stages of their journey. The TV ads feature the airline's trademark music, 'Rhapsody in Blue' and have an uplifting, inspirational tone.

As well as these main campaigns, the airline also uses ambient media, such as taxis and tube trains branded inside and out in United colours. Recent work furnishing the interiors of London taxis in United colours and materials is designed to give business travellers a taste of experiencing the brand.

The airline also uses sponsorship, particularly in sport. It was one of the official sponsors of the US Olympic Team at Sydney 2000. It also sponsors British yacht racing.

Brand Values

Brands are important in all markets, but especially in the airline industry. As a commodity market, brands are one of the biggest differentiators determining customers' choice of airline. In the age of the international alliance, the strength of individual names within groups will make brands even more important in the future.

United has over 70 years of brand heritage. A key aspect of its brand is its commitment to service, encapsulated in the Customer Satisfaction Philosophy which it first introduced in 1997. This includes a United Commitment to its customers that strives to provide them respect, courtesy and fairness in the air and on the ground. This is a sweeping policy that incorporates pricing, refunds and all aspects of customer service by United and its code-sharing partners.

The Customer Satisfaction Philosophy is summed up in 'six ways to succeed', namely that United Airlines service should be: worldly, easy, honest, precise, active and engaging. The brand is known simply as 'United'. This is designed to express how the airline is united to create a better journey, united in the interests of customers and uniting travellers with their destinations.

Things you didn't know about United Airlines

United flies more than 235,255 passengers every day.

In 1999 United carried over 87 million passengers.

United employs over 10,200 pilots and 23,856 flight attendants.

United operates 42 Boeing 777-200s and 44 747-400s – two of the biggest aircraft in the world.

The average age of its passenger fleet is 10.1 years.

Market

It seems odd to think of a world without payment cards. We spend an estimated £1.6 trillion per year using payment cards and Visa, which is the world's leading financial brand, has a 60% share of this gigantic market.

Commercial cards take up an increasingly important slice of this market. As companies seek efficiencies by allowing employees to charge purchasing and work expenses to a corporate account, the usage of commercial cards is high. Research shows that they are used by 79% of all corporations. In Europe, the commercial payments market is estimated to be worth £533.3 billion. Visa has 2.4 million commercial cards in Europe, creating an annual transaction volume of £8.7 billion.

In 1999, commercial cards were used for an estimated 94 million payments in the UK – a 14% increase on the year before. With more and more small and medium sized enterprises (SMEs) using corporate cards, this is expected to be one of the fastest growing areas of plastic card use for the next few years. By 2009, the number of commercial card payments is expected to reach 369 million.

The commercial card market has changed dramatically since the early 1990s. Then it predominantly consisted of fuel and business cards. The traditional business card was designed for travel and expenses (T&E) payments. Although 69% of corporate T&E expenses are still placed on commercial cards, Visa products are increasingly being segmented to suit more specific needs. There are now several different types of commercial card: business cards for SMEs, which are used to separate business and personal spending; corporate cards, which are used by bigger companies to control travel and expenses costs; and purchasing cards, which are used to procure low value items within large companies. All of these options allow companies to keep a tighter rein on their expenditure and gather more intelligence about spending patterns.

These factors mean that there are now 39 different types of bank-issued commercial cards on the market, compared to thirteen in 1995. In the same period, the number of bank-issued commercial cards in use in the UK has leapt from 520,000 to 1.1 million.

Achievements

Visa cards are the most widely held and accepted payment cards in the world and are as close as there is to a global currency.

Visa recently cemented its dominance of the payment card market when its billionth card was issued. That is enough for one in four of the world's adult population to own one. This is an unprecedented achievement for a financial brand and demonstrates Visa's formidable global power. Very few brands can demonstrate such international recognition and reach – Visa now claims to be as ubiquitous as Coca-Cola and McDonald's.

Visa has helped to drive uptake of payment cards among the population. In 1970, when just £2 billion was spent on credit cards predominantly in the US, customers had to show an impressive banking history to get one. But now, Visa's one billion cards are used to spend £1.06 trillion at nineteen million outlets in more than 300 countries and territories. Students, pensioners, millionaires and business people can all use Visa cards, with products tailored to suit them.

Visa's commercial card activities have enjoyed similar success. For example, over 1,500 private sector companies and public bodies, including Glaxo Wellcome, 3M and BT, have adopted the Visa Purchasing card, launched in 1994.

Visa is also at the forefront of adopting new technology. Smart Debit/Chip applications have been added to all UK Visa magnetic strip cards issued since 1998 and will supersede cards carrying only a magnetic strip by the end of 2001. Over five million UK Visa chip cards – which are safer when it comes to fighting fraud – have been issued.

History

Visa started life in 1958 in the US, when the Bank of America launched its BankAmericard programme. During the 1960s, the Bank of America began licensing its blue, white and gold charge card to other US banks, leading to the formation of a new entity, National BankAmericard Inc, in 1970. This was jointly owned by the banks issuing the card and was in charge of administering the programme in the US.

It was not until 1977 that the Visa name first appeared. Three years earlier, the programme had expanded beyond the US market under the management of a new international body, called IBANCO. It came up with the Visa name to give the programme a single, global, identity. IBANCO subsequently became Visa International and the National BankAmericaCard Inc became Visa USA.

Credit cards first appeared in the UK in 1966, when Barclays Bank launched the Barclaycard. Barclays soon adopted Visa and, through its card division, became the country's largest Visa issuer. Other banks quickly followed and the UK soon became one of the world's leading credit card markets. Visa Debit Cards were introduced in the UK in 1987 and there are now 23 million cards in circulation. There are currently more than 75 British banks and building societies issuing Visa cards in the UK.

Product

Visa's commercial product portfolio can be divided into three product areas: business, corporate and purchasing. Visa Business is designed for small businesses with 1-50 employees. It is for all general purchasing needs, not just T&E. It is also well suited for the specific payment needs of small businesses, such as payment of utility bills, office equipment and computer hardware and software.

The Visa Corporate card is issued to large businesses or corporations and is designed for purchasing all T&E requirements. It is also especially suitable where management control information is important, giving the cardholder's company detailed management information and spend analysis. Other options include travel insurance and emergency cash and local currency billing.

Launched in the UK in 1994, the Visa Purchasing card is typically issued to large corporations and public sector organisations and is primarily designed for purchasing low value items like office equipment and stationary, although it can also be used to pay for consultancy and temporary staff. It empowers staff to deal directly with suppliers in virtually paper-free transactions, replacing purchase orders and requisition forms. At the end of each month, companies can receive a full management information report, detailing spending by employee, supplier and category of purchase.

In 1997, Visa struck a deal with Her Majesty's Treasury to issue Government Procurement Cards to all central UK Government departments and agencies. Today, Visa Purchasing is available throughout Europe and Visa is the market leader with around 90% market share.

Visa Multinational is a unique offering, providing the benefits of a single contact for multinational corporations, with the advantage of local bank support and service. This benefits overall expense management through global control and allows regional offices to draw on the services of local Visa member banks.

Recent Developments

Visa's European division recently launched an aggressive strategy to capture a majority share of the £0.8 trillion business-to-business e-commerce payments market. Electronic payments in this sector are booming and Visa intends to assert a leading position for its brand.

Currently 54% of all online consumer sales are attributed to Visa and the company wants to mirror this success in online business-to-business sales. To achieve this, Visa is developing secure payment and data technology designed for the business-to-business e-commerce market. It is also entering into strategic third party alliances with leading e-commerce systems providers to ensure they support Visa as the preferred payment system.

Visa sees developments like its global invoice specification – which is the world's first truly inter-operable global electronic invoice system – as crucial to the flourishing of business-to-business e-commerce.

Promotion

Visa has a rich heritage of global brand support. It is one of the world's biggest advertisers, using a full variety of marketing channels. Its sponsorship of the Sydney 2000 Olympic Games has been one of its highest profile activities, with Visa being one of eleven worldwide companies who participated in the Olympic Partner Programme. As well as providing a showcase for Visa's products to a huge business and consumer audience, the Olympic sponsorship underlines Visa's muscle as a truly global brand.

The company has sponsored the three previous summer Olympics (Seoul, Barcelona and Atlanta) and four Winter Olympics (Calgary, Albertville, Lillehammer and Nagano). It will also sponsor the 2002 Olympic Winter Games in Salt Lake City and the 2004 Summer Games in Athens.

The Olympic sponsorship holds great attractions for Visa's business partners, such as issuing banks and merchants. It gives them the opportunity to leverage the value and global recognition of the Olympics brand to benefit their customers.

Visa is also well-known for investing in high-profile advertising. Its 1996 'Visa Family' campaign ran across eleven countries and increased awareness levels for the brand by up to 40%. The latest 'The Future Takes Visa' campaign is running across the EU and positions the brand as a leading-edge payment system that can be used no matter how technology changes in the future. The theme of the advertisements is to make people feel positive about the future and to think about Visa as a brand that they can use with confidence.

On a more business-to-business level, Visa Business sponsored the Department of Trade and Industry's annual UK Innovation Lecture. The multi-media event, which linked 50 venues by satellite, explored the issues set to dominate and challenge the business environment for the next ten years.

Visa Purchasing also sponsored the 1999 Kelly's Awards for Excellence in Purchasing and Supply in association with the Chartered Institute of Purchasing and Supply. The awards were created to recognise the importance of the supply chain as a critical management function within business, by identifying and rewarding outstanding performance.

Brand Values

Visa is one of the strongest brands in the world. Unprompted awareness has been at 60% for the last three years. Levels of brand preference are almost three times Visa's closest competitor, Mastercard.

Because of the impact of the internet, e-commerce and sweeping changes in the financial services market, Visa has developed a new brand positioning. This is: 'Visa is the transaction system – payment today, information tomorrow and through various channels – which gives you confidence that you can get what you want, when and where you want it, now and in the future.' Visa's core values are trust, reliability, flexibility, convenience and security.

Visa wants its brand to constitute the 'gold standard' of international payments.

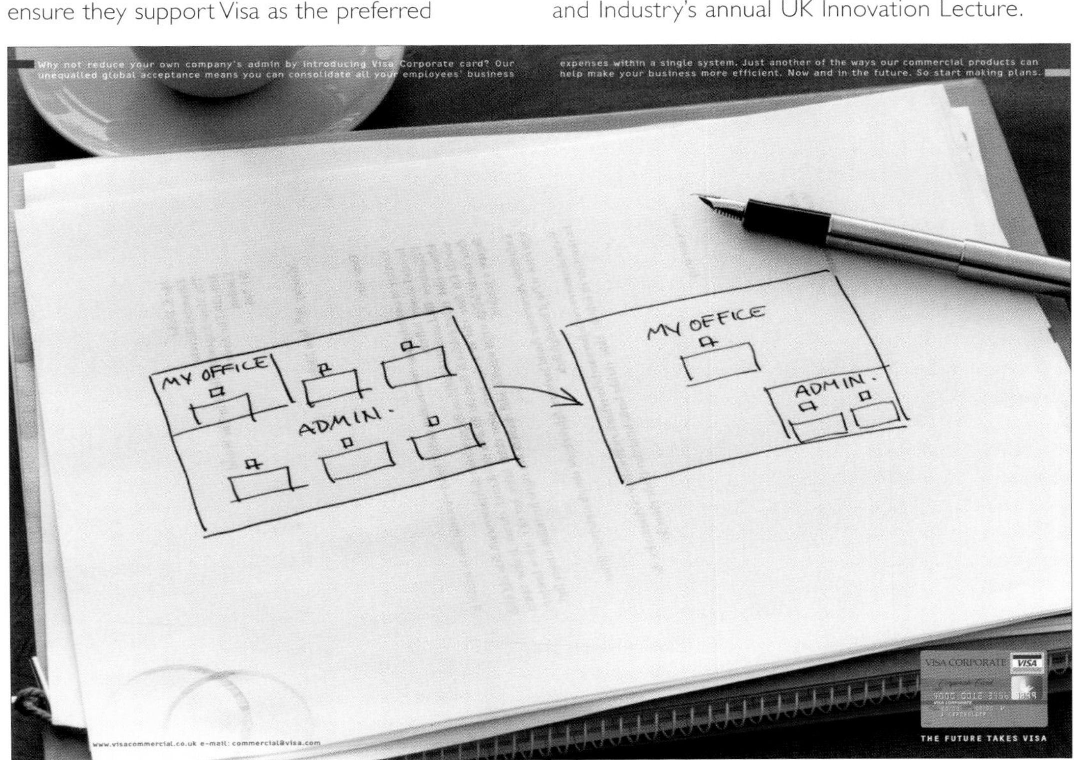

Things you didn't know about Visa

When stacked one on top of the other, all the Visa cards in use in the world would be 120 times the height of Mount Everest. Laid end to end, they would reach around the world – twice.

Over 623,000 cash machines around the world accept Visa cards.

Visa is the first payment card to break the $1 trillion barrier for card transactions.

The UK is the largest European market, accounting for 35% of all cards.

Over 600 transactions are made on Visa cards per second worldwide.

In Europe, Visa has 2.4 million commercial cards, 86 card-issuers and an annual transaction volume of £8.7 billion.

THE DOCUMENT COMPANY XEROX

Market

Xerox may be best known for inventing the photocopier, but its business sector is now much wider than this product alone. Nowadays, it is in the business of providing 'document solutions', supplying products and services which meet a wide variety of business needs.

This encompasses any service which helps companies better manage and share their information. In the age of technology convergence, companies have to cope with sweeping changes in the way that business gets done. Computing, imaging, communications, database marketing and the internet are all coming together, as companies combine technology with knowledge to change the way they do business and gain competitive advantage.

They are looking to companies like Xerox to provide the technology and knowledge to help them process, integrate and optimise information in this chaotic and fast-changing business landscape.

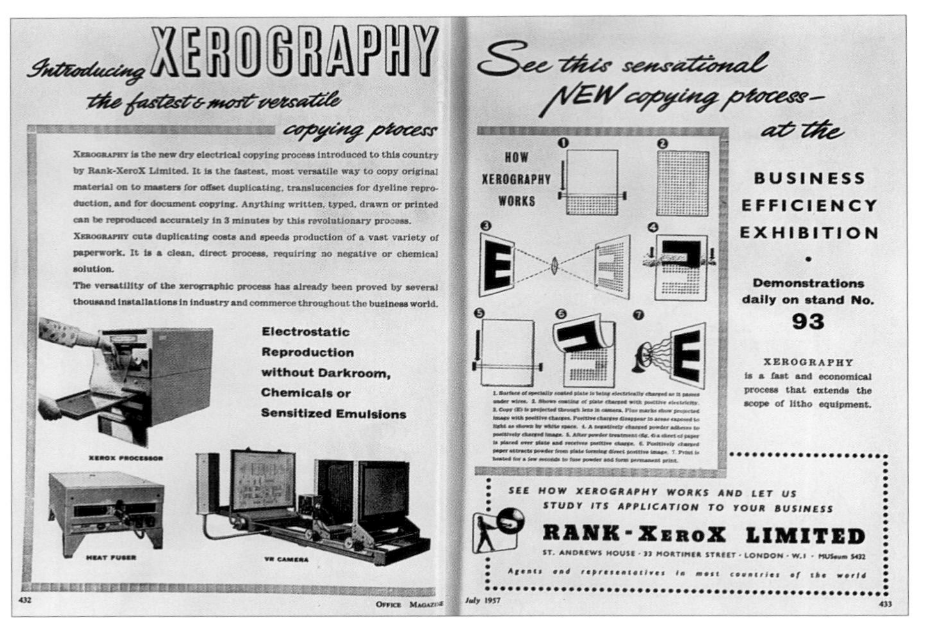

Achievements

The photocopier is one of the most important inventions of the modern age. Indeed, Fortune magazine recently recognised this when it included the Xerox photocopier in its Products of the Century League. Alongside the paper clip, the Post-It® Note, the Intel microprocessor and the Apple Macintosh, Xerox's ground-breaking invention was judged to be a product which has helped to revolutionise the workplace.

A measure of its success is the Xerox brand name which is often used to describe a photocopy, no matter what type of machine is used. This is an achievement enjoyed by a very small handful of the world's most powerful brands, all of whose names are used to generically describe a product category. Alongside Hoover, Post-It® Notes, Apsirin and Tarmac, Xerox is part of an exclusive club. According to Interbrand, Xerox is the world's 23rd most powerful brand, worth £7.5 billion. This means that Xerox has a higher brand valuation than Nike, Budweiser, Dell, BP, Shell, Apple and even Pepsi-Cola.

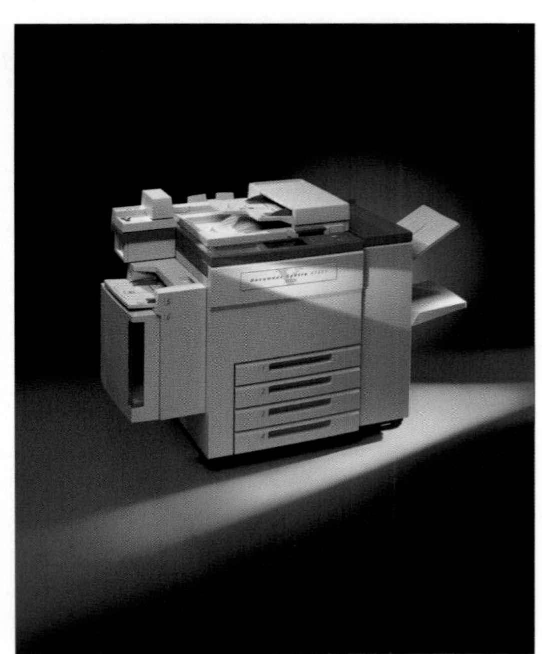

In the US, Xerox was recently voted the number one Office Equipment Brand in a Landor/Harris ImagePower survey. Of the executives interviewed in the survey, 61% said they knew Xerox 'very well'.

The company, which ranks 87th in the Fortune 500, has a legendary track record of innovation. Its fabled Palo Alto Research Centre developed the first fax machine, laser printer and the graphical user interface – including the mouse which was first taken up by Apple and is now standard on Microsoft Windows PCs.

Since 1980 Xerox and Fuji Xerox have won 25 national quality awards in twenty countries. These include the most prestigious quality awards in the US, Europe and Japan. Xerox has done particularly well against its Japanese counterparts being the first non-Japanese corporation to regain market share after losing it to Japanese competitors.

One of the company's most notable achievements has been its effort to reinvent itself from a black and white analogue copier company to a global enterprise meeting the demands of converging technology with network-connected digital products, solutions, services and support.

History

The process of photocopying documents was invented by Chester Carlson in New York City in 1938. Having worked for a printer as a teenager, Carlson knew the difficulty of getting words in hard copy and was looking for a more efficient duplication process. His invention of electrophotography was patented in 1939.

Despite the potential of his invention, Carlson spent a discouraging ten years searching for a company to develop the technology into a useful product. Businesses at the time didn't believe there was a market for an electronic copier when carbon paper did the job satisfactorily.

Some twenty companies, including IBM and General Electric, were among those to reject the idea. Eventually, in 1947, the Haloid Company – a New York photographic paper manufacturer – acquired the licence to make the copying machine. One of the first things Haloid and Carlson agreed upon was that the word 'electrophotography' was too unwieldy, changing to a term derived from Greek, 'xerography'. Soon after, Haloid coined the word 'Xerox' as the trademark for the new copiers and, in 1958 the company changed its name to Haloid Xerox.

In 1956 when Haloid wanted to expand its operation into Europe it formed a joint venture with the Rank Organisation known as Rank Xerox Ltd. This was an extremely productive partnership, and then in the 1990s Rank Organisation started to divest some of its share to Xerox Corporation until 1997 when Rank Organisation sold its last remaining shares to Xerox.

The enormous success of the Xerox 914 – the first automatic office copier to use ordinary paper – prompted the company to change its name again, to the Xerox Corporation in 1961. The 914 – so called because it could copy sheets

as large as nine by fourteen inches – sold 10,000 units in its first two years on the market. It made Xerox into a rising star, causing its net revenue to leap from £1.7 million in 1960, to £15.1 million in 1963.

The 914 was eventually discontinued in 1974. In its lifetime it sold 200,000 around the world. Other hit products were the 813 desk-top copier, introduced in 1963, and the 2400 (named after the number of copies it could make in an hour) in 1964.

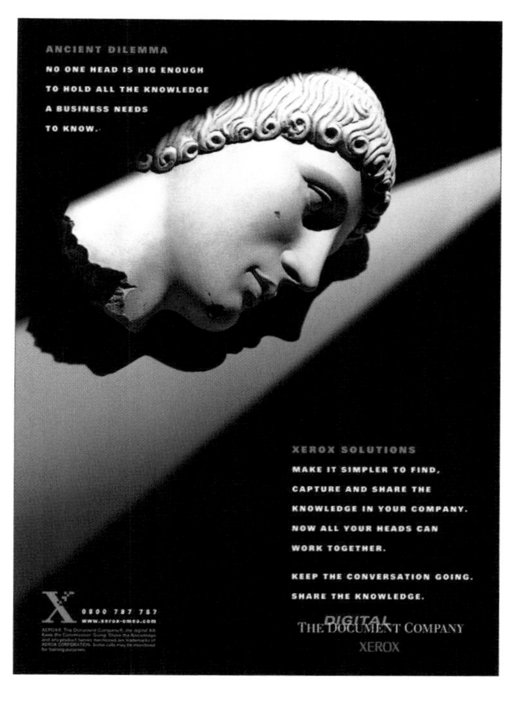

However, Xerox did not only give us the photocopier. It also produced the first ever fax machine, the Telecopier I, in 1966 and the first ever laser printer, the 9700, in 1977.

Product

Xerox's core expertise is in the production and management of documents. They can be colour or black and white, paper or digital, and for the small office, the network or the global enterprise. Xerox offers a broad range of 'document solutions' products and services, such as copiers, printers, fax machines, scanners, desktop software, digital printing and publishing systems and outsourced document management.

Office products include a wide range of copiers, printers and multifunction systems. Designed to increase productivity, products such as the Xerox DocuPrint N32 and the Document Centre 400 Series. Xerox also makes a wide range of products using ink jet technology designed for the growing small office/home (SOHO) market, and most recently the 'M' Series, which copies, prints, faxes and scans in black and white and colour.

These products are produced in partnership with the Sharp Corporation and Fuji Xerox.

On a larger scale, Xerox is a leading player in the high-end digital printing and production market. Its DocuTech, DocuPrint and DocuColor ranges are widely used in publishing and graphic arts, enabling companies to deliver just-in-time, mass-customised and on-demand solutions. Just-in-time printing is becoming an important growth area as companies seek to reduce storage costs and wastage by matching print runs to demand.

Xerox also supplies solutions for the eBusiness market. Among the services offered by Xerox eSolutions is ContentGuard. This enables people to put their copyrighted work on the internet while keeping control over who sees it. This is one of the ways in which Xerox is developing new ways of allowing people to visualise and share information over the internet.

Xerox also offers a wide range of network, consulting, customer training and outsourcing services to support companies' document management requirements. It also supplies software to help companies share information over networks. DocuShare – a web-based application – helps project teams keep up to date, while DigiPath is designed for printing and publishing applications.

Recent Developments

The Xerox Corporation recently teamed up with 3M to develop a new Electronic Paper product. This is a digital document display with the portability of a plain sheet of paper, which is still in prototype.

Developed at the Xerox PARC, electronic paper represents a new kind of display. Like paper, it is user-friendly, thin, lightweight and flexible. But like a computer display, it is also dynamic and rewritable. This combination of properties makes it suitable for a wide range of applications, including electronic paper newspapers and magazines, textbooks and paper displays.

The 3M collaboration is another example of Xerox's ongoing efforts to leverage its £1.1 billion annual investment in research and technology to deliver new products, develop research-based strategic alliances, spawn a series of entrepreneurial spin-off companies and license its rich portfolio of patents and inventions to other companies.

Xerox has also introduced a new range of personal and networked products to expand its retail presence to more than 10,000 stores. It is investing £200 million in worldwide marketing and advertising over the next two years to support the move. A new range of digital copier/printers aimed at the SOHO market is an example of the new product drive.

Xerox is also expanding its distribution capacity. Retail outlets carrying Xerox products will jump more than 40% and the number of Xerox resellers and dealers will grow by more than 30%.

Xerox was recently selected by KMWorld magazine as the 'Knowledge Company of the Year' for 1999. Xerox was cited for Eureka, a knowledge-sharing best practice that enhances customer service by increasing Xerox service teams' ability to diagnose, solve and prevent equipment problems whilst in the field. KMWorld is a leading publication in the knowledge management and business intelligence industry.

Promotion

Xerox utilises a wide range of promotional tools, including TV and print advertising, direct mail, point of purchase, trade shows and sponsorship. All channels share the same theme. This, called the 'Knowledge Campaign', is based on the premise that between the realms of e-mail, paperwork, and internet, most offices are drowning in information but starved of real knowledge. The focus is to show how Xerox can help customers find document solutions to problems they most need to solve. The 'Knowledge Campaign' shows how sharing knowledge through documents – in whatever form – is key to any company's success.

The print campaign, using business press, presents a problem/solution approach, expressed as 'Ancient Dilemma.... Xerox Solution'. Each of the ads highlights a different product and demonstrates how it can solve a business problem.

Since 1994, when it was the official copies sponsor of the Winter Olympics at Innsbruck, Xerox has been a worldwide sponsor of the Olympic Games. This allows it to use Olympic logos in its communications and Xerox equipment to be showcased during the competition. At the Sydney 2000 Olympic Games, Xerox provided over 2,800 machines for use in the massive administrative effort that supported the competition. In 1999 Xerox also sponsored the Rugby World Cup.

Brand Values

To reflect its new wider-ranging positioning in the market, Xerox styles itself The Document Company Xerox. Its core values centre on being the global leader in document management. It aims to provide solutions that provide a bridge between the paper and digital worlds and enhance business productivity through the sharing of knowledge.

Things you didn't know about **Xerox**

The first ever photocopied image said '10-22-38 Astoria'. This was the date, October 22nd 1938, that the inventor of 'xerography', Chester Carlson, created the image in his laboratory in Astoria, New York.

The word xerography is derived from the Greek for 'dry' and 'writing'.

Xerox invests over £1 billion in research and development every year.

Xerox is the second largest printer company in the world.

Xerox manufactures products in fifteen countries, and has offices in 150 countries.

Market

Yellow Pages has supported the growth and development of businesses in the UK for over 30 years. In this time it has become the leading directory in the UK and a trusted household name. It is an invaluable and indispensable information bridge between buyers and sellers, keeping businesses in touch with existing and potential customers 365 days a year.

As we move into the twenty-first century, the Yellow Pages brand is increasing in strength. People do business differently these days. The internet has fuelled the quest for evermore flexible and rapid access to information, and other technological advances mean that expectations are high, and competition is fierce.

Of course Yellow Pages is still most famous for being the distinctive yellow directory. But these days fulfilling its role as a business information bridge means it is more than that: 'Yell.com', an award-winning website, was launched in 1996 to ensure that Yellow Pages keeps up with the fast-moving pace of communications technology. 'Talking Pages' has expanded the peripheries of the familiar yellow directory with its 24-hour phone information service. 'Business Pages', a directory exclusively targeted at businesses, and 'The Business Database' which supplies business-to-business data have all ensured that Yellow Pages continues to link businesses and their customers in the fast paced world of business.

Now, more than ever, Yellow Pages is part of everyday life. It is used by almost half of the adult population in the UK every month, and the Yellow Pages product portfolio is used almost 1.5 billion times a year (Source: Saville Rossiter-Base 1999, NOP Business 1999 and Yellow Pages internal stats. 1999).

Needless to say, the more times that Yellow Pages is used each day, week, month, and year, the more that the advertisers within it are likely to benefit.

Brand Achievements

Households in the UK receive a new Yellow Pages directory every year. Some 28 million directories are distributed to homes and businesses across the country. With this kind of access, brand awareness is extremely high with 98% of adults having a Yellow Pages directory at home (Source: Saville Rossiter-Base 1999).

Yellow Pages generates £262 million daily for companies that advertise within it (Source: Saville Rossiter-Base 1999). It is hardly surprising then that over 80% of those advertisers will re-advertise the following year. And with a range of products and services that are constantly being reassessed and improved, the Yellow Pages team are working all the time to ensure that they will keep on returning. It is service like this that has cemented Yellow Pages' position as a Superbrand.

46% of adults use Yellow Pages regularly which means that the directory is used over 100 million times per month (Sources: BMRB 1999 and Saville Rossiter-Base 1999). With such a high level of penetration, Yellow Pages represents a crucial source of new business for companies nationwide. More than 350,000 advertisers place over 650,000 advertisements in Yellow Pages to promote their goods and services (Source: Yellow Pages Sales Data).

YELL.COM™

90% of advertisers state that they consider placing an advert in the Yellow Pages directory to represent value for money. Existing advertisers are consistently happy with their investment in the Yellow Pages – 83% are satisfied with the response from their advert (Source: Saville Rossiter-Base 1999).

Companies in the UK qualify for a free discretionary 'line' entry in the directory for their business, which means that there are about two million entries nationwide. That is, two million companies with potentially different advertising requirements. For this reason, Yellow Pages' sales teams are highly trained in order to recognise and recommend the appropriate advertising programme for an individual company.

Yellow Pages takes a caring and individual approach to every company within the directory, advising them every step of the way, and even designing their advertisements, if required. Yellow Pages' success is due in part to the extent that it is committed to helping its customers. It works hard to support businesses and to provide the right service for their needs.

This commitment to service and continuous improvement led to Yellow Pages winning the 1999 European Quality Award for Businesses Excellence.

History

Although directories are closely associated with telephones, they actually pre-date Alexander Graham Bell's invention by two centuries. The first versions can be traced back to Elizabethan times when street directories were published detailing the names and addresses of residential and business premises. By the 1840s Kelly's London Post Office directories began to emerge.

The arrival of the telecommunications era offered further potential for the publishers of directories. In 1966, the General Post Office, which was the controller of most UK telephony at the time, introduced and developed Yellow Pages as a national business.

The first Yellow Pages was launched in Brighton and in the early years it was bound into the standard telephone directories. The first advertisement in Yellow Pages was sold in 1966 and by the mid 1970s, Yellow Pages had attained nationwide coverage and was bridge building across the country. Yellow Pages became a registered trademark in the UK in 1979.

And with the development of products like Yell.com, Talking Pages, Business Pages and The Business Database, Yellow Pages is more committed than ever to keeping up with the new developments in technology.

Product

Yellow Pages is the UK's most comprehensive classified directory. But it is more than that. It has a range of supporting products and a breadth of distribution that make it the market leader.

Recognised as an essential advertising tool by companies of every size all over the country, Yellow Pages acts as a shop front to a business. Firms that advertise in it receive an average of 387 calls a year from people responding to their ad (Source: Critical Research 1998).

Yellow Pages is best known for the Yellow Pages directory. But increasingly, the goal of bringing buyers and sellers together is being accomplished through other media, particularly the internet. The product portfolio shows the breadth of the Yellow Pages umbrella.

Yell.com, the award winning website was launched in 1996 in anticipation of the huge increase of internet usage. Yell.com is host to an exciting and diverse range of interactive products and services, which include Yellow Pages on-line, a UK specific web directory, and comprehensive travel, property, entertainment, shopping and business specific channels. Yell.com also offers website design services as well as a range of advertising opportunities.

Talking Pages, the 24-hour telephone information service, provides details about businesses and services throughout the country. Customers can call for the latest information about anything from a business's prices, to special offers and opening hours.

Business Pages, the business-to-business classified directory was launched in the 1980s. It covers only businesses that supply goods and services to other businesses, and covers six major metropolitan regions throughout the UK.

The Business Database, launched in 1986 has become a leading supplier of data for business-to-business direct marketing in the UK and contains 1.5 million business locations.

Recent Developments

In 1999 Yellow Pages developed an award-winning redesign of the directory. This included a new cover, a clearer format that is easier to navigate and a new typeface that makes information easier to read. There is an increased emphasis on local information sections, and colourful, more eye-catching graphics. The directory is now more user-friendly than ever with advertisements that stand out more, attracting additional customers for advertisers.

The redesign also introduced 'White Knock Out' ads which give advertisers the option of making their advert even more distinctive by placing a white ad on yellow paper.

Yellow Pages is constantly striving to assess and improve the services that are offered by the products in its portfolio. It is currently trialing colour advertising. Business Pages has recently introduced a sixth directory covering the Thames Valley and Central area. This means that the national business community is even more efficiently served. And Talking Pages has recently gone one step further with the introduction of a new level of service: 'Call Completion'. This service minimises time and effort for consumers because operators can transfer callers directly to the company they have requested.

Promotion

Yellow Pages knows that high brand awareness means high usage, ensuring that Yellow Pages advertisers continue to reap the benefits of placing an ad in the directory. Yellow Pages has always recognised the importance of building its brand through strong advertising campaigns. The 'let your fingers do the walking' campaign ran for thirteen years throughout the 1970s and early 1980s and put Yellow Pages on the map.

Yellow Pages has had incredible success with some of the most memorable television campaigns. For example, the 'not just for the nasty things in life' TV campaign began with a character called JR Hartley who uses Yellow Pages to trace a book he had written in younger days. This was the starting point for one of the UK's longest running and most famous ad campaigns which has since been followed by other highly successful ones such as 'Life' and 'Cleaners', which received a gold award at the 1999 British Television Advertising Awards.

High profile campaigns like this have helped to increase the existing awareness and usage of Yellow Pages, and to ensure that Yellow Pages is working harder for its advertisers.

Yellow Pages regularly communicates with the business community, both advertisers and non-advertisers, through a whole range of media and promotional activity. Designed to ensure companies are aware of the range of services available, the importance of Yellow Pages is perhaps best demonstrated by the fact that it receives over 100,000 sales enquiries from companies a year.

Brand Values

Yellow Pages won the 1999 European Quality Award for business excellence.

Team work and a progressive outlook ensures an exceptional standard of customer service, on both a national and local level. Yellow Pages prides itself on being trustworthy and professional in its actions and in its high level of respect for its customers and colleagues.

Yellow Pages continually strives for improvement in their product portfolio and its level of service to advertisers and consumers alike at the same time as maintaining a socially and environmentally responsible outlook. Above all, Yellow Pages is customer focused, which is how it has become such a trusted part of everyday life.

As well as working for the business community, Yellow Pages has strong ties to the local community and is a sponsor of the Marie Curie Cancer Campaign and the Reading Half Marathon.

® Registered trade mark of British Telecommunications plc.
TM Trade mark of British Telecommunications plc.

Things you didn't know about Yellow Pages

Some 28 million Yellow Pages directories are distributed to homes and businesses across the country every year.

The book 'Fly Fishing' by JR Hartley was not written until 1991 – eight years after the commercial was first aired. It became a Christmas best-seller.

More than 350,000 advertisers place over 650,0000 advertisements in Yellow Pages every year.

Yellow Pages is most often used to help people find the information about the automotive, restaurant and construction sectors.

By laying a year's worth of Yellow Pages directories end to end, a yellow path could be built stretching from London to Beijing.

On average nearly 40 people use Yellow pages every second of every day in the UK.

Brand Guardians

ABTA

KEITH BETTON
Head of Corporate Affairs

After spells with Shell International and British Telecom, Keith moved to the travel industry in 1986. After three years with leading PR consultancy Biss Lancaster he joined ABTA, and became Head of Corporate Affairs. Apart from being the travel industry's main media spokesperson, he co-ordinates the highly-successful ABTA Convention and is ABTA's brand guardian.

IAN REYNOLDS
Chief Executive

After leaving the London School of Economics Ian began his career at Shell-Mex and BP. He joined IBM in 1968 and progressed through a series of sales management appointments. He was Director of IBM UK Holdings from 1987 to 1994 and served variously as Director of Sales, Marketing and Services and Personnel and Corporate Affairs. In 1994 he became Chief Executive of ABTA.

American Express

BEN COCKE
UK Trade Marketing & Communications Manager, Corporate Services

Ben spent three years working for American Express in Hong Kong on graduation in 1990 and subsequently returned to London, working for several years with Renault Financial Services as Communications Manager before returning to American Express in 1999. He is currently responsible for Marketing and Communications for American Express' corporate UK clients and multi-national clients across Europe.

JO SHALE
Director, Communications & Acquisition Corporate Services

Jo joined American Express in 1998 from McCann Erickson Worldwide where she was Account Director responsible for managing the communications mix for a portfolio of multi-national brands.
Over the last ten years she has occupied a number of sales and marketing management positions both agency and clientside. Jo has a strong academic background in economics and advanced marketing.

Andersen Consulting

JAMES E MURPHY
Global Managing Director of Marketing & Communication

James E Murphy has had this position since 1993.
Previously, Jim was chairman and CEO of the Americas operations of Burson–Marsteller where he served as the senior management representative on the Andersen Consulting account for the Young & Rubicam Inc group of companies.

TERESA L POGGENPOHL
Global Director of Brand, Advertising and New Media

Teresa L Poggenpohl is the Global Director of Brand, Advertising and New Media for Andersen Consulting. Prior to her current role, Teresa served as Global Director of Market Research where she created Andersen Consulting's first global research function. She has been with Andersen Consulting since 1986.

Cap Gemini Ernst & Young

CINDY GREENER
Marketing Director

Cindy Greener is currently Marketing Director for Cap Gemini in the UK. Managed international strategic planning function for part of TI Group. Managed automotive component factories for part of TI Group. General manager and headed up research and development for part of Panavision. Left school at sixteen to be an engineering fitter and welder. MBA qualified.

MICHELLE PERKINS
In charge of Public Relations

Australian. Bachelor of Social Sciences from Mathew Flinders University in Australia.
CIM diploma in the UK. Member of the CIM. Running the UK press office since 1997. In charge of Public Relations for UK & Ireland. Been with Cap Gemini Ernst & Young since 1995 – previous roles in Finance & retail sectors.

Castrol

RICHARD BUITENHEK
Director Castrol Brand Marketing

Prior to current role spent fifteen plus years in marketing and sales related roles. Worked with strong international consumer brands distributed through multi-channel outlets in both mature and dynamic growth markets.
The Castrol brand is the company's most valuable asset, as brand guardian the current challenges are to build the value and equity of the Castrol brand and proactively market it in the areas of sponsorship, e-mail and new brand-broadening opportunities.

Dun & Bradstreet

BARBARA JAMES
Head of Marketing Communications

Barbara James joined Dun & Bradstreet in 1988 as Sales and Marketing Manager for the company's Business Training division, progressing through the company to her current role as Head of Marketing Communications.
Today, Barbara's focus is to develop a marcomms strategy that supports the Dun & Bradstreet business in its evolution into an internet enabled organisation and to transition the existing customer base through the web.

easyJet

TOBY NICOL
Head of Communications

Toby joined easyJet in late 1999 from Charles Barker BSMG Worldwide where he gained big brand and aviation experience, with a brief to maintain and build the easyJet brand. As head of communications for the airline, Toby is responsible for all aspects of media, government relations and campaigning.

JAMES ROTHNIE
easyGroup Director of Corporate Affairs

James Rothnie originally joined easyJet when it was an airline with three aircraft. He helped to grow the airline's brand through media activity and defending the company from the agressive tactics of the major airlines as easyJet spearheaded its entry into different European markets. He now promotes the brands of all the easyGroup companies and ensures that the same brand values are mirrored throughout the easyGroup.

Knight Frank

JOHN MARTIN FRICS
Senior Partner

John Martin became Senior Partner of Knight Frank in 1996. His early career was spent specialising in all aspects of the retail and leisure markets working with clients such as Land Securities, MEPC, Prudential and Standard Life. Since becoming senior partner, the firm has doubled in size, formed a strategic alliance with Grubb & Ellis in the US and bought out the partners in its Australian business to give Knight Frank 100% control.

Legal & General

KATE AVERY
Retail Customer Director

Legal & General has recognised the requirements to be customer centric if they are to continue to deliver market beating products and services. Kate is responsible for the end to end customer experience, which includes product design, customer access (internet, face to face) and ongoing servicing.
Kate joined Legal & General in 1996 after a career in financial services spanning banking to stockbroking.

CAROLINE FAWCETT
Customer Communications Director

Caroline Fawcett is responsible for Legal & General's Brand Management and Customer Communications Policy. Caroline has over fifteen years experience in Financial Services marketing, having worked for insurance companies in both the US and the UK. Brand development and internal alignment have been her major passions for the last few years.

ACAS

JANET GAYMER
Head of the Employment Law Department

Janet Gaymer is Head of the Employment Law Department at the City firm of solicitors Simmons and Simmons. In May 1995 she was appointed to the council of ACAS. She has twice been voted the 'Experts Expert' in a survey undertaken by Legal Business and in 1997 received The Times Woman of Achievements in the Law Award.

BILL MORRIS
General Secretary of the Transport & General Workers Union

Bill Morris was appointed to the ACAS Council in 1995 and is currently General Secretary of the Transport and General Workers Union (T&G). His industrial duties have included executive responsibility for the Union's four transport sectors, the car industry, energy and engineering and white collar workers. In February 1999 he was appointed a member of the Royal Commission on the reform of the House of Lords.

ACNielsen

BRIAN CHADBOURNE
President

Brian Chadbourne is ACNielsen's president for Europe.
Prior to this appointment in June 1999, Chadbourne held key leadership positions in Europe and the United States, developing a wealth of consumer products experience working with blue chip companies including International Flavors & Fragrances, United Biscuits and Rowntree Mackintosh.

MARIO LEESER
Group Executive for Europe, Managing Director for UK

Mario Leeser is ACNielsen's Group Executive, Central Europe and Managing Director for the UK.
Prior to this, Leeser held senior level international positions for ACNielsen Europe preceded by sixteen years at Dun & Bradstreet Information Services in general management assignments in Australia, Austria and Peru.

Bartle Bogle Hegarty

NIGEL BOGLE
Chairman

Nigel began his advertising career at nineteen as a trainee at Leo Burnett in 1967, finally becoming one of the agency's eight Account Group Heads. In 1973 he left to become a founding partner of TBWA; where he was joint managing director with John Bartle, and John Hegarty was Creative Director. This partnership led to their agency's foundation in 1982. Bartle Bogle Hegarty has twice been awarded agency of the year by Campaign, and twice won agency of the year at Cannes International Advertising Festival.

JOHN HEGARTY
Chairman & Creative Director

John started in advertising as a junior Art Director at Benton and Bowles in 1965. In 1970 he became a founding shareholder in Saatchi & Saatchi becoming its deputy Creative Director in 1972. In 1973 he left to help found the London office of TBWA. In 1980 TBWA became Campaign Magazine's first ever agency of the year. In 1982 he started Bartle Bogle Hegarty. John's credits include 'Vorsprung durch Technik' for Audi, and Levi's 'Bath' and 'Launderette'. His awards include two D&AD Golds and six Silvers, Cannes Golds and Silvers, and British Television Gold and Silvers.

Budget

RODDY GRAHAM
Sales & Marketing Director, Budget UK

Roddy Graham joined Budget UK in the Autumn of 1998 as sales and marketing director. He is responsible for strengthening Budget's operations and market position in the UK. Mr Graham has a wealth of experience in the UK contract hire, rental and fleet sector, having previously worked for Highway Vehicle Management and Hertz UK.

ROELAND MOENS
Vice President, Sales and Marketing, Budget Rent A Car International

Roeland Moens is Vice President of Sales and Marketing for Budget International, a position he has held since November 1998. His previous senior car rental positions included country general manager for the Benelux at Hertz, head of the Iberian peninsular at Europcar and latterly director of Europcar UK.

Clifford Chance

MICHAEL BRAY
Chief Executive Officer

Michael Bray is the Chief Executive Officer of Clifford Chance. He took a first class honours degree in Law at Liverpool University.
Michael joined Clifford Chance in 1970 and became a partner in 1976. Areas in which he has specialised include corporate debt restructuring, project and acquisition finance and financial leasing arrangements.

KEITH CLARK
Chairman

Keith Clark is the Chairman of Clifford Chance. He gained a scholarship to St Catherine's College, Oxford, took a first class degree in Jurisprudence and gained a postgraduate Bachelor of Civil Law degree.
Keith joined Clifford Chance in 1971 specialising in banking and finance, sovereign loans and leasing arrangements. Since 1981 he has been particularly involved in sovereign debt restructuring.

Compaq

HAMISH HAYNES
Marketing Communications Director

Hamish Haynes is responsible for Compaq's brand and image across the company.
Haynes has been with Compaq since 1986 and has a career spanning eighteen years in the IT industry. Previous Compaq roles have included consumer director, consumer marketing manager, retail sales manager, regional manager (public sector) and dealer sales manager. Prior to joining Compaq, he was regional manager of First Computer, running its southern retail branches.

JO McNALLY
Vice President & Managing Director

Jo McNally is responsible for the entire sales, marketing and service operation in the UK and Ireland. McNally has taken the UK company from a $1 company when he set up in February 1984 to a £1 billion company at the close of the 1997 financial year. His computer industry background includes over fourteen years inside ICL and Honeywell Information Systems, which equipped him with the front-line sales experience needed to pull Compaq, in just over six years, alongside IBM as a leading UK supplier of business PCs.

The Gallup Organization

CAROLYN DYER
Director of Analysis & Consulting

Carolyn Dyer joined Gallup in 1996 as a Consultant Analyst. Previously she was Director of Personnel, Training and Development for the Bavard Group. Her first Executive appointment, in 1993 was to the post of Head of Personnel for Alloa Pubs and Restaurants Limited.
Carolyn's responsibilities include the recruitment, positioning, productivity and development of European-based Researchers, Analysts and Managing Consultants in Gallup's Survey and Strengths Management practices.

JILL GARRETT
Managing Director

Jill was born and educated in Birmingham and graduated in Economics from the London School of Economics. She joined The Gallup Organization in 1994.
Jill's work involves strategic analyst consultancy with executive teams and includes selection, development, team building and positioning. She has also researched excellence in a range of roles from Motor Car Technicians to Business Banking Officers, from Corporate Consultants to Salvation Army Leaders.

Glaxo Wellcome

GEOFFREY POTTER
Director, Corporate Communications & Community Affairs

Geoffrey Potter was born in 1949 in Hull, Yorkshire, he graduated BA (Econ) (first class honours) in Political Theory and Institutions at the University of Sheffield in 1970. He is responsible for the central Corporate Communications of Glaxo Wellcome embracing corporate reputation, media relations, employee communications, scientific and educational affairs, therapeutic and science communications, sponsorship and co-ordination of global community affairs.
He was elected a Fellow of the Institute of Public Relations in 1998. Mr Potter is married and lives in Hertfordshire with his wife, Sarah, and their two children.

LSE

ANTHONY GIDDENS
Director

Anthony Giddens is the most widely-read and cited social theorist of his generation. His ideas have profoundly influenced the writing and teaching of sociology and social theory around the world. He is the author of 32 books, published in 29 languages. Many books have been published about him and his work. In 1999 he was the BBC Reith Lecturer.

LYCRA®

KAREN M JONES
European Brand Manager

Karen Jones was appointed European Brand Manager for DuPont LYCRA® in 1999.
Recruited to the marketing department of JET petrol in 1986, Karen moved to DuPont Printing & Publishing as Marketing Manager in 1989. Five years later she transferred to LYCRA® in the UK where she also ran the global Wool plus LYCRA® programme.
Karen has a degree in German and is a member of the Chartered Institute of Marketing.

LINDA W KEARNS
Global Brand Manager

Linda W Kearns is currently the Global Brand Manager for DuPont LYCRA®. She joined DuPont in 1984 as a marketing research analyst in the Corporate Business and Marketing Group of External Affairs.
Linda graduated from the Massachusetts Institute of Technology with a BS degree in mathematics and holds a Masters Degree from Princeton University. She and her husband, Jim, live in Newark, Delaware, and have two children, Emily and Jake.

Michael Page International

TERRY BENSON
Chief Executive

Terry Benson is Chief Executive of Michael Page International. He joined the company in 1979 initially concentrating on UK business development. He was appointed Chief Executive in 1995. His blunt and direct management approach has been the driving force behind the company's unrivalled global expansion.

Microsoft

SHAUN ORPEN
Director of Corporate Marketing

Shaun Orpen joined Microsoft in 1988. In his current role as Director of Corporate Marketing, Shaun is responsible for the integration of all cross-company marketing services and is currently spearheading an initiative focusing on two of the overriding company principles - customer and partner loyalty; and image and brand excellence.

NEIL THOMPSON
Head of EMEA Image & Communications

Neil Thompson joined Microsoft in 1992 and following various roles is now Head of EMEA Image & Communications. Neil has overall responsibility for the Microsoft Brand, Corporate PR, Community Affairs and niche product marketing. Neil's main objective is to build a positive focus for the Microsoft Brand and maximise revenue opportunities for niche products.

One 2 One

DAVID HENSON
Director, Business Unit

David joined One 2 One in 1999 from Dolphin Telecommunications, briefed with developing the organisation, processes and product needed to help the brand become a major player in the business market.
David started his career at BT, moving to Bull Information Systems, where he was responsible for bringing a new business unit to the market. During his time as Sales & Marketing Director at NB3, he led the repositioning of the company as a major mobile supplier to the business sector.

COLIN MORLEY
General Manager, Brand Development & Communication

Colin joined One 2 One in January 1996 following years of experience in the food industry, with companies including Spillers Food, Quaker Oats and Weetabix. Colin has been responsible for new brand positioning for One 2 One, with work including the award winning Who Would You Most Like To Have A One 2 One With? campaign and its development to the new Welcome 2 Your World vision.

Post-it® Notes

JO SCHILLER
Product Manager

With an honours degree in Business Studies from Brighton University, Jo Schiller, was appointed from a senior marketing role in 3M Specialty Tapes and Adhesives to develop the Post-it® Products vision for the twenty first century. She believes fervently that the brand reflects everything that 3M stands for - innovation, quality and reliability. Her enthusiasm is reflected in current advertising programmes.

JOHN WALKER
General Manager, 3M Stationary and Office Products

Following an honours degree in Physics from Southampton University, John Walker has been responsible for building on the brand strength of some of 3M's major assets, such as Scotchbrite, Post-it, and Scotch brands. He believes passionately in the responsibility of manufacturers to build, communicate, defend and deliver real and meaningful brand values to the consumer.

Reed Executive

KATY NICHOLSON
Marketing and Communications Director

Katy started out in publishing, then joined Reed as Marketing Manager for professional divisions in 1989, becoming Group Public Relations Manager in 1996. In 1998 she left Reed for the PR Agency world, working on brands including BT, Cisco, RAC, Dixons, and Tesco, before returning to her current position in 2000.

JAMES REED MA, MBA
Chief Executive

James was appointed Chief Executive of Reed Executive PLC in February 1997. His early career was spent with BBC Television, Help the Aged, Saatchi & Saatchi PLC, and The Body Shop PLC. He is committed to providing innovation, value and continuous improvement to all Reed clients.

Reuters

JEAN-CLAUDE MARCHAND
Group Marketing Director

Swiss born Jean-Claude Marchand has board responsibility for the Reuters brand and ensuring a coherent marketing focus on customer needs across business divisions. He chairs Reuters Information Division. He began his career at Reuters as a sales executive, and after a period as Sales and Marketing Manager for Asia, he returned to manage continental Europe. He headed the Global Sales & Operations Group before taking up his present position in February 2000.

MARCUS FERRAR
Global Director of Public Relations

British born Marcus Ferrar is responsible for Reuters brand communications, comprising brand advertising, public relations and sponsorship. He served for sixteen years as a Reuters correspondent, including in Eastern Europe during the cold war and in Portugal during the revolution. After posts in general management and marketing, he assumed his communications role in 1993. For five years, he also conducted investor relations in Europe. His hobby is mountaineering (Matterhorn, Mont Blanc).

Sheraton

JOHN P GREENLEAF
Senior Vice President, Marketing

John is responsible for the development, product management and marketing efforts in North America for Starwood's hotel group, which includes St Regis, Luxury Collection, Westin, Sheraton, Four Points and W. Greenleaf formerly served as vice president, brand manager for Sheraton Hotels & Resorts.

JANE M MACKIE
Vice President, Brand Manager

Jane is responsible for the development and implementation of marketing strategies for the hotel chain and its more than 200 properties in North America. Mackie, a fourteen-year Sheraton veteran, most recently served as vice president, brand manager for Four Points Hotels, Starwood's fastest growing brand.

Siemens

FIONNUALA TENNYSON
Head of Corporate Communications

Fionnuala Tennyson manages the company's external and internal communications.
Prior to joining Siemens she was Communications Manager at London Electricity. Previously she was Public Relations and Development Manager at the Institute of Public Relations. This position followed a stint with the Advertising Association as External Affairs and PR Director. Ms Tennyson began her career in advertising with Saatchi & Saatchi and McCann-Erickson.

ALAN WOOD
Chief Executive

Alan Wood, Chief Executive of Siemens plc, is responsible for the overall management and strategic development of Siemens' businesses in the United Kingdom.
He is also Chairman of the Confederation of British Industry's National Manufacturing Council (NMC).
Alan Wood attained a first class honours degree in mechanical engineering from Manchester University and an MBA from Harvard University.

Toyota

MATTHEW HARRISON
General Manager, Vehicle Marketing

After graduating from Hull University with a BSc (Hons) in Financial Accounting, Matthew joined Ford Motor Company where he held a variety of positions in Ford of Britain's Sales Operations, its European Marketing Department and its global Brand Development function.
He joined Toyota in February 2000 and has responsibility for product planning, marketing programmes and brand management at Toyota (GB).

PAUL PHILPOT
Marketing Director

After graduating from Loughborough University with a BSc (Hons) in Finance, Paul joined Midland Bank for a short career in Financial Services. In 1988 Paul joined Ford Motor Company, where he rapidly progressed through the Sales and Marketing functions.
Joining Toyota (GB) in 1997 as General Manager, Vehicle Marketing, Paul took over full responsibility for Toyota's expanding Marketing Team in 1999.

United Airlines

GRAHAM ATKINSON
Senior Vice President, Marketing

Graham Atkinson is Senior Vice President-Marketing for United Airlines. He is based at the company's world headquarters in Chicago.
Named to the position in July 1999, he is responsible for all of United's global marketing strategies, advertising and communications, including the development and integration of products, brand management and distribution.

BRANDON O'REILLY
General Manager for UK & Ireland

Brandon O'Reilly is United Airlines' General Manager for the UK and Ireland. He is based at United's UK headquarters at London Heathrow.
Appointed to this position in 1998, he is responsible for all aspects of the airline's activities including sales, marketing, airport operations, cargo, administration and reservations.

Mintel

Everyone at Mintel, from production to direct sales, is an ambassador for our brand. It is not right to focus on any one individual within the group, as we all share the responsibility and limelight in these circumstances. The brand is represented in every communication to or from Mintel – press, telephone, email, face-to-face.
However, if you would like to speak to one of our 150 brand guardians, why not contact our Head of Research, Paul Rickard or Head of Marketing, Steve Charlton.

Motorola

RICHARD L FOSS
Vice President of Global Brands

Richard L Foss (Rich) is vice president of Global Brands for Motorola's Personal Communications Sector and is leading the effort to develop world-class consumer insights, cutting edge product designs and end-to-end solutions - all aligned to global consumer needs.
Prior to joining Motorola in 1999, Rich spent 21 years with The Procter & Gamble Company (P&G).

GEOFFREY FROST
Vice President & Director of Consumer Communications

Geoffrey L Frost is vice president and director of Consumer Communications of Motorola. His main area of responsibility is global consumer communications, including advertising, public relations, merchandising and sponsorship opportunities for Motorola's consumer products. Before joining Motorola in 1999, Frost served as Global Director of Advertising and Brand Communications for Nike, Inc.

Powergen

EDMUND WALLIS
Chairman and Chief Executive

Edmund Wallis was appointed to the Board of Powergen plc on 22 October 1998, having been chief executive of Powergen UK plc since March 1990 and Chairman since July 1996. A non-executive director of Mercury European Privatisation Trust plc and a non-executive director of London Transport, he was also formerly non-executive chairman of LucasVarity plc.

Psion

DAVID LEVIN
CEO

David Levin (38) joined Psion as CEO in February 1999 from Euromoney Publications PLC, where he had been Chief Operating Officer since 1996. Prior to that he worked for Bain & Co focusing on acquisition, integration and strategy. David also worked for Apax Partners & Co as an Associate Director until 1994.

ALASDAIR SETON-MARSDEN
Marketing Director

Alasdair Seton-Marsden (37) joined Psion as International Marketing Director in September 1999 from Spring PLC, where he was the Marketing Communications Director.
Alasdair has marketing experience on both client and agency side having worked in both New York and London with a number of major blue chip companies. He was responsible for setting up the first New Media unit at Saatchi & Saatchi plc and more recently worked for Microsoft where he was responsible for marketing communications to the broad business audiences.

Ryman

MALCOLM COOKE
Group Director

Group Director for the holding company with specific responsibilities for the trading aspects of Ryman including Marketing and Buying. Has been responsible for the Ryman Brand for over ten years and prior to that held similar positions in large retail organisations. He also holds similar responsibilities for La Senza and Contessa.

THEO PAPHITIS
Chairman & Chief Executive

Chairman and Chief Executive of the Ryman Group of companies, purchased in 1995. A Greek Cypriot by birth he was previously involved in property and property finance. He also built up a successful Mobile Telephone business and is now, in addition to Ryman, Chairman of La Senza, Contessa, Movie & Media Sports (a sports advertising & sponsorship company) and Millwall Football Club.

Shell

RAOUL PINNEL
Global Head of Brands & Communication

Raoul Pinnell developed an early interest in business whilst at school, Bradfield College, leaving to pursue Business Studies, subsequently followed by a post-graduate Diploma in Marketing. Following seventeen years with Nestle, five years at Prudential and three years at NatWest. Shell International appointed him to the post of Global Head of Brands & Communications in 1997.

SIMON SAVILLE
Global Brand Standards Manager

Simon Saville joined Shell in 1985, attracted by the opportunity to create fuels and lubricants with improved marketing propositions.
He spent 2.5 years in Japan, focusing on the technical marketing and manufacturer liaison.
On return to the UK, he was on an international basis for Shell's fuels differentiation strategies and initiatives in the mid-90s, a time when Shell was consolidating its position as the leading supplier of branded fuels worldwide.
Since 1996 he has been responsible for the Shell brand strategy and identity on a global basis.

Sun Microsystems

LOUISE PRODDOW
Marketing Director

Louise has been at Sun since 1994 and has been instrumental in the strategic development of the UK marketing department. Having created and built up a marketing communications team, with a strong focus on brand development, demand creation and integrated marketing, she was also responsible for delivering the .com UK e-commerce and new media programmes.

SHANKER TRIVEDI
Vice President, Computer Systems (UK & Ireland) & Managing Director

Shanker is responsible for managing Sun Microsystems business in UK and Ireland. His vision is to double Sun's business over the next three years by building even closer relationships with customers and business partners through delivering better network computing solutions.

Tarmac

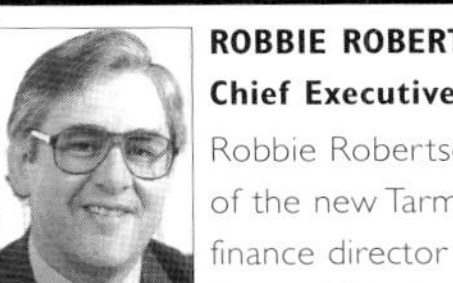

ROBBIE ROBERTSON
Chief Executive

Robbie Robertson is Chief Executive of the new Tarmac Group. A former finance director of Anglo American South Africa, he headed Anglo American Corporation of South Africa's London office before moving to Minorco, becoming Chief Executive of its industrial minerals business, now Anglo Industrial Minerals, in 1997.

TONY TRAHAR
Chairman

Tony Trahar is chairman of the new Tarmac Group and Chief Executive of its parent company, Anglo American plc. Tony qualified as a chartered accountant in 1973 joining Anglo American soon afterwards as a management trainee. He has been a director since 1989 holding a range of executive responsibilities across the business.

Xerox

ANOUSH GORDON
Director, Integrated Marketing

Functionally responsible for marketing in UK.

ROB WALKER
Managing Director

Responsible for all marketing and operational activity of sales and service throughout the UK.

Yellow Pages

PHILLIPA BUTTERS
Head of Design

Head of Design for Yellow Pages, Philippa Butters ensures they only work with agencies that deliver exciting and innovative design solutions for the product and its range of service brands.
Philippa has received numerous awards including the Grand Prix Award at the 1999 Design Effectiveness Awards for her work on the Yellow Pages directory re-design project.

NIGEL MARSON
Marketing Communicators Controller

Marketing Communications Controller for the Yellow Pages Group, Nigel Marson, is responsible for all external communications for the Yellow Pages portfolio of products including the leading UK portal, Yell.com.
Under his leadership, Yellow Pages has won a string of advertising and design awards and usage has significantly increased across the entire portfolio.

Directory

ABTA
Association of British Travel Agents
68 - 71 Newman Street
London
W1T 3AH

ACAS
Advisory, Conciliation
& Arbitration Service
Brandon House
180 Borough High Street
London
SE1 1LW

ACNielsen
ACNielsen
ACNielsen House
Headington
Oxford
OX3 9RX

American Express
American Express Service Europe Ltd
Portland House
14th Floor
Stag Place
London
SW1E 5BZ

Andersen Consulting
Andersen Consulting LLP
2 Arundel Street
London
WC2R 3LT

Avis
Avis Rent-A-Car Ltd
Trident House
Station Road
Hayes
Middlesex
UB3 4DJ

Bartle Bogle Hegarty
Bartle Bogle Hegarty Ltd
60 Kingly Street
London
W1R 6DS

BT
BT
BT Centre
81 Newgate Street
London
EC1A 7AJ

Budget
Budget Rent a Car International Inc.
41 Marlowes
Hemel Hampstead
HP1 1XJ

Cap Gemini Ernst & Young
Cap Gemini Ernst & Young
130 Shaftesbury Avenue
London
W1D 5EU

Castrol
Castrol International
Burmah Castrol House
Pipers Way
Swindon
SN3 1RE

Clifford Chance
Clifford Chance LLP
200 Aldersgate Street
London
EC1A 4JJ

Compaq
Compaq Computer Ltd
Hotham House
1 Heron Square
Richmond
Surrey
TW9 1EJ

Dun & Bradstreet
Dun & Bradstreet Ltd
50 - 100 Holmers Farm Way
High Wycombe
Buckinghamshire
HP12 4UL

easyJet
easyJet
easyLand
London Luton Airport
LU2 9LS

The Equitable Life
The Equitable Life Assurance Society
Walton Street
Aylesbury
Buckinghamshire
HP21 7QW

FedEx Express
FedEx Express
35 - 37 Amersham Hill
High Wycombe
Buckinghamshire
HP13 6NU

The Gallup Organization
The Gallup Organization
Drapers Court
Kingston Hall Road
Kingston-upon-Thames
Surrey
KT1 2BG

Glaxo Wellcome
Glaxo Wellcome plc
Glaxo Wellcome House
Berkely Avenue
Middlesex
UB6 0NN

Goldman Sachs
Goldman Sachs International
Peterborough Court
133 Fleet Street
London
EC4A 2BB

Hewlett-Packard
Hewlett-Packard Ltd
Cain Road
Bracknell
Berkshire
RG12 1HN

HSBC
HSBC Holdings plc
10 Lower Thames Street
London
EC3R 6AE

ICL
ICL Plc
26 Finsbury Square
London
EC2A 1SL

JCB
JC Bamford Excavators Ltd
Rocester
Staffordshire
ST14 5JP

Knight Frank
Knight Frank
20 Hanover Square
London
W1S 1HZ

Legal & General
Legal & General Assurance Society Limited
Temple Court
11 Queen Victoria Street
London
EC4N 4TP

LSE
The London School of Economics and Political Science
Houghton Street
London
WC2A 2AE

LYCRA®
DuPont (UK) Ltd
94 Regent Road
Leicester
LE1 7DD

Mercury Asset Management
Mercury Asset Management Ltd
33 King William Street
London
EC4R 9AS

Merrill Lynch
Merrill Lynch Europe plc
Ropemaker Place
25 Ropemaker Street
London
EC2Y 9LY

Michael Page International
Michael Page International
39 - 41 Parker Street
London
WC2B 5LN

Microsoft
Microsoft Ltd
Microsoft Campus
Thames Valley Park
Reading
Berkshire
RG6 1WG

Mintel
Mintel International Group Ltd
18-19 Long Lane
London
EC1A 9PL

Motorola
Motorola Ltd
Midpoint
Alencon Link
Basingstoke
Hampshire
RG21 7PL

Nokia
Nokia UK Ltd
Headland House
The Chord Business Park
London Road
Godmanchester
Cambridgeshire
PE29 2NX

One 2 One
One 2 One Personal Communications Ltd
Maxwell Road
Imperial Place
Borehamwood
Herdfordshire
WD6 1EA

Post-it® Notes
3M UK plc
3M House
PO Box 1
Market Place
Bracknell
Berkshire
RG12 1JU

Powergen
Powergen Plc
53 New Broad Street
London
EC2M 1SL

Psion
Psion Computers Plc
Alexander House
85 Frampton Street
London
NW8 8NQ

Reed Executive
Reed Executive plc
Marketing Department
94 Baker Street
London
W1M 1LA

Reuters
Reuters Group
85 Fleet Street
London
EC4P 4AJ

Ryman
Ryman Ltd
Swallowfield Way
Hayes
Middlesex
UB3 1DQ

Shell
Shell International Petroleum Company Ltd
OMM/3 Shell Centre
London
SE1 7NA

Sheraton
Starwood Hotels and Resorts Worldwide Inc
777 Westchester Avenue
White Plains
New York
10604

Siemens
Siemens plc
Siemens House
Oldbury
Bracknell
Berkshire
RG12 8FZ

Sony
Sony United Kingdom Ltd
The Heights
Brooklands
Weybridge
Surrey
KT13 0XW

Sun Microsystems
Sun Microsystems Ltd
Guillemont Park
Minley Road
Blackwater
Camberley
GU17 9QG

Tarmac
Tarmac Plc
PO Box 8
Millfield Road
Ettingshall
Wolverhampton
WV4 6JP

Toyota
Toyota (GB) plc
The Quadrangle
Redhill
RH1 1PX

United Airlines
United Airlines
United House
Southern Perimeter Road
Heathrow Airport
Hounslow
Middlesex
TW6 3LP

Visa
Visa International
PO Box 253
London
W8 5TE

Xerox
Xerox (UK) Ltd
Bridge House
Oxford Road
Uxbridge
Middlesex
UB8 1HS

Yellow Pages
Yellow Pages
Queens Walk
Reading
Berkshire
RG1 7PT